Advance Praise for *Escaping Maya's Palace*

"This is a stunning and audacious work of grand social theory. It is utterly fascinating, vigorously argued, and as evidence based as one could ever imagine. Sclove exposes modernity as a covert struggle, stretching out over four centuries, between economic growth and psychospiritual self-realization. . . . An intellectual tour de force with momentous implications."
> —Penny Gill, professor emeritus of politics, Mount Holyoke College, and author of *What in the World Is Going On?*

"Mind-blowingly insightful . . . Sclove's book unmasks fatal defects in economic thought together with surprising opportunities for social and environmental salvation."
> —Richard B. Norgaard, professor emeritus of ecological economics, University of California, Berkeley, and author of *Development Betrayed*

"*Escaping Maya's Palace* is profound, powerfully original, and politically and spiritually sophisticated at a level that is very rare. It could be life changing for many people and a catalyst for integrating deeper psychospiritual awareness into social-change movements!"
> —Sally Kempton, author of *Meditation for the Love of It*

"By unearthing buried insight within one of the world's oldest and most revered works of philosophical and spiritual wisdom, Sclove illuminates a toxic flaw at the core of modernity. His suggested remedies are generous, far-reaching, and distinctly practical."
> —Langdon Winner, professor emeritus of political science and humanities, Rensselaer Polytechnic Institute, and author of *The Whale and the Reactor*

"An amazing and soul-nourishing book that courageously defies the taboo against integrating spiritual wisdom into modern scholarship. Sclove's revelation of the deep structure of the *Mahabharata* is a major contribution to the scholarship on this foundational Indian epic. His ensuing critique of modern society is profound and pointed."
> —Frédérique Apffel-Marglin, professor emerita of anthropology, Smith College, and author of *Subversive Spiritualities*

"Richard Sclove is a Renaissance man for our times, weaving insights from a dozen disciplines into a dazzling string of revelations. His book presents a compelling new rationale for creating more self-reliant and culturally progressive local economies."
—Michael H. Shuman, economist, attorney, and author of *The Local Economy Solution*

"This profound book presents a paradigm for others to follow in reconstructing a holistic study of society. It should be read by all historians and by everyone interested in understanding how we reached this point of impending social and environmental catastrophe. It's a masterpiece."
—Gerald Friedman, professor of economics, University of Massachusetts Amherst, and author of *Reigniting the Labor Movement*

"*Escaping Maya's Palace* is a remarkable book. Sclove argues that 'We should seek to evolve equal and ample opportunities for realizing our psychospiritual potential.' He explores that principle by providing an original interpretation of a psychologically insightful myth (ancient India's *Mahabharata*), a social-theoretic examination of how social dislocation has intensified egoism, and a psychosocial study of the unhappy consequences of intensified egoism for human well-being. If you are open to considering fundamentally different ways of thinking about the largest human challenges, Sclove's book will give you a truly thoughtful and deeply informed point of entry."
—Joshua Cohen, Marta Sutton Weeks Professor of Ethics in Society and professor of philosophy and law, emeritus, Stanford University, and coeditor, *Boston Review*

"Through in-depth historical analysis, psychological inquiry, and sharp critical theory, Richard Sclove unpacks some of the world's deepest problems with a sobering and truthful clarity. Filled with wisdom, *Escaping Maya's Palace* is a handbook for healing."
—John Zorn, saxophonist, composer, and producer

"An enlightening feast of psychological and social insight that only the rare intelligence of a scientist turned social theorist and spiritual seeker could dream up."
—Chellis Glendinning, psychologist and author of *My Name Is Chellis and I'm in Recovery from Western Civilization*

"Drawing on many disciplines, Sclove argues that the intensity of craving in humans has been shaped by historical forces writ large. It's a provocative and fascinating thesis! This book should be of interest to all who care about the future development of individuals and the fate of our world."

— Robert Roeser, Bennett Pierce Professor of Caring and Compassion and professor of human development and family studies, Penn State University

"This wonderful book engages psychology, history, anthropology, Eastern spirituality, and social theory to disclose the depth of difficulties confronting contemporary societies. It offers ways to move us to a more benign, more spiritual, and more psychologically and politically healthy world."

— Ervin Staub, professor emeritus of psychology, University of Massachusetts-Amherst, and author of *The Roots of Goodness and Resistance to Evil*

Praise for *Democracy and Technology*

"Remarkably ambitious, superbly accessible, and urgently needed— a gold mine of fundamental insights and suggestive provocation . . . This is the most far-reaching work I have seen on the political nature of technological change."

— David F. Noble, author of *Forces of Production*

"Mr. Sclove is refreshing in the way he rejects ideas so nearly universally held that most people have never thought to question them."

— *New York Times*, Sunday Book Review

"A welcome addition to an essential debate . . . This book provides a provocative and thorough analysis of the challenges facing us on the threshold of the twenty-first century."

— US Congressman George E. Brown, Jr., chairman, House Science Committee

"Tightly reasoned and far-ranging in examples and erudition . . . cogent and illuminating . . . seminal . . . Sclove writes in the hallowed and constructive tradition of Paul Goodman, Ivan Illich, Paulo Freire, Lewis Mumford, and E. F. Schumacher."

— *Annals of the American Academy of Political & Social Science*

Escaping
Maya's Palace

Escaping Maya's Palace

DECODING AN ANCIENT MYTH
TO HEAL THE HIDDEN MADNESS
OF MODERN CIVILIZATION

Richard Sclove

KARAVELLE
PRESS

BOSTON LONDON NEW DELHI

KARAVELLE
PRESS

Boston, Massachusetts

Copyright © 2022 Richard Sclove

www.EscapingMayasPalace.com

Edited and designed by Girl Friday Productions
www.girlfridayproductions.com

Design: Paul Barrett
Editorial management: Dave Valencia
Image credits: cover © iStock/Stefan90

ISBN (paperback): 978-1-7354533-0-9
ISBN (e-book): 978-1-7354533-1-6

Library of Congress Control Number: 2021924704

Then Krishna, the Lord of the Universe, commanded Maya, "Build a palace of such magnificence that people in the entire world of men will be unable to imitate it, even after examining it with care, while seated within." Maya was delighted, and he joyfully built a palace for the Pandavas resembling the palace of the Gods.
                    —*Mahabharata*, Book 2

Contents

List of Figures

Readers can view or download larger versions of the figures at
www.EscapingMayasPalace.com/figures.

Introduction

Chapter 1

SEEING EARTH FROM VENUS

Suffering, stunting, and mortal threats in modern civilization

One night when our daughter was six years old, I took her outside to look at the sky. It was the spring of 1997, and this was no ordinary evening. Holding hands on the sidewalk outside our two-story wooden house, we could see stars, the crescent moon, and a planet. And something else: a fuzzy ball of light dwarfing every other celestial object, with more white light streaming out far behind it. Comet Hale-Bopp.

There was a soft magic in the air as we talked about what we were witnessing. I told Lena that comets like Hale-Bopp are rare. In my forty-three years, I'd never seen anything like it. After watching in silence for a while, we turned toward the lone planet we'd spied hanging in the sky. I guessed it was Venus. Lena's chin-length blond hair, in transition from ringlets to wavy, shifted in the breeze as she scrutinized the small bright ball of light.

"Daddy," she asked, "if there were people on Venus looking at us, would Earth be a teeny light in the sky like Venus?"

It was an astonishing question coming from a young child. We'd been discussing how a dot of light in outer space could be a world as enormous as ours. From that Lena had managed to flip perspective, speculating that from far away, our planet too might appear as nothing but another luminescent dot suspended in the heavens. She looked up at me expectantly for a reply. But in switching perspective, she had already found the answer to her question. All she needed was my affirmation.

At around the same age Lena posed another question. "Daddy, why are there soldiers who hurt people?"

For that one I didn't have a ready response. A child's questions about the world's irrationality, cruelty, and suffering aren't easy to answer. Slavery, genocide, poverty, nuclear weapons, melting ice sheets, dithering politicians. How do we explain such things to our children? We may not know the answers ourselves.

But what if there were a way to address the world's woes by emulating Lena's question about Venus? If we learned to consider intractable problems from a fresh point of view, might we discover a hidden thread linking many of society's problems together?

That will be our quest in this book: a sleuthing expedition across two millennia to diagnose and heal the secret insanity of modern civilization. We'll discover that this insanity is rooted in a distortion in psychological development and that it bears responsibility for countless painful and dangerous symptoms, personal as well as social. We're troubled by the symptoms but don't trace them back to their source. That's because one of this malady's startling features is that it prevents those afflicted—which is pretty much all of us—from understanding it.

To get started toward repairing our civilization, we need a vantage point that isn't corrupted by our psychological disorder. We'll find one in an improbable place: not by peering at Earth from a faraway planet but by burrowing deep within an ancient myth.

THE TIME CAPSULE

Two thousand years ago, a team comprising some of our most sage and adept ancestors—"wise men from the East," although probably not the same ones who visited newborn Jesus—prepared a time capsule for our benefit. Compassionately, they filled it with lessons indispensable to navigating core challenges that, in the fullness of time, have come to confront the modern world. Lacking weather-resistant containers, these distant benefactors didn't entrust their teachings to an actual capsule. Instead, they buried their insights as a hidden layer of meaning within the lines of a popular epic: the *Mahabharata*—the "great story of the descendants of Emperor Bharata."

One might wonder how a text composed in Sanskrit and passed down from ancient India can assist a scientifically advanced civilization. The *Mahabharata* is up to the job because its principal authors had once suffered from our ailment but, as enlightened sages, could explain it in a way that is only possible for someone who has come out the other side. Properly decoded, the *Mahabharata* describes a camouflaged psychological disorder with symptoms much like ours—except, in the legend, the heroes break away from their affliction. Ensconced in a palace of deception built by a demon named Maya, they manage to escape. In the details of their story lies much wisdom for our time.

A sweeping tale of morality on and off the battlefield, the *Mahabharata* is also renowned as one of the longest books ever written, stretching out to no less than seven times the length of the *Iliad* and the *Odyssey* combined. Decoding the *Mahabharata*'s concealed meaning, and then working out its implications for the modern world, will require knitting together scholarship drawn from more than a dozen disciplines.

Our decryption of the *Mahabharata* may call to mind analogous decryptions sensationalized in movies such as *The Da Vinci Code* or *Raiders of the Lost Ark*. Except instead of titillating with make-believe ancient secrets, we'll be recovering actual lost wisdom and then using it to work out a groundbreaking social critique.

On its surface, the *Mahabharata* is a straightforward myth about a ruinous war, but we'll learn to interpret that story as an allegory of the epic inner voyage from building an ego to attaining spiritual enlightenment—the "hero's journey" in the vernacular of mythologist Joseph Campbell. Because a version of this allegory appears in virtually all cultures, you can interpret the social critique that we will be working out in light of your own religious or spiritual tradition or from a nonreligious stance. The argument that we will craft works equally well under any of these orientations, although its meaning and moment will vary somewhat as a result.[1]

We'll interpret the *Mahabharata* allegorically for several reasons: First, read in this way, the saga offers indispensable insights into human psychological and spiritual development, including hard-to-detect deviations from health. Second, the *Mahabharata* encrypts many of its psychological insights beneath its surface narrative. By unraveling the concealment, we'll also be grinding and polishing a lens that will prove vital to dispelling the illusions that conceal our own plight. Third, because the *Mahabharata* is far removed culturally from modern societies, it allows us to explore its psychological insights with a dispassion that is hard to muster if we leap straight to considering circumstances in which we're enmeshed. Finally (if least importantly), it's difficult to resist the delicious irony of using an ancient saga to dissipate pretensions enshrouding our technologically advanced civilization.

Admittedly, the notion of initiating a critique of modernity from a remote starting point may sound unpromising. Yet perhaps it had to be thus. In effect, we will be exemplifying what Freud sought in adapting the Oedipus myth and psychologist Bruno Bettelheim accomplished with fairy tales: showing that age-old stories sometimes embody wisdom that we can absorb in no other way.[2]

Throughout our journey, we will be executing a double decryption:* In Part I, we'll decode a secret story that flows beneath the *Mahabharata*'s surface narrative. Then in Part II, we'll use that

---

* My use of the pronoun "our"—as in "our" journey or expedition—does not presuppose that you will agree with every step in the argument. "Our" extends an invitation to participate as an active member of this expedition, testing

decoding in combination with modern scholarship to unravel core mysteries of modern civilization. By the end we'll understand things we've never imagined about the predicament of today's world together with practical actions we can take to suffer less, flourish more, and be able to contemplate humanity's future with greater optimism.

A VOYAGE OF DISCOVERY, HEALING, AND LIBERATION

Let's glimpse ahead. Over the past several centuries, the global economy has subjected communities and traditions, as well as our relationships with nature and the world of spirit, to steady disruption. This is widely known.

But the disruption runs deeper than that.

With the *Mahabharata*'s help, we'll learn that this chronic dislocation produces corresponding effects in our interior lives. Egoism—the sense of being a small, separate "me"—intensifies, distorting and impeding psychological growth. (To the extent that growth beyond egoism takes people into terrain that we commonly identify as spiritual, it's actually "psychospiritual" development that is impeded.)

Significant symptoms of this psychological alteration emerged in the seventeenth and eighteenth centuries, rippling out with particular vigor from northwest Europe: Growing numbers of people began to exhibit intensified craving for personal possessions, as well as for addictive substances like sugar, alcohol, coffee, tea, and tobacco. They innovated and worked harder—or found ways to make other people work harder—to be able to pay for goods that they imagined, falsely, would extinguish their newly instilled craving. Meanwhile, as consumerism circled back to stimulate further economic dynamism, social dislocation ramped up.

In short, contrary to conventional economic theory and popular belief, modern capitalism *causes* rather than allays insatiable hunger. Moreover, to the extent that this hunger folds back to fuel the quest for further economic growth, that means that *modern economies have grown dependent on perpetuating psychological and spiritual stunting.* Should people's dislocation-amplified cravings ever miraculously diminish, consumer demand would drop and the market economy as we know it would collapse.

If this is true, many further questions arise:

---

whether you agree at each stage. It's in the nature of an expedition that team members may not concur with every decision, but it is still "their" expedition.

- Could this transformation in human psychology possibly have influenced world history, including the balance of power among global regions?
- Might intensive egoism and craving bear some responsibility for engendering contemporary social ills beyond addiction? What about other leading mental and physical disorders, such as depression and heart disease? How about broken families, broken political systems, terrorism, refugee crises, and climate change?
- And if amplified egoism is a distinctly modern phenomenon with momentous social ramifications, how could we not have known?

For the sake of argument, let's imagine the worst—that humanity has spent the past four centuries evolving a civilization in which billions of people unwittingly endure immense suffering and risk terrible dangers, even the mounting peril of driving our civilization over a cliff, in order to *prevent* access to higher ranges of self-realization. That would be madness—the hidden madness of modern civilization.

By exposing this insanity together with its causes, we open opportunities to overcome it. There are ways to envision damping down dislocation and establishing more deeply nurturing relationships with one another and our world, beginning with personal actions at the local level. We can stretch our political visions beyond what we've inherited from the European Enlightenment and the Industrial and Silicon Valley eras—and beyond the incomplete analyses of conservatives and liberals, greens and libertarians—to address not only our deepest fears but also our highest hopes for personal and planetary healing. We can make our civilization safe for the soul.

The insights that we will hammer out won't amount to a master key for explaining everything about modernity and its ailments. But they will fill in many gaps. Nor will acting on those insights usher in a utopia. Human failings predate the birth of our malady and will persist even if it is cured. But effecting a cure promises to improve our personal well-being, our prospects as a civilization and a species, and our opportunities to advance psychologically and spiritually. We will still have science and technology, many societies may continue to rely on competitive markets, and we will want to hold fast to modern ideals of social justice, democracy, peace, and sustainability. But these will all gradually assume different forms than we have known.

Speaking for just a moment to those of a scholarly bent: One of our discoveries will be that by integrating the perspective of those who have transcended egoism into our research repertoires—a strategy that is professionally taboo—we can make better sense of human psychology, world history, and many contemporary social ills and perils.

(If you're skeptical, I invite you to suspend disbelief long enough to review the evidence.) By demonstrating that the taboo is counterproductive, we also clear the way to launching promising new avenues of research across many disciplines and applied professions. As just one example, the fields of economics and public-policy analysis are ripe for psychospiritually informed top-to-bottom makeovers.

Karl Marx looms quietly in the background of this story, but in unexpected ways. Some argue that Marx's critique of capitalism was too harsh. Capitalist societies have continued to evolve, in many cases moderating the traumatic excesses that Marx and Engels witnessed during the heyday of the Industrial Revolution, such as brutally oppressive and exploitative factory work. But in other respects, the bearded patriarch of modern radicalism may have judged capitalism too forgivingly. Besides Marxian social *injustice* (in which some people benefit at the expense of others), capitalism also produces extensive social *irrationality* (hindering the psychospiritual self-realization of everyone, rich and poor alike, and at great personal and social cost).

THE *MAHABHARATA* IN MODERN TIMES

A word about our guidebook's track record: The *Mahabharata*'s standing as a text foundational to Indian culture is beyond dispute. The culmination of a TV serialization that aired from 1988 to 1990 garnered 92 percent of the Indian television audience. But outside of India, the *Mahabharata* has captured much less attention. Even so, the notion that insights drawn from the epic might be capable of informing contemporary circumstances has notable precedents. This is especially so for a portion known as the *Bhagavad Gita* (the *Song of God*), the fame of which has spread far beyond India's shores.[3]

Appearing as a section within one of the *Mahabharata*'s eighteen books, the *Bhagavad Gita* is widely considered the Hindu analogue of the Bible or the Koran. Many Indian spiritual teachers have felt it almost a mandatory rite of passage to prepare a line-by-line annotation of the text. During his years of resistance to British colonial rule, Mahatma Gandhi took time in 1926 to prepare one such commentary, which he discussed with his ashram's residents after morning prayers. Gandhi often described the *Gita* as a spiritual touchstone that guided his political life, including his unwavering commitment to nonviolent social change.

The *Bhagavad Gita* has been known and influential in the Western world for more than two centuries. Ralph Waldo Emerson and Henry David Thoreau both turned to it for inspiration. In 1845, after spending a "magnificent day" in the *Gita*'s good company, Emerson commented in his journal that: "It was the first of books; it was as if an empire spoke to us, nothing small or unworthy, but large, serene, consistent, the voice of an old intelligence which in another age and climate had pondered and thus disposed of the same questions which exercise us."[4]

The following year Thoreau borrowed Emerson's *Gita* to read as he lived in contemplative solitude beside Walden Pond. In his subsequent ruminations upon his two-year "abode in the woods," Thoreau writes: "I bathe my intellect in the stupendous and cosmogonal philosophy of the Bhagvat Geeta . . . in comparison with which our modern world and its literature seem puny and trivial. . . . The pure Walden water is mingled with the sacred water of the Ganges." He would return to the *Gita* over many years, reading it in three different translations.[5]

In 1893 a previously unknown Hindu monk, Swami Vivekananda, delivered a series of electrifying lectures to a throng of seven thousand at the World Parliament of Religions in Chicago. Thirty-year-old Vivekananda had arrived in the US only two months earlier, penniless and uninvited. Quickly unmistakable in his saffron-colored robe and turban, through sheer force of personality and towering intellect he became the Parliament's most popular speaker.

Amid Vivekananda's listeners sat L. Frank Baum, an undistinguished man in his late thirties. Seven years later Baum published his magnum opus, *The Wonderful Wizard of Oz*, which ascended rapidly in popularity to become America's de facto national fairy tale. There is plausible evidence that Baum crafted central characters in his magical story from Vivekananda's summation of the *Bhagavad Gita's* several paths of yoga (practices for attaining union with the divine). The heart-challenged Tin Woodman represents the yogic path of devotion; the brain-bereft Scarecrow symbolizes the yogic path of knowledge; and the courage-aspiring Lion exemplifies the yogic path of selfless, ethical action in the world.[6]

The *Mahabharata's* influence within popular culture has continued. The *Bhagavad Gita* relates a conversation between a warrior named Arjuna and his friend Krishna. During their dialogue, Arjuna learns that Krishna is an incarnation of God—a being known in subsequent Hindu thought as an *avatar*. Krishna is unusual in other ways. For instance, he has blue skin. Now think of the 2009 film *Avatar*, one of the highest box-office-grossing movies of all time. In it, a poorly educated, paraplegic former soldier is coupled with an "avatar"—his technological agent—in the form of a big blue humanoid body. *Avatar's* director, James Cameron, acknowledges that he was influenced subconsciously by his acquaintance with the *Mahabharata* and other Hindu myths.[7]

The *Bhagavad Gita* has also played a role in world-historic events. While an undergraduate at Harvard, J. Robert Oppenheimer began reading ancient Sanskrit texts in translation. He was sufficiently captivated that later, as a charismatic young physics professor at Berkeley, he studied Sanskrit during his spare time and read the *Gita* in its original language, later calling it "the most beautiful philosophical song existing in any known tongue." An oft-read copy sat by his desk, and he frequently gave away English translations to friends. A decade afterward, in 1945, words from Krishna in the sacred text flashed unbidden through Oppenheimer's mind as he oversaw the top-secret test explosion of the world's first atomic bomb in the chill of a New Mexican desert morning. As the powerful detonation overpowered the predawn darkness: "If the radiance of a thousand suns were to burst into the sky, that would be like the splendor of the Mighty One." Then, as the gaze of overawed scientists followed an ominous mushroom cloud boiling high into the sky: "I am become Death, the shatterer of worlds."[8]

Many believe that the American effort to develop the atomic bomb during World War II would not have succeeded without Robert Oppenheimer's unique combination of scientific and administrative gifts. The most careful student of the subject argues, in turn, that to proceed with his assigned wartime tasks, Oppenheimer drew upon his interpretation of the *Gita* to overcome his ethical reservations.[9]

In short, even if you have never heard of the *Mahabharata*, but you have watched *The Wizard of Oz* or *Avatar*, the *Mahabharata* has already textured your life. Indeed, considering the *Gita*'s role in the history of the atomic bomb, and the bomb's enduring influence in world affairs, there is arguably no modern human life that hasn't been touched by the *Mahabharata*. And that impact shows no sign of declining. For instance, Steve Bannon, the former chief strategist for Donald Trump, is reputedly a great devotee of the *Gita*, reading it as justifying a cataclysmic war to restore a moral world order—precisely the opposite of Gandhi's subtler allegorical interpretation.[10]

In contrast to Bannon's apocalyptic rhetoric, the intent of our effort to decode the *Mahabharata* is to reveal insights more conducive to constructive social influence. The *Mahabharata* has long exerted a peculiar power upon many of those who have encountered it, but its unmined riches remain more extensive than anyone has suspected.

A LITERARY PUZZLE

For me, the lid of the long-sealed time capsule bearing the *Mahabharata*'s hidden message began twisting itself open in April 2011, as I participated in a nine-day silent meditation retreat in Northern California's Sonoma Ashram. Although my formal education includes training as a social theorist, through my sideline as a student of Eastern spirituality I was familiar with the *Mahabharata* in modern renderings. Now, sitting by candlelight in my ashram bedroom, alone and erect on a meditation cushion hours before sunrise, I found myself pondering a literary puzzle.

Early in the saga, a young but unwaveringly righteous and self-composed king, Yudhishthira (the earthly son of Dharma, the god of moral duty and lawful behavior), suddenly steps out of character and recklessly agrees to wager his newly won kingdom in a dice match with his sworn enemies. After swiftly losing twenty-one successive throws of the dice, he and his family are forced into exile. Why would an epic—composed, recomposed, and augmented over the course of centuries—retain such a glaring psychological contradiction during a pivotal moment in the story's grand narrative?

Moreover, because of that dice match, thirteen years later a climactic war will rage in which much of Yudhishthira's extended family, along with almost all his enemies and allies and millions of foot soldiers, will perish. Why choose to have a devastating war hinge on an unexplained, onetime character aberration?

Part I of this book unfolds a new interpretation of the events surrounding Yudhishthira's baffling dice match. It shows that the *Mahabharata* is built upon a beautifully coherent structure that previous modern interpreters have not detected, a structure that encodes a nuanced model of human psychospiritual development. Once we know that structure, we can use it to peel away additional layers of narrative camouflage, discovering that at the time of his downfall, Yudhishthira was living in an artfully contrived palace of regression and illusion ("Maya's Palace"). From this standpoint, his gambling losses are something different, and more instructive, than the calamity commonly supposed.

In Part II, we'll tease out insights from our *Mahabharata* decryption to inform a wide-ranging inquiry into modern psychology, world history, and the evolution of a perverted relationship between psychological development and economic-and-technological development. In Part III, we'll apply these lessons to chart a course for the future. In the myth, Yudhishthira escapes bondage within his palace of regression; in our times, we often don't. Why, and what can we do about it?

As we critique modernity, we will be using our novel interpretation of the *Mahabharata* as an illuminating alternative stance—analogous to six-year-old Lena's shift in planetary perspective—and as such a source of framing and hypotheses for our inquiry. But at no point will we treat the *Mahabharata* as authoritative. For any claim concerning modern psychology, history, or society, we will seek corroboration in modern scholarship.

As we reinterpret the *Mahabharata*, you may find that certain words get in your way. If the names of Hindu gods—particularly the saga's supreme God-in-the-flesh, Krishna—displease, you are welcome to substitute an alternative God, prophet, or higher power. Or, if you're allergic to theism, you might try swapping in a suitable psychological concept—such as Carl Jung's collective unconscious—or a prized secular value, such as Truth, Freedom, Love, Peace, or simply "my truest and best self." As Gandhi remarked, "There is no god higher than truth."

LESSONS UNLEARNED

Back in Sonoma I sat in meditation posture, crossed legs grousing their customary complaint that, in their good judgment, it was past time to shift position. Faltering in my attempt to maintain concept-free meditative concentration, I continued pondering the conundrum of Yudhishthira's complicity in a game of chance that brought his downfall and exile. On its face, his behavior represents a serious gambling addiction. In layman's terms, a behavior is addictive when you do it and receive no reward or, at best, a fleeting one. But then, rather than quit, you try it again and—when that turns out no better—again, again, and again ad infinitum.

By that measure Yudhishthira's gambling behavior is not only addiction but addiction ratcheted up. After all, if you lose four, five, or perhaps even six throws of the dice in a row, you figure you've had a string of miserable luck. But Yudhishthira persists in gambling despite ten, fifteen, and then more successive losses. That's more than bad luck; the game must be rigged. Yet despite the emerging bald evidence that he has entered an unwinnable contest, Yudhishthira plunges ahead to stake and lose his kingdom, his family, and even his freedom.

The story gnawed at me. Dimly I sensed that there might be a significant message here or that something not so unfamiliar was being portrayed. Where else, I mused, have I ever witnessed behavior like this? Sitting upright with my mind calmed by a week of reduced sensory input—no conversation, TV, phone, newspaper, novels, or recorded music, limited food, and long hours of eyes-closed meditation—the characteristics of ordinary bustling life began to stand out in unaccustomed sharp relief. From this stance it dawned on me that in everyday life I almost never see Yudhishthira-like irrationality and compulsiveness . . . except, oh, maybe at least a thousand times each day in my own life and in the lives of everyone I know or observe.

Think about it. We feel some inner lack, so we seek external stimulation or distraction: We surf the Web, listen to a podcast, or catch a movie. We seek external validation that we are real, that we matter, by counting our Facebook "likes" or number of Twitter followers. We look for satisfaction from outside ourselves—through a chocolate bar, new clothes, or a new-model car. And when we're lucky there's a reward—some fulfillment—but it's oh-so-fleeting. Have you noticed that even that second swallow of perfectly chilled microbrewed beer doesn't pack nearly the explosive pleasure that you get from the first sip? So we try again, perhaps piling on more of the same activity, or this time something different. But always it's some source of external gratification or distraction, and always with an outcome that, if positive, proves ephemeral at best. And yet, rather than drawing the obvious conclusion that the entire grand game is rigged and seeking a way to opt out and move on, we continue trying again and again.

That is so much of our lives. It is so much of my life. To co-opt ironically one of the great aphorisms of Hindu spirituality: "I am That."

OK, so Yudhishthira the compulsive gambler may have stepped out of character for Yudhishthira, but he's as near to me as my skin. This, I was now convinced, bore further inquiry. Returning home to rural western Massachusetts, I began delving more deeply into the message that the epic might be trying to convey in having a devastating war hinge on an unexplained character shift. Even more intriguing: What can it mean that Yudhishthira's momentary aberration has become the modern behavioral norm?

Part I

DECODING THE
MAHABHARATA

Chapter 2

THE WAR WITHIN

The Mahabharata *as psychospiritual allegory*

THE SURFACE STORY: A GREAT
WAR AND ITS CAUSES

The *Bhagavad Gita* opens as two enormous armies face off for a long-anticipated fight to the finish. One army has been assembled by the five Pandava brothers; the other is under the command of one hundred brothers who together constitute the Kaurava clan. The Kauravas are the Pandavas' cousins. The winner in this war will become the undisputed ruler of the royal city of Hastinapura and its kingdom.

Duryodhana, the firstborn son of blind King Dhritarashtra, heads the Kaurava clan. The leader of the Pandavas is their oldest brother, Yudhishthira; his brother Arjuna is his most able and spiritually evolved warrior. In the interest of keeping these characters memorable, for now you can think of Yudhishthira, Arjuna, and the other Pandavas as the "good" guys and of Duryodhana and the Kauravas as the "bad" guys.*

Just before the hostilities commence, Arjuna asks Krishna—his charioteer and best friend—to drive out between the two massed armies. Fearing that this war will prove an abomination, Arjuna grows faint of heart and slumps into despair. He has no desire to shed the blood of his close relatives, including elders for whom he feels profound affection and respect. He lowers his mighty bow and tells Krishna that he will surrender rather than fight.

Krishna replies by explaining why Arjuna must do battle. His core answer is that as a member of the warrior caste, Arjuna has a duty (dharma) to fight. The correct way to fulfill duty is for its own sake, non-selfishly, without attachment to the results, which are in the hands

---

* There is a guide to *Mahabharata* names, places, concepts, and pronunciation at the back of this book.

ᵉ of selfless, detached action amounts to a spiritual
ᵢhna calls karma yoga (ethical action in the world).
ᵎ describes two other spiritual paths. Jnana (pro-
nuh") yoga is the path of wisdom secured via inten-
ᵢtudy or meditative practice. This is an arduous path
ᵢvely few people are suited. Bhakti yoga is the heart-
ᵎf devotion to God. Bhakti is accessible to all people and
ᵉ into karma yoga when an ethical action is consecrated
to God aᵤ₊ ᵣformed as an act of worship. We've already encountered
these paths as embodied in the respective inner quests of the Cowardly
Lion, brainless Scarecrow, and heart-lacking Tin Man in *The Wizard of
Oz*. Krishna doesn't mention the yoga of physical postures—known in
India as hatha yoga—that has grown popular in our day.

To assist Arjuna's grasp of bhakti, Krishna decides to reveal a
small secret that he has been keeping for many years: Krishna is God.
Literally. Lest Arjuna have any doubt, Krishna bestows on his friend
immortal eyes and then reveals himself as the embodiment of the
entire cosmos throughout and beyond all time and space. All the suns
and stars of all possible universes blaze in his inner firmament, while
beasts, gods, and the entirety of the Kaurava and Pandava armies are
swallowed up and crushed in his "numerous mouths that are spiky
with tusks and horrifying." Arjuna is overawed and convinced, steeled
to resume his battlefield duties.[1]

The inspired grandeur of the *Bhagavad Gita* appears as an episode
in Book 6 of the *Mahabharata*'s eighteen books. The reasons why the
impending battle between the Pandavas and Kauravas must take place
are laid out in Books 1 and 2.

Owing to convoluted patrimonies, the sovereignty of the kingdom
of Hastinapura is in doubt. Yudhishthira of the Pandavas appears to
have the strongest legal claim, but Duryodhana of the Kauravas has
become accustomed to thinking of himself as heir apparent. He and
his brothers grew up in Hastinapura, whereas the Pandavas spent their
childhood years far off in a forest.

Unable as young men to resolve their conflict, the competing clans
agree to divide the kingdom. Duryodhana will rule in Hastinapura.
Meanwhile, the Pandavas move west to the forested Khandava Tract,
where they construct a prosperous city and begin developing a new
kingdom. Before long, Yudhishthira attempts to formalize his expanding wealth and power by undertaking the rite of Royal Consecration,
which will sanctify him as the "King of Kings" (emperor of the known
world). In preparation, he and his brothers form strategic alliances
with adjacent kingdoms while forcing the submission of more distant
lands in all directions.

The Royal Consecration proceeds, with tribute flowing in to
Yudhishthira from all of India and as far away as China, Greece,

and Rome. Upon seeing his cousin's newfound wealth and power, Duryodhana becomes envious and challenges Yudhishthira to a dice match, which he accepts. Duryodhana assigns his uncle Shakuni—a master wizard in the arcane arts and tricks of dicing—to play on his behalf. As the stakes swiftly escalate, Yudhishthira proceeds to lose twenty successive rolls of the dice. In short order, the normally composed and wise young king has wagered away his entire kingdom. As if that weren't enough, next he gambles each of his four brothers away into slavery, followed by himself, and finally their communal wife, Draupadi.

While Yudhishthira stands silent and stunned, Draupadi is subjected to the outrage of being dragged into court by her hair during her menstrual period, nearly stripped naked before the assembled men of power, and labeled a whore (because she has multiple husbands). Rather than submit to slavery, she displays the steely presence of mind to dispute Yudhishthira's right to have staked her in a bet after he had already become enslaved.

Fair-minded family elders find themselves unable to decide the merits of Draupadi's argument. Finally, Duryodhana's blind father, Dhritarashtra, feeling remorse at Draupadi's degradation, negates the twentieth and final dice match, and magnanimously restores the Pandavas' freedom, wealth, and kingdom. But then he consents, under emotional pressure from Duryodhana, to allow a final winner-take-all throw of the dice. The loser will have to go into exile for thirteen years. Astonishingly, Yudhishthira agrees and is, yet again, outdiced by the wily uncle Shakuni. The Pandavas depart in dignity for the forest but, inasmuch as Duryodhana has no intention of relinquishing his crown or ceding any territory, the groundwork has been laid for a future war to avenge Draupadi's humiliation and decide who finally shall become king.

This is the background for the conflict that—four books later in the *Mahabharata*'s gigantic sweep—will become the setting for the *Bhagavad Gita*'s brink-of-war, divine revelations.[2]

THE *BHAGAVAD GITA* AS SPIRITUAL ALLEGORY

On its surface the *Bhagavad Gita* tells the tale of firming a wavering soldier's resolve to perform his duty. However, the text itself tells us that it can be read allegorically. For instance, the impending battle of the *Mahabharata* takes place on the field of Kurukshetra (the field of the Kurus, a name for the interrelated Kaurava-Pandava dynasty). But in the *Gita*'s thirteenth chapter, Krishna explains that "This body, Arjuna, is called 'the field.'"[3]

In other words, the central "battle" of the story can be interpreted as a struggle between the lower self (i.e., the ego, as represented by Duryodhana and the Kauravas) and the higher spiritual self (the soul, represented in the *Gita* by Arjuna). Krishna is saying that this battle cannot be shirked, because at stake is whether our baser instincts or our most noble capabilities will gain sovereign command of the inner kingdom. As one of the text's modern translators writes: "We find in the *Gita* that there is going to be a great battle for the rule of the Kingdom; and how can we doubt that this is the Kingdom of Heaven, the kingdom of the soul?"[4]

Perhaps the strongest external evidence for interpreting the *Gita* as an allegory of spiritual development is that a book ostensibly about girding emotionally for war was a constant spiritual touchstone for Mahatma Gandhi, our modern world's foremost practitioner of non-violent political action: "When disappointment stares me in the face and all alone I see not one ray of light, I go back to the *Bhagavad-Gita*. I find a verse here and a verse there, and I immediately begin to smile in the midst of overwhelming tragedies."[5]

If the *Bhagavad Gita* is widely interpreted in spiritual terms, the remainder of the *Mahabharata* is commonly read at face value as an intricate legend about interfamilial disagreement, duty, and war. There is also a wide range of scholarly interpretations of the epic's moral teachings, narrative structure, cosmological symbolism, and so on. Many prior interpretations of the *Mahabharata* are ingenious and compelling. That said, a complementary interpretive strategy might be to see whether our understanding of the epic is enriched if we apply the *Gita*'s well-worked spiritual correspondences (e.g., Kauravas = the ego, Pandavas = the soul) throughout the *Mahabharata*'s eighteen books.[6]

There is a noteworthy precedent for this approach, although it has attracted relatively little attention. Scholars today rely extensively on a nineteen-volume Sanskrit critical edition of the *Mahabharata* that was synthesized from more than seven hundred extant manuscript versions by an international team of specialists who toiled over four decades. (I start to have a panic attack every time I try to imagine integrating hundreds of versions of a multi-thousand-page text.) The general editor of this Herculean endeavor was V. S. Sukthankar, an Indian scholar with a doctorate in Sanskrit from Berlin's Humboldt University. In his day few, if any, could speak with more authority on the *Mahabharata*.

In 1942 Dr. Sukthankar prepared four lectures on "The Meaning of the *Mahabharata*" for delivery at the University of Bombay. His final lecture laid out what he characterized as the saga's deepest, metaphysical meaning. At this level, he says, the entire *Mahabharata* represents the internal "battle royal" between the "divine" or "transcendental self" and "one's lower self, the empirical ego." He insisted that "The ancient commentators are clear about it. The unsophisticated Indian, whose property the epic is, knows it instinctively. It is sheer stupidity on the part of the modern critic to have missed the obvious—because the epic itself is also very clear about it."[7]

Given his stature, one might have expected this interpretative strategy to gain considerable traction. But nobody heard Sukthankar's fourth lecture. He died without warning at age fifty-five, only hours before he was scheduled to deliver it. His lecture notes did not appear in print until fifteen years later, and then only in a rarely read book and with their distinguished author no longer there to champion his ideas.

Starting from Sukthankar's premise, we will use the *Bhagavad Gita*'s spiritual symbolism to work out a novel reading of the larger epic. This interpretation offers insights uniquely suited to advancing our understanding of modern psychological and social circumstances.

A WORD ON WORDS

Before tackling the *Mahabharata*, we need to clarify a few terms, including several that we've already encountered. (Don't worry, there won't be a pop quiz.)

Mainstream psychology envisions psychological growth terminating with the formation of a robust, well-integrated ego. The supposition is that there's nowhere further to go. As people mature, they may become more compassionate or altruistic, but these are regarded as healthy ego traits, never as the fruit of transcending ego-identification.

To acknowledge the possibility of ego-transcendence, I will use the words "egoic" and "egoism" to refer to psychological states or transformations during which people remain ego-identified. "Ego-transcendence," by contrast, denotes the *post-egoic* developmental range, which may culminate in stable enlightenment. Thus, I will not apply "ego-transcendence" to episodes of mystical transport that arise and fall away while someone remains developmentally ego-identified.[8]

The minority of psychologists who acknowledge the possibility of ego-transcendence commonly use the term "transpersonal" to characterize development beyond egoism. I will also use that term. However, "transpersonal" does not imply shedding a distinctive personality. People liberated from the ego-function remain full of distinguishing character traits.[9]

To avoid confusion with the tenets of Freudian psychology, today many psychologists prefer to use the word "self" instead of "ego." In keeping with transpersonal psychology and spiritual teachings, I will continue to use the term "ego," but without adopting Freud's definition. Instead, I'll define the ego initially as the unconscious process of establishing a psychological boundary and identifying with what is on the inside. Further distinctive characteristics of egoism will emerge as our inquiry unfolds.[10]

Developing beyond ego-identification means moving into terrain that our culture commonly designates as spiritual. For that reason, I will speak of the full spectrum of human self-realization as involving "psychospiritual development." (While it is customary to think of development beyond ego-identification as distinctively spiritual, actually spiritual development commences at birth, unfolding along with other aspects of development, such as cognition and morality.[11])

The term "psychospiritual" need not involve a belief in God (or gods). In the *Mahabharata* and Hinduism generally, psychospiritual growth is presumed to involve developing a mature relationship—or even oneness—with divinity. But Buddhism and Western transpersonal psychologies typically envision ego-transcendence in philosophical, psychological, or scientific terms. Here the term "psychospiritual" is intended to be neutral, allowing any of these possibilities.

Similarly, I will use the word "soul" to designate that aspect of the self—the higher self—that steps forward as ego-identification softens. As you read, you can leave it at that, with the meaning of soul not further elaborated, or you can supply your own richer understanding, be it secular, spiritual, or religious. Our argument works equally well with different definitions of soul, although richer conceptions will lend it added meaning and significance.

If the concepts of ego and soul feel in any way questionable, you can think of them simply as constructs—tools for thinking about human nature and our potentials. The question concerning a psychological construct is whether it is illuminating and helpful. For instance, does it make the world more intelligible, help explain social phenomena, and facilitate human flourishing? We can't answer these questions in advance; we must proceed with our inquiry and assess the plausibility and usefulness of our conclusions. In other words, buckle your seat belt and let's see where we arrive.

In the interpretation that follows, we will dwell especially on Book 2 of the *Mahabharata* in which the dice match occurs and which caches a key to unlocking a deeper interpretation of the entire epic.

Chapter 3

THE STORY BENEATH
THE STORY

*An epic secretly patterned on stages of
psychospiritual development*

A PATTERN IN THE NARRATIVE

To make sense of Yudhishthira's baffling dice game, we must explore the wider context in which it is situated—to wit, a recurrent pattern in which the Pandavas journey back and forth between society and wilderness. As they move between forest and city, the brothers acquire progressively greater skills, moral refinement, and spiritual attainment. Their moves from forest to city occur after they have resolved challenges they encounter while living away from royal urban life. Their countermoves from city back to forest are generally provoked by their conflict with the Kauravas.

From a modern perspective, a plausible hypothesis would be that the forest episodes represent, at least in part, inner work in the realm of the deep unconscious (i.e., mostly out of reach of the egoic Kauravas). In terms of concepts developed by psychologist Carl Jung, this can include engaging with beasts, demons, princesses, and gods—beings that represent buried psychic material that people must confront and assimilate in order for healthy personal development to continue. In contrast, royal city life offers the comforts, stability, and belonging of well-ordered community life, as well as the challenge of cohabiting with an envious and hostile egoic self.[1]

This underlying developmental pattern can be depicted as an upward spiral that alternates, across the spiral, between successive stages of:

- **Pandavas Apart from Kauravas**, generally in a wilderness setting that provides space for performing soul work in the deep unconscious; and
- **Pandavas Together with Kauravas**, typically in a royal setting that offers the opportunity, via conflictual engagement, to differentiate from the ego, while testing and integrating prior soul work. (See Figure 1. Readers can view or download larger versions of Figure 1 and other figures at www.EscapingMayasPalace .com/figures.)

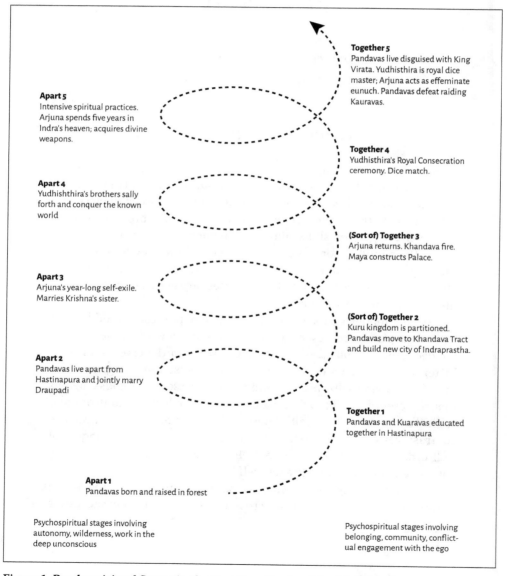

Together 5
Pandavas live disguised with King Virata. Yudhisthira is royal dice master; Arjuna acts as effeminate eunuch. Pandavas defeat raiding Kauravas.

Apart 5
Intensive spiritual practices. Arjuna spends five years in Indra's heaven; acquires divine weapons.

Together 4
Yudhisthira's Royal Consecration ceremony. Dice match.

Apart 4
Yudhishthira's brothers sally forth and conquer the known world

(Sort of) Together 3
Arjuna returns. Khandava fire. Maya constructs Palace.

Apart 3
Arjuna's year-long self-exile. Marries Krishna's sister.

(Sort of) Together 2
Kuru kingdom is partitioned. Pandavas move to Khandava Tract and build new city of Indraprastha.

Apart 2
Pandavas live apart from Hastinapura and jointly marry Draupadi

Together 1
Pandavas and Kuaravas educated together in Hastinapura

Apart 1
Pandavas born and raised in forest

Psychospiritual stages involving autonomy, wilderness, work in the deep unconscious

Psychospiritual stages involving belonging, community, conflictual engagement with the ego

Figure 1. Psychospiritual Stages in the First Four Books of the *Mahabharata*

Recognizing this pattern also enables us to identify deviations from it, depicted in Figure 1 as "(Sort of) Together" Stages 2 and 3. These have their own crucial stories and secrets to tell. There is also an upward movement—along the spiral's implied, core vertical axis—from egoic separateness, fragmentation, and dualistic perception toward deepening integration, moral clarity, wholeness, and nondualism. "Nonduality" denotes transcending the experience that one is sharply separate from other people and one's surroundings.

In his four lectures on the *Mahabharata*, Dr. Sukthankar pointed out many indications that the epic's composers wrote from a nondualist stance: "All great works of Indian art and literature . . . represent but so many pulsating reflexes of one and the same central impulse towards seeing unity in diversity." He maintained also that a typical untutored Indian reader is not troubled by inconsistencies in the *Mahabharata*, "because apparently by automatic mental adjustment he instantly reaches the plane of thought on which the mind of the poet is working." By implication Sukthankar was referencing a nondual plane on which contradictions resolve.[2]

When writing from a standpoint in which the bounded, dualistic consciousness of ego has been transcended, there is no sharp distinction between "outer" wilderness (nature) and "inner" wilderness (unconscious). To the ego, both are "not me" and not controlled by me. Hence the movement toward transcending ego entails coming to terms with the "Forest" within and without.*

SYNOPSIS, SYMBOLISM, AND STRUCTURE IN THE *MAHABHARATA*

Our purpose in reviewing narrative stages in early books of the *Mahabharata* is fourfold. First, we need to become sufficiently familiar with the story to be able to undertake a deeper interpretation of it. Second, we want to find out whether understanding the Kauravas and Pandavas as symbols, respectively, of the ego and the higher self indeed yields a coherent psychospiritual interpretation of the *Mahabharata*. Third, we must verify that the narrative alternates between Apart and Together Stages. Finally, we want to learn whether, as they move from Forest to city and back again, the Pandavas are also *developing* internally—that is, maturing psychologically and spiritually. Establishing these two final points will tell us if we're justified in mapping the Pandavas' life journey as an ascending developmental spiral.

---

* Henceforth I will capitalize the word "Forest" when referring to such deep inner developmental work.

As we probe the *Mahabharata,* the question may arise of whether the teachings we're unearthing were placed there by the authors intentionally or subconsciously. Are we playing more the role of archaeologists (striving to disclose an ancient culture's self-understanding) or depth psychologists (using concepts from our own time to probe that culture's unconscious dimensions)? I suspect that we're blending those two roles. But what matters are the insights that we can lift from the ancient source material and direct toward a new understanding of the modern world.

My synopsis of each narrative step appears in italics, followed by some preliminary psychological and spiritual interpretation. It is not important to absorb the details in what follows; what matters is discerning whether a trajectory of psychospiritual growth runs beneath the surface story. (Note: this is where we begin to undertake real-world *Da Vinci Code*–style decryption of ancient secrets.)

Apart Stage 1: *Prior to the Pandavas' conception, their father, King Pandu, retires with his two wives to a remote forest, where he pursues the life of a celibate spiritual renunciate. Eager to have children, his wives recite sacred words* (mantras) *that enable them to be impregnated by the gods. The five Pandava brothers, each the fruit of a different god, are born and spend their earliest years in the Forest.*

The *Mahabharata* doesn't dwell on the Pandavas' childhood. However, in the ancient Indian imagination, wilderness was a domain of mythic creatures, gods, and supernatural adventures; in modern depth psychology, it is a terrain of subconscious psychospiritual effort and self-realization. In allegorical terms, the *Mahabharata* is indicating that the soul is born of gods in the domain of myth and magic.

Together Stage 1: *Upon King Pandu's death, Forest sages escort the brothers to the royal city of Hastinapura. There the Pandavas receive scriptural and martial-arts instruction in the company of their envious Kaurava cousins. Provoked by the teasing horseplay of Bhima (Yudhishthira's strongest brother), young prince Duryodhana and his allies try unsuccessfully to drown and poison their playful tormentor. In recognition of Arjuna's prowess, the accomplished warrior Drona teaches Arjuna to use the invincible Brahma-Head weapon, warning that it should only be used against a superhuman opponent.*

The Pandavas' journey into society is facilitated by Forest sages, suggesting that their developmental path is being guided by a higher wisdom. This is their first move from a wilderness setting into a social context in which they find themselves at odds with their egoic cousins. The Kauravas' envy and attempt to murder Bhima display the ego's perception of the higher self as a threat, perhaps even a mortal one.

In the *Mahabharata*, divine armaments, such as the Brahma-Head weapon, symbolize inner spiritual powers. It is noteworthy that Drona imparts such powers only to a student who has shown himself worthy, and never without providing moral instruction in the conditions under which these special powers may be used.

Apart Stage 2: *The eldest Kaurava brother, Duryodhana, prevails upon his blind father, the regent king Dhritarashtra, to send the Pandavas away to a provincial town. There Duryodhana tries to have them burned alive in a combustible house. Forewarned, the Pandavas escape. To evade further assassination attempts, they live incognito in various wild Forests. Along the way, brother Bhima kills a threatening Rakshasa (a man-eating giant) and marries the Rakshasa's sister, who is able to take on the guise of a beautiful woman. Their physical union is exuberant: "In secret corners of the woods, on mountain ridges blossoming with trees, by lovely ponds abloom with lotus and water lily, . . . there she assumed a superb body and made love to the Pandava."[3]*

The Kauravas' and Pandavas' grandfather—the renowned sage Vyasa—advises the Pandavas to move to the outlying town of Ekachakra. There, Bhima vanquishes another fearsome Rakshasa, this time as an act of selfless service to a local Brahmin and his village. Finally, Arjuna wins a royal archery contest in the kingdom of Panchala. The prize is Draupadi, daughter of Panchala's powerful king. Draupadi becomes the Pandavas' joint wife.

While in Panchala the Pandava brothers encounter Krishna for the first time. They perceive him as a gallant human prince, not a deity. Krishna benignly witnesses the Pandavas' decision to wed Draupadi collectively, and later he sends a wedding gift.

This is rich material. A Jungian psychologist might posit that in escaping to the Forest, the Pandavas are finding safety from the Kauravas by concealing themselves back in the deep unconscious. Within this context, brother Bhima's transition from killing a man-eating Rakshasa to protect his family to killing a Rakshasa to protect others represents moral advance—that is, considering the interests of a wider circle of people. (Vyasa—who urges the Pandavas to go to Ekachakra—is more than the Kurus' grandfather; when he first appears in the *Mahabharata*, we are told that he is also the epic's author.)

The brothers' joint marriage to Draupadi is another indication of developmental progress. It wasn't customary in ancient north India for brothers to share a wife, so this detail may be a tip-off that the Pandava brothers are not really five different people. It's fine to think of them that way while they are engaged in their sundry adventures, but at a deeper level they are aspects of a single being—internally differentiated and evolving, but a unitary psyche. As the *Mahabharata* translator J. A. B. van Buitenen observes, "The Pandavas act as one organism whose limbs it is impossible to amputate." With their marriage to Draupadi, the limbs of that organism are becoming more tightly cohesive.[4]

This stage of the story is also when the Pandavas first encounter Krishna, who approves of their unusual marriage arrangement by offering a gift. The timing of this meeting suggests that the brothers' marriage—which represents their psychological integration—enables them to begin, albeit in a partial way, to know God and to be known by God. In other words, the union of their plurality into oneness brings greater closeness to God. In contrast to Bhima's prior union with a Rakshasa, which satisfied carnal and reproductive drives, wedding Draupadi serves higher psychospiritual-developmental needs.

If Draupadi contributes to the Pandava brothers' integration, what of the opposing Kaurava clan? There's a parallel construction between the two clans, except that Draupadi completes and unifies the Pandavas, whereas the Kauravas' single sister, Duhsala, accomplishes nothing analogous for her one hundred brothers (only several of whom are fleshed out as distinct characters). The symbolic implication is that the ego is less evolved, harmoniously integrated, and whole.

(Sort of) Together Stage 2: *The Pandavas return to Hastinapura, where Duryodhana wants to kill them. To prevent war, Dhritarashtra partitions the kingdom, giving the Pandavas the undeveloped Khandava Tract as their portion to rule. The Pandavas build a prosperous new city, Indraprastha.*

In ancient India, partition was one customary solution to the problem of inheritance within joint family systems. However, in modern psychological understanding, partitioning, or "splitting," represents a failure to integrate positive and negative aspects of the self into a unified whole. If so, the necessary next developmental step, in which the soul continues its healthy conflict with the ego, could be thwarted. Underscoring this possibility, the decision to split the kingdom comes neither from Krishna nor from the sage Vyasa but from the Kaurava patriarch Dhritarashtra, who is "blind"—i.e., deficient in wisdom.[5]

Apart Stage 3: *Arjuna inadvertently violates a pledge among the Pandavas to grant privacy to the brother whose turn it is to lie with Draupadi. Consequently, Arjuna voluntarily exiles himself to the Forest for a year. There he has romantic and sexual adventures, goes on a spiritual pilgrimage, and, with Krishna's permission, abducts and marries Krishna's sister.*

While off by himself in the Forest, Arjuna continues his developmental trajectory: he enters Krishna's family circle, thus coming into a more intimate relationship with God.

(Sort of) Together Stage 3: *Arjuna returns from self-exile to Indraprastha. During a local pleasure outing, Arjuna and Krishna encounter the wandering Fire God (Agni), who is voraciously hungry to consume the trees and wildlife of the great Khandava Forest (the undeveloped portion of the newly established Pandava kingdom). Indra, the king of the gods, protects this Forest because a great snake named Takshaka lives there. Upon Arjuna's supplication, Agni gifts Krishna and Arjuna divine weapons, including the mighty Gandiva Bow; Arjuna is overjoyed. Battling Indra and allied gods, who pour down torrential rains, Arjuna and Krishna assist in burning down the entire Khandava Forest. As Takshaka's house is about to be swallowed in flames, a panicked demon named Maya rushes out from the door. Krishna and Agni prepare to slay him, but Arjuna intervenes to spare Maya's life.*

Grateful for being rescued, the demon Maya offers a boon. Arjuna needs nothing and suggests talking to Krishna, who asks Maya to build an assembly hall in Indraprastha for the Pandavas. Maya proceeds to construct the most magnificent palace the world has ever seen. Not long after, Yudhishthira conceives the wish to perform the Royal Consecration ritual that will anoint him emperor of the world.

This stage counts as "togetherness," since Arjuna is reunited with his family in their home capital city. But the togetherness is limited, because under partition the Pandavas remain cut off from engagement with the Kauravas.

Lord Indra tries to extinguish the Khandava fire, but Arjuna and Krishna thwart him with their newly acquired divine weapons. Might Arjuna's readiness to take arms against the supreme God of heaven—who is also his true father—constitute an act of hubris? Likewise, what of Yudhishthira's aspiration to become world emperor? We'll take up these and other questions in short order.

Apart Stage 4: *In support of Yudhishthira's imperial ambition, his four brothers disperse in four directions and before long succeed in conquering the known world, including Greece and Rome to the far west and Lanka (today's Sri Lanka) in the far south.*

The Pandavas' grand aspirations find fulfillment more swiftly than anyone might reasonably have expected.

Together Stage 4: *Upon the brothers' return to Indraprastha, Yudhishthira's Royal Consecration ritual proceeds. Duryodhana attends the ceremony. He burns with envy and is humiliated when the Pandavas see him duped by several architectural illusions—including banging into a transparent door and mistaking a crystal floor for an indoor pool of water—that Maya has built into the palace. Seeking to appease Duryodhana, Dhritarashtra orders the swift construction of an assembly hall in Hastinapura that will rival the palace that Maya has* built for the Pandavas. The Pandavas accept an invitation to a dice match in the new hall, where Yudhishthira gambles everything away. Dhritarashtra voids the match, but when Yudhishthira loses a final roll of the dice, the Pandavas are forced into a thirteen-year exile.

Unpacking the symbolic meaning of this fourth Together Stage will be our task in the next two chapters.

The *Mahabharata*'s Apart/Together pattern is now well established. But what of the additional claim that as the Pandavas move back and forth from Forest to city, they are also developing psychospiritually? There has so far been clear evidence of such development: the Pandavas have acquired mundane skills and some spiritual capability (i.e., Arjuna's Brahma-Head weapon), advanced morally (i.e., killed a Rakshasa for the benefit of unfamiliar villagers), and become better integrated with each other through wedding Draupadi.

But afterward, during the two "(Sort of) Together" Stages in which the Pandavas are cut off by partition from their normal conflictual engagement with the Kauravas, evidence of inner development becomes less obvious. For instance, both Arjuna and Yudhishthira exhibit indications of grandiosity. During the ensuing Apart Stage 4, the Pandavas conquer the world but, again, with little indication of corresponding inner growth; Arjuna's announced objective is simply to "swell our coffers."[6]

If we're to be justified in representing the *Mahabharata* in terms of an ascending spiral structure, we need to see if the Pandavas' psychospiritual development resumes.

Apart Stage 5: *Living frugally in the Forest, the Pandavas share many adventures and practice spiritual purification, meditation, and yogas. Arjuna undertakes austerities that enable him to journey alone to the highest heaven, the abode of the supreme God, Indra. Arjuna lives there for five years, acquiring invincible divine weapons as well as skill in the customarily feminine arts of singing and dancing. During this time, the other Pandavas and Draupadi pilgrimage high into the Himalayas.*

Meanwhile, Duryodhana and his Kaurava allies venture into the Forest, planning to humiliate and possibly kill the Pandavas. Instead, they are captured by Gandharvas (flying spirits that mediate between the gods and men). Yudhishthira intervenes to have the Kauravas freed. This only deepens Duryodhana's shame, anger, and envy.

This long Apart Stage 5 Forest sojourn differs notably from Apart Stage 2. Now provincial villages are left far behind. The Pandavas are moving deeper into the unconscious. By undertaking spiritual practices, they rise out of the wild Forest into the loftier realms of the Himalayas and, in Arjuna's case, the heavenly abode of the gods. In modern psychospiritual terms, this is moving from the ordinary personal unconscious toward supraconsciousness, or the Jungian collective unconscious.

The literal meaning of yoga is "union"—that is, any practice that, in full fruition, brings wholeness and union with God. Arjuna's celestial stay is prolonged but not permanent—i.e., his spiritual realization is high but not yet stable. The "weapons" that the gods bestow upon Arjuna during this time are spiritual powers that, as when he acquired the Brahma-Head weapon, he is carefully taught how and when to use. These are weapons that he will eventually need to defeat the Kauravas.

Together Stage 5: *The terms of the final dice match required that the Pandavas spend twelve years in Forest exile, and then a thirteenth year living unrecognized in society. They decide to spend that final year residing disguised in the northwest Indian realm of King Virata. Yudhishthira becomes Virata's palace dice-master. Arjuna pretends to be an effeminate eunuch, donning dresses and jewelry as song-and-dance teacher to Virata's womenfolk.*

Suspecting that the Pandavas might be hiding in Virata's kingdom, the Kauravas mount a large cattle raid. The Pandavas join forces with Virata to repulse the attack.

The journey toward liberation requires integrating elements of one's internal makeup that have previously been inaccessible or repressed. In Together Stage 4, dice gambling was Yudhishthira's downfall. Now, rather than reject that truth (his distressing "shadow" side, in Jungian terminology), he comes to terms with it by fulfilling the role of Virata's dicing master. Likewise, Jung argued that maturation requires men to acknowledge and integrate their feminine aspect, and vice versa. The great warrior Arjuna took singing and dancing lessons in Indra's heaven (Apart Stage 5), and here he completes this inner journey by bending gender, donning women's clothes, and teaching dance and music to Virata's female household.[7]

If the Pandavas' psychospiritual development falters during Stages 3 and 4, that is not the case in Stage 5, in which they practice meditation and yoga, develop further spiritual capabilities, and move toward wholeness by integrating their shadow and feminine aspects. In Stage 4 the Pandavas laugh without compassion at a humiliated Duryodhana. By contrast, in Stage 5 Yudhishthira displays consummate compassion in arranging to free a defeated Duryodhana from captivity.

A DEVELOPMENTAL DOUBLE HELIX

In the stages that we have explored, we have found ample evidence that the *Mahabharata*'s surface narrative is patterned by a trajectory

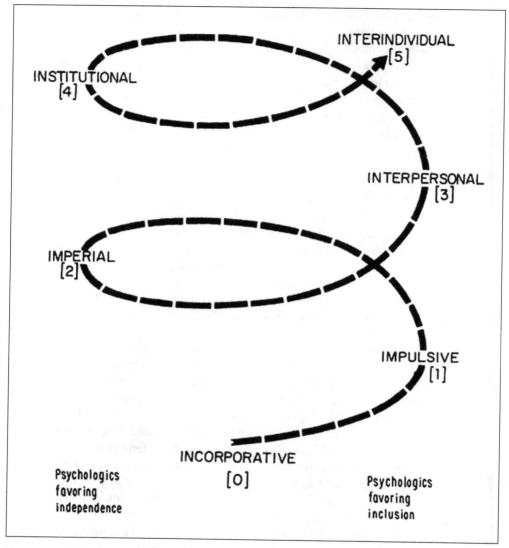

Figure 2. A Helix of Evolutionary Stages. From THE EVOLVING SELF: PROBLEM AND PROCESS IN HUMAN DEVELOPMENT by Robert Kegan, Cambridge, Mass.: Harvard University Press, Copyright © 1982 by the President and Fellows of Harvard College. Used by permission. All rights reserved.

of psychospiritual development that can plausibly be represented as an ascending spiral.

The Mahabharata's spiral pattern is analogous to certain modern theories of psychological development. For instance, Harvard University psychologist Robert Kegan depicts human development in terms of an upward spiral alternating between successive stages of autonomy versus belonging or interpersonal relatedness (see Figure 2). Within Kegan's model, growth to a new stage is provoked when crisis or contradiction (e.g., conflict with the Kauravas) emerging within one's current stage can only be resolved by disembedding from that stage and moving on toward the next (e.g., the next Forest sojourn).

While there are striking similarities between Kegan's and the *Mahabharata*'s models, there are also differences. Notably, the spiral trajectory in Kegan's model represents the dance of a unitary evolving self—an ego—that is conceived as developing in relationship with a succession of supportive contexts. In contrast, the *Mahabharata*'s spiral dance involves two internally complex entities (the egoic Kauravas and the soulful Pandavas) *coevolving* in relationship with an alternating

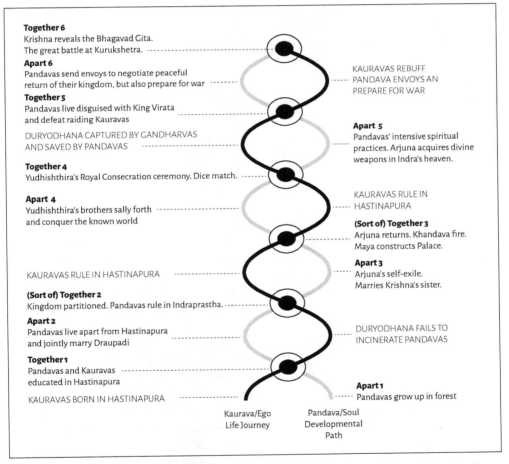

Figure 3. The *Mahabharata*'s Double-Helix Developmental Logic. Figure 1 re-rendered as a double helix in which ego and soul develop through ascending stages that alternate between independent self-actualizing experiences ("Apart") and conflictual interaction ("Together"). A sixth Apart/Together sequence, extending through the *Bhagavad Gita* and the Kurukshetra war, is shown at the top.

succession of supportive contexts. Thus Kegan, like most Western developmental psychologists, is concerned with understanding ego maturation, while the *Mahabharata* focuses on a soul that develops by differentiating from—and ultimately evolving beyond—the ego.

The contrast between Kegan's unitary model of ego maturation and the *Mahabharata*'s ego-and-soul tango toward ego-transcendence suggests that it would be more accurate to pair the spiral in Figure 1 (depicting the Pandavas' development) with a mirror-image spiral documenting corresponding events in the lives of the rival Kauravas. Psychospiritual development results from the dance between these two spirals (see Figure 3). The Kaurava counterspiral can be viewed as a "life journey" rather than a "developmental path," because it is not evident that the Kauravas are capable of much development.[8]

The *Mahabharata*'s surface story embodies the sort of conventional narrative logic that one finds in any coherent tale. We've now elucidated a second, developmental logic that is encoded in the epic's underlying structure. But there's more.

EIGHTEEN STAGES TOWARD SELF-REALIZATION

Translator J. A. B. van Buitenen observes that there is "a peculiar fascination with the number eighteen in the *Mahābhārata*. . . . There are eighteen books, eighteen armies [at war on the field of Kurukshetra], eighteen days of battle, eighteen chapters of the *Bhagavadgītā*."[9]

Mahabharata scholars haven't settled on the significance of the number eighteen. But our discovery of the epic's subsurface trajectory of psychospiritual development opens up new possibilities. An important clue appears in a study by psychologist Daniel P. Brown, who spent twelve years comparing three ancient Asian spiritual traditions: Hindu Yoga (as represented by Patanjali's *Yoga Sutras*), Theravada Buddhism (*vipassana* meditation), and Mahayana Buddhism (Tibetan *mahamudra* practice). He found that all three share "a common underlying structure of *eighteen* distinct stages . . . which unfold in an invariant sequence."[10]

While Brown didn't include the *Mahabharata* in his comparison, the *Yoga Sutras* and the *Mahabharata* were drinking from a common cultural well. Hence, one plausible interpretation of the *Mahabharata*'s repeated use of the number eighteen—and particularly the narrative's traditional division into eighteen books—is that it symbolizes successive stages in psychospiritual development. See Figure 4, which places a central column running up between the double helix of Figure 3 and subdivides it into eighteen segments. (There is no need to study this figure closely; we'll return to it in Chapter 18, below.)[11]

We'll find evidence supporting this eighteen-stage interpretation as we continue to unpack the symbolic meaning of the narrative. But it

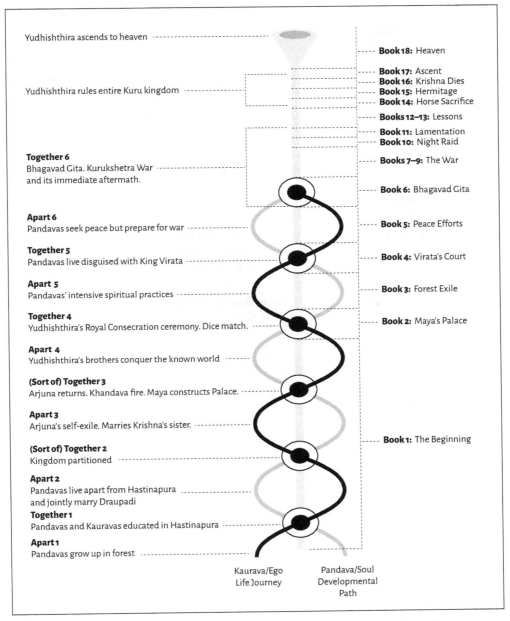

Yudhishthira ascends to heaven

Yudhishthira rules entire Kuru kingdom

Together 6
Bhagavad Gita. Kurukshetra War
and its immediate aftermath.

Apart 6
Pandavas seek peace but prepare for war

Together 5
Pandavas live disguised with King Virata

Apart 5
Pandavas' intensive spiritual practices

Together 4
Yudhishthira's Royal Consecration ceremony. Dice match.

Apart 4
Yudhishthira's brothers conquer the known world

(Sort of) Together 3
Arjuna returns. Khandava fire. Maya constructs Palace.

Apart 3
Arjuna's self-exile. Marries Krishna's sister.

(Sort of) Together 2
Kingdom partitioned

Apart 2
Pandavas live apart from Hastinapura
and jointly marry Draupadi

Together 1
Pandavas and Kauravas educated in Hastinapura

Apart 1
Pandavas grow up in forest

Book 18: Heaven

Book 17: Ascent
Book 16: Krishna Dies
Book 15: Hermitage
Book 14: Horse Sacrifice

Books 12–13: Lessons

Book 11: Lamentation
Book 10: Night Raid

Books 7–9: The War

Book 6: Bhagavad Gita

Book 5: Peace Efforts

Book 4: Virata's Court

Book 3: Forest Exile

Book 2: Maya's Palace

Book 1: The Beginning

Kaurava/Ego
Life Journey

Pandava/Soul
Developmental
Path

Figure 4. The *Mahabharata*'s Eighteen Books as Stages in Psychospiritual Development

is pertinent that the *Mahabharata*'s eighteen books vary enormously in length: Book 12 is nearly one thousand pages long in English translation, whereas, taken together, the final three books run barely forty pages. Thus, it's clear that the epic's division into eighteen books has nothing to do with the practicalities of splitting a long text into manageable portions.

It appears that the *Mahabharata* exhibits a remarkable hidden structure. Beneath the surface narrative there is a subsurface logic, in which:

- Episodes of *spiritual instruction and effort* (Forest experiences) alternate with
- *Soul-ego conflict* (this results in the double helix depicted in Figure 4), thereby
- Advancing stages in *psychospiritual self-realization* (indicated by the central column that is divided into eighteen segments).

To be sure, the number eighteen, representing steps toward psychospiritual self-realization, is not a human invariant. Comparisons of many systems of spiritual development have found that their number of stages varies or that they are not conceptualized in terms of stages.[12]

Now get ready. The *Mahabharata*'s subsurface developmental trajectory is about to become a decoder ring that explains Yudhishthira's aberrant behavior during the dice match—the scene that is pivotal to the epic's first two books and all that comes after.

Chapter 4

THE PALACE OF ILLUSION

An escape from psychological stunting

Yudhishthira's transitory gambling addiction occurs at the culmination of the period during which the kingdom is partitioned. By delving into the *Mahabharata*'s subsurface structure, we've learned that partition involves a deviation from the epic's recurring episodes of Pandava-Kaurava conflict. What might it signify that a deviation in subsurface pattern coincides with a deviation in Yudhishthira's customary character?

To begin: Who is the demon Maya that Arjuna rescues during the Khandava fire? In Sanskrit, the name Maya is close in spelling and pronunciation to the word *maya*, meaning "illusion." In the more technical method of English transliteration, the demon's name is written *Mayā*, with the first *a* pronounced "uh" and the second *ā* (with a horizontal line) pronounced "ah." In contrast, the word for illusion is written as *māyā*, in which both syllables have the "ah" sound. When a demon named Maya builds a palace incorporating numerous architectural illusions (*māyā*), it seems fair to view Maya as the architect of illusion.

Upon seeing Maya, Agni (the Fire God) and Krishna close ranks to slay him. Maya screams for help, and Arjuna rides to the rescue. Thus, Arjuna is susceptible to the entreaties of the creator of illusion precisely when he is exhibiting the puffed-up self-regard without which he wouldn't dare battle the king of the gods and his allies who are trying to extinguish the fire. It is perhaps not accidental that this occurs during partition, when the normal pattern of Pandava-Kaurava conflict is interrupted. In this way the *Mahabharata*'s multiple layers of logic inform one another, allowing us to use clues from one level to decode meanings in another.

So, Maya builds the Pandavas an assembly hall worthy of the gods. Soon after, a visiting sage named Narada arrives and questions

Yudhishthira at length about whether he is virtuously fulfilling the duties of a king. After replying, Yudhishthira asks no further questions about what is expected of a king; instead, he is eager to know if his assembly hall is the world's most magnificent. Narada assures him not only that his palace is unsurpassed but also that his deceased father in heaven, King Pandu, wishes him to undertake an extravagantly costly Royal Consecration sacrifice that will install him as the King of Kings. Yudhishthira finds the prospect alluring. Thus, the young ruler of a newly founded kingdom no sooner takes occupancy of the world's grandest palace than he aspires to be recognized as emperor of the world. Might these represent additional hints of ego-inflation?[1]

Still, when your brothers include the formidable Bhima and the unsurpassable Arjuna, and Krishna is your patron, sometimes circumstances turn your way. Before long, Yudhishthira, ensconced sumptuously in his Palace of Illusion, manages to in fact become sovereign of the known world. He becomes wealthy, famous, admired, and potent beyond compare, sort of like Jeff Bezos, Beyoncé, Nelson Mandela, and Alexander the Great rolled into one.

WHY DOES HE GAMBLE?

Why, near the end of the Royal Consecration, does Yudhishthira accept Duryodhana's challenge to gamble? And why does he continue to play even though the game is clearly rigged?

Yudhishthira says that he is bound by moral law (dharma) to do so. Translator J. A. B. van Buitenen explains that the *Mahabharata*'s Royal Consecration dramatizes a much older Vedic (scripturally prescribed) kingship affirmation ritual, the *rajasuya*. The last stage of the *rajasuya* was a mandatory dice match. Thus, Yudhishthira, as the paragon of dharma, has no choice but to accept the challenge to gamble.[2]

But while this can explain why Yudhishthira agrees to the dice match, it does nothing to explain why he agrees to gamble on the terms offered or why he loses his accustomed composure. For instance, the dice match that concluded an ancient Vedic *rajasuya* was pro forma. The game had to be played, but the newly consecrated king couldn't lose. In contrast, in the *Mahabharata*, Duryodhana's wily uncle Shakuni practically announces his intention to cheat before the game has even begun, boasting that cheating without detection is part of an expert gambler's skill—that, in effect, the dice are going to be loaded. Based on this admission, Yudhishthira could certainly have challenged the legitimacy of the game at any point.[3]

Thus, the *Mahabharata* has, without explanation, introduced a twist, turning the mandatory dice game upside down from a match the king can't lose into one he can't possibly win. Inverting the outcome of the *rajasuya* dice match might be a clue that other incidents in Book 2 are the opposite of what they seem.

A different interpretation of the dice match, for which there is also textual support, is that Yudhishthira's gambling, and indeed everything in the epic, exemplifies fate or destiny—in effect, the expression of Krishna's will. This is a coherent way to read the text (albeit one that diminishes the drama of human emotions and motives, since the answer to every question about why the characters act as they do is ultimately "because God so determines"). However, even if one believes that destiny is in the driver's seat, this alternative reading does not preclude the possibility that the forces at play in the surface story—i.e., divine determination—might be different from those operating beneath it.[4]

The *Mahabharata* refers to the dice match many times before and after. A key commentary occurs during the Pandavas' subsequent Forest exile, after they've had time to reflect on what might have gone wrong. Yudhishthira's mighty brother Bhima berates him for gambling away their kingdom: "Others have stolen our kingdom. . . . A Law that is a scourge for both ourselves and our allies is a vice, king: it is not Law, it is *wrong* Law." Bhima is arguing that Yudhishthira may have tried to uphold dharma, but he erred in discerning what dharma demanded.[5]

Yudhishthira, crucially, agrees and explains further:

> They are doubtless true, O Bharata [Bhima],
> Your biting words that hurt and destroy me. . . .
>
> For I took the dice desirous to take
> Duryodhana's kingship and kingdom away. . . .
>
> On seeing the dice would always favor
> The wishes of Shakuni, even and odd,
> I'd still have been able to check myself,
> But anger destroys a person's calm.
>
> One cannot restrain oneself if valor
> And power and pride are girding one, brother.[6]

Here, Yudhishthira explains that their downfall in the dice game was not, after all, owing to the requirements of dharma. Nor, in his understanding, was their calamity an expression of God's all-determining will. With the benefit of hindsight, Yudhishthira concedes that he consented to gamble based on a small-minded wish to deprive Duryodhana of his status as a king, coupled with a greed-fueled ambition to absorb the Kauravas' kingdom. Even as it became obvious the game was rigged, Yudhishthira persisted in gambling because anger, power-lust, and pride—emotional states typical of egoism—destroyed his equanimity and self-mastery. Scholars who rely on dharma to try to explain Yudhishthira's gambling are, in effect, discounting this passage.

As a result of gambling, Yudhishthira loses everything, becoming initially enslaved and subsequently exiled. But that is only the surface story.

ILLUSION REVEALED

It is commonly taken for granted that Maya's illusory works encompass several overt architectural gimmicks—e.g., a water pond that looks deceptively like a glass floor—that humiliate Duryodhana when he visits the Pandavas' new palace. But deeper works of illusion are secretly in play, enough to ensnare even the steady mind of Yudhishthira.

Living in Maya's incomparable palace, Yudhishthira perceives himself as the commander of all known kings. The dice game reveals this as an illusion, for Yudhishthira lacks sovereignty over even his own emotions. And because of that deficit of inner sovereignty, *he actually controls nothing*—a truth that becomes manifest when his absence of self-mastery induces him to lose outer sovereignty and plummet into slavery.

Yudhishthira controls nothing because he has devolved deeply into egoism, lapsing into being driven by conditioned wants and automated responses. In this state, Yudhishthira can't control anything—no matter his titular world stature—because he lacks autonomous agency. "He" has become an "it"—a puppet subservient to emotional impulse. Ego-inflated, insatiably acquisitive, and desperately addicted, this is no sovereign—only a pretender to the throne, an impostor.[7]

The insight that surmounting egoism is essential to freedom is a point of convergence between Eastern spirituality and Western secular ethics. For instance, in terms of the philosophy of Immanuel Kant, curbing our egoism through moral behavior—and thereby realizing freedom from egoic impulses and conditioning—is a highest-order human good.[8]

But Eastern and Western traditions differ in one core respect regarding morality. Most Western traditions understand a mature ego as the end-stage of human development. Morality can be invoked to ride herd over the ego's baser impulses, but our egoic propensities are presumed to endure. In contrast, the East has understood identification with the ego as an intermediate developmental phase. Hence Eastern traditions evolved embodied practices—such as the karma, bhakti, and jnana yogas introduced in the *Bhagavad Gita*—as vehicles for transcending ego-identification.

Ethical training is integral to Eastern spiritual practice not only because it is morally right but also because it is developmentally effective. Striving to behave ethically exemplifies a "fake-it-till-you-make-it" strategy—that is, attempting to emulate an enlightened person who abides in nondual awareness, discerning no difference between the good of others and herself. This effort to behave *in the manner* of an enlightened person can be a component of the path toward *becoming* enlightened. The spiritual efficacy of ethics is implicit in all the great religious traditions, as well as in Yudhishthira's lifelong struggle to fulfill dharma.[9]

In the *Mahabharata*, the dice game doesn't *cause* Yudhishthira's loss of sovereignty; it *reveals* it. Wily Shakuni isn't, after all, the wicked uncle who steals away the emperor's clothes. Unknowingly, Shakuni functions as the clear-seeing child who shouts out that this emperor isn't wearing any clothes. The illusion of ego is that I am a small separate me—I am my thoughts, feelings, body, stories about myself, and so on. I am bounded and finite. I see the world dualistically, in terms of me and not-me.

Bounded—and unaware that it creates and sustains its boundedness—the ego feels cut off from the currents of love, compassion, equanimity, and intuitive knowing that, according to the world's wisdom traditions, flow through unbounded non-egoic awareness. The only steady state that the ego knows is that of emptiness and lack, engendering the constant fear that it will never have enough to feel safe, satisfied, or real. And this anxiety is well founded, because emptiness is intrinsic to the ego's bounded-off structure.[10]

To be strongly ego-identified doesn't have to mean living in abject misery. We may even, like the youthful Pandavas while dwelling in Maya's Palace, experience ourselves as inwardly content with our outward success. But inevitably, in the ego-state there remains an underlying stratum of emptiness (as exemplified in Yudhishthira's lust for Duryodhana's kingdom). At any moment we may imagine that we need "just one more thing" to feel content—an object or circumstance that in practice recedes into a perpetual string of "one more things." Egos are prone to compulsive and addictive behaviors because those are common symptoms of inner emptiness, ego's core disease (or dis-ease). Seeking to fill the unfillable, egos slip easily into repetitive patterns of futile outward seeking.

Ultimately, the only enduring solution is to transcend the egoic state, allowing the boundary defining the ego to soften or dissolve away. But the ego subconsciously resists this prospect more than anything else because, from its standpoint, boundary dissolution looks like annihilation, death. An apparent death, yes, but what is dying is the illusion of separateness that stands in the way of freedom and wholeness. In the words of Thich Nhat Hanh, a modern Zen teacher,

"Nothing has a separate self. . . . To really understand this is to be free from fear."[11]

Egoism and Moral Regression

Was Yudhishthira this severely ego-laden all along? No. According to our structural reinterpretation, something went awry. It began with partition: When Dhritarashtra split their kingdom, the Pandavas were cut off from struggle with the Kauravas. This led them to skirt necessary inner work, and as a result Yudhishthira and his brothers began to manifest egoic tendencies.

An important tip-off for discerning the Pandavas' inner state involves the gods. The Pandavas don't encounter Krishna or other gods "just as they are" (whatever that might mean). The gods appear as the Pandavas are able to experience them, based on their stage of psychospiritual development. Thus, when the Pandavas first meet Krishna (in Book 1), they encounter him as a friendly human being. That they can see him at all shows that they have begun to advance psychospiritually, but they are not yet able to perceive indications of his divinity. Only much later, on the verge of battle in the *Bhagavad Gita* (in Book 6), is Arjuna able to experience Krishna in his transcosmic glory.[12]

In this light, perhaps the strongest evidence that the Pandavas have slid into intensified egoism is how the gods appear to them after the partition of their kingdom and prior to their twelve-year Forest exile. Some half dozen years after the Pandavas have established their new domain, Arjuna and Krishna meet Agni—a god who is compulsively preoccupied with his own voracious hunger (reminiscent, in fact, of a pitiably insatiable "hungry ghost" in Buddhism). When asked, Agni doesn't hesitate to give Arjuna celestial weapons (spiritual powers) but fails to instruct him in their proper use.

Gifting supernatural weapons without moral instruction is abnormal behavior in the *Mahabharata*. Both before and after this moment, when Arjuna receives spiritual weapons—from Drona in Book 1 or from the gods in heaven in Book 3—care is taken to teach him how and when to use them. There is good reason for such precaution, as spiritual powers for which we aren't properly prepared tend to generate ego-inflation, as happens to Arjuna when he takes up arms against Indra and the other gods and helps raze the entire Khandava Forest. His compatriot Krishna participates enthusiastically in the gruesome slaughter. For instance, the two warriors

> started a vast massacre of the creatures on every side. Indeed, whenever the heroes saw live creatures escaping . . . they chased them down. . . . As the Khandava was burning, the creatures in their thousands leaped

up in all ten directions, screeching their terrifying screams. Many were burning in one spot, others were scorched—they were shattered and scattered mind-lessly, their eyes abursting. Some embraced their sons, others their fathers and mothers, unable to abandon them, and thus went to their perdition. . . . All over, the souls were seen writhing on the ground, with burning wings, eyes, and paws, until they perished. . . . When they jumped out, the Partha [Arjuna] cut them to pieces with his arrows and, laughing, threw them back into the blazing Fire.[13]

There is no heroism in this faunacide. Bloodthirsty killers, sport-ing celestial weapons against which no earthly foe can prevail, glee-fully massacre innocent animal families. This is not the Arjuna we have known before, nor is this the Krishna that we have known or will come to know later. Arjuna's behavior, as well as the behavior of Agni and Krishna as seen through Arjuna's eyes, betoken a person who has slipped into a deeper state of egoism than we have previously seen. More self-centered, he now exhibits limited capacity for moral reflec-tion or restraint.

Similar developmental regression is on display during Duryodhana's humiliation by Maya's architectural illusions. As Duryodhana is fooled in successive quick episodes, the Pandavas (except Yudhishthira) take turns laughing at him. Exhibiting their own now-intensified egoism, their behavior has become unseemly, reflecting no compassionate con-sideration for Duryodhana's feelings. Even Krishna joins in the mock-ery, mirroring the Pandavas' inner state.

The appearance (or nonappearance) of the gods reveals a simi-lar story concerning Yudhishthira. Throughout the Pandavas' rule in Hastinapura, Krishna has become a routine presence in their lives. He is a friend and powerful ally and—although they cannot yet perceive him as a god—owing to his power, sound counsel, and generosity, he exceeds all other men in their esteem.

During one of the later stages of the Royal Consecration, the great Kaurava sage and elder Bhishma tries to explain to the Pandavas and the other kings in attendance that Krishna is God supreme: "Krishna alone is the origin of the worlds as well as their dissolution. . . . Krishna is everywhere at all times." Bhishma's words do not fully register with anyone in the room. Lacking his attainment, they can't absorb this information. But the words draw our attention to a subsequent telling absence. As van Buitenen notes, "The ubiquitous presence of Krishna in *The Assembly Hall* [*Mahabharata* Book 2] makes his absence at the cli-max, the game of dice, the more conspicuous." According to Bhishma, Krishna cannot really be absent during the dice match, because he is all-pervasive. The fact that he is suddenly absent from their view tells us that Yudhishthira and his brothers have slipped into an intensified form of egoism. Not only can they not perceive Krishna as God, they can no longer perceive him at all.[14]

Krishna's absence aside, Yudhishthira, like his brothers, exhibits his own regression and ego-intensification. Despite having already become the wealthiest and most powerful person within his ken, underneath he remains relentlessly discontent. Finally, he becomes so overwhelmingly greedy that he risks his stupendous wealth, territory, and stature for a shot at stripping his rival cousin Duryodhana of his own kingship.

Regression and Dis-integration

The nature of the Pandavas' regression and ego-intensification bears further attention. Regression means returning to a prior, less developed psychological stage. But the Pandavas have never previously been egoic in the way that they become after partition.

In suddenly exhibiting powerful egoic drives, the Pandavas do retrogress in certain respects. Prior to partition, the young-adult Pandavas exhibit basically upright noble characters. Brother Bhima kills a man-eating ogre for the benefit of a village that he's just encountered for the first time. In sharp contrast, after partition Arjuna merrily commits ecocide and faunacide (the Khandava fire), the Pandavas show no compassion to a humiliated Duryodhana, and Yudhishthira becomes so lustful for territory, power, and status that he is willing to risk the enslavement of those he holds most dear. In Yudhishthira's case, egoic drives have usurped the primacy of morality in his psychological makeup.

Egoism has also fragmented the Pandavas' customary unity. Instead of functioning as a single organism, Yudhishthira gambles away his family's freedom without even consulting them. We took note of the ego's limited wholeness in the previous chapter, when we contrasted Draupadi's role in unifying the Pandavas with the absence of any comparable unifying cement among the one hundred Kaurava brothers.

Thus, the Pandavas are moving backward along several dimensions, including emotionally, morally, and in their degree of integration. Yet along other developmental dimensions, there is no regression during the Pandavas' Maya's Palace interlude. Their capacity for instrumental reason (i.e., for crafting effective means to get what they want) and their martial, leadership, and other practical skills remain unsurpassed. Arjuna even continues to excel in his command of supernormal spiritual powers, deploying the divine Gandiva Bow that he requests from Agni.

In short, outer partition (the cutoff from the Kauravas) finds its counterpart in a corresponding inner dis-integration. Before partition, the Pandavas exhibit harmonious, integrated development of all their individual and collaborative capabilities. But now there is an inner split into two nonintegrated developmental tracks—one continuing forward while the other turns and presses backward. Finally, the latter regression becomes so intense that it culminates in the Pandavas losing all that they've achieved outwardly.

Subtle developmental insights are being conveyed here. On the one hand, we see that outer circumstances and inner development are portrayed as interdependent. Yet partition differs from their other developmental contexts in causing the Pandavas' development suddenly to become nonintegrated.

Unaware of what has happened, the Pandavas are driven by new egoic traits that they don't understand to achieve outwardly, yet without commensurate moral consideration. Indeed, *their unsurpassed outer achievement partly depends on their emotional and moral regression.* The ego's sense of lack and consequent unquenchable craving compels them to strive outwardly with new intensity. At the same time, their amplified outward striving is now less inhibited by moral restraint, because they feel more sharply distinct from others and thus less predisposed to take their views and interests into account.

Finally, the Pandavas remain intrinsically more capable than the Kauravas. For that reason, when egoic drives usurp the fulfillment of dharma as the focus of the Pandavas' energies, they begin to manifest an egoism that is ramped up in its ability to pursue its aspirations. Reveling in their new palace, the Pandavas have gone beyond acting like cousin Duryodhana—now they're like Duryodhana on steroids. After all, even at his most ambitious Duryodhana never comes close to achieving universal sovereignty.

Thus, Yudhishthira can almost become king of the world while still only a young adult because, in effect, he is crazed to achieve it, natively more capable than his comparably motivated Kaurava cousins, and now less morally restrained in pursuing what he craves.

Properly decoded, the *Mahabharata* is teaching that when psychospiritual development does not involve sufficient differentiation (e.g., from the ego) and integration (e.g., moral development stably integrated with other developmental dimensions), "outer" achievement may no longer correspond to "inner" attainment.

THE OPPOSITE OF WHAT IT SEEMS

On the *Mahabharata*'s surface level, partitioning the kingdom appears as a sensible compromise, Duryodhana epitomizes evil, Yudhishthira's character shift is inexplicable, the dice game is a catastrophe, the Pandavas' loss of their kingdom is unjust, and exile to the Forest is a further calamity. But from the standpoint of the epic's subsurface developmental spiral, that customary reading is inside out. Partition initiates a sequence of moral and spiritual regression, whereas the events surrounding the dice game set the Pandavas back on the path toward self-realization.

Yudhishthira's momentary backslide into a gambling addiction is no longer a mystery. It is the culminating consequence of a developmental disruption. Conventional readings of the *Mahabharata* regard the first outcome of the dice match (enslavement) and the second (exile) as roughly equivalent disasters. Either way, the Pandavas lose their kingdom. However, from the standpoint of the saga's underlying developmental structure, they play complementary constructive roles. Temporary enslavement reveals that the Pandavas' sovereignty has been illusory. Exile, by contrast, is a coveted first-class ticket back onto an upward-spiraling trajectory of psychospiritual development.

Had the Pandavas suffered the misfortune of *not* being driven into exile, they would have readily returned to life-as-before, stagnating developmentally in their great Palace of Illusion. We know because that is what, in fact, they begin to do immediately after Dhritarashtra restores their freedom and kingdom, and prior to the concluding dice throw that sends them into exile: "Riding their cloudlike chariots," the Pandavas and Draupadi "started . . . *in cheerful spirits* for their good city Indraprastha."[15]

While Duryodhana's intentions are malevolent, they ultimately redound to the Pandavas' benefit. This is conveyed most clearly at the end of the *Mahabharata*: Ascending to heaven, Yudhishthira is outraged to find Duryodhana seated resplendently among the gods. The message is that Duryodhana correctly fulfilled dharma, providing the Pandavas with the conflict without which they could not have succeeded in their psychospiritual journey. In this respect, the *Mahabharata* is indicating that the ego-function is spiritually constructive when ego-identification is limited in intensity and duration, but that it becomes developmentally pathological if it escapes those constraints.

But if exile from Maya's Palace is a boon, how is it that none of the Pandavas can see this?

Chapter 5

MAYA'S ARTS OF DECEPTION

How is the stunting camouflaged?

THE SOCIAL PRODUCTION OF ILLUSION

To understand why and how the Pandavas' developmental setback is shrouded in illusion, we need to distinguish the structure of
Duryodhana's misperceptions from Yudhishthira's. The architectural
illusions that fool Duryodhana don't fool anyone else. They are self-
evident, causing Duryodhana only momentary bewilderment and then
angry humiliation. In contrast, the illusion that fools Yudhishthira into
believing himself sovereign also deceives everyone around him. Thus,
in this case the process of seduction into delusion has been so gradual
and pervasive that *an entire society has succumbed*. When just one person is deluded, others can point out the mistake. But when everyone is
deluded, who is there to help?

The 1978 Jonestown massacre, in which hundreds of Americans
were induced to live under harsh circumstances in a South American
jungle prior to poisoning their own children and committing mass
suicide, comes to mind as a stark modern example. However, the
Mahabharata's pertinence resides partly in the fact that its plot centers on people who are psychologically healthy, widely admired, and
conventionally successful, unlike the Jonestown victims, whom we are
too easily tempted to categorize as socially marginal, duped cult members and thus "nothing like me."[1]

THE EGO AS MASTER OF SELF-
SERVING SELF-DECEPTION

Two basic processes are at work in camouflaging the Pandavas' regression and arrested development. The first involves the structure of the
ego. The second involves social reinforcement.

As they regress into egoism, the Pandavas develop a paramount interest in perpetuating the ego-function and its sovereignty. The principal tool for achieving this is illusion—specifically any illusion that contributes to masking the reality that something fundamental has gone awry in their psychospiritual development.

The capacity to generate such illusions is significantly intrinsic to the ego-function itself. In erecting the boundary through which it distinguishes itself from "other," the ego becomes obsessed with filling its resulting painful hollowness with things or experiences from "outside." This leads the ego to a preoccupation with outer striving and a concomitant tendency to evaluate its progress based on outer achievement, in part as a means of deflection.

At all other times Yudhishthira is concerned most centrally with learning to fulfill dharma, but in Maya's Palace he becomes focused outwardly on expanding his territory, power, and public stature. Thus, *his inner value structure has altered, conforming to egoic priorities rather than the call of morality and spiritual liberation.* Yudhishthira comes to believe that ritual affirmation of his imperial status will confer sovereignty and eventually take him to heaven, whereas in truth only psychospiritual growth can fulfill those aspirations.

Then, in short order, the Pandavas' egoic drives and diminished moral restraint help them actually achieve what they now most crave—outward success. Interpreting based on their crimped egoic value structure, the Pandavas furthermore construe this "success" as confirmation of their internal worth and that they are continuing to "develop." Arjuna's acquisition of the Gandiva Bow—a supernatural power deployed here in the service of egoic ambitions—reinforces the illusion of spiritual progress, because the ego is happy to misinterpret transnormal capabilities as automatic evidence of spiritual attainment. Thus, both outer and selected inner achievements deflect attention from the reality that the Pandavas' emotional and moral development has regressed.

And even when they do try to attend to dharma while living in Maya's Palace, their ability to discern it falters, again distorted by self-interest. Recall that during the dice match, Yudhishthira explains that dharma requires that he accept the challenge to gamble and then, even after it is clear the game is rigged, that he continue to play. But later—in Book 3, when the Pandavas are experiencing their next Forest interlude—Yudhishthira can see that his prior perception of dharma was false, conceding that he wagered recklessly from overweening egoic ambition, not from the dictates of true dharma.

From this developmentally more advanced stance, Yudhishthira realizes that his previous assessment of his *inner satisfaction* was also illusory. While living in Maya's Palace, he had imagined himself content with his imperial conquests, opulent life, and social adulation.

Pumped-up egos easily convince themselves that they are doing and feeling great, especially when they are outperforming competitors. Yet in retrospect, Yudhishthira realizes that his contentment had been another self-imposed mental trick. In truth he remained so empty and unfulfilled that he was willing to risk everything—his kingdom and even his freedom—just for a chance to acquire a bit more territory and humble his rival Duryodhana.

The Pandavas' shift in value orientation from a primary preoccupation with fulfilling dharma to achievement in the outer world latently realizes the ego's paramount purpose of preventing ego-transcendence and thus perpetuating its sovereignty. (By "ego-sovereignty" I mean the ego's usurpation of controlling power within the person, including over the soul and the self-realization process.)

Misidentifying with the Ego

There is a more concrete way to think about the Pandavas' process of self-delusion. Up until now, episodes of strife with their cousins have enabled the Pandavas to differentiate from the ego. When that developmentally healthy struggle is aborted by partition, so is the process of differentiation. As a result, the Pandavas begin to dedifferentiate—that is, to *misidentify* with the ego.

Almost anyone who has tried to meditate has had a taste of differentiating from the ego-mind. Meditators soon discover that they can—at least momentarily—stand apart from their thought processes, observing thoughts float by without participating in them. This is called "witness consciousness," and it involves distancing oneself from one aspect of the ego-function.

We might say that with partition, it is as though Duryodhana, rather than separating from the Pandavas, instead becomes secreted away within them. As a result, the Pandavas start to *see through Duryodhana's eyes and to be animated by his emotions and ambitions.* This surreptitious assimilation of Duryodhana's psyche involves the Pandavas:

1. regressing, fragmenting, and stagnating developmentally; and yet
2. concurrently *seeing themselves and the world as Duryodhana would.*

The Pandavas can't see their developmental regression because they all begin simultaneously—without possibly being able to realize it—to see through Duryodhana's eyes and cogitate with his mind.

When we proposed earlier that the Pandavas exhibited "intensive" egoism while living in Maya's Palace, it's because they had shifted from *coexisting* with a ripening ego (i.e., with the Kauravas, in Book 1) to *misidentifying* with the ego and so manifesting egoic psychology (in Book 2). During this period, Yudhishthira transitioned from an initial ego-inflation (enjoying being treated almost as a god) to insatiable acquisitiveness (for territory, power, and stature) to uncontrollable addiction. This suggests a trajectory of gradually *intensifying* ego-identification.

The denial, rationalization, and other mental tricks through which the Pandavas misconstrue their situation are not far removed from the ego-defense mechanisms recognized by mainstream psychology. In both cases, these mechanisms are means of coping with anxiety. But the difference is that the mechanisms familiar to modern psychology *support* healthy development—or signal mental disorder when they don't—whereas the Pandavas' defense mechanisms *distort and inhibit* development.[2]

Ego-Based Social Reinforcement

By themselves, ego-protective distortions in perception and reasoning would not necessarily suffice to sustain the Pandavas' illusion that they are continuing to progress. Ego-distorted perception requires social reinforcement. Duryodhana proves it: As an egoic being he too is susceptible to illusion and deluded by Maya's Palace. But in his case, there is no social reinforcement. The Pandavas witness him being duped and the illusions in question quickly dissipate.

We can lift a shade to expose the mechanism of socially reinforcing egoic self-delusion by momentarily roaming further afield in world literature. According to the modern Sufi master Idries Shah, Hans Christian Andersen's "The Emperor's New Clothes" is based on a much older Moorish story—"The Three Impostors."[3]

In the Moorish version, fear of being proven hereditarily illegitimate induces a hapless king and all the men in his court to imagine that everyone other than himself can see a miraculous species of cloth. Each person has been told that the magic cloth is invisible to a person whose birth was illegitimate. Unable to see the fabric and fearing that he might after all be a bastard (prior to DNA testing, who could know these things for sure?), every single man, beginning with the king, pretends that he can see the cloth. No one dares defect from this tacit conspiracy of deceit, because the first to do so risks humiliation and loss of all status and power. Indeed, all the nobles compete to see who can outdo the rest in describing how marvelous the cloth appears.

Meanwhile, readers know that the "invisible" cloth is a fiction perpetrated by three devious tailors who plan to make a killing selling absolutely nothing. And for quite a while, they pull it off. Egoic insecurity, vanity, and greed—manifested here in each man's readiness to emulate the rogue tailors in lying ("Yes, I can see the beautiful cloth")—induce an entire society into the collective delusion that "everyone else can see what I cannot." Through lying, each man thus *becomes* the fraud that he wants to believe he is not.

It would be easy to misread "The Three Impostors" as a spot of cute entertainment, although it is surely that. But it is also a technically precise exposé of a hidden process through which human beings, as they become enslaved to their own programmed egoic emotions, trick one another into imagining themselves sovereign and free.

And how do people typically react if someone pierces the veil of illusion? In "The Emperor's New Clothes," one innocently candid pair of eyes suffices to shatter the society-wide conspiracy of deceit. The truth-teller must be a small child or someone else with nothing to lose in speaking truthfully. (In the Moorish tale, it's a poor man who tells the king: "It is of no interest to me whose son I am. So I can tell you that in fact you are riding about without any clothes on!") This reinforces the teaching that egoic perception and behavior are conditioned by self-interest. The socially marginal truth-tellers are not unusually perceptive, smart, or psychospiritually evolved. They simply lack the objective interest, shared by everyone else, in lying about what's in front of their eyes.[4]

The Tenacity of Socially Reinforced Illusion

But is it really that easy to end communal illusions that stabilize everyone's egos? If it were, wouldn't we all be spiritual illuminati?

The *Mahabharata*'s assessment of the tenacity of ego-protective social illusions is more realistic. Recall the patriarch Bhishma's attempt to reveal Krishna's divinity during Yudhishthira's Royal Consecration ceremony. Shishupala, the most imperious of the attending kings, objects, belittling first Bhishma and then Krishna himself. Growing impatient, Bhishma responds, "Whichever man's spirit hastens to death, let him now challenge Krishna . . . to a duel until he is felled and enters the body of this God!" Krishna listens with forbearance to Shishupala's jeers until a line is crossed, and the avatar calmly terminates the discussion by pitching his discus to decapitate Shishupala. As rain showers down from a cloudless cerulean sky, lightning streaks, and the earth quakes, the other kings observe "a sublime radiance rise forth" from the corpse, greet Krishna, and enter his body, fulfilling Bhishma's supernatural prophecy.[5]

Even so, the dogged grip of mutually instilled illusion is not so easily relaxed. The kings concur that they have witnessed a miracle. But not one entertains the possibility that Krishna might be its agent (which would amount to conceding that the worth of Krishna—who, to them, is a mere prince—shines more brilliantly than their own).

Some stare dumbfounded, others are silent; some secretly approve of the arrogant Shishupala's execution, while yet others continue fuming at the assertion that Krishna is their superior. They can contrive to preoccupy themselves with anything except the truth. Not even the most dramatic imaginable demonstration can vanquish their shared ego-protective illusion.

And all of this involves the matter of Krishna's divinity, a reality declared by Bhishma and moments later evidenced publicly. In the alternative case of Yudhishthira's faux sovereignty not a single character—not even Bhishma—is able to detect the subtler illusions in play.

The Proof Is in the Placement

The placement of the story of Shishupala immediately before Yudhishthira's gambling contest supports our reading of Maya's Palace as a domain of growth-inhibiting illusion. In the conventional reading in which the dice game presents as a calamity, the location of the Shishupala episode becomes arbitrary and its meaning is trivialized. First, we read an odd story about a bunch of squabbling kings. Then in the ensuing, seemingly unrelated episode, virtuous would-be emperor Yudhishthira inexplicably shifts character and loses a rigged dice match. In this widely accepted reading, the cohesiveness of the *Mahabharata*'s plotline falters.

But in our inverted structural reading, the lessons in the social reinforcement of illusion that are conveyed in Shishupala's story offer vital insight for unlocking the hidden meaning of Yudhishthira's ascent toward the emperor's throne and subsequent exile: we meet a roomful of kings who are blinded by egoism from the obvious truth that their superiority is an illusion. How much clearer a clue could there be to watch out for something similar in the dice match that follows immediately after? The placement of the Shishupala episode affirms the *Mahabharata*'s coherence when it is read as an allegory of psychospiritual development.

WHO (OR WHAT) IS MAYA?

Once we know what to look for, it's no longer difficult to discern the mechanisms of social reinforcement that camouflage Yudhishthira's egoism. For instance, as soon as he takes up residence in Maya's Palace, Yudhishthira is generous with his wealth but also begins to behave and be treated "as the Gods wait on Brahma in heaven." The implication: sitting at the pinnacle of a social hierarchy can prove ego-inflating. Tempted not long afterward to become the King of Kings, Yudhishthira is speedily affirmed in his colossal ambition by all his self-serving friends and counselors. Who is going to say no to becoming a confidant of the emperor of the known world?[6]

It is evident that the members of Yudhishthira's retinue are less intensely ego-identified than he is. They do not, for instance, manifest addictive behaviors. But they are also not sufficiently evolved to escape the web of illusion through which the Pandavas' egos conceal and preserve their sovereignty.

Unmasking Duryodhana's easy susceptibility to illusion also contributes to reinforcing the Pandavas' self-delusion. Content to laugh at Duryodhana for his perceptual blunders, the regressing Pandavas buttress their now-unwarranted sense of superiority, also deflecting attention from their own deeper illusions. Intrinsically more capable than Duryodhana, when they set themselves to excelling, they do so in every way—including in generating a system of illusion so subtle that, unlike the visual tricks built into Maya's Palace, it's nearly impossible to detect.

This may finally unmask Maya's identity. Of the few oddball survivors of the Khandava inferno, van Buitenen explains that "The oddest of them all is Maya, . . . oddest in an Indian sense. . . . He is completely *alone*, which in the Indian context is an astonishing feature. . . . In India personages of any kind, however demoniac, come in families."[7]

So who is this mysterious Maya? I see only one candidate for the role: Yudhishthira, his family, and their retinue—the people complicit in deluding themselves and one another based on egoic propensities. The confounding oddity that Maya has no family is a clue that "he" is actually an "it"—the symbol for a self-camouflaging social process. The persona of the architect of illusion is part of the illusion.

Hence illusions that the Pandavas conjure—under the guise of Maya, their collective alter ego—induce them to remain in growth-retarding circumstances that they also generate (i.e., Maya's Palace). This mechanism is labyrinthine for a reason: if it were more transparent it wouldn't be effective in thwarting ego-transcendence.

NESTED NARRATIVES

The *Mahabharata* encodes an additional hint to its underlying developmental logic. The epic is constructed as a nested set of stories within stories, each of which has its own narrator. But there is no omniscient, all-revealing voice. Remember, even the gods appear and speak here in relation to the Pandavas' current developmental stage.

The *Mahabharata*'s narrative structure is convoluted, but the details are less important than understanding what is being communicated by the nested structure itself. Vyasa, an enlightened sage, composes the *Mahabharata* and teaches it to his several disciples. One of these is named Vaisampayana, whom Vyasa later asks to recite the story to Arjuna's not yet especially well-evolved great-grandson, King Janamejaya. Present to overhear Vaisampayana's telling is a paid orator named Ugrashrava, the son of another Vyasa disciple. Afterward Ugrashrava imparts the story to a group of Brahmin sages who are conducting an arduous twelve-year Vedic ceremony. The story the Brahmins absorb includes events related through the eyes of subsidiary narrators, such as Sanjaya, a court adviser and charioteer, who in turn reports back on the Kurukshetra War to blind King Dhritarashtra.[8]

Each narrative layer is told and heard by people at different developmental stages. Thus, the *Mahabharata* is, like much modern storytelling, multi-perspectival—except that the *Mahabharata*'s perspectives are hierarchically ordered:

- The epic's creator, Vyasa—whom we do not hear speaking the story directly—is an enlightened master.
- Vaisampayana, who relates Vyasa's composition to Arjuna's regal great-grandson, is Vyasa's advanced spiritual disciple.
- Ugrashrava is not a disciple; he is only the son of another Vyasa disciple and thus not spiritually as advanced as Vaisampayana. The Brahmins to whom he tells the story are experts in the formalities of ritual but seem self-impressed and, in that respect, egoic.
- The charioteer Sanjaya has been specially equipped by Vyasa to serve as the surrogate eyes for "blind" (i.e., clueless) King Dhritarashtra through the temporary power of being able to see events at a distance. However, there is no indication that Sanjaya is otherwise spiritually evolved.

In other words, all of the narrators are linked in some way to the enlightened author Vyasa, but each subsequent telling involves less evolved narrators. And characters in the story who are at higher developmental levels can understand things that those at lower levels cannot, as when Bhishma can see that Krishna is God while the Pandavas and other kings cannot.

As readers, mostly we're hearing (1) the recollection of Ugrashrava (who is spiritually untutored) of (2) Vaisampayana's trained recitation of (3) Vyasa's original telling of what various characters did and said, often as conveyed through the eyes of lesser narrators on the scene. This could be a clue that the epic can be interpreted at different levels, but that we're going to have to work out deeper levels of meaning for ourselves, because Ugrashrava—the one relaying the story to us—lacks the spiritual attainment to do that work for us.

This nested narrative structure reflects a sophisticated theory of knowledge: *all knowledge is stage-specific*. This is different from postmodern relativism (i.e., "anything goes" or "my view is as good as anyone else's"). Relativism can be useful for respecting and interrelating competing perspectives that all originate from within the same stage of psychospiritual development. But relativism is misplaced when it comes to comparing knowledge arising from different stages. Knowledge evolved from a higher developmental stage encompasses and transcends knowledge evolved from a lower stage. We know something about this from observing young children who—while inquisitive and prone to delight and wonderment—also see the world in more simplified terms than do adults.[9]

Throughout its eighteen books, the *Mahabharata* shows us the world through its central characters' eyes. In each case, what they know reflects their developmental station. But the Pandavas' ego-identified stage has a unique property: its psychological processes are distorted in the interest of perpetuating itself, rendering it a particularly opaque, sticky, and thus developmentally hazardous stage.

The *Mahabharata*'s stage theory of knowledge also suggests why the epic, once decoded, becomes a useful tool for understanding modern psychology: there are aspects of our psyches that can only be grasped by looking back from a more evolved, post-egoic stance.

MAYA'S MODERN PALACE?

This book's introduction concluded with me seated on a meditation cushion wondering why the *Mahabharata*'s authors chose to have a cataclysmic war hinge on Yudhishthira's unexplained gambling addiction. Now we understand that his addiction is a symptom of psychospiritual development gone awry. In addition, we've learned why the Palace-bound Pandavas are unable to detect their developmental peril: the ego is adept at deploying self-deception to preserve ego-sovereignty.

That raises a new question: Why have centuries of *Mahabharata* readers and scholars *also* failed to understand the Pandavas' peril, misinterpreting their subsequent exile as a calamity? Let's juxtapose several observations:

- Yudhishthira's addictive gambling bears some psychological resemblance to modern consumerism.
- Yudhishthira's addiction is the culminating symptom of a developmental disorder.
- Prior symptoms include his sudden unbounded desire to acquire more territory, wealth, power, and renown. These cravings are less specifically targeted than an addiction—e.g., to gambling or vodka. Thus, Yudhishthira's character shift while living in

Maya's Palace is, if anything, more directly analogous to modern consumer acquisitiveness than I initially suspected.

- Modern readers have consistently misinterpreted the Pandavas' plight in the same way that the Pandavas do, failing to discern their moral regression and arrest.

Uh-oh.

Is it conceivable that we haven't been able to detect in the Pandavas *what we can't detect in ourselves*? Sharing Yudhishthira's insatiability and perceptual blinders, might we also share the developmental disruption that is their underlying cause? This amounts to hypothesizing that imprisonment in Maya's Palace—that is, unknowing arrest in intense ego-identification—has become the norm in modern societies. From this perspective, consumer insatiability or an unquenchable yearning for power, wealth, or stature would become indicative surface symptoms.*

Various social scientists and spiritual teachers who have reflected upon the modern psychospiritual project concur that modern psychospiritual development is truncated. Ken Wilber, in his book *Integral Psychology*, judges that over the course of modern adolescence we experience "the emergence of the logical mind and adaptation to its new perspectives," but that then, "around age twenty-one, . . . many individuals' overall development tends to become arrested." Psychologist Chellis Glendinning judges, "In a society fraught with psychological distress, in which certain forms of dysfunction like workaholism and sexual addiction are accepted as normal . . . nearly everyone manifests some truncation of full maturity."[10]

Robert Kegan has organized human psychological development into five successive stages or "orders" (plus, implicitly, a sixth order beyond ego-identification). For American adults he reports, "Among a composite sample of people from a wide range of socioeconomic backgrounds in the U.S., 79 percent have *not* reached the fourth order. . . . And only a tiny percentage of people in the studies are *beyond* the fourth order." In *Arrested Adulthood*, sociologist James Côté argues that increasing numbers of modern people live in perpetual "youthhood," never progressing into a stable and responsible adult-ego stage.[11]

Philosopher and transpersonal psychologist Michael Washburn notes that "For most people, the mental-egoic stage is virtually coextensive with life itself. No wonder so few developmental theorists have looked upon the egoic stage *as a stage*, much less a stage that prepares the way for a higher transegoic stage of life."[12]

---

* Henceforth I will use "Palace" or "Palatial" capitalized, as well as "Maya's Palace," as equivalent metaphors for unrecognized arrest in intense ego-identification.

Thus, a number of observers agree that modern psychological and spiritual growth tends to halt well short of our full potential. On the other hand, they are not in consensus on whether this situation is historically aberrant—that's the stance of Glendinning and Côté—or intrinsic to the human condition. And only those with a transpersonal perspective, such as Wilber or Washburn, understand this truncation as arrest in ego-identification.

(As an aside: arrest in ego-identification need not retard all aspects of development. Recall, for instance, that when the Pandavas become ego-arrested and regress morally, the evolution of their leadership and martial capabilities continues to advance.)

In this respect the *Mahabharata* offers a sense of proportion concerning our modern situation that is at once sobering and exhilarating. The period during which the Pandavas are strongly ego-identified runs from the back of Book 1 (partition and the Khandava Forest fire) all the way through the end of Book 2 (the dice match and exile). Then again, the epic comprises *eighteen* books in all. From the *Mahabharata*'s perspective, it looks as though modern societies may have become mired in Book 2 of an available eighteen-book developmental trajectory.

If true, that would indicate that millions and even billions of people may have suffered stunting—and in some cases misery—unnecessarily. But it also means that there could be a collective opportunity to escape Maya's Palace into a world of possibility beyond the ego's imagination.

Developmental trajectories that escape intense ego-identification have the potential to reduce suffering directly in two basic ways: First, they can protect people from experiencing discontent as relentless, autonomy as impaired, and morality as ego-compromised as that exhibited by the Pandavas after they become entrapped in Maya's Palace. Second, they can improve people's prospects for ego-transcendence.

In terms of the outer limits of possibility, Daniel P. Brown of Harvard Medical School explains that the great Asian meditation traditions promise something "quite radical: nothing short of a life without the experience of emotional pain. . . . Disciplined deployment of attention, which may permanently alter human information-processing, may alleviate all traces of everyday unhappiness." Brown isn't saying that enlightened people never encounter severe adversity—only that having transcended the ego-function, they no longer experience suffering as a result. More recently, Brown has argued that spiritual practice can furthermore foster a stable flourishing of positive mental states, as well as greater capability to work compassionately on behalf of the well-being of others.[13]

On the other hand, if arrest in strong ego-identification has become ubiquitous—perhaps much more so than in ancient India—there's a question whether it might have some not-yet-identified social basis that would need to be altered to lessen the intensity of egoism and improve access to the higher ranges of psychospiritual development.

I am not upholding the *Mahabharata* or Hinduism as an ideal template for human development. It's certainly possible to characterize psychospiritual growth in terms other than a war metaphor or distinct developmental stages, whether eighteen or some other number. For our purposes it will suffice to demarcate psychospiritual growth into just three broad phases—pre-egoic, ego-identified, and post-egoic (the last corresponds to the *Mahabharata*'s Books 3 through 18).

Likewise, the *Mahabharata*'s idealization of ancient India's caste system holds little promise as a model of social organization for a modern world that has evolved a more egalitarian social-justice ethos. The *Mahabharata* is merely one nuanced exemplar of the hero's journey into the higher ranges of self-realization, albeit one especially astute about the wiles through which the ego-function can entrench its sovereignty.

Even if our hypothesis about modern developmental arrest holds up, that doesn't mean that many people will suddenly opt to abandon all other pursuits in a single-minded quest to ascend into the higher ranges of psychospiritual fulfillment. As a recent research article puts it: "In ethnography and history . . . everywhere in the world we find spiritual experts—shamans, priests, sorcerers, and sadhus—and yet nowhere in the world is there a society in which all are experts."[14]

The *Mahabharata* points toward a vast, humanly more accessible but—for modern societies—largely uncharted middle ground. That middle ground lies far short of universal attainment of the highest stages of human self-realization. After all, when the Pandavas escape from Maya's Palace, they do not suddenly find themselves enlightened. They are still sixteen books—more than four thousand pages and many further intermediate developmental attainments—away from their final stable attainment of spiritual liberation. But moving toward the middle ground would mean no longer accepting social arrangements that leave most people suffering and stunted well short of their potential, trapped unaware in Maya's Palace.

Part II

DECODING MODERN CIVILIZATION

Chapter 6

A PROCESSION OF ADDICTS

Why are so many of us addicted, anxious, or depressed?

In the *Mahabharata*, Yudhishthira's brief bout of addiction reveals that his sovereignty was an illusion. Spiritually, his development was stunted. So if we want to know whether our modern psychospiritual development is in trouble, inquiring into addiction provides a useful point of entry.

A DISLOCATION THEORY OF ADDICTION

According to psychologist Bruce Alexander, addictive behaviors have always existed, but today they are more prevalent and socially damaging all around the world. For instance, from 1980 to 2018 the number of Americans dying from drug overdoses increased tenfold. In 2020, drug overdoses were responsible for an estimated ninety thousand US deaths, up 34 percent from just three years earlier. Since 2009, more Americans have died annually from drug abuse than from motor-vehicle crashes; many of these people are addicted to prescribed opiate painkillers, such as OxyContin, or became heroin users after taking such painkillers. Worldwide, the prevalence of alcohol, cocaine, and opioid addiction increased notably from 1990 to 2010.[1]

As of 2016, the US National Institute on Drug Abuse estimated the annual economic cost of substance abuse in the United States, including lost productivity and health- and crime-related costs, as in excess of $700 billion—about 4 percent of the nation's gross domestic product. This includes over $190 billion related to illicit drugs, $295 billion for tobacco, and $225 billion for alcohol. A year later the White House Council of Economic Advisers determined that earlier estimates of the economic cost of the opioid crisis "greatly understate" the total amount, which they pegged at $504 billion for 2015. Since that time, the number of opioid overdose deaths has continued to skyrocket. Compounded over decades, the financial loss is staggering. And these figures omit hard-to-quantify costs such as failure in school or family dissolution.[2]

Looking at addiction in broader terms, Alexander sees it "spinning out of control," ranging far beyond drugs, alcohol, and smoking to compulsive gambling, shopping, eating, sex, video gaming, television viewing, and internet surfing. People can also become addicted, he argues, to work, wealth, power, fame, and notoriety. One recent study estimates that 47 percent of US adults exhibit "maladaptive addiction"—that is, addiction associated with such adverse repercussions as reduced autonomy, financial loss, emotional trauma, or impaired social relationships or physical health. Gabor Maté, a medical doctor who works with heroin addicts, observes that "Misplaced attachment to what cannot satiate the soul is not an error exclusive to addicts. . . . Our designated 'addicts' march at the head of a long procession from which few of us ever step away."[3]

Attempting to understand why addiction is growing more common, Alexander made a striking discovery: there are many examples of societies that have persisted for centuries without exhibiting any appreciable incidence of addictive behaviors, but when something goes wrong, addiction becomes endemic. This has, for instance, happened repeatedly among American Indian communities, reflecting their histories of lethal infectious epidemics imported from Europe, displacement from accustomed territories, genocide, heavy-handed government interventions (e.g., children removed forcibly from their homes into distant boarding schools), and other disruptions of traditional ways.

Importantly, eruptions of societal addiction can also reverse. A 1975 study of American soldiers in Vietnam reported that a great many servicemen used heroin while at war and, among them, 20 percent became addicts. Yet after returning to the US, 95 percent of the addicted soldiers recovered from their heroin habits, an astonishingly high remission rate. The explanation: The controversial war was not only stressful and traumatic, as wars normally are, but also atypically unclear as to the ends being pursued and their legitimacy. Under these conditions, soldiers were highly vulnerable to opiate addiction. Once restored to their home social networks, the vast majority were able to recuperate.[4]

Alexander has found that a common thread running through all these historic examples is sustained dislocation—the experience of having vital bonds with one's community, nature, or the spirit world upset or dissolved. Dislocation cuts people off from the nourishing environment that we need in place for "psychosocial integration"—that is, to establish a healthy sense of identity, belonging, and meaning.

Addiction is, by Alexander's definition, always harmful to the addict, society, or both. But it is also, in a limited and tragic sense, functionally adaptive for the addict. Addiction represents an effort to compensate for a devastating loss of wholeness, purpose, and well-being:

> The barren pleasures of a junkie . . . are more sustaining than the unrelenting torment of social exclusion and aimlessness. At the other end of the social hierarchy, endlessly amassing expensive merchandise and organizing it for display and consumption provides an equally narrow sense of meaning for affluent North Americans bereft of richer purposes. . . . To say that an addiction is 'adaptive' is not to imply that it is *desirable*, either for the addicted person or for society, but only that, as a lesser evil, it may buffer a person against the greater evil of unbearable dislocation.[5]

While social dislocation can have many causes, Alexander's research ties the unprecedented prevalence of addictions in the modern world to the spread of global capitalism, a system widely recognized for tilting the balance from deep and enduring human relations more toward instrumental, cash-mediated transactions within incessantly shifting social worlds. Market-driven dislocation is distinctive not because it is more disruptive than episodic calamities such as wars or natural catastrophes, but because it is perpetually sustained. Research affirms that chronic stress is more influential in inducing addiction than is a traumatic event (while the two in combination are more influential still). Plagues, wars, or floods can be ruinous, but they eventually pass, generally allowing stable social relations and settings to reemerge.[6]

Alexander argues that prior to the advent of a global market economy, widely prevalent addiction was exceedingly rare. He observes that during the Middle Ages, when "alcohol consumption and drunkenness on festive occasions was widespread in Europe, . . . a few people became 'inebriates' or 'drunkards,'" but mass alcoholism only emerged with the birth of global capitalism after 1500 and then intensified in step with industrialization and European colonization through the nineteenth century.[7]

Capitalism is not, moreover, the only social order that can produce sustained dislocation. Twentieth-century communist systems often did so as well. In the case of the former Soviet Union, Alexander attributes extensive alcoholism to a dislocating industrial model that originated in the capitalistic West, amplified by Stalin's forced collectivization of agriculture and the stress of living in a police state. Today's China generates dislocation by hybridizing political autocracy with industrialization and growing reliance on market forces.[8]

Alexander's dislocation theory cannot foresee precisely who, among a group experiencing identical dislocating forces, will become addicted. One can imagine that factors such as genetic predisposition, an abusive upbringing, and other contextual circumstances contribute to variations in individual susceptibility.[9]

On the other hand, some of these other factors are interdependent with dislocation. For instance, abusive parenting can contribute to later addiction, but disruptive macroeconomic forces—such as regional economic decline—can ratchet up family stresses and abusiveness.

INTEGRATING DEVELOPMENT INTO ALEXANDER'S THEORY

The *Mahabharata* offers additional perspective on addiction's significance: it is a symptom of disrupted psychospiritual development. It is addiction that shows Yudhishthira that he has lost self-mastery and that helps us understand that the Pandavas had fallen away from their path toward liberation.

For Alexander's purpose—to explain the social causes of addiction—it isn't crucial to investigate addiction as a symptom of impaired development. But crossing that threshold can augment his argument for how deeply damaging dislocation is.

Alexander credits Erik Erikson's "cross-cultural and psychoanalytic research [as] the single most important predecessor" influencing his theory. Alexander adopts Erikson's concept of psychosocial integration and then articulates dislocation as its antithesis. But Erikson's central point was that achieving psychosocial integration is core to progressing through stages in psychological development. Any pathologies, such as addiction, that are concomitant with faulty psychosocial integration thus represent *symptoms* of life-limiting developmental impairment.[10]

For instance, "basic trust" is the core positive attitude associated with the first stage in Erikson's developmental model. In a 1950 essay he enumerated forces of dislocation—including immigration, industrialization, and urbanization—that he deemed culpable in impairing young American mothers' ability to impart a sense of basic trust to their infants. He speculated that mass addiction among teens and adults may be an expression of failure to establish basic trust on a wide scale, indicating that addiction can serve as a "canary in the coal mine" for widespread developmental distortion. More recent studies find that there are additional ways, besides those hypothesized by Erikson, in which dislocation can carve a developmental pathway toward addiction.[11]

Many subsequent psychological studies recognize environmental factors such as crippling poverty, social disorder, or dysfunctional family lives as central causes of developmental impairment. Psychologists such as Robert Kegan argue conversely that stable "holding environments" (the opposite of dislocation) are necessary for successful psychological development. Maté summarizes extensive evidence that the most severe addictions result from trauma that has distorted neurological and psychological development.[12]

Thus, modern psychology supports the idea that addiction can be a symptom of dislocation-induced developmental distortion. Conventional psychology, however, admits no possibility of development past ego-identification and thus has no basis for considering that addiction might represent a symptom of *ego-arrested* development in which ego-identification intensifies and becomes protracted or permanent. But to be able to formulate such an interpretation requires a transpersonal perspective.

Mainstream psychology understands psychological development as involving: (1) building and (2) maturing an ego. Transpersonal psychology, on the other hand, extends this sequence into: (1) building an ego, (2) identifying—or misidentifying—with that ego, and then (3) disidentifying and moving into a post-egoic range of development. From this perspective, chronic dislocation induces egoic emptiness and cravings that increase people's susceptibility to addiction. This is what the *Mahabharata* portrays as occurring after the Pandavas agree to partition and begin living in Maya's Palace.[13]

From a mainstream standpoint, a basic reservation about the transpersonal perspective is whether there even *is* a general human potential for post-egoism. The standard way to address mainstream skepticism has been to try to document instances of people who operate post-egoically and the conditions under which that occurs. The alternative approach that we'll pursue is to see if a transpersonal perspective—and, in particular, what people who have transcended egoism say about the rest of us—can help us make better sense of diverse social phenomena that are otherwise inexplicable.[14]

The question of "ego-arrested" development aside, it is consonant with both the *Mahabharata* and modern developmental psychology to extend Alexander's dislocation theory to encompass addiction as a sign of perturbed psychological development. When we see a dislocated society frothing over the top with addiction, we're also seeing a society in which developmental self-realization has gone widely awry.[15]

DISORDERS BEYOND ADDICTION

Yudhishthira's gambling addiction isn't the only sign that the Pandavas' psychospiritual development has faltered. There is also his prior unbridled acquisitiveness and Arjuna's hubris and reduced capacity for moral reflection, as well as the Pandavas' failure to act compassionately toward a humiliated Duryodhana. These additional tokens of the Pandavas' ego-arrest don't qualify as pathological by modern standards (well, Arjuna's merciless Khandava slaughter might), but they raise the question of whether a modern developmental disorder that has become widespread could be showing itself in ways besides addiction.

Epidemiologists and social scientists have found evidence that dislocation contributes to mental and social disorders such as depression, suicide, anxiety, attention deficit hyperactivity disorder (ADHD), reactivity and impulsiveness (which may, in turn, contribute to poor decisions, violence, or criminal acts), reactionary fundamentalism, and political fanaticism.[16]

The World Health Organization reports that among all the diseases afflicting humanity, depression is currently the leading cause of illness and disability worldwide. In 2015, an estimated 322 million people suffered this misery (4.4 percent of the world's population). From 2007 to 2017, the number of American teenagers who had experienced a recent episode of depression jumped 59 percent. Epidemiological studies indicate that dislocation—including neighborhood disorder, unemployment, inadequate care during childhood, loneliness, and disconnection from others—contributes to depression.[17]

Many people who suffer from addiction also suffer from ADHD; the same stresses contribute causally to both. Along similar lines, a study of US college students and children found that anxiety levels increased significantly from 1952 to 1993, with the decline in social connectedness a major factor in accounting for the difference. Inasmuch as dislocation contributes to depression, anxiety, and addiction—and one disorder can also cause or predispose for the others—not surprisingly they often occur in conjunction with one another. For instance, up to 58 percent of Americans who experience depression in a twelve-month period also experience anxiety.[18]

From 1999 to 2016 the suicide rate in the United States grew 30 percent. Among the contributing factors were depression, substance abuse, economic stress such as job loss or home eviction, and weakening social ties. Among Americans aged ten to twenty-four, the rate of suicide surged 56 percent from 2007 to 2017.[19]

A six-member research team's review of mental-health assessments administered to more than seventy-five thousand US college and high-school students from 1938 to 2007 found that the number of students exhibiting symptoms indicative of psychopathologies such as depression, anxiety, schizophrenia, narcissism, or hypomania multiplied roughly fivefold over the course of these seven decades. The researchers hypothesize that the factors that have contributed most to causing this expanded scope of suffering are social values associated with a dislocated culture: "As American culture shifted toward emphasizing individual achievement, money, and status rather than social relationships and community, psychopathology increased among young people."[20]

Rising trends in the occurrence of mental illness over the past several decades have also been reported for the UK, China, and many other countries. Some of this increase is attributable to change in the size and age-distribution of national populations; however, there is also evidence of mental-health disorders growing more prevalent in conjunction with modernization, urbanization, intensive use of digital media, and periods of acute economic distress (such as during and after the global financial crisis of 2008). Whether the incidence of any given disorder is stable or growing, the extent of human suffering is vast.[21]

Genetics is another factor in this picture. For instance, schizophrenia, depression, and anxiety are thought to have genetic components. But unlucky genes are not the sole cause of these illnesses and can't account for temporal variations in their prevalence. Social and other environmental circumstances activate genetic potentials.[22]

Physical Ailments

People experiencing psychological illness tend also to live more physically impaired and shorter lives. Addiction to smoking cigarettes causes lung cancer and emphysema, but, says the US Department of Health and Human Services, it also "harms nearly every organ of the body." This can include—listen up, men—damage to sperm and erectile dysfunction. Excessive alcohol consumption can lead to liver disease, many types of cancer, heart disease, stroke, and dementia—not to mention a healthy fraction of motor-vehicle fatalities. The Centers for Disease Control hold binge and heavy drinking responsible for killing nearly ninety thousand people annually in the US, on average subtracting thirty years off the lifespan of those who die.[23]

Drugs and alcohol are not the only addictive substances that can cause physical harm. Modern food science combines tasty new combinations of fat, salt, sugars, and low-chew textures into a vast array of addictive processed foods. ("Betcha can't eat just one"—the famous 1960s advertising tagline for Lay's potato chips—unabashedly celebrated this engineered irresistibility.) Eating this way has contributed to an epidemic of obesity and follow-on diseases, such as osteoarthritis, type 2 diabetes, cardiovascular disease, Alzheimer's disease, stroke, liver disease, and many kinds of cancer. A 2013 study estimates that from 1986 to 2006 overweight and obesity played a role in 18 percent of adult deaths in the United States. Worldwide, the incidence of overweight and obesity increased 29 percent over the past three decades.[24]

Turning from addiction: Depression can harm the immune system and increase the risk of developing heart disease, diabetes, and drug and alcohol abuse; it is also the major cause of suicide worldwide. Anxiety has been linked to heart disease and stroke. People suffering mentally may also die sooner because they exercise less, eat worse, or earn less income. A review published in 2015 of 203 studies from twenty-nine nations found that mental illness tends, on average, to be associated with a ten-year reduction in lifespan, and this reduction is trending worse over time.[25]

SOCIOECONOMIC VARIATION

Because dislocation tends to be imposed most harshly on our world's structurally weaker members, there can be significant racial, class, or other biases in who develops follow-on pathologies. For instance, in 2014 a poor person in the US was about 17 percent more likely to suffer from alcoholism and twice as likely to abuse drugs or be addicted to them compared to someone living above the federal poverty level. To the extent that a society stigmatizes and blames those experiencing such afflictions, the personal harm of addiction is often compounded by subsequent social disdain or punishment (e.g., incarceration for possessing illegal drugs, which has contributed to appalling racial injustice in the composition of US prison populations).[26]

Then again, demographic variation in the incidence of diseases that are influenced by dislocation is not always straightforward. For instance, within the US in 2014, non-Hispanic white adults suffered from a serious mental illness about 20 percent more frequently than Hispanics and about 30 percent more frequently than Black Americans. From 2005 to 2015 the incidence of depression increased significantly among white Americans but not among Black Americans. In high-income countries such as Germany and the United States, people at the bottom of the income ladder are about twice as likely to experience depression as those at the top, but there is no such variation in low- to middle-income countries such as Mexico or South Africa.[27]

Overall, within modern societies it is generally true that people living in poverty are more susceptible to mental and physical illness than those who are wealthier; they also have less access to treatment. But they are not alone in bearing scars related to stress and disconnection. For instance, in the contemporary United States obesity is prevalent across *all* income levels. Among women obesity is more common at lower income levels, but in men there is a modest tendency running in the opposite direction.[28]

One study of affluent suburban youth in the Northeast US found higher incidences of anxiety, depression, and substance abuse than among youth in impoverished inner-city neighborhoods. Weak social bonds resulting from affluence (e.g., low-social-interaction suburban neighborhoods in which houses are far apart and parents are preoccupied with ambitious careers) are hypothesized as contributing factors. Other studies interpret some of this adolescent tribulation as symptomatic of a culture that does not provide healthy avenues for spiritual connection and growth.[29]

Celebrity drug-and-alcohol-rehab centers exemplify the reality that even great fortune and fame does not automatically confer protection against the ill effects of dislocation and can even contribute to causing such effects. Apart from suffering from the same disorders that plague the poor—albeit often at a lower rate—people in the higher economic tiers become disproportionately susceptible to other conditions, such as narcissism and workaholism. For instance, in 2008 nearly half of US professionals worked at least sixty-five hours a week.[30]

While narcissism and workaholism are not highly stigmatized—both are sometimes applauded—they can become problematic. Compulsive overwork can harm family and social life, lead to burnout, and contribute to stress-related illness. Self-involved narcissists are sometimes poorly suited to the demands of healthy parenting, just as leaders who are exceptionally narcissistic sometimes endanger their organizations or entire societies (a fear expressed by many before and during Donald Trump's presidency).[31]

Thus, while there are demographic variations in exposure and health outcomes, no social sector escapes the influence of chronic dislocation. Just recall that in recent decades evidence of mental illness has been rising among US college students—a group that is, by definition, relatively privileged.

MENTAL DISORDERS AND PSYCHOLOGICAL DEVELOPMENT

Dislocation contributes to mental illnesses beyond addiction. But in such instances is there also an underlying disturbance in psychological development? Often, yes. In the words of a prominent psychologist: "Psychopathology is not a condition that some individuals simply have or are born to have; rather, it is the outcome of a developmental process." For instance, unhealthy developmental trajectories resulting from adverse childhood circumstances have been shown to provide fertile ground for incubating ADHD, depression, anxiety, schizophrenia, and personality disorders. Roughly 40 percent of the populations in today's high-, middle-, and low-income countries experience such adversity.[32]

Researchers also see a two-way street running between developmental perturbation and mental disorders. For example, growing up in difficult circumstances can limit teenagers' maturity and push them toward drug abuse. Habitual drug abuse can, in turn, interfere with how they mature—or don't—thereafter.

This doesn't mean that all developmental abnormality is dislocation-derived. Genetics can be a contributing factor. Death of a parent during infancy, childhood abuse, or family dysfunction not attributable to dislocation can also impair development.

Nor is it true that developmental irregularity lies beneath every instance of mental illness. For instance, sometimes a single defined bout of depression can be a symptom—a "dark night of the soul"—accompanying psychological maturation. Arjuna's despondency on the eve of the Kurukshetra War and Yudhishthira's dismay at the culmination of the cataclysmic war are afflictions of this essentially constructive, transitional sort. But this is different from the also-common modern situation in which mental woes recur or even linger to plague people for years or a lifetime, often reflecting developmental impairment. A study published in 2011 found that 19 percent of adult Americans experience an episode of major depression during their lifetimes. Unlike Arjuna and Yudhishthira, more than half of these people suffer one or more recurrences in succeeding years. Federal data indicates that in 2018 more than fifteen million Americans had been taking antidepressant medication continuously for at least five years.[33]

Of course, independent of psychological development, there are some important ways in which health has improved in the modern era. For instance, advances in water and sewage management have greatly reduced infant mortality and the incidence of waterborne infectious diseases. But deepening dislocation—and the impaired psychological growth with which it is intertwined—has increased our susceptibility to a wide range of ailments, including addiction, anxiety, and depression as well as follow-on physical illnesses such as cancer, heart disease, and diabetes.[34]

SYMPTOMS OF EGO-ARREST?

Some transpersonal psychologists contend that many of today's mental afflictions are specific to egoic psychology. For instance, egoic traits such as insecurity and emptiness can manifest in, respectively, anxiety or addiction. If so, one might wonder if escaping ego-identification could help cure or prevent mental disorders. Recent research with psychedelic drugs sheds light on this possibility. Hallucinogens such as LSD and psilocybin commonly produce temporary effects that scientists characterize as "loss of ego boundaries," "ego-dissolution," or "ego-transcendence." Those ingesting these drugs frequently report life-altering mystical experiences as part of the package.[35]

But you probably knew that.

However, new research suggests that just a few doses—sometimes even one dose—administered in a therapeutically supportive environment (typically including soft music and lighting and a reassuring psychotherapist or two) have also proven extraordinarily effective in providing relief from today's most common psychological disorders: addiction, anxiety, and depression. Beneficial effects have persisted through follow-up assessment periods that have so far ranged up to two and a half years. Leaders in psychiatry, psychotherapy, and neuroscience are among those attesting to the significance of these findings.[36]

This research is recent and has involved only small groups of patients, so the results must be considered provisional. Still, if temporary ego-dissolution can effect long-term cures of many psychological ailments, that is consistent with the proposition that a healthy portion of modern suffering is an outgrowth of ego-arrested development—just as in the case of Yudhishthira and his family.[37]

Chapter 7

UNINTERRUPTED
DISTURBANCE

Modes of dislocation

The evidence we've reviewed so far suggests that the disruptiveness of the global economy distorts psychospiritual development, heightening susceptibility to a wide spectrum of pathologies. To further untangle the hidden history of psychospiritual development, we need to understand ways in which modern dislocation is distinctive. We'll start by focusing on more recent modes of dislocation.

MARKET-DRIVEN DISLOCATION

Since the dawn of the Industrial Revolution, many theorists have reckoned with the psychological effects of capitalism. French sociologist Émile Durkheim (1858–1917) observed that the dynamism of industrial capitalism *destabilizes* the social world, while increased specialization in the division of labor *weakens people's connections* with one another and with society overall. Believing these forces at fault for the increasing frequency of suicide, Durkheim was a pioneer in theorizing a link between market-driven dislocation and psychopathology.[1]

To the mid-twentieth-century economist Joseph Schumpeter, capitalist innovation and productivity involves a process of "creative destruction." Profit-seeking entrepreneurs introduce new types of businesses and production methods. When these succeed, they often out-compete prior businesses, disrupting the lives of people and communities. For instance, during the third quarter of 2019, the US economy created 7.3 million new jobs and eliminated 7.3 million old ones. That sounds like a wash, except there is no assurance that those thrown out of work will land new jobs or, if they do, in the same geographic location or at the same skill and wage levels. Moreover, the emotional pain caused by unemployment can be severe—often even worse than suffering the death of a loved one. Mainstream economic histories nonetheless celebrate creative destruction as the dynamic responsible for modern economic growth, although occasionally they may acknowledge that it has also "paradoxically . . . eroded the cement of society."[2]

Economic historian Karl Polanyi (1886–1964) argued that the groundbreaking innovation behind the rise of modern capitalism was the "disembedding" of the economy from society. Previously, economic processes were enmeshed within the wider society, and thus were compelled to conform to traditional values. Many of these social mores were not admirable in modern terms—in fact, they could encode terrible inequality and injustice—but they inhibited chronic dislocation. For instance, the powers that be in most preindustrial societies were suspicious of innovation, regarding it as a threat to their privilege and clout.[3]

In contrast, in a capitalist society various social segments come to tolerate or embrace innovation . . . at least if they anticipate that their well-being will not take a hit. Moreover, to the extent that no actor exerts decisive power over all innovation—and especially as globalization intensifies—societies come increasingly under the sway of social forces that they cannot fully control.

Polanyi explained that whenever conditions have approximated the abstract ideal of autonomous laissez-faire markets, the consequences have proven dire:

> To allow the market mechanism to be sole director of
> the fate of human beings and their natural environ-
> ment . . . would result in the demolition of society. . . .
> Robbed of the protective covering of cultural institu-
> tions, human beings would perish from the effects of
> social exposure. . . . Nature would be reduced to its
> elements, neighborhoods and landscapes defiled. . . .
> No society could stand the effects of such a system.[4]

The upshot is that Polanyian disembedding involves replacing traditional constraints on economic activity with a new system of constraints and incentives that permit chronic social turbulence while seeking to prevent system self-destruction.

Marx and Engels offered a famously concise encapsulation of the disruptive effects of market dynamism in *The Communist Manifesto* (1848): "Constant revolutionizing of production, uninterrupted disturbance of all social conditions, everlasting uncertainty, and agitation distinguish the bourgeois [i.e., industrial capitalist] epoch from all earlier ones. All fixed, fast-frozen relations . . . are swept away, all new-formed ones become antiquated before they can ossify. All that is solid melts into air, all that is holy is profaned."[5]

The disruptive sequence of events that has continued to unfold since those lines were penned confirms their enduring truth. During just my own lifetime I've experienced a heavily unionized industrial economy that emerged in the aftermath of World War II, offering substantial numbers of workers lifetime employment with generous benefits and supporting a robust middle class. In short order this devolved into a deindustrialized service economy and then an increasingly globalized postindustrial knowledge economy in which entire regions experienced dizzying transformation and sometimes steep economic decline. This segued into a pair of bursting economic bubbles, including the worldwide recession that began in 2008 with the housing-market collapse, succeeded next by a gig economy in which technological nomads skip from job to job with no job benefits or tenure. Along the way, economic inequality has steadily increased, with inflation-adjusted wages stagnating and many parents forced to work two or three jobs to get by, while their children are in the care of other people. During this same time, a vertiginous array of technological and consumer innovations—ranging from interstate highways and birth-control pills to fast food and the internet—has wrought further upheavals in social life.

To be sure, it's not been all bad. For instance, job safety has improved, a much wider range of occupations has opened to women and people of color, and the air we breathe is far cleaner than when I was a child.

Modes and Dynamics of Dislocation

Once an economy becomes unfettered from customary societal constraints, the capacity to evolve novel modes of dislocation becomes unlimited. But in general, dislocation involves shifting combinations of the following basic elements:

- *Destabilizing* social settings and traditions through change that is rapid, unpredictable, and sometimes chaotic
- *Weakening people's integration* into the worlds of community, nature, and spirit
- *Fragmenting* daily life—for instance, by reapportioning experiences that were formerly unitary into distinct locations, times, and social spheres

Together these elements can contribute to cascades of follow-on psychological and social repercussions, ranging from cultural ferment and creativity on the one hand to disorientation, diminished social cohesiveness, and deficits in belonging and meaning on the other.[6]

Social inequality is a compounding stressor in causing dislocation or limiting people's ability to cope with it. However, because social stratification and oppression long predate the emergence of capitalism, inequality can't by itself account for the elevated modern incidence of addiction and various other psychopathologies or explain why ego-identification may have become atypically intensive and tenacious.

Historically, dislocation has been bound up with the integration of local economies into national and global markets, eroding local economic self-sufficiency. This increases local vulnerability to distant disturbances that can't be influenced from the local level. It can force local businesses to change or shut down in response to translocal competitive pressures; in other cases it replaces locally controlled enterprises with branches of national and multinational corporations that are guided from afar with little attention to local repercussions. All of this can not only deprive people of stable developmental contexts, but also limit their power to shape the world in which they live.

As local economies are dissolved and digested into their national and global counterparts, a special magic is born: During bad times, global business cycles and other macroeconomic perturbations contribute to dislocation via disruptive deprivation. During good times, Schumpeterian creative destruction accomplishes much the same thing. Thus, dislocation becomes inescapable.

Sometimes communities find themselves sitting in the way of a new economic development project—perhaps a factory, highway, or waste dump. In this case the "dislocation" can entail forced physical displacement, often reflecting the inability of a targeted community to resist superior political and economic power. As creative destruction proceeds, many people are transferred, move to pursue new job opportunities, or become unemployed. Throughout the second half of the twentieth century, roughly one in five Americans moved each year. Even for those who stay in place, this turnover in community membership can be unsettling. Years ago, one of my graduate-student friends was mulling over the ceaseless demolition of buildings in older cities such as Boston and concluded that modern urban life is akin to "nuclear war in slow motion."[7]

Capitalism always includes government involvement, whether in undertaking development directly or in acting in the background to issue currency, enforce contracts, support research and development, and so on. In Polanyi's terms, this means that the state has an ambiguous role vis-à-vis market-driven dislocation: governments must prevent dislocation from escalating to the point of societal self-destruction, but at the same time they become an enabling mechanism through which dislocation is facilitated, contested, and channeled. For instance, governments can limit dislocation through environmental or workplace-safety regulations, by providing a robust social safety net, or by establishing social mechanisms for overseeing innovation. Alternatively, they can accelerate dislocation by restricting consumer class-action lawsuits, making it more difficult for workers to organize, hindering the ability of poor people and people of color to vote, resisting environmental protection, deregulating the financial industry, removing campaign spending limits, or negotiating trade agreements that privilege globalization over community and regional stability (all of which have happened in the United States in recent years).

Another distinctive capitalist market dynamic involves pricing ("commodifying") more and more dimensions of life. Trees, wildlife, lakes, geological strata, and fishes become "natural resources." Drinking water is bottled and sold. People become "consumers," "workers," or simply "eyeballs." Today, human organs and sperm are for sale, and wombs can be rented. In 2012, an advertising agency pushed the envelope by hiring homeless people in Austin, Texas, to function as mobile Wi-Fi hotspots. As one aspect of this process, market values—such as productivity, income, consumption, and wealth-based status—tend increasingly to ascend over other social values.[8]

Among the consequences of this societal shift toward commodification is the desacralizing of daily experience, which involves alienation simultaneously from other people, nature, and spirituality. As Kant observed, attributing a price to something voids its sacredness: "Everything has either a *price* or *dignity*. Whatever has a price can be replaced by something else as its equivalent; on the other hand, whatever is above all price and therefore admits of no equivalent has a dignity."[9]

Capitalism also incentivizes calculative social relations—conceiving others as means to our own ends. This can erode community life, weakening our emotional connections and moral relations. The way we experience ourselves shifts as we come to know ourselves more often as consumers or strategizing advantage-seekers than as whole persons or moral agents. Advertising amplifies the propensity to experience life in transactional terms.

Community cohesiveness is further corroded by privatizing services that were previously procured free of charge through ties of kinship, reciprocity, or friendship. Paying to see a movie or to download recorded music versus gathering to sing and tell stories are everyday examples.[10]

The repetitive mindlessness of many jobs in the lower tiers of workplace hierarchies can make people feel powerless, their lives bereft of purpose and meaning. Indifferent treatment by bureaucracies can prove similarly alienating (although bureaucracy is ancient in origin and neither unique to capitalism nor limited to economic affairs).

Economic development can also modify or destroy local ecosystems, harming health, stressing livelihoods, and depriving people of the direct experience of being integrated within the natural world. Large-scale environmental modifications—such as deforestation or climate change—are increasingly prompting human mass migrations or tensions that spill over into violence.[11]

Within societies that tolerate great disparities in wealth and in which social safety nets are not notably robust, poor communities experience especially intense social stresses. These can include elevated rates of unemployment, mental illness, crime and incarceration, and increased exposure to environmental toxins.

In the case of the United States, dislocation has been amplified through the legacies of colonization, slavery, and immigration. Black slavery, for example, involved an almost incomprehensible intensity of dislocation sustained over many generations, persisting in new guises after legal emancipation. At the same time, slavery played a central role in creating the modern world economy, thus contributing to dislocation across the globe.[12]

Non-slave immigration to the US has encompassed people impelled to emigrate by intolerance, persecution, or economic distress in their countries of birth, or who uprooted themselves in the quest for economic advancement. Upon arrival they encountered further dislocation. During the century of peak open immigration from 1820 to 1924, roughly thirty-six million new people came to the US, a transfer of populations among continents that was unprecedented in world history. Beyond the exceptional trauma of the intervening Civil War, during this period the nation was transforming from an agrarian to a substantially urban and industrial society, further compounding the experience of unfamiliarity and dislocation. Those groups already settled in the US experienced the influx of immigrants, with their distinctive languages and cultures, as one more dislocating force.[13]

Chaotically Layered Waves of Dislocation

If we reflect on this procession of change, is modern dislocation primarily episodic or a constant discordant buzz? The answer is both . . . and more: a chaotic layering involving successive patterns and waves of dislocation.

Sometimes we encounter dislocation through disruptive events—a steep economic downturn or the close-by roar of a gang of earthmovers. But we may also confront dislocation in our everyday lives—particularly in neighborhoods in which there is extensive poverty, chaos, and crime. Or we can experience subtler forms of dislocation, as in "neighborhoods" where neighbors don't know each other's lives or names and where there are no local gathering places. A 2018 survey of twenty thousand US adults found that nearly 50 percent do not have daily meaningful social interactions, such as quality time with family or an extended conversation with a friend.[14]

Interwoven with this mishmash of abrupt, steady, and subtle dislocation are further transformations that unfold more gradually. Consider the successive waves of reinvention in white Western family structure and gender relations since the 1700s. There has been a progression from a preponderance of rural extended families that were relatively self-sufficient economically to families in which all members (including children) worked outside the home for pay, followed by middle-class nuclear families with a single (usually male) breadwinner, to today's growing numbers of single-adult, blended, or multiracial households in which most adults are working outside the home for pay . . . unless they are home-based teleworkers.

Meanwhile, modern cultures are in greater flux than is historically typical. We see this expressed in swiftly shifting codes of conduct in homes, workplaces, and other face-to-face or online social settings. All of this unsettles identities, relationships, meanings, and purposes, while leading successive generations to inhabit partially different cultural universes. For example, the generation that lived through the Great Depression and World War II is a world away from children who've grown up with cell phones and social media.[15]

And then there is an occasional, massively disjunctive event: an epic tsunami, a war of unimaginable stupidity or brutality, a burst of cultural upheaval that upends all orienting certainties, the out-of-the-blue destruction of twin office towers, or a global pandemic. The event is always something different and unanticipated. But now there are at least two more twists: First, the competitive muscle of capitalism is a new and formidable factor in engendering episodic macro-crises. Second, these extraordinary disruptive events now burst into a baseline social order that is itself incessantly disorienting and disruptive.

No previous civilization has come close to enduring dislocation of this relentless intensity.

TECHNOLOGICAL DISLOCATION

The market-based economy is not the only significant force driving dislocation. Technologies coevolve roughly in tandem with market dynamics, producing their own complementary dislocations. (I use the word "technology" in the broad sense of material culture. This encompasses not only cutting-edge high technologies but also automobiles, air conditioners, electric power systems, and all other instrumentally useful material artifacts, as well as their accompanying institutions and practices.)[16]

In the early 1970s, futurist Alvin Toffler sold six million copies of *Future Shock*, a book that held the furious *pace* of techno-economic transformation—more than any particular functional attributes of modern technologies—responsible for disparate psychological disorders. However, for our purposes the rapidity of technological innovation can be regarded as just another aspect of capitalism's disruptive dynamism.[17]

Beyond that, technologies contribute to dislocation through their specific design characteristics. For instance, the social consequences of adopting private automobiles are vastly different from the effects of building mass-transit systems.

The Device Paradigm

Philosopher of technology Albert Borgmann argues that modern life is latently constituted by the "device paradigm." The central values embedded in this paradigm are convenience and efficiency. Modern technical devices provide ever more narrowly specified goods and services with ever-increasing speed, efficiency, and effortlessness. In contrast, societies not dominated by the device paradigm rely on "integrative practices." Integrative practices are more burdensome and inefficient. But compared with devices, each one provides many goods and services (rather than one narrowly specified commodity), and it does so in a way that is experientially rich and psychologically integrative.[18]

Borgmann's classic example of an integrative practice is a wood-burning open hearth inside an eighteenth-century European or American household. The hearth provided warmth for people's bodies as well as heat for cooking, bathing, washing, and drying clothes. It cast light and threw evocative dancing shadows. It created a natural focal point for gathering and socializing, generating emotional warmth and closeness.

Using a hearth involved many physically taxing, time-consuming burdens: felling trees, sawing and splitting logs, hauling wood and water, building and tending a fire, caring for the horses or oxen used to drag large logs, growing and harvesting crops, and so forth. But just as the hearth created conviviality, so these supporting activities fostered richly collaborative relationships between adults, children, animals, and the wider world of nature.

Now contrast the world of the hearth with its modern substitutes. Today we heat our homes by adjusting a thermostat, which automatically regulates the central heat coming from a basement furnace. We cook our food using convenient appliances such as a stove, microwave oven, or toaster. We secure light by flipping a wall switch. Lacking the conviviality provided by a steadily lit hearth, we seek solace in front of a TV or computer screen.

Our modern device world is more antiseptic, convenient, and physically less burdensome. But it is also experientially less dense and rich. We are no longer inherently in relationship with the means of our own subsistence, nature, the seasons, animals, other people, or a stable community setting. In these respects, we are literally dis-integrated from the world, which becomes another mode of dislocation.

Living this way, we're sometimes vaguely perplexed, sensing that something is amiss. We've got all this stuff that's expected to make us happy, but our lives can feel empty and fragmented. How does this come to pass?

Ends and means in a world of integrative practices are tightly bound to one another. People living by the hearth know where their wood, food, and water come from. They are enmeshed collaboratively in a directly experienced social and environmental setting. In contrast, the device paradigm achieves convenience by materially separating ends from means, and by ensuring that the means (such as the global petroleum industry, national electric grids, interstate trucking and rail networks, regional water and sewage treatment systems, and the telecommunications networks and computers that constitute the internet) recede experientially into the background. These marvelous infrastructures make our lives of convenience possible precisely by being removed from our daily direct experience.

The exception is that many of us spend a portion of our days toiling within one of these infrastructures. But even then, we are reliant on many devices in conducting our work, while experiencing only a minor fragment of the total multi-infrastructural system upon which our lives depend.

The modern separation of ends and means hides the totality of our supporting infrastructures deep in the background. Meanwhile, we conduct our lives in a foreground comprising ubiquitously convenient commodities. One of my friends, who has lived in developing countries where the device paradigm is less dominant, describes life in the foreground as "like living on a movie set"—superficial and inauthentic.

The device paradigm is dis-integrative in other ways that complement market-driven dislocation. For instance, by physically separating technical ends from means, the paradigm promotes instrumental relationships. Rather than experience ourselves in terms of interdependencies and belonging, the paradigm predisposes us to act strategically for our own benefit.

The device paradigm also increases dislocation by supplanting local interdependencies with others that are more diffuse and remote. For instance, many of the background infrastructures we've grown reliant on are complex, geographically distributed, managed by distant bureaucracies, and responsible for producing social and environmental impacts far removed from where we sit as device-users or consumers. On all these counts we become implicated in dislocating communities elsewhere—even around the world—in ways that we don't directly experience and can't easily modulate if we do learn about them. Conversely, we become less able to influence circumstances originating elsewhere that shape our lives, which is both disempowering and dislocating.

Contrasting Efficiencies

When Borgmann explains that devices are "more efficient" than integrative practices, he is thinking in modern Western cultural terms. A psychospiritual-development perspective would explain the same points differently. Devices aren't "more" efficient; they're *differently* efficient. Devices are efficient at accomplishing specific instrumental tasks. Integrative practices are less efficient at accomplishing any one such task, but impressively efficient at doing many things simultaneously. This includes stabilizing relationships with other people and the natural world, which is favorable to psychospiritual development and, as such, antithetical to the dis-integrative device paradigm.

As an example of contrasting efficiencies: using devices frees us from many physical burdens. We no longer have to chop wood with an ax, slop the pigs, or haul heavy buckets of water. But eliminating that toil has distanced us experientially from the natural world and from the meaning that can be intrinsic to using our bodies physically for life- and society-sustaining purposes. This has furthermore contributed to a devastating epidemic of obesity and life-threatening diseases that are concomitant with a sedentary lifestyle. Some psychologists believe that meaninglessness contributes to addiction, anxiety, depression, and suicide.[19]

Seeking to avoid the adverse health repercussions, many compensate by joining a gym or health club. There in their "leisure" time they (and I) spend hours a week sweating, pumping, and spinning—like so many pet hamsters—on exercise devices that produce no further meaningful social service. In other words, we work sedentarily for pay, in part so that in our off-hours we can afford to perform activities as physically taxing and boring—but now more meaningless—than those that people formerly did in order to support themselves and contribute to their communities. When we stand back from the individually "efficient" devices to look at the overall life that results, their efficiency becomes less self-evident.

From the previous chapter we can infer that in weakening our relationships with one another, stable communities, and the natural world, the device paradigm is also contributing to altering pathways of psychological development in ways that can increase people's susceptibility to mental disorders and distress. A growing body of research supports this inference.[20]

"It Belongs with the Others"

We can better understand some of the device paradigm's implications for psychological development through a contrasting example. In the early 1930s a brilliant Russian psychologist named Alexander Luria conducted psychological tests with peasants in the remote steppes of central Asia. Their answers reveal how a less fragmented/more integrative mode of life contributes to a psychology of wholeness.

Operating under the premises of Marxist social theory, Luria engaged his informants on the assumption that they lived at a lower stage of economic and, correspondingly, psychological development. Expecting to find proof of his cultural superiority, not surprisingly, he found it. But his data tell a more interesting story.[21]

In one experiment Luria worked with three men—identified as Peasants I, II, and III, and aged respectively twenty-five, thirty-two, and twenty-six—who had never or rarely visited a city. In our terms, these were men who lived in a world dense in integrative practices. Luria wanted to test their ability to engage in abstract thinking using analytical categories.

Luria began by showing the men drawings of a hammer, saw, log, and hatchet and asking them which one of the four items did not belong with the others. His supposition was that if the men could think analytically, they would see that the hammer, saw, and hatchet are all "tools," and therefore conclude that the log "does not belong."

That is not how the peasants saw it:

Peasant I: "They're all alike. The saw will saw the log and the hatchet will chop it into small pieces. If one of these things has to go, I'd throw out the hatchet. It doesn't do as good a job as a saw."

Peasant II: "I also think they're all alike. You can saw the log with the saw, chop it with the hatchet, and if it doesn't split, you can beat on the hatchet with the hammer."

Luria judged the men cognitively inferior because they seemed incapable of categorizing analytically. However, an alternative interpretation would be that the three men saw the world in terms of meaningful wholes within which everything "belongs" . . . including themselves.

Luria tried again: "But these three things are tools—right?"

Peasant I: "Yes, they're tools."

That's an important data point; the twenty-five-year-old knew the category "tool" and how it was used.

Luria: "What about the log?"

Peasant II: "We say it's a tool because everything's made out of wood, so it belongs with the others."

Writing decades later, psychologist Abraham Maslow argued that seeing potentials latent in a situation—such as that the log belongs with the tools because it is a potential component of a tool—represents a developmentally superior mode of perception. Likewise, developmental psychologist Michael Basseches maintains that knowing objects as interrelated rather than analytically distinct represents a higher stage of dialectical reasoning, contributing to desirable psychological integration and wholeness. That turns the tables, suggesting that in some respects Luria's peasant informants may have outdone the Stalinist-era professor of psychology from Moscow University in—of all things—dialectical reasoning.[22]

Luria persisted: "Yet you can use one word—tools—for these, isn't that so?"

All three subjects: "Yes, of course."

Luria: "And you can't use that word for a log?"

All three: "No."

Luria moved in for the kill: "If I asked you to pick the three things you could call by one word, which would you pick?"

I: "I don't understand."

II: "All four of them."

III: "If we don't pick the log, we won't have any need of the other three."

The wholeness evident in these peasants' perception and reasoning contrasts with our modern dis-integrated psychology. And there's another lesson: they experienced themselves and the world holistically not because they were spiritually illuminated but because that is natural to human cultures that have not suffered the onslaught of relentless dislocation.[23]

Differentiated Lifeworlds and Fragmented Selves

The device paradigm contributes to dislocation in another way. Operating in concert with capitalism's drive toward profit, productive efficiency, and a specialized division of labor, the device paradigm fragments our lives into functionally distinct contexts and roles, posing a further challenge to psychological integration and wholeness.[24]

In separating ends from means, the device paradigm also separates people internally, for instance dividing us each into family-selves, consumer-selves, worker-selves, citizen-selves, and so on. Think again of the contrasting practice of maintaining an eighteenth-century hearth. In that world, work, consumption, physical exercise, self-development, socializing, and leisure were integrated into a seamless holistic experience. In the world of the hearth, people were known and knew themselves as whole, spatially and temporally consistent selves. In the modern market and device world, we are instead known in terms of distinct personas and roles that manifest according to the particular foregrounded setting—home versus workplace, shopping mall, school, voting booth, and so on—in which we find ourselves at the moment.

Without some division of labor and contextual differentiation, we wouldn't have vaccines against infectious diseases, silicon chips, and solar photovoltaic cells. There wouldn't be as much great literature, art, public architecture, or cinema. But in embracing modern contextual hyper-differentiation, there's a developmental price to pay. This is especially so if there is no adequate compensatory effort to establish stable contexts for experiencing integration and wholeness.

Might devices also interfere with experiencing sacredness? Philosopher Erazim Kohák suggests that integrative practices facilitate access to a primordial sense of the sacred. By "primordial" he means a sensibility that is humanly innate but that becomes covered over by a more instrumental and analytical engagement with the world.[25]

The *Mahabharata* offers a developmental interpretation of how this might come about. During the dice match, the Pandavas' unity is shattered: Yudhishthira stakes and sacrifices his brothers' and Draupadi's freedom. Crucially, this is also when Krishna is absent. The lesson is that as Yudhishthira becomes intensely ego-identified, he becomes more distinctly separate and thus more cut off from all else, including Krishna (i.e., divinity). One might speculate that the disintegration from other people and nature that is intrinsic to the device paradigm could involve a corresponding firming in ego boundaries, impeding access to the sacred.[26]

On Being No Place at Once

In the past several decades the device paradigm has taken a new turn related to personal computers and smartphones. Like prior single-purpose devices, these new devices remain dependent on a recessive background, but each accomplishes a wide range of tasks. Integrated via the internet and cellular networks, microprocessor-based devices establish new relationships and lifeworlds—a qualitatively new foreground—with unique dislocational and dis-integrative propensities.

MIT professor Sherry Turkle, who has published extensively on human-technology interaction, has studied cyber-dislocation. Many children and teens are starved for attention; even when they are nominally with their parents, the adults are obsessively engaged on their smartphones. While pretending to listen to one another, professionals text during meetings. Teenagers sit or walk side by side, absorbed into their personal smartphone screens.[27]

Turkle worries that people are seeking virtual communities in compensation for the erosion of face-to-face social life. But the substitution is problematic. Online relationships are thinner and more tenuous. Rather than develop intimacy or work through conflicts, we move on. This risks depriving us of the contextual stability that's necessary to healthy differentiation and integration.

Virtual life can also corrosively exacerbate one of the problems it was intended to address. As more people spend time online, and are thus less available for face-to-face interaction, *other* people are impelled to go online in compensation, setting up an unwelcome feedback loop. With opportunities for in-person social life contracting, we grasp harder and more defensively for less satisfactory virtual substitutes.[28]

As face-to-face relations weaken, people also feel starved for validation that they matter. The result is obsessive checking of tweets, texts, and Facebook posts—which only takes them further away from direct engagement, compounding the initial techno-alienating dynamic. According to the CEO of the ironically named Virgin Mobile cell-phone service, 20 percent of customers will interrupt sex to take a phone call.

Some of us are spread so thin among so many places simultaneously that we exist in a state of "being no place at once." In effect, attention deficit disorder is being upgraded from psychological impairment to societal norm. According to a leading study of how Americans use their time, "many Americans never experience anything fully, never live in the moment."[29]

The results are disturbing from the standpoint of psychospiritual development. Americans have fewer friends than they used to. Families, even when in the house at the same time, are dispersed in separate rooms with their respective entertainment and communication devices. Children and teens exhibit new and more extensive symptoms of fear and isolation. Today's college students evince less empathy than their counterparts of decades past. Recent research links teen and young-adult social-media use to increased risk of depression and suicide. For instance, a study published in 2017 found that American adolescents who spend three hours or more a day using electronic media are 34 percent more likely to exhibit signs associated with the risk of committing suicide. Similar trends are emerging worldwide; a 2021 study of adolescents in thirty-seven nations found that loneliness and sadness have increased in step with the use of the internet and smartphones.[30]

Online social networks can be a salutary adjunct to face-to-face relationships, including for connecting people who share specialized passions or challenges. But online relationships are not so great for sharing a walk, an embrace, and the delicate scent of a flower in the woods. When virtual life displaces in-person social interaction, we pay a price. Life in cyberspace is alienating us from a foreground that was already impoverished and dislocating.

Chapter 8

THE WANTS OF MANKIND

The social history of insatiability

According to an article in *World Psychiatry*, depression, substance abuse, and other mental disorders are now the leading causes of disability throughout the world, on average stripping away twenty years of full health from every person five years and older.[1]

In Chapter 6, we concluded from the extent of modern mental illness that impairment in psychological development has grown extensive. In Chapter 7, we explored the rampant dislocation that drives the problem. But how ubiquitous and tenacious are such distortions in psychological development? We know that people who don't exhibit mental illness are not necessarily free of distorted psychospiritual growth. For instance, growing up under adverse social circumstances can harm psychological development—as revealed in poor academic performance, behavioral problems, or a weakened sense of moral agency—without necessarily causing mental disorders such as depression or addiction.

The *Mahabharata* suggests another window for determining how pervasive modern developmental impairment has become: insatiability. Consumer insatiability is ubiquitous and typically persists through a lifetime. But is insatiability a human constant? Or is it possibly a symptom of developmental distortion? If the latter, we would be a major step closer to understanding how Yudhishthira's momentary psychological aberration became the new normal.

RICKSHAW-WALLAH ECONOMICS

In 2006 and 2007 my family and I lived for nine months in the northern Indian city of Varanasi, which is mentioned in the *Mahabharata* and situated some four hundred miles southeast of the saga's principal settings. In modern Varanasi, devices such as motorized vehicles and cell phones are layered upon a life that is still rich in integrative practice. For instance, my most common mode of transportation was to walk or hire a bicycle rickshaw.

The men who pedal rickshaws are called rickshaw-wallahs. Generally, they are delighted to convey visitors who hail from more developed nations, knowing that they can charge at least 50 percent above the going rate paid by an Indian customer—and sometimes much more. Often when I was walking around busy parts of Varanasi, rickshaw-wallahs vied eagerly for my patronage. But sometimes in the late afternoon when I'd ask a wallah for a ride, he'd decline. Why?

At the time, Varanasi rickshaw-wallahs typically lived on the equivalent of about two dollars and fifty cents a day. (That was meager, but not quite as little as it sounds, because the cost of living was far below that in the United States or Europe.) With such an income a family was far from affluent, but together with a wife's earnings they could get by. When a lounging rickshaw-wallah brushed aside my request for a ride, my inference was that he had already hit his target income for the day. Even though he would have earned a healthy bonus by ferrying a foreigner, evidently he valued his leisure more than the goods, status, or security that additional income would have provided. In economic and psychological terms, he was satiable.

This doesn't mean that rickshaw-wallahs wouldn't have preferred to be rich. If someone had offered one the equivalent of a thousand US dollars—a lump sum slightly more than his typical annual income—without doubt the gift would have been gleefully accepted. But his desire for more did not burn vigorously enough to motivate a reclining wallah to transport me once he'd decided that he was done working for the day.

To a modern Westerner this species of economic conduct may not be especially familiar. Employers expect that offering a higher wage will prompt employees to work longer or harder. But in human terms, the behavior of a Varanasi rickshaw-wallah isn't exceptional. For instance, anthropologists have observed comparable propensities in nomadic hunter-gatherer cultures. The portion of each day devoted to subsistence activities is short compared with modern norms and often far from intense:

> Hunting and gathering are social events and contexts for socializing. The Batek, for example, do not "view work as a burden. . . . Most men and women approach their economic activities enthusiastically." . . . Mbuti approach their hunting in a similar way . . . : "The overall pace of the hunt is so leisurely that old people

and mothers with infants may join. Between casts of
the nets, the hunters regroup . . . to share tobacco or
snacks of fruit and nuts gathered along the way, . . . to
flirt and visit, to play with babies."[2]

The propensity to work in order to meet basic subsistence needs—
and only intensively when necessary—and otherwise to turn to noneconomic pursuits is not a unique attribute of rickshaw-wallahs
or remote tribal societies. It was not uncommon in late-medieval
Western Europe and even into the early modern period. For instance,
when wages rose after the fourteenth-century Black Death created significant labor scarcity, many English peasants began upgrading their
diets and purchasing sturdier shoes. A minority took advantage of
increased income to improve their housing and to purchase a variety
of useful consumer items, such as metal basins, ceramics, tablecloths,
and bed linen. But a substantial number of peasants appear to have
taken advantage of higher wages to simply work fewer days.[3]

A study based on precious rare evidence—the life stories of peasants in an early-fourteenth-century village in southern France, as
recorded in their own words—found that:

> For them the working day was punctuated with long,
> irregular pauses, during which one would chat with
> a friend, perhaps at the same time enjoying a glass of
> wine. . . . Whenever they could, they tended to shorten
> the working day into a half day. . . . More generally, the
> case of Montaillou corresponds to . . . rural life almost
> everywhere in the West before the time of Adam
> Smith. . . . Production for the market is not neglected
> (mostly sheep, with poultry and eggs as a subsidiary
> contribution), but the main effort is directed toward
> the more or less satisfactory subsistence of the family
> itself rather than towards "the creation of accumu-
> lated surpluses." . . . The refusal to over-exert oneself
> is reflected in all the naps taken, the time spent sit-
> ting in the sun and the many allusions to days off and
> saints' days.[4]

Over the next several centuries such relaxed behavior became
less common in many areas throughout Eurasia. Growing numbers of
people found new ways to augment their income. Simultaneously, the
quantity and range of economic goods imported, produced, and consumed started to increase dramatically.

THE RISE OF CONSUMERISM

Notable economic changes emerged in the mid-seventeenth century, especially in the Netherlands, the adjacent Low Countries, Britain, and the northwest corner of France. In the language of economics, "consumer aspirations" were climbing. More people began to work, earn, and consume well beyond the level requisite to mere subsistence. In the case of the English middle classes (the so-called "middling sort") this included purchasing kitchenware, candlesticks, window curtains, books, clocks, paintings, the latest clothing fashions, and new kinds of food and furniture.[5]

Intellectuals took note of this altered psychological landscape. Scottish political economist James Steuart reasoned in 1767 that in former times, "the wants of mankind being few," people could be induced to "labour beyond their wants" only by the institution of slavery. In contrast, Steuart saw that "men are forced to labour now because they are slaves to their own wants." He was sanguine about this new enslavement, judging it responsible for increasing industriousness, food production, and population.[6]

Reflecting in 1784 on the life he knew in America and Europe compared with that of American Indians, Benjamin Franklin observed of the latter that "Having few artificial Wants, they have abundance of Leisure for Improvement by Conversation. Our laborious Manner of Life compar'd with theirs, they esteem slavish & base."[7]

Historian Jan de Vries provides a useful review of theories that have tried to explain this rise in consumer acquisitiveness. De Vries rejects advertising as a contender because that doesn't explain why people suddenly became more susceptible to the arts of commercial persuasion. Many historians argue instead that mass consumerism was driven by the attempt of lower classes to emulate those above. De Vries and others find this line of explanation oversimplified. It can't account for consumer goods, such as hand-printed cotton clothing and wooden chests, that were refined as they emanated upward from below.[8]

David Hume (1711–1776) proposed that human desires were aroused by exposure to novel consumer goods arriving from overseas—tea from China and brightly colored cotton cloth from India, for example. This amounts to assuming that people exhibited insatiability when confronted with new consumption opportunities.

This is plausible, but it begs certain questions. Just as the efficacy of advertising doesn't explain *why* advertising is effective, the mere availability of new wares doesn't explain why people would want them, much less want them badly enough to work longer or harder to acquire them. As a leading historian of consumerism observes, the preference for new goods was "neither pre-existing nor stable but had to be created." For instance, coffee did not become popular in Europe until a century after its introduction.[9]

De Vries also considers seventeenth- and eighteenth-century innovations in moral reasoning that defended private consumption as a route to civic virtue, the advance of the arts and sciences, and economic growth. But while that helps us understand why the clergy and various intellectuals did not *oppose* consumption, this doesn't explain what *animated* popular consumption in the first place. Surely few people were purchasing fashionable wardrobes and refined tableware based on elite philosophical expositions.[10]

Cultural historian Colin Campbell attributes the escalation of consumer craving to the rise of Romanticism, which cultivated an inner capacity for fantasy and countered Puritanism's moral asceticism and frugality. But even if Romanticism was a contributing factor, Campbell's theory is narrowly particular to England and, even there, doesn't fully explain the underlying drive to consume once external

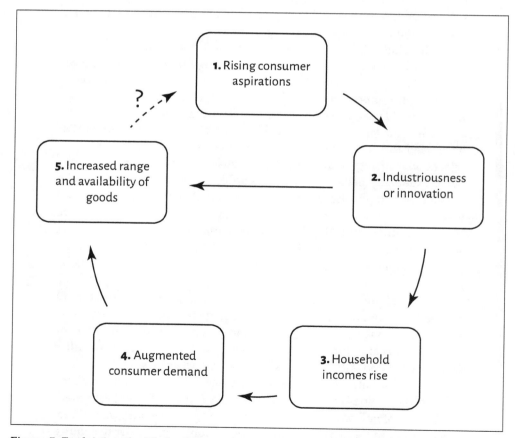

Figure 5. Explaining the Birth of Consumerism. "Industriousness" in Step 2 means extend- ing work effort beyond that needed for an adequate subsistence. "Innovation" can be techno- logical, organizational, financial, or entrepreneurial.

constraints diminish. After all, people might have chosen to direct their expanded cultural liberty and awakened imaginations into new social, educational, and artistic pursuits without folding consumerism into the mix.[11]

Figure 5 presents a basic model of how consumption and production became dynamically linked during the early modern period (which I take to run roughly from 1500 to the late 1700s). The dashed arrow running from Step 5 back to Step 1 has an accompanying question mark, reflecting the lack of consensus among historians about how to explain the rise of consumer acquisitiveness. Perhaps taking psychological development into account can shed light on the matter.

FUNCTIONAL SATIABILITY VERSUS INSATIABILITY

In seeking to understand the transition toward society-wide insatiability, I am not claiming that premodern peoples—any more than contemporary Varanasi rickshaw-wallahs—were exemplary or spiritually enlightened. As best one can ascertain, our premodern forebears exhibited everyday cravings of the sort that the Buddha identified 2,500 years ago as a root cause of human suffering. On the other hand, we can't be certain whether the Buddha was speaking of wants as intense or insistent as those we experience today. To look at the lives of hunter-gatherers and many peasant societies, one would doubt it. But if one simply assumes without reflection that the intensity of craving is invariant throughout history, that forecloses any inclination to wonder whether historical forces can alter that intensity.

Something distinctive does seem to have occurred in portions of Europe in early modern times. We know that at other times and places, various people experienced a powerful craving for "more"; the plundering by the Vikings and Spanish conquistadors are obvious examples. Even hunter-gatherers, who are generally content with a modest material standard of living, "delight in abundance when circumstances afford it and . . . consume ostentatiously what they have." (Although in the case of tribal foragers such behavior may express norms of sharing and maintaining equality more than personal craving.)[12]

But the difference is this: Varanasi rickshaw-wallahs, modern mobile hunter-gatherer groups, and many premodern European peasants—when not coerced into intensive labor—display enough contentment with their material lot in life that they are "functionally satiable." By this I mean that given a choice between routinely working past the satisfaction of basic subsistence needs versus simply "being" or pursuing noneconomic activities, they tend to opt for one of the latter. Yes, confronted with a windfall opportunity to consume more, they may take it. But under ordinary circumstances their cravings aren't sufficiently potent to motivate sustained industrious effort beyond subsistence.[13]

In contrast, in early modern Europe widespread and intensified craving moved to the fore as a significant animating social force. This differs from Yudhishthira's boundless acquisitiveness just prior to the dice match not in intensity but in becoming so pervasive and persistent that all of society reorganized in response to it.

CONNECTING THE DOTS

Upon reflection, it is evident that modern capitalism depends on there being extensive insatiability in the form of modern consumerism. This becomes apparent when social circumstances interfere with the *expression* of insatiability. For instance, whenever there is a sharp economic downturn, consumer demand drops, and market economies start to collapse into a tailspin. We saw this dramatically in the fall of 2001; as *Time* magazine later noted: "After the 9/11 terrorist attacks, President Bush didn't call for sacrifice. He called for shopping. 'Get down to Disney World in Florida,' he said. 'Take your families and enjoy life, the way we want it to be enjoyed.'"[14]

In times of economic contraction, it's not that our insatiable craving withers. Instead the money available for consumption declines. Keynesian economic theory responds to such crises by recommending new government expenditure or policy interventions to rebuild consumer purchasing power. The danger of economic depression would be the same if today's insatiability were ever to transition back to functional satiability. However, the latter has never occurred in modern market societies.

Some scholars and social critics contend that there are times when consumer craving in a society can prove inadequate, but that commercial marketing intervenes to stimulate acquisitiveness and keep an economy humming along. In its strongest form the contention is that insatiability is appreciably an artifact of advertising.[15]

There is little disagreement that advertising can induce people to buy product A rather than product B. But there is no consensus on the extent to which ads can entice people to increase their total consumption (i.e., to do more than simply switch from purchasing one bundle of goods to another). Moreover, any *susceptibility* to the influence of advertising depends on having previously become sufficiently insatiable to succumb to the stimulus. For instance, living in an environment well saturated in ads, Varanasi rickshaw-wallahs may nonetheless decline clients once they've hit their target incomes.[16]

Normally we don't take note of the essential role of insatiability within capitalist economies. That's because insatiability is a taken-for-granted background circumstance. But as we've seen, anthropology and history both indicate that insatiability is not a universal human trait. This implies that wherever there is a modern market society, there must be an underlying cause present to ensure that the distinctive psychology necessary to keeping that society in operation is instilled and maintained.

Could the cause be a mysterious chemical in the water people drink, the influence of sunspots, the work of a powerful magic genie, or perhaps a combination of the three? Any one of those conjectures is possible, I suppose. But given the precise spatial and temporal conjunction of insatiability with dynamic market economies, doesn't it seem more likely that some process integrally related to the market is the motor inducing and sustaining the transition into insatiability?

So let's recap some of the things we know: Wherever there is capitalist market dynamism, there is:

- Extensive propensity to addiction;
- Corresponding impairment in psychological development, induced by market-driven social turbulence and dis-integration; and also
- Consumer insatiability . . . which "just happens" to bear a family resemblance to addiction.

Considering this consistent conjuncture of phenomena, one can opt to fantasize about some mysterious independent cause (genies, sunspots, or whatever) being responsible for the insatiable psychology. But isn't market-induced dislocation and ensuing alteration in psychological development—which we have already established as an important contributing cause of insatiability's kissing-cousin, addiction—the more obvious candidate for the job?

As an analogy: If "Bill" (symbolizing addiction) and "Fred" (symbolizing insatiability) are born nearby to different mothers, yet share physical characteristics that distinguish them from other children, might we not hypothesize shared paternity? One might say that consumerism and addiction both reflect an unquenchable thirst, the former for novelty and the latter for repetition.

On this basis we can conjecture that *addiction and consumer insatiability are both products of a dislocation-induced shift in psychological development.* One way to find out if this hypothesis is true would be to examine the juncture in European history when the expression of mass insatiability became decisively established. If the birth of consumer insatiability on a mass basis coincided with the emergence of widespread addiction, that would suggest that a developmental abnormality closely akin to that which induces addiction is the prime candidate for causing society-wide insatiability as well.

Establishing this would go beyond merely observing that modern market economies can't operate in the absence of insatiability. First, we would be explaining what *causes* insatiability to arise where and when it's systemically needed. Even more strikingly, it would show that modern market economies are miraculously capable of *inducing and sustaining* the very psychology upon which their operation depends. And because insatiability, unlike addiction, is not only extensive but

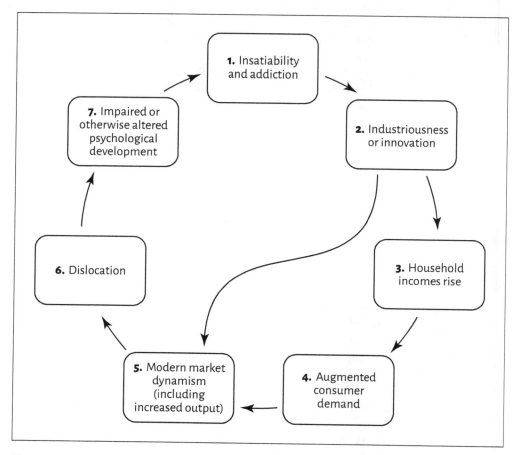

Figure 6. Developmental Abnormality, Addiction, and Insatiability in the Modern World. The insatiability that animates industriousness and innovation (Step 1 → Step 2) can be oriented toward a variety of objectives, including consumer goods (Step 4, our primary focus in this chapter) or simply wealth (Step 3). Consumer goods and wealth can, in turn, be either ends in themselves or means to other ends, such as personal identity, status, or power.

Regarding Step 7: A developmental shift leading to health disorders such as addiction qualifies, on that basis, as an impairment. If consumer insatiability proves symptomatic of a similar developmental alteration, the latter will qualify as an impairment to the extent that insatiability, its repercussions, or its underlying developmental cause is detrimental to individual or societal well-being. For instance, in the *Mahabharata*, Yudhishthira's insatiable acquisitiveness is problematic because it betrays his persistent discontent and is, like addiction, a symptom of ego-arrested development and its accompanying compromised morality.

omnipresent in contemporary market societies, this in turn would confirm modernity is inextricably intertwined with altered psychological development. (The extent to which this developmental alteration qualifies as an "impairment" remains to be seen.)

Such a hypothesis amounts to synthesizing (1) Bruce Alexander's dislocation theory of addiction, as we have extended it developmentally, with (2) the cycle of modern consumption and production portrayed in Figure 5. This is depicted visually in Figure 6. Economic historians have elucidated the causal chain running clockwise from Step 1 through Step 5. Likewise, in Chapter 6 we established the causal chain that continues to run clockwise from Step 5 back to developmental impairment and addiction. What is missing is that historians haven't satisfactorily explained the arrow leading from Step 7 into Step 1. Alexander does explain that arrow, but depicts it as causing addiction, without considering that it might also be causing generalized consumer insatiability. Thus, to complete a case for the plausibility of Figure 6, the challenge is to see whether the appearance of widespread insatiability and addiction coincided historically, suggesting shared causal origins.

ADDICTIVE SUBSTANCES IN EARLY MODERN EUROPEAN HISTORY

Reflecting back upon his magisterial *Civilization and Capitalism* volumes, historian Fernand Braudel commented in 1976, "I do not think we should consider the appearance of a great number of foodstuffs [in postmedieval Europe] as mere anecdotal history. Sugar, coffee, tea and alcohol have each had a long-term and very important influence upon history." Notice that all Braudel's listed "foodstuffs" happen to be stimulants or otherwise psychoactive substances with addictive potential. As globe-encompassing capitalism developed across the fifteenth to eighteenth centuries, psychoactive comestibles represented a significant portion of what was being brought back to Europe. To Braudel's short list we can add tobacco and, in less dramatic quantities, cocoa, opium, cocaine, and marijuana. In tandem with these import trends, European domestic production of alcoholic beverages, especially beer and distilled liquors, also grew vigorously. Anthropologist Sidney Mintz dubs all these substances "drug foods." In the words of two historians of world trade, "Colonial empires were built on the foundation of drug trades," and drugs "must be recognized as a foundation of the world economy, not an aberration."[17]

Many of these items, such as distilled liquors, were known to Europe during the Middle Ages or before, but primarily as medicines available only in limited quantities. Drug-food production and use only began to expand significantly during the 1600s, often soaring further from the mid-eighteenth century onward.

Production rocketed in part because the Atlantic slave economy—based on the power to extract labor without paying for it—made it profitable. Tobacco, coffee, sugar, and rum were all produced on American and Caribbean slave plantations. But in a market economy production is only profitable when there is consumer demand. Why was there robust demand for these new drug foods?

Drug foods can serve diverse functions. Besides pleasing our palates, stimulants such as coffee, tea, and sugar can improve work productivity. Alcohol helps people to relax and recover, or in higher quantities to cope with misery. Although premodern peoples didn't understand why, in modern biological terms, drinking alcoholic beverages, or those made with boiled water such as tea and coffee, was generally a healthier option than drinking unpurified water. Such items are also not infrequently consumed in convivial social settings. And as with other consumer purchases, choosing to ingest drug foods can also establish one's individuality, group membership, and social status. In preindustrial Europe, it was also understood that moderate on-the-job consumption of relatively low-alcohol beverages, such as ale, supported the ability to work.[18]

This explains why people found the drug foods appealing, but not why they turned toward this set of consumer goods so much more aggressively than others. For more than three hundred years—from Columbus's footfall in the Americas until well into the nineteenth century—drug foods were linchpins of transcontinental trade. For most of that period they—together with gold, silver, and slaves (whose labor was heavily directed toward growing drug foods)—surpassed in significance all other items of world trade. Could the fact that drug foods have the potential to become addictive be part of the explanation?[19]

Amid the sea of drug foods transiting into Europe in growing amounts, mass consumption began soonest and grew most quickly in Britain and other European areas that first evolved dynamic consumer societies. We'll consider the history of drug foods in Britain, which became the dominant actor in building and shaping global capitalism.

From the 1660s to 1770s the value of groceries imported into England and Wales—mainly tobacco, sugar, and caffeine drinks—rose from 17 percent to over one-third of the monetary value of all imports. By 1790 taxes and tariffs on drug foods generated roughly 60 percent of total British public revenue. The attempt to impose the same taxation regime on the American colonies led to the Boston Tea Party and contributed to provoking the American Revolution (and a subsequent Yankee preference for coffee over tea).[20]

Some further specifics:

Tea

The British were the first Europeans to fall in love with coffee, but discriminatory taxes induced them to switch over to tea imported halfway around the world from China. By the 1780s, at the dawn of the Industrial Revolution, annual tea consumption in England is estimated to have been two pounds per person. This was some ten times greater than the average consumption in continental Europe at that time and roughly twice the rate at which the tea-cultivating Chinese were drinking tea as late as the 1840s. By 1880, the English had more than doubled their tea intake to an annual average of five pounds per person.[21]

Sugar

Similarly, around 1750 yearly sugar consumption is estimated to have been on the order of two pounds per person in continental Europe while variously estimated at ten to seventeen pounds in England. Even by 1800 continental European sugar consumption is estimated at only 2.6 pounds per person. By that time annual English sugar use had jumped to eighteen to twenty-four pounds per person. By the 1890s, it soared to just below ninety pounds (that's a remarkable quarter pound per person *each day*, much of it incorporated as an ingredient in other foods).[22]

Alcohol

Alcohol was consumed widely during the Middle Ages, often throughout the day. However, mostly this was low-alcohol ale, and there is little evidence of alcoholism. Coming into the early modern period, alcohol consumption shifted among competing beverages in response to availability, cost, government policies, and changing tastes. However, generally there was a progression from the predominance of low-alcohol beverages (such as ale or hard cider) to higher-alcohol beer (the addition of hops allowed longer fermentation times) and distilled spirits.[23]

During the peak popularity of gin in the mid-eighteenth century, there were many thousands of venues selling gin in London alone. (London was then home to some 675,000 people—about 12 percent of England's population.) Historian John Burnett hazards the informed guess that annual gin consumption in the capital—the national epicenter of fervor for gin—was "very much more" than ten gallons per adult. That implies on average something in the vicinity of a weekly quart per person. And since not all adults were drinkers, and not all drinkers were gin-drinkers, we can infer that those who indulged in gin were downing a *lot* of it. Moreover, the quaffing of gin was layered upon substantial beer consumption. Not ordinarily given to colorful metaphors, de Vries observes that preindustrial economic dynamism "floated like a cork on an expanding pool of alcohol."[24]

For all of these drug foods, while there were geographic, class, and gender variations in what was consumed when and in what quantities, the dramatic increase in British consumption occurred across all economic strata.[25]

CONTEMPORANEOUS DISLOCATION

There was a marked increase in craving for drug foods in conjunction with the development of capitalism. But was there also chronic dislocation?

Well in advance of the seventeenth century, various societies across Eurasia, Africa, and the Americas engaged in long-distance trade, and some took steps toward developing dynamic market societies and consumer cultures. For instance, there were a variety of precursor developments in commercially vibrant Renaissance Italy. There one finds aspects of a budding middle-class consumer society. There was also upper-class anxiety about market-induced social dislocation, but this seems to have been anxiety about a development that remained substantially checked by an extensive system of market regulations promulgated by the Church, guilds, aristocrats, and municipalities. Wine had been enjoyed on the Italian peninsula since antiquity, but during the Renaissance there is more evidence that people were eating nutritious whole foods than immoderately consuming addictive drug foods.[26]

In the case of England, there was a confluence of dislocating developments during and prior to the seventeenth century. One was Britain's central role in developing a vigorous Atlantic trading economy. Domestically, beginning in the late 1500s large landholders responded to new market incentives by evicting tenants and encroaching on the tradition of peasant access to common-use lands, a process known as "enclosure." More than one thousand English villages and hamlets vanished entirely. This produced poverty and dislocation in the English countryside, incidentally establishing a pool of people who could be drafted into building ships and ports, crewing sailing vessels, clearing Caribbean plantation lands, and colonizing overseas.

British merchants became active in trading African slaves and commodities such as timber, fish, and the drug foods tobacco, sugar, rum, and coffee, as well as routing imported tea, spices, textiles, and porcelain through the Atlantic from Asia. The accompanying profits and institutional innovations stimulated the domestic English economy and contributed to follow-on dislocating trends.[27]

One such trend was urbanization, which during the early modern period proceeded more rapidly in England than anywhere else in the world. By 1750—at the peak of the "Gin Craze"—London was the world's largest city, a disorderly sprawl in which familiar rural customs were thrown into topsy-turvy disarray. Newcomers to the city experienced dislocation on several fronts simultaneously: from prior rural traditions and economic activities, familiar social relationships, and closeness with animals and nature, as well as nature-based spiritual sensibilities.

Concentrated profits from the Atlantic trade also contributed to the rising power of the British merchant and commercial class. The ensuing English Civil Wars (1642–1651) and Glorious Revolution (1688) ushered in a constitutionally constrained monarchy and an empowered Parliament dominated by the landed gentry and urban bourgeoisie. It is estimated that the nation's population declined by nearly 4 percent during the English Civil Wars. (To put that in perspective, it is 50 percent higher than the fraction of population loss during the US Civil War, which remains America's deadliest war.) War also empowered agricultural, merchant, and other capitalist entrepreneurs, working through Parliament, to greatly strengthen their property rights in relation to the monarchy. This all set the stage for deep dislocation in the countryside, where most people still lived and worked.[28]

Over the century and a half that followed the Glorious Revolution (thus running through the early period of British industrialization), traditional local rights of peasants and the rural poor to the use of common lands devolved increasingly—via judicial and legislative machinations biased toward the upper class—into the exclusive property rights of wealthy landlords and large tenant farmers, expressed in a new wave of enclosures. With traditional village life overturned, more and more people were thrown by default into the embrace of an increasingly dynamic, globally integrated capitalist economy and its endemic dislocation.[29]

Substantial numbers of those land-dispossessed were forced by circumstances into urban squalor, beggary, crime, prostitution, or indentured servitude in North America. Whereas formerly rural family members worked interdependently, now increasingly husbands, wives, and children worked in separate paid occupations—including handcrafts and retailing—sometimes in the home and sometimes in a small shop. Growing numbers of unmarried young women left home to become live-in domestic servants. As industrialization took hold, there was further incessant revolutionizing of systems of production, drawing former agricultural laborers and other working-class men, women, and children into factories, subjecting them to a capitalist work regimen that was closely supervised and notably non-leisurely, and replacing self-reliance and artisanal skills with machine-tending.

The experience of dislocation varied based on geographic location, class, gender, and so on. Cultural historian Dror Wahrman's study of the development of the sense of self in eighteenth-century England fills in details for a core segment of the middle class: people who were urban or urban-oriented and literate or semiliterate. In the century prior to industrialization this population experienced multiple sources of dislocation, including:

- The perceived withdrawal of God from active involvement in the world.
- Tumultuous metropolitan settings populated—in London, especially—by a steady stream of rural migrants who did not fit the mold of established urban cultural categories.
- The emergence of a consumer culture of unprecedented vigor, together with the invention of modern financial instruments and the commodification of more and more aspects of life: "Traditional values metamorphosed into detached and manipulable commodities. . . . Identity itself was in danger of coming out of the commercializing smelting kiln without real substance, referent, or true value."[30]

These dislocations produced a century-long stretch of enormous fluidity in personal identity, exemplified in an exceptional enthusiasm for attending masquerade balls. As anxieties accompanying dislocation intensified, the members of this subculture finally evolved—just at the onset of industrialization—a more inward-oriented, steady, and well-bounded sense of self, perhaps amounting to an inner strategy for achieving some shelter from the storm.

Of the dislocating forces that Wahrman identifies, the emergence of a market-mediated consumer culture stands out for initiating an *enduring* process of dislocation, which was something new in British history. At the same time, all these dislocations were in some measure symptomatic of the churning action of the new North Atlantic trade economy.

Wahrman's treatment provides one indication that people of the middling sort typically did not know dislocation of the harshness visited upon the lower classes. But they nonetheless lived during a time in which their culture and social relations were in unaccustomed flux, and they became unsettled and disoriented as a result. These are also precisely the English folk who whirled and twirled at the epicenter of the new "consumer class," avidly acquiring fashionable new goods, ingesting drug foods, and participating in novel forms of entertainment.

WHEN IS IT "ADDICTION"?

According to Bruce Alexander, under the influence of dislocation it's a sure bet that a portion of drug-food consumption will tip over into addiction. For the early modern period, there isn't a great deal of quantitative data bearing on the matter; the science of epidemiology did not get underway until the mid-1800s. But there is evidence pointing in Alexander's direction.

There are many competing definitions of addiction. Here's one recently formulated by an international team of health researchers: "A repeated behaviour leading to significant harm or distress. The behaviour is not reduced by the person and persists over a significant period of time. The harm or stress is of a functionally impairing nature." Alexander adds that the harm can be "to the addicted person, society, or both."[31]

Many historians adopt a looser definition. In the case of drug foods, they don't necessarily require that the consumption be detrimental to health or to performing social responsibilities; hence one might, for instance, become addicted to drinking tea. On the other hand, they become more confident that they are observing addiction when people continue to consume not only over the long haul but also despite countervailing incentives, such as harm caused to loved ones, mounting financial costs, or legal penalties.[32]

For our purposes, all these definitions are germane. It makes sense for health professionals to adopt a definition restricted to behaviors known to warrant prevention or therapeutic intervention. In contrast, here we are looking for evidence of distorted or arrested psychological growth. Powerful insistent cravings that result in repetitive consumption—whether or not satisfying the medical definition of addiction—can represent such evidence, especially when they occur in conjunction with dislocation. (The differences between scientists' and historians' definitions of addiction may, in any case, be narrowing. Both caffeine and sugar are currently being investigated by scientists for their addictive potential.)[33]

Historians have relied on a variety of indications to judge that addiction grew widespread in England. As early as 1604, when tobacco use was limited primarily to the elite, King James I wrote that "many in this kingdom have had such a continual use of taking this unsavory smoke, as now they are not able to forbear the same, no more than an old drunkard can abide to be long sober."[34]

In the succeeding century, attempts to legislate reduced gin consumption proved largely ineffective. Likewise, when government duties doubled the price of imported tea, the English turned readily to smuggled sources; at times during the first half of the eighteenth century an estimated 75 percent of the tea consumed was illegal. Stiff tariffs on imported tobacco provoked a similar response. This is suggestive. People prized their tobacco, tea, and high-octane spirits enough to flout the law.[35]

Rising prices sometimes prompted people to rein in their consumption or substitute one drug food for another. But not always. As economist Mark Koyama observes, "even as the price of tea and sugar rose at the end of the eighteenth and during the first part of the nineteenth century, the quantity consumed increased. The reason for this appears to be a simple one: addiction."[36]

Even if we adopt the health scientist's proviso that the consumption in question must result in significant harm or functional impairment, we can still infer that there was extensive addiction. For instance, based on what we now know about the consequences of immoderate drinking, eighteenth-century gin and beer consumption must have been harmful to many Englishmen and their families. From 1718 to 1751, deaths associated with alcoholic liver disease jumped sharply, and historians suspect that gin mania boosted London mortality rates in other ways. It's also likely that children fared poorly if one or both parents were habitually drunk.[37]

And while in the tavern, why not enjoy a pipe or two of tobacco? Throughout the century many Englishmen appear to have smoked several pipefuls a day. This was assuredly unhealthy. (Today we know that tobacco smoke is equally endangering whether conveyed through a pipe or a cigarette.) British sea captains and slave traders also supplied tobacco to sailors and slaves, inducing addiction so that, thereafter, tobacco provisions could be used to secure—or coerce—obedience.[38]

Opium, in the form of an alcohol-based tincture called laudanum, was administered medically to people of all classes from the eighteenth century forward. Imports of opium more than tripled between 1827 and 1859, and they continued to increase for the remainder of the century. Among those who became addicted were the poets Samuel Coleridge and Lord Byron. But consumption became most problematic in the gritty industrial cities of north England and in the lowland Fens area to the east, where land enclosures had degraded the lives of agricultural laborers. Some workers turned to laudanum as a respite from the bleakness of their lives; in the Fens opium was often added into beer. Moreover, addiction was not limited to adults. Many working women of necessity entrusted their infants' care to others, and it became common practice to dose babies with laudanum to keep them sedated: "The young 'uns all lay about the floor . . . like dead 'uns, and there's no bother with 'em. When they cry we give 'em a little of it [laudanum]," explained a Fenlands nurse. Drugged babies became disinterested in eating, and mortality climbed as a result.[39]

Among those early to conclude that addiction followed in the wake of dislocation was Karl Marx's longtime collaborator Friedrich Engels, who attributed alcohol abuse by industrial workers—including "many a mother [who] gives the baby on her arm gin to drink"—to economic exploitation, social stress, and squalor. Charles Dickens wrote in 1836 that "Gin-drinking is a great vice in England, but wretchedness and dirt are a greater; and until you improve the homes of the poor, or persuade a half-famished wretch not to seek relief in the temporary oblivion of his own misery, . . . gin-shops will increase in number and splendour."[40]

Recall, finally, that Bruce Alexander's definition of addiction encompasses harm "to the addicted person, *society, or both.*" By that standard, the great bulk of European drug-food consumption could count as addiction, because the tobacco, coffee, sugar, and rum imported into Europe were procured through the enslavement of—literally—millions of people.[41]

Reviewing the history of early modern Britain, we've seen that mass consumerism, including a dramatic surge in drug-food intake with indications of extensive addiction, emerged within a society experiencing the birth of a socially disruptive, disorienting and—for many of those of lower social station—brutally stressful, capitalist political economy. This supports the notion that insatiability and addiction are twin symptoms of chronic dislocation.

Chapter 9

MAYA'S MODERN ARCHITECTURE

Summarizing our theory thus far

Our overall purpose in the previous chapter was to investigate whether dislocation-induced impairment in psychospiritual growth is pervasive in the modern world. But in addressing that question, we have stumbled onto a great deal more.

Our sleuthing suggests that ceaseless dislocation contributes, behind everyone's back, to instilling the craving needed to keep the production and consumption circuits of modern economies in perpetual motion. This indicates that Figure 6 in the preceding chapter is a fair representation of the psychosocial dynamics integral to the operation of a global market economy. That doesn't mean that other causes play no role in driving consumption, but dislocation-derived craving establishes a susceptible psychological substratum upon which other factors can operate.

In Chapter 6 we determined that many mental and physical maladies that have grown prevalent in modern times are at least partially products of dislocation and an ensuing impairment in psychological development. The European history that we reviewed in Chapter 8 indicates that consumer insatiability is likewise a product of dislocation and an altered trajectory of psychological growth. In some people the developmental tilt toward insatiability may be expressed in other ways—such as a relentless drive toward wealth, power, or celebrity. But to the extent that relatively few people fail to succumb in some measure, we can infer that dislocation-altered development has become rampant in modern times. It's the new normal.[1]

It is doubtless that insatiability varies in intensity. One can find modern people who are content to live on modest means, are caring and generous to others, and so on. Likewise, functional satiability did not vanish entirely with the transition to industrial economies. For instance, there were early nineteenth-century English factory workers who resisted the new, tightly supervised work regimen, even though their refusal to show up on demand limited their income and consumption possibilities. (See Figure 7.)[2]

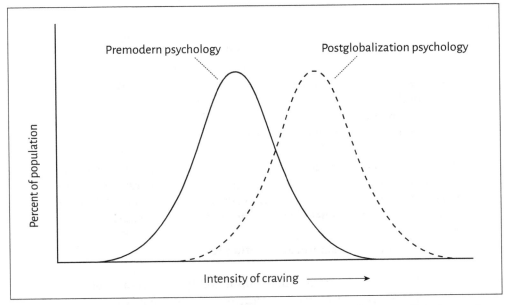

Figure 7. **The Modern Shift in Trajectories of Psychological Development. This figure shows trajectories of psychological development shifting under the influence of global capitalism. The solid-line bell curve on the left suggests how the intensity of craving might have been distributed across the population of premodern Europe, ranging from people whose cravings were relatively modest (toward the left) and greedily intense (toward the right). The dashed-line bell curve to the right indicates how this distribution shifted toward greater intensity of craving as dislocation mounted.**

**   Modeling the distribution of craving with a bell curve is consistent, for example, with the evidence that a minority of late-medieval English peasants took advantage of higher wages to significantly increase their consumption, while many others prioritized leisure time over higher income. (See Chapter 8, above).**

**   Another indication that the intensity of craving may have been relatively modest during the late-medieval period is that drug-food consumption among the English peasantry was limited mostly to ale. An important dietary staple for England's lower social orders, ale was high in nutritional value, low in alcohol content, and understood (correctly) to protect against disease. For these reasons, its price was regulated to ensure that it remained affordable. Ale consumption did not display telltale indicators of addiction—such as continued consumption despite countervailing incentives—that characterized consumption of the later drug foods.**

Exactly how many people manage to escape the developmental alteration that underlies insatiability, and why they do so, is a research question for the future. But we can surmise that they must represent a rather small proportion of modern populations, based on the simple fact that the aggregate strength of our insatiability suffices to fuel global capitalism's steady growth.

GLOBAL CAPITALISM AS THE ENGINE OF MALADY AND DISCONTENT

According to our culture's dominant self-understanding, capitalism is the world's greatest invention for satisfying human wants. This is worse than an oversimplification. Certainly, today's markets are stupendous at producing all manner of services and stuff. But this is also a system that depends on instilling and perpetuating a psychology that is insistently unappeasable. In this way capitalism secretly causes the core craving that it pretends to satisfy.

This discovery challenges the core justification for capitalism—i.e., the promise to *deliver the goods and experiences* that will provide satisfaction. In reality, capitalism does the opposite, secretly *delivering the psychology* that pushes satisfaction ever further out of reach (while incidentally rendering people more susceptible to unnecessary misery, disease, and untimely death).

This discovery is significant in other respects:

- The realization that intense insatiability is a product of social forces opens it to critical scrutiny in a different way than if it were simply a universal human trait, an inalterable fact of how the world is. We can only *adapt* to inalterable facts, but it is possible to *critique and alter* facts that are caused by human activity.
- Whereas addiction and other dislocation-induced maladies are *unfortunate side effects* of the global political-economic system, insatiability is *essential*. In other words, if we could prevent addiction and other system-stimulated illnesses, the overall system would remain intact and we would be better off. But were the system to become unable to generate insatiability, it would collapse.
- When this system causes harm, insatiability—as an essential system component—bears some of the responsibility.

Step 7 in Figure 6 left it an open question whether the developmental shift that causes insatiability qualifies as an "impairment." We can now see that it does, because the shift is deleterious to well-being in several ways (with more to come in later chapters):

- Insatiability signifies *chronic discontent*. People who are insatiable never have enough, always want "more," and are often anxious that it may prove unattainable. When intense insatiability is seen as just a fact of human nature, people become resigned to it and adapt. But once we understand that our political-economic system *induces* that insatiability, our condition is revealed in a new light. Having recognized insatiability as a distinctively modern phenomenon, Durkheim observed that "Insatiability is rightly considered a sign of morbidity [i.e., sickness].... Inextinguishable thirst is constantly renewed torture."[3]

- Insatiability also functions as a driving force in sustaining a political-economic system that increases our susceptibility to many *mental and physical afflictions.*
- The psychosocial system depicted in Figure 6 forms a closed loop in which each step becomes a contributing cause of its own perpetuation. Thus pervasive insatiability contributes to *triggering* the developmental impairments that cause insatiability and extensive illness, and in that respect it functions as a *society-wide impediment to healthy development.*

Perhaps an analogy can help convey our plight. Imagine a civilization in which everyone suffers constantly from poison-ivy rashes, and the accepted treatment is to apply a lotion . . . made from crushed poison-ivy leaves. And that's not the extent of the irrationality: growing and processing the poison ivy needed to make all of that (secretly itch-producing) lotion emits pollution that increases people's susceptibility to many serious mental and physical diseases.

This would be crazy . . . but no more so than the global social order in which we now live—a political-economic system that secretly causes the problem it promises to solve, together with a great deal of unnecessary suffering.

MODERN DEVELOPMENTAL DISTORTION IN TRANSPERSONAL TERMS

Our discovery that the global economy is built upon a self-sustaining impairment in psychological development, while dramatic, makes no reference to an available post-egoic range in human development. On the other hand, no modern scholarship suggests any kind of interdependence between impaired psychological development, addiction, and consumer insatiability. It is the *Mahabharata* that prompted us to imagine that these phenomena might be intertwined, and it does this based on a transpersonal model of psychospiritual development that explains insatiability as an outcome of arrest in abnormally intense ego-identification. The fact that the *Mahabharata* anticipates and helps explain what we have concluded—that addiction and insatiability are twin symptoms of distorted psychological development—lends credence to the transpersonal perspective from which that prediction derives. "Credence" doesn't mean decisively established, but it is a meaningful step in that direction.

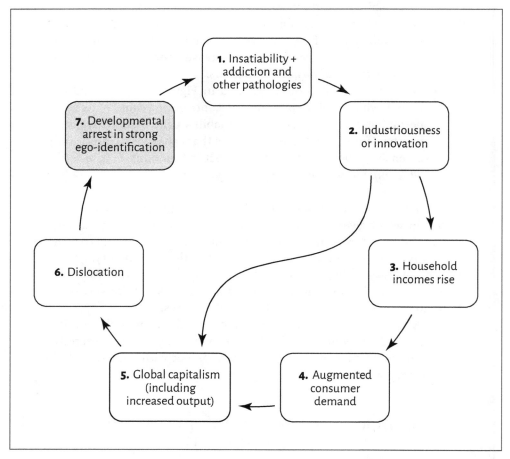

Figure 8. A Transpersonal Model of the Disruption of Psychospiritual Development in Modern Civilization. This diagram modifies Figure 6 in several ways. Step 7 (highlighted by shading) substitutes transpersonal text for the less-specific phrase "impaired psychological development." (Now that we have established ways in which insatiability is detrimental to well-being, the words "or otherwise altered" in Step 7 of Figure 6 become unnecessary.) Consistent with Chapter 6, Figure 8 modifies Step 1 by adding "other pathologies," which is shorthand for various illnesses besides addiction that can derive from dislocation-induced developmental impairment, such as depression, anxiety, ADHD, and follow-on physical diseases such as cancer, heart disease, and obesity. And Step 5 replaces "Modern market dynamism" with "Global capitalism," reflecting the reality that modern dislocation is the result of political-economic processes operating worldwide, including even in contemporary communist nations, such as China and Vietnam, that have become deeply integrated into the global economy.

Figure 8 modifies Step 7 of Figure 6 to incorporate the transpersonal component that we have derived from the *Mahabharata*. Here "impaired psychological development" is fleshed out as "developmental arrest in strong ego-identification." From now on I will refer to the causal wheel shown in Figure 6 as the "psychologically conventional formulation" of our model of capitalist psychosocial dynamics and to the modified depiction in Figure 8 as the "transpersonal formulation."

In this transpersonal variant of our theory, the developmental abnormality shown in Step 7 *involves* arrest in intense ego-identification, but it need not be *limited* to that. For instance, one can imagine that among people who are strongly egoic, somewhat different developmental pathways lead toward insatiability alone versus, say, toward insatiability coupled with mental illness.

Notice that advertising plays no part in our explanation of the origins of modern insatiability. Advertising can channel incessant craving and may well amplify it. But the foundation of modern insatiability is rooted in a distortion in psychological development (per our conventional formulation) or, more specifically, in arrest in intense ego-identification (per our transpersonal formulation). Indeed, one might reasonably conjecture that it is their egoism that renders modern people distinctively susceptible to the blandishments of advertising.

THE COVERT DYNAMICS OF A DISLOCATED CIVILIZATION

Dislocation is intrinsic to modern capitalism. But dislocation is more than an unfortunate consequence or, as in Schumpeter's notion of creative destruction, a necessary feature of innovation and growth. On the one hand, *too much* dislocation is socially and ecologically destructive. That is why Karl Polanyi argued that a true laissez-faire economy would soon self-destruct and that at least a measure of government oversight and intervention is essential.

But, unbeknownst to Polanyi or anyone else, it appears that *too little* dislocation could also lead capitalist market economies to collapse based on insufficient consumer insatiability. In this respect modern markets are revealed as wondrous perpetual-motion-and-growth machines. Provided that they don't self-destruct through excessive dislocation, they can feed indefinitely upon their own psychological byproduct—to wit, insatiability.

All of which might be fine . . . except that people cannot assume their assigned roles as insatiable consumers without tending to suffer the sense of insufficiency that is innate to unquenchable craving, as well as a deepened propensity to mental illness and to ensuing life-shortening, debilitating, and anxiety-provoking physical disorders. Moreover, in later chapters we will find that the extent of our psychosocial troubles is much greater than this.

Chapter 10

IN THE SWEETNESS
OF OUR REPOSE

Objections and refinements

Might more late-medieval English peasants have chosen higher income over leisure if their economy had, without imposing dislocation, simply offered them more enticing consumer wares? Along similar lines, some anthropologists suggest that nomadic hunter-gatherers exhibit functional satiability only because their wandering makes it impractical to accumulate more than a few modest possessions. In the absence of indisputable evidence, how certain can we be that modern insatiability is a product of sustained dislocation?[1]

As we saw in Chapter 8, Varanasi rickshaw-wallahs offer a counterinstance to the notion that an abundant range of purchase possibilities is sufficient to stimulate insatiable acquisitiveness. Varanasi is bustling with shops offering traditional crafts—such as world-renowned, locally woven silk fabrics—as well as a vast array of contemporary consumer goods. Yet there are wallahs who, once they've hit their daily earning target, decline rides even to foreign visitors whom they could charge multiple times the going Indian rate. This represents an instance of functional satiability trumping tangible consumer offerings.

Then again, maybe there's something idiosyncratically aberrant about Varanasi rickshaw-wallahs. Can we find a more general test for the objection that functional satiability is only an artifact of the absence of alluring consumption opportunities?[2]

NEW WORLD OPPORTUNITIES

As it happens, the historical encounter between Europeans and North American Indians offers a wealth of instances in which members of a consumer society and of traditional subsistence societies had a chance to trade places, literally stepping into one another's shoes and moccasins. Were the natives who tasted the European lifestyle clamoring for the opportunity to transform their tribes into consumer cultures, while the Europeans were desperate to get back to materially abundant Western civilization? Not exactly.

Of the early centuries of European settlement and colonization in North America, historian Howard Zinn writes: "One fact disturbed: whites would run off to join Indian tribes, or would be captured in battle and brought up among the Indians, and when this happened the whites, given a chance to leave, chose to stay in the Indian culture. Indians, having the choice, almost never decided to join the whites."[3]

In the aftermath of the Seven Years War (1756–1763), St. John de Crèvecoeur asked in some perplexity:

> By what power does it come to pass, that children who have been adopted when young among these people [i.e., American Indians], can never be prevailed on to re-adopt European manners? Many an anxious parent I have seen last war, who at the return of the peace, went to the Indian villages where they knew their children had been carried in captivity; when to their inexpressible sorrow, they found them so perfectly Indianized, that many knew them no longer, and those whose more advanced ages permitted them to recollect their fathers and mothers, absolutely refused to follow them, and ran to their adopted parents for protection against the effusions of love their unhappy real parents lavished on them![4]

That speaks to children, who were at a malleable stage of life. But what of their elders? Of the many colonial adults who chose to remain with their adoptive tribes, historian James Axtell finds that "they stayed because they found Indian life to possess a strong sense of community, abundant love, and uncommon integrity . . . and, as two adult converts acknowledged, 'the most perfect freedom, the ease of living, [and] the absence of those cares and corroding solicitudes which so often prevail with us.'"[5]

In 1676 a native Micmac chief from eastern Canada's Gaspé Peninsula explained his peoples' preference for their materially simpler way of life to a group of French sea captains:

> Thou reproachest us . . . that our country is a little hell in contrast with France, which thou comparest to a terrestrial paradise. . . . Thou sayest of us also that we are

the most miserable and most unhappy of all men, . . .
lacking bread, wine, and a thousand other comforts
which thou hast in superfluity in Europe. Well, my
brother, . . . all miserable as we seem in thine eyes, we
consider ourselves nevertheless much happier than
thou in this, that we are very content with the little that
we have. . . . And, whilst feeling compassion for you in
the sweetness of our repose, we wonder at the anxieties and care which you give yourselves night and day in
order to load your ship. . . . Which of these two is the
wisest and happiest—he who labours without ceasing
and only obtains, and that with great trouble, enough
to live on, or he who rests in comfort and finds all that
he needs in the pleasure of hunting and fishing?[6]

Half a century later, in 1721, the New England Puritan minister
Cotton Mather remained baffled by persistent tribal indifference to the
material allure of modern civilization:

Tho' they [i.e., American Indians] saw a People Arrive
among them, who were Clothed in *Habits* of much
more Comfort and Splendour, than what there was
to be seen in the *Rough Skins* with which they hardly
covered themselves; and who had *Houses full of Good
Things*, vastly out-shining their squalid and dark
Wigwams; And they saw this People Replenishing
their *Fields*, with *Trees* and with *Grains*, and useful *Animals*, which until now they had been wholly
Strangers to; yet they did not seem touch'd in the
least, with any *Ambition* to come at such Desirable
Circumstances.[7]

If, as the objection runs, people act functionally satiable only when
lacking consumption opportunities, then these stories of intercultural
exchange and comparison ought to have run in the other direction.
Instead, the historical reality is consistent with our thesis that modern
consumer insatiability is a product of sustained dislocation.

In fairness, there were confounding factors at work. (In the real
world, there always are.) For instance, American Indians who found
their way into the Europeans' world were most often treated as inferiors,
whereas Europeans in the Indians' world were assimilated as equals.
This means that Indians who returned home may have been saying
"no" to being disrespected rather than "no" to consumer abundance.

On the other hand, returned Indians did not seem to miss the
trappings of comfort and affluence they experienced in white society.

From the outset, Indians engaged in trade for selected European artifacts—such as glass beads, small metallic objects (which were prized for their spiritual value), and blankets—but this conformed to traditions of exchanging goods with other tribes for religious purposes or to cement intersocietal ties, including via long-distance trading networks. With time they shifted toward swapping food and animal pelts for items, such as axes and guns, which had utilitarian more than spiritual value. But rarely did they relinquish their subsistence lifeways or seek to emulate European material accumulation. Again, this indicates that insatiability is not a human universal.[8]

INDUSTRIOUSNESS UNDER DURESS

Jan de Vries envisions early modern European consumerism as largely a matter of "free choice." He contends that many people, including in the working class, worked harder so that they could earn more and buy more. In contrast, we've found reason to believe that often the new interest in consumption reflected inner compulsion driven by distorted psychological development.

But there were other factors at play. Some historians contend that preindustrial working-class industriousness was driven more by external duress than any newly awakened desire to consume. For instance, one study finds that whereas construction workers in London may have begun to work harder than would have been required for mere subsistence (thus conforming to de Vries's perspective), during the same period rural farming families in southern England were most likely working harder just to get by.[9]

In the mid-eighteenth and early nineteenth centuries, this case becomes even more clear-cut. As wealthy landowners and large tenant farmers pushed more and more of the rural peasantry and poor off the common lands from which they had derived much of their livelihood, many in the latter groups were utterly immiserated. Some became dependent on what meager local poor relief was available, or on street alms or crime. Others found no better option than securing one of the newly invented factory jobs where for many—especially those working in unskilled machine-tending jobs—the living and working conditions were horrendous and the wages poor. These people worked extra hard because they had no choice.[10]

Figure 9 alters Figure 6 and 8 to reflect these realities. First, the route from global capitalism (Step 5) to dislocation (Step 6) is shown to have involved the state (shaded Step 5b). In preindustrial England this included modifications in property rights and other laws that contributed to the deteriorating material circumstances of the rural peasantry and wage laborers. Initially the early modern state was a terrain of contest between upper-class factions that sometimes found their interests at odds (e.g., landed aristocracy versus wealthy tenant farmers). Later, as wageworkers became more strongly organized, they too began to establish influence within the state apparatus, as the state navigated an uneasy tension between encouraging economic growth (and thereby, unknowingly, sufficient dislocation to sustain consumer insatiability), influencing the distribution of burdens and wealth, and tempering intolerably destructive dislocation. (Step 7 remains neutral between the conventional and transpersonal formulations of our theory by including the language from both.)

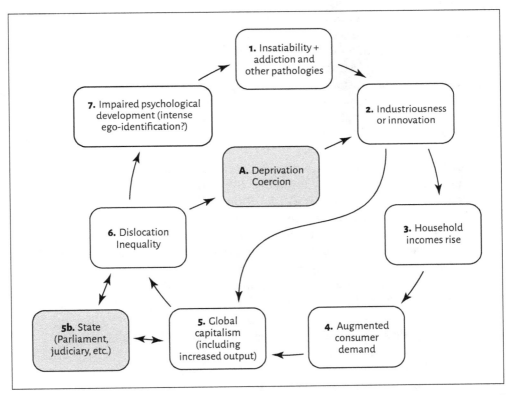

Figure 9. State Intervention and Duress as Additional Factors in Modern Psychosocial and Political-Economic Dynamics.

Figure 9 also adds "Inequality" to Step 6 and introduces shaded Step A in order to indicate that some people were working harder not because they were becoming acquisitive consumers, but because worsening material circumstances meant that their survival depended on it. Factory owners often wielded the power to impose long workdays, intensive pacing, and rigid work rules as a condition of employment. Also, among those compelled to work under duress were literally millions of American Indians, Africans, African Americans, and dispossessed Englishmen, Irishmen, and others who were enslaved, indentured, forced ("impressed") into becoming sailors, brutalized, or who died in order to procure sugar, rum, tobacco, coffee, and cotton—and gargantuan profits—for the European market.[11]

Those forced to work harder contributed to economic growth and dislocation as producers, but typically lacked the wherewithal for significant discretionary consumer expenditure. On other hand, material deprivation often translated into increased consumer demand for *non*discretionary goods. For instance, the destruction of local subsistence economies meant that many villagers who had been locally self-sufficient became wage laborers who now had to turn to the market to purchase necessities of life—such as buying food rather than growing vegetables or grazing a cow on common land. Starting in the mid-nineteenth century, Western imperial powers imposed this dynamic as an intentional strategy, disrupting local self-reliance within their colonies to force peasants into wage work or into growing monocrops for export and, by necessity, to become consumers.[12]

Complementary and Intertwined Dynamics

Notwithstanding the modifications introduced in Figure 9, whether people were animated by insatiable acquisitiveness, poverty, or coercion, they were experiencing dislocation and tending to exhibit symptoms of distorted psychospiritual development.

Duress and insatiable craving are, furthermore, not mutually exclusive forces. Not only are both often operative simultaneously within a *society*, but they may also be active simultaneously within many *individuals*, including both up and down the class ranks. For instance, when their income or creditworthiness permitted, early modern workers often exhibited proto-consumerism—e.g., buying novel goods such as tea-brewing paraphernalia, tobacco pipes, crockery, or more fashionable clothing.[13]

Of course, tea pots, teacups, and tobacco pipes were consumer wares that enabled drug-food consumption, and thus another indication of dislocation-driven craving. The fact that many of those experiencing duress (Step A) were also driven toward addictive consumption (Step 1) provides evidence that they—as much as the more affluent and obviously insatiable consuming classes—were subject to developmental impairment (Step 7).

For those of meager income it was thus entirely possible to become industrious in response to two simultaneous forces:

- Diminished *economic capacity* to meet basic needs (i.e., the interior pathway from Step 6 to Step 2 that runs through Step A); and

- Dislocation that impairs psychospiritual development, thereby instilling *emptiness and craving* (i.e., the exterior pathway from Step 6 to Step 2 that runs through Steps 7 and 1).

The double impetus to industriousness implies that if duress recedes across a modern capitalist society, inner emptiness is likely to step forward as a dominant animating force. For example, as their economic productivity and output increased during the nineteenth century, many workers were also organizing to demand higher wages and improved working conditions, including shorter work hours. When they succeeded, their material deprivation and oppression diminished, but typically their dislocation and craving did not evaporate but rather changed form. Generally, they did not revert to premodern functional satiability.

Under the influence of global capitalism, even those well removed from hand-to-mouth bare subsistence can experience both psychological and material deficits. For instance, today, living in a dislocated world in which bonds of communal affection are thin and unstable, and there are no longer strong traditions of mutual aid, people who are comfortably middle class may be stirred to industrious endeavor by: (a) the need to pay for subsistence goods that were previously provided cooperatively or communally; (b) an insatiable yearning for non-subsistence consumer goods (the "one more thing" that I hope is going to make me happy); as well as (c) the *fear* of future deprivation (e.g., the realistic recognition that it is possible to slip downward from the middle class).

For our purposes, it isn't crucial to know what proportion of early modern Europeans were insatiable consumers, immiserated proletarians, or a hybrid of the two. Of course, it mattered enormously to them, as it does to historians and should to our moral sensibility. But whatever the statistics and extent of suffering, modern civilization is distinctively grounded in—and sustained by—perpetuating insufficiency.

PSYCHOLOGICAL "VERSUS" CULTURAL CHANGE?

There is ambiguity in the extent to which the transition to insatiability involved only psychological change or also accompanying cultural change. For instance, human societies that exhibit functional satiability often discourage the display of personal wealth or inculcate a norm mandating that wealth be shared. In that case, how much does sustained dislocation establish insatiability not only by intensifying egoism but also by altering cultural norms regulating personal wealth and consumption?

It's neither easy nor essential to know. Part of what it means for an economy to disembed, in Karl Polanyi's sense, is that prior cultural norms are ruptured. This contributes to altering psychospiritual development. Likewise, when there is any widespread shift in trajectories of psychospiritual development, this will assuredly contribute to innovations in cultural beliefs and practices. Cultural and psychological changes go hand in hand, reinforcing one another.

But is it possible that the European transition from functional satiability involved no shift in psychological development, but *only* a relaxation of cultural constraints? This was Émile Durkheim's view. Lacking a worked-out conception of psychological development, Durkheim inferred that dislocation must be unleashing an insatiability that is humanly innate—contained by societally imposed norms and manifesting when those norms break down.[14]

Durkheim's theory rules out the possibility of a Yudhishthira—someone who becomes insatiably acquisitive not because social norms have collapsed (customary norms are robustly intact while the Pandavas are living in Maya's Palace), but because circumstances cause him to deviate from a healthy trajectory of psychospiritual development. Likewise, Yudhishthira's insatiability subsides not as the result of any restoration of cultural restraint—to the contrary, he is exiled to the wilderness—but from inner growth.

So far our inquiry weighs against Durkheim's supposition. Consider the consistency with which two species of insatiability—addiction and consumerism—have emerged simultaneously throughout modern history. Many psychologists already recognize that addiction can be a symptom of a dislocation-induced developmental disorder. If one species of insatiability signals an underlying developmental disorder, is it not plausible to imagine that the other species might as well?

Or if, as Durkheim assumed, all people are latently insatiable, it's peculiar that European settlers who lived for a time among American Indians so often chose to remain under a regime of tribal "cultural repression." In fact, there are first-person accounts from Europeans who experienced tribal life as notably *less* constrained culturally than the lives of relative material abundance that they had previously known.[15]

THE ROLE OF RESISTANCE

They hang the man and flog the woman,
Who steals the goose from off the common,
But let the greater villain loose,
Who steals the common from the goose.
        —Seventeenth-century English protest poem

Inasmuch as capitalism causes dislocation and often extensive misery, there have always been those who objected to the way our society is structured. But such resistance has often proved a poor match against the forces driving capitalist expansion. Indeed, through violence that sought to break down residual communal or class solidarity, over the past few centuries state repression has often compounded market-induced dislocation.

Segments of the peasantry and working class, men and women alike, fought back at various times against rising food costs in a market economy, the privatization of common lands, and exploitation in factory and field. They struggled for the right to organize and vote. In some cases they formulated revolutionary visions, striving to establish a more just and humane social order.[16]

Enslaved Black people frequently resisted their oppression by such means as working slowly, breaking tools, or trying to escape. There were also many hundreds of rebellions on slave ships and plantations throughout the Americas. But the enslavers' powers to retaliate were such that few revolts succeeded—the most notable exception being the Haitian Revolution (1791–1804), which resulted in the first postcolonial independent nation under the rule of people of African descent.[17]

Figure 10 depicts some of the causal understanding that informed resistance movements. This figure modifies Figure 9 in several ways. The first alteration is to add a bold dashed arrow running directly from global capitalism (Step 5) to augmented household incomes (Step 3). This reflects the poor and working-class perspective that while some people were getting wealthier by working hard (Steps 2 → 3), a fortunate few in the upper classes were getting rich off the backs of the enslaved or laboring poor without necessarily having to work much at all. Workers with this perspective might insist: "The bankers and bosses aren't working harder to satisfy their insatiability. They're making *me* work harder!"

Related to this, resistance movements commonly experienced their dislocation as involving not merely deprivation, but also coercion, deepening inequality, and other forms of injustice—hence the word "injustice" added to Step A. Variants of this social-justice critique have accompanied capitalism since its early days and reflect a prior legacy of opposition to medieval oppression. Proponents of capitalism have tended to counter that they have earned their wealth and power through personal effort that contributes to the social good (i.e., denying the bold arrow running from Step 5 to Step 3). Any deprivation is the result only of other people's lesser innate capacities or their decision not to better their circumstances through industrious effort (i.e., denying the dashed arrows running from Step 6 to Steps A and 2).

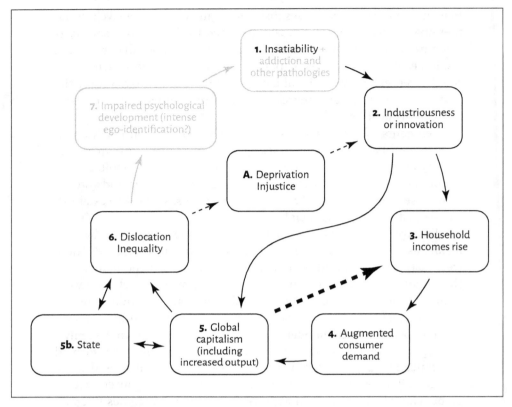

Figure 10. Perceived Causal Relationships That Informed Historical Resistance to Capitalism

The other crucial change in Figure 10 is to fade out Steps 7 and 1 from Figure 9. This captures the omission—from the opposing world-views of *both* capitalism's enthusiasts and its resisters—of our discovery that modern economic dynamism depends on distorting psychological development and instilling persistent discontent (i.e., insatiability). Capitalism has always evoked sharply polarized responses, but *these have all reflected an incomplete understanding of the extent of harm— against all social classes—for which capitalism is responsible . . . and upon which it secretly depends.*

On the other hand, within Step 1, the word "insatiability" remains visible, as does the arrow from Step 1 into Step 2. That's because— without anyone grasping the psychosocial forces at play—insatiability was nonetheless taken for granted as a social background condition.

INDUSTRIOUSNESS WITHOUT INSATIABILITY?

Figure 6 depicts a basic model of the psychological stimulus to industri-ousness and innovation that is integral to modern consumer societies.

But working more than is needed for basic survival occurs under other circumstances. For example, some non-nomadic tribal societies, especially those with access to abundant food resources, evolved cultures in which people readily contributed to activities that were productive well beyond the level required for subsistence.

In the 1920s and '30s, Bronislaw Malinowski studied one such culture: the Trobriand Islanders of the western Pacific Ocean. Trobrianders devoted more effort than mere subsistence would have required to activities such as canoe-building, vegetable gardening, and complex multi-island ceremonial activities. Their motives included pride in displaying, sharing, and exchanging culturally prized items (notably ritually important yams and rarely worn ceremonial body ornaments), pleasure in skilled production, and above all a commitment to perpetuating valued ancestral patterns of life.[18]

However, their psychology and social-psychological conditioning differed notably from that found in modern market societies. Trobriand activities that we would designate as "economic" were subordinate to long-established cultural patterns. Trobriand wealth was culturally regulated so that no one could accumulate more than their village's chief. (This is analogous to premodern European sumptuary laws that regulated the clothing people could wear based on social class.) Trobriand wealth in ceremonial body ornaments was also in constant circulation rather than permanently possessed by individuals. A great deal of productive activity was not easily distinguishable from socializing, social bonding, and worship.

Trobriand perception and reasoning were deeply holistic—reminiscent of Luria's three Russian peasants—which could indicate an absence of the sharp dualism and predominance of instrumental reasoning that are associated with intensive ego-identification.[19]

Unlike modern consumers, Trobrianders exhibited no taste for novelty in consumption. Much to the chagrin of European traders and employers, neither money nor European consumer wares nor even superb imitations of native crafts could tempt Trobrianders away from the call of tradition. Many Europeans concluded that the Trobrianders were incurably lazy, when in reality they were eager to throw themselves into hard work . . . but not in response to the incentives that would motivate a modern consumer. Trobriand Islanders became functionally satiable once they had fulfilled their designated roles within a culturally valued patterned activity. Thus, without suffering dislocation and impaired psychological development, people may find reasons to act industriously.

Even in the modern world, industriousness needn't be motivated solely by duress or psychological neediness. From a transpersonal perspective, when the ego usurps sovereignty, the soul is eclipsed but may still find expression in creativity or in selfless service. For instance, when we see people perform before an audience seeking adulation, that's fulfilling an ego need. But when they perform to bring joy, or when they find dignity and meaning in the act of performance, that is the soul finding a foothold.[20]

Chapter 9 suggested that people's susceptibility to advertising and the lure of new consumer goods likely presupposes a developmental distortion that induces insatiability. American Indian and Trobriand responses to their encounters with Western civilization are consistent with this hypothesis. These non-dislocated peoples didn't merely decline the opportunity to embark down the path toward a Western consumer lifestyle. Rather, they did so *despite* strenuous efforts by Western missionaries, clerics, educators, traders, merchants, soldiers, adventurers, and others to convince them that their lives would be greatly improved through doing so.

Chapter 11

A BUTTERFLY DREAMING

How is the distortion of psychological development concealed?

> Once Chuang Tzu dreamed he was a butterfly, flut-
> tering happily hither and thither, not knowing he was
> Chuang Tzu. Suddenly he awoke and found himself
> to be Chuang Tzu. Now he does not know whether
> Chuang Tzu dreamed he was a butterfly or he is a but-
> terfly dreaming he is Chuang Tzu.
> —Chuang Tzu, fourth century BC

If today's global political-economic system deleteriously alters psychological development, that raises an obvious question: We pride ourselves on living in a scientific civilization and "the Information Age"—a
civilization that exceeds all that have come before it in its capacity to
explain the world in which we live. If so, how can the truth of our modern psychosocial circumstances still be a secret?

The question is worth exploring if only to forestall the skeptical
retort that prolonged failure to detect a dynamic so consequential is
inconceivable, and so our theory must be wrong. But we'll see that the
question matters for a second, more important reason.

EXPLAINING A SECRET'S SECRECY

Note first that it isn't as though our theory has previously been
advanced but rejected. It has never previously been formulated at all,
either in its conventional or transpersonal version. Even someone who
remains skeptical might concur that it's odd that a theory along our

lines has never even been entertained, notwithstanding several centuries of reflection on the nature and causes of modernity.

One explanation could be that our argument involves an inordinately challenging chain of reasoning. But many ideas in philosophy, rocket science, and so on seem no less difficult. Our world is hardly deficient in cadres of people with the intellectual chops to think their way through complex terrain.

Then again, from the standpoint of our theory's conventional formulation, no alternative explanation springs immediately to mind. Establishing that insatiability arises from dislocation and an ensuing, nonspecific impairment in psychological development (as per Figure 6) doesn't suggest anything about why no one has previously forged this thesis.

But that isn't true for the transpersonal formulation (Figure 8). The Pandavas fail to detect their developmental disorder because they are seeing through the distorted eyes of their own egoism. Thus, perhaps it's been hard for anyone to detect our modern predicament because in our day—as then—intense egoism has a built-in propensity to perpetuate itself by obscuring its stunted nature and the ill effects that result.

To nail this down, let's see if we can identify ideas and social processes that inhibit formulating a developmental-distortion theory of modernity and whether these can plausibly be attributed to the ego's impulse to protect its sovereignty.

MASKING IN EVERYDAY LIFE

Several everyday beliefs are important to masking our psychosocial circumstances. These are not necessarily ideas that people are aware of consciously, but they lurk in the cultural background:

The first is the belief that insatiability is normal. In the modern world, insatiability has become so ubiquitous that most of us take it for granted. Yet as we've seen, pervasive insatiability is a product of social and economic forces that alter psychological development.

The second belief grows out of our insatiability: We find it natural to measure worth, including self-worth, based on material gains or achievement. Just think of how common it is to rank nations based on their gross domestic product, or how much attention our society devotes to the lives of the rich and famous. Of course, we also rely at times on other measures of value, such as selflessness, courage, creativity, and political freedom. But the pride of place commonly accorded to material measures of worth is significant for what it *diverts* people from considering: psychospiritual self-realization as an alternative metric of value.

Building on this cultural background, there is a belief dynamic that is functionally foundational to modern societies:

1. **The Core Myth:** For a capitalist market economy to function, most people must take it for granted that consumption and/or wealth (or perhaps power, stature, or fame) will produce enduring contentment. From a transpersonal perspective, egoic psychology is predisposed in this direction—that is, toward expecting that "outside" objects and experiences will redress "inside" yearning and deficits.

2. **The Myth Is Never Fulfilled:** It must nonetheless be guaranteed behind their backs—as it will be, so long as people remain dislocated, dis-integrated, and insatiable— that any satisfaction will remain transitory. Otherwise, people's acquisitiveness would scale back, and the economy, which depends on high consumer demand, would collapse.

3. **Nonfulfillment Is Masked:** People must fail to register the contradiction between (1) and (2). The two beliefs I discussed just above—that insatiability is universal and that material worth is the primary metric of value— contribute to this masking by limiting critical reflection.

The modern myth of satisfaction-via-consumption is analogous to something Malinowski wrote of the Trobriand Islanders: "The mythical world . . . must always be beyond what actually exists, yet it must appear just within reach of realisation if it is to be effective at all." Our core myth induces us to keep scratching rather than try to cure the cause of the itch. There are dissenters, but mass culture embraces the myth.[1]

Insatiability and a material metric of value were also operative in the case of the Pandavas while living in Maya's Palace. However, in modern times these background beliefs have become more pervasive, entrenched, and normalized. Like fish who don't know what water is because they've never been out of it, we no longer know from experience what it's like to live in a society not organized to instill and perpetuate insatiability.

MISSED CHANCES TO UNMASK

If everyday beliefs contribute to concealing our psychosocial situation, why haven't elite knowledge systems come to our rescue? Explaining why we haven't entertained the thought that modern psychological development might be distorted is different from explaining why, say, sixteenth-century scholars didn't invent quantum mechanics. The latter couldn't have happened because countless preparatory steps were not yet in place. In contrast, not a few of the subsidiary ideas necessary for formulating a dislocation theory of developmental disorder were available during the early modern period or even before.

For instance, various medieval-era European mystics and proto-scientific alchemists knew that psychospiritual development past egoism is possible (although they wouldn't have used such words to express the insight). During the Enlightenment, the French philosopher Jean-Jacques Rousseau began articulating a theory of child-and-adolescent psychological development in his book *Emile, or On Education* (1762). Europeans had also known since the seventeenth century that many indigenous cultures found no allure in European material accomplishments and that Europeans adopted into such cultures often found them morally superior.[2]

Eighteenth-century Scotland experienced a burst of intellectual ferment that became a source of ideas that influenced America's Founding Fathers as well as British industrialization. This period, known as the Scottish Enlightenment, also saw the articulation of ideas that could have contributed to propounding a dislocation theory of insatiability. In Chapter 8, we noted that James Steuart's influential *Inquiry into the Principles of Political Economy* (1767) identified insatiability as a new driver of industriousness ("men are forced to labour now because they are slaves to their own wants"). In that same year, Adam Ferguson—a founder of the discipline of sociology—published *An Essay on the History of Civil Society*, in which he lamented that commercialism was weakening social relations, reducing them to self-interested calculation and contracts.

Rather remarkably, during this period Adam Smith—the patron saint of modern economic thought—in his second most influential work, *The Theory of Moral Sentiments*, explained that the belief that consumption can provide enduring contentment is illusory. Any man who labors all his life to accumulate power, wealth, and possessions, wrote Smith, in the end "in his heart . . . curses ambition, and vainly regrets the ease and the indolence of youth, . . . which he has foolishly sacrificed" striving to procure consumer goods ("baubles and trinkets") that "can afford him no real satisfaction" and "will always appear in the highest degree contemptible and trifling." Smith observed that it is nonetheless "this deception which rouses and keeps in continual motion the industry of mankind." Thus Adam Smith, of all people, identified consumer satisfaction as an illusion necessary to perpetuating market dynamism. He was almost making our argument for us.[3]

Hence, several building blocks for a dislocation theory of psychospiritual distortion and arrest were available to thinkers of brilliance living in a time of intellectual freedom and exuberance. For instance, it would not have been a great stretch for some contemporary to have wondered if the thinning of communal bonds of affection (a concern expressed by Ferguson) might have had something to do with explaining the coincident birth of insatiability-driven industriousness described by Steuart.

But that didn't happen. Competing ideas were elaborated in their stead. For instance, various intellectual currents—including the European Enlightenment's skepticism of religious dogma, the Calvinist belief in predestination, and the Newtonian articulation of a mechanistic model of the universe—contributed to marginalizing European spiritual insights that managed to survive religious suppression. Meanwhile, thinkers such as Steuart and Smith were not perturbed by their psychological observations. Steuart assessed people's new enslavement to their wants favorably because it increased human industriousness and population. For the same reasons, Smith judged the self-deceptive myth of consumer satisfaction to be socially beneficial.[4]

The birth of modern consumerism also coincided with the construction, initially in Europe and later in America, of unilinear stage theories of human history. These theories ranked human societies in terms of discrete stages ordered hierarchically along a single line, stretching from "primitive" to "civilized." All societies were supposedly destined to progress through these stages in the same sequence, albeit at different dates and rates. Beyond legitimating genocide, slavery, imperial conquest, and colonization, these theories played a central role in the early stages of masking, reducing attention to dislocation and its psychospiritual downside.[5]

Most unilinear stage theories were explicitly materialist, basing their metric of historical progress on technological indicators such as harnessing fire, farming, and metalworking. However, even nonmaterialist stage theories, such as Hegel's psychospiritual theory of history, invariably "found"—because they presupposed—that their own society surpassed all others. None entertained the possibility that progress along one dimension (such as economic productivity or political freedom) might sometimes involve backsliding along another dimension (such as psychospiritual growth).[6]

Even Karl Marx's critique of capitalism postulated a fixed historical sequence that begins with primitive communism and marches along through ancient societies, feudalism, and capitalism before culminating in advanced communist societies. This model pegged precapitalist societies as outdated stepping-stones to a superior postcapitalist future.

Concurrently, the Romantic Movement—which valued emotion and intuition over reason, celebrated untamed nature, and had appreciative things to say about non-modern cultures—emerged as a force opposing Enlightenment thought, industrialization, and evolutionary-stage theories. Romanticism might thus have become an earlier platform for critical theorizing along our lines. And to some extent it did, as in the writings of William Blake, Henry David Thoreau, and John Ruskin. However, the Romantic critique of industrialism never found enough traction in the general culture to displace the wider conviction that Western civilization represents the apex of human achievement.[7]

Over time, the likelihood of exposing insatiability as a problematic historical development diminished among intellectuals for the same reason that it did in the population at large: normalization. The empirical social sciences were born toward the end of the early modern period, in the mid-1700s. From then on, fewer Western people had any experience of functional satiability except, at best, via observation or secondhand reports of people, such as peasants or indigenous tribes, who were increasingly disparaged as backward and indolent. Insights such as Steuart's into the historical emergence of insatiability were largely forgotten.[8]

MAINSTREAM ECONOMICS VERSUS PSYCHOSPIRITUAL DEVELOPMENT

The discipline of economics has become the dominant voice in explaining market economies, and a potent force in informing public policy and teaching us how to think about our society generally. Mainstream economic theory has commonly conceived of people as rational egoists (so-called *Homo economicus*): egoic in being preoccupied exclusively with our self-interest, rational in selecting efficient means to advance our interests. Conventional economic theory furthermore takes it for granted that our interests and desires ("preferences") are not affected by economic activities or institutions. Often the theory takes a further step in imagining that our preferences do not change over time. Finally, the theory assumes that it's morally wrong for public policy to influence what people want. This is the doctrine of "consumer sovereignty," which treats our desires as sacrosanct and morally insulated from critique.

All these assumptions are problematic, and together they render economic theory vulnerable to the charge that it embodies inherent contradictions and fallacies. For instance, routine features of market operation—such as emulating one another's consumer purchases, advertising, and economists' own policy prescriptions—all influence what people desire, do, and buy, violating the assumption that the economy does not shape human wants, as well as the doctrine of consumer sovereignty. But from our standpoint the more basic short-coming is that in modeling people as rational egoists, economic theory makes no allowance for psychological development.[9]

For instance, economic theory endorses a market system that is intended to allow *Homo economicus* maximum opportunity to sat-isfy his or her preferences. What could be wrong with that? Nothing . . . except that the modern techno-economy distorts psychospiritual growth and elevates the prevalence of grave psychological and physical maladies, all while *depending upon* the secret ability to cause the insis-tent craving that it is supposedly going to quell. Mainstream economic theory is the pivotal intellectual apparatus sustaining the secret, thereby legitimating the system it misrepresents. This is not some eas-ily corrected theoretical oversight; it reflects profoundly consequential omission and distortion at the theory's core.[10]

The Behavioral Turn

Recently behavioral and experimental economists have taken the con-structive step of using insights from social psychology and economic experiments to improve upon some of the less plausible assumptions of mainstream economics. But any attempt to integrate psychological development remains primitive. (There is certainly no inkling that mar-ket economies might instill insatiability by distorting development.)[11]

For instance, relaxing the supposition that people act exclusively to advance their narrow self-interest, some behavioral economists are investigating settings that can induce people to internalize a norm of cooperation. This approach has merits. But it's one thing for people to learn to *conform* to a social norm; it's another for them to *evolve* until higher ethical principles emerge as a natural expression of their being. "'Socialization' or 'internalization' is not moral *development*," explains one psychologist.[12]

A parable may help make this distinction clearer:

The Caterpillars Who Learned to Share

There once was a beautiful species of butterfly that was naturally unselfish and communitarian. Whenever one butterfly detected nec-tar-laden flowers, it invited others to share in the bounty. The but-terflies also exhibited one unique biological property: they were able to mate and lay eggs during either their butterfly or caterpillar stage. Both caterpillar and butterfly eggs could grow into caterpillars that later matured into new butterflies.

One day a group of these butterflies settled on a remote island. There the succeeding generation of caterpillars discovered a leaf for which they had a particular fondness. Unbeknownst to them, eating this leaf prevented them from developing into butterflies. Within a generation or two there were no butterflies left on the island.

The caterpillars didn't notice. They lived on, munching their favorite leaves and producing new generations of leaf-munching caterpillars.

Now, unlike their butterfly forebears, these caterpillars were a rather selfish lot. When one of them found the favored leaf, it hoarded it until it had consumed the entire amount. Nonetheless, there were enough of these leaves that the caterpillar community survived and reproduced.

Over time, some of the island's caterpillars found themselves drawn to intellectual pursuits. Caterpillar historians recorded the great trials and accomplishments of each succeeding generation of caterpillars. Caterpillar agronomists and economists took an interest in optimizing propagation of the plant that sported their favorite leaf. Caterpillar storytellers recounted the heroic tale of the first caterpillars that, as it was told, arrived on the island long ago, floating across the tossing sea while clinging precariously to a slippery branch.

There were even some caterpillars who believed that all would be better off if they could only learn to cooperate and share their favorite leaves. They ran experiments to discover the conditions under which caterpillars were prone to become sharers, hoping to encourage that behavior.

Of course, none of the learned historians, clever economists, or well-intended experimentalist caterpillars ever tried to account for the striking failure of any caterpillars to develop into butterflies. The thought never entered their heads that becoming anything more than a caterpillar was a possibility.

All Trees, No Forest

Since it doesn't acknowledge the possibility of psychospiritual development, economic theory naturally doesn't consider the effects of economic processes and psychospiritual development upon one another. The cognitive process through which economics obscures this interaction is instructive because it reveals the discipline's reliance on assumptions characteristic of egoism itself. To show this, let's examine the economic concept of "externalities."

Mainstream economic theory is much captivated by the elegant mathematics of self-setting prices that efficiently balance supply and demand. On the theory's periphery lurks the topic of externalities. An externality is conceived as any way in which a transaction between two agents in a competitive market spills over and affects someone not directly party to the transaction. The term "externalities" is telling; it's a tip-off that economics is wedded to a dualistic way of thinking in which there's a sharp distinction between self and other, inside and outside. In other words, economic thought *internalizes* premises characteristic of the egoic psychology that it imputes to *Homo economicus*. (There is even some evidence that the mainstream economics profession self-selects for people who are, on average, more prone than others to think and behave like *Homo economicus*.)[13]

In theoretical terms, economists believe that they have externalities well under control. One normal proposal is to examine each instance of adverse externality as it arises, assign to it a "shadow price" reflecting harm that it delivers to innocent bystanders, and impose that shadow price as a tax on producers so that their behavior takes into account their spillover influence on others. An example would be to enact a carbon tax on fossil-fuel combustion to limit climate-altering greenhouse-gas emissions.

Remember, however, that an externality is literally anything that you experience without being a direct party to the transaction that caused that "anything" as a byproduct. For example, imagine walking down a street in your city or town. As you stroll along, almost everything that you experience—including the sidewalk beneath your feet, the buildings and vehicles around you, the clothing and behavior of passers-by, and the quality of the air you breath—are "externalities." You did not personally pay for any of these things in a voluntary bilateral transaction in a perfectly competitive free market.

Virtually every market-distributed commodity or event displays such spillover effects. Some are anticipated, most are not, ranging from the aesthetic, psychological, and biophysical to the ecological, economic, and political. Indeed, competitive markets often reward firms for displacing costs onto other people in the form of externalities. And many consumer purchases are *intended* to excite the admiration and envy of other people, which is another external effect. In short, externalities are not a rarity; they are utterly pervasive.

Some economists might, upon reflection, agree. But they would argue that the great majority of these externalities are innocuous and can safely be ignored. Notice, however, the fragmented way in which economic theory has framed the concept of externalities. Even if most externalities are *individually* innocuous, *taken together* these externalities appreciably constitute the world in which we live . . . including the techno-economic dislocation that is responsible for distorting psychospiritual development.

But, displaying a non-holistic style of thinking, economic thought camouflages all of this. (While non-holism isn't exclusive to egoism, it is often characteristic of it, as symbolized by the fracture of the Pandavas' customary unity when Yudhishthira devolves into intense egoism during the dice match.)

In effect, Adam Smith's miraculous Invisible Hand—a metaphor for explaining how private self-interest procures overall societal benefit—is really an Invisible Sleight of Hand, obscuring the heavy psychospiritual price we pay in return for the species of economic growth and technological innovation that our civilization has embraced. (Perhaps this is what the Micmac chief we encountered in Chapter 10 was trying, in his own eloquent way, to explain to the French sea captains.)

Acknowledging the obfuscation intrinsic to conventional economics doesn't imply a flip-side turn toward demonizing all aspects of market life. Markets can serve constructive purposes. The danger lies in idolizing competitive markets and allowing them to frustrate higher levels of human flourishing.

THE TABOO

An unwritten taboo constrains inquiry into our psychospiritual circumstances. It states that as a scholar, *Thou shalt not acknowledge the potential for psychospiritual development past ego-identification.* A follow-on injunction, even stronger than the first, is: *Thou shalt not integrate a post-egoic perspective into research, and particularly not into critical social inquiry.* With few exceptions, violating either limb of this taboo—let's call it "the Taboo"—is toxic to a scholar's career.[14]

There is no constraint against studying religious ethics or religion and spirituality as cultural systems that produce sundry social, biological, or psychological effects. But researchers who dare affirm that moving into the terrain of post-egoism might be possible or—even more scandalously—that adopting a post-egoic stance can prove intellectually fruitful are putting their professional reputations, access to funding, and publication opportunities on the line. As a 2018 report puts it, "Researchers wishing to explore some of these domains [e.g., transpersonal or mystical experiences] may encounter reluctance, resistance, or even ridicule from the scientific and academic community."[15]

One consequence is that the Taboo prohibits writing a book like this one. If you aren't allowed to acknowledge the possibility of ego-transcendence, then you can't conceptualize intense ego-identification as a developmental distortion and halt. Nor, without adopting a post-egoic viewpoint, can you perceive resistance to ego-transcendence . . . or the successful enactment of that resistance through such means as the Taboo. Among all the elements that contribute to masking, the Taboo's distinctive potency is that it has taken a great bulk of the world's most brilliant people off the hunt.

The roots of the Taboo trace back to the European Enlightenment's rejection of religious dogma and to Karl Marx's contention that belief in a heavenly afterlife supports popular acquiescence to injustice in this life. Both skeptical orientations have proven their intellectual value. But neither required dismissing the idea that it is possible to transcend ego-identification. The Taboo is also rooted in the modern denigration—for instance, in unilinear stage theories of history—of innately spiritual, indigenous ways of knowing, which helped justify slavery, colonization, and imperialism and which continues to justify extractive exploitation of indigenous natural resources.[16]

There was a time when the Taboo's strength ebbed. During the cultural ferment of the 1960s and early 1970s, humanistic and transpersonal psychologists began integrating spirituality into developmental psychology, with a focus on supporting psychological thriving and, in some cases, ego-transcendence. Some of their research even appeared in the pages of august professional journals, such as *Science* magazine. But by the 1980s, the Taboo was back in full force. Without identifying any fundamental flaws in transpersonal research programs, mainstream psychological scholarship disowned them.[17]

Some might counter that the Taboo safeguards critical social inquiry from New Age woo-woo fantasies and other intellectual dead ends. However, that is nothing but unfounded supposition. The Taboo can't derive from rigorous evaluation of forbidden social-scientific research because it has been so effectual that there has been virtually no research to evaluate.

Alternatively, one might imagine that the Taboo reflects academe's pervasive secular rationality. But it doesn't. A 2004–2005 survey of 40,670 faculty members at 421 colleges and universities across the US found that an astonishing 81 percent judged themselves spiritual, 64 percent said they're religious, and 61 percent engaged in practices such as prayer or meditation.[18]

Through my former work as a senior staff member at the Mind and Life Institute (cofounded by the Dalai Lama) and the Center for Contemplative Mind in Society, I came to know dozens of researchers—some of them renowned in their fields—who admitted privately to pursuing a spiritual practice oriented toward enlightenment. Yet they maintained that were they to acknowledge post-egoic spiritual development within their teaching or research—even if framed in secular, scientific terms—they would be discredited.

In the mid-1990s, I participated in a multi-college faculty seminar on integrating spirituality into higher education that was convened by David K. Scott, a physicist who had become the chancellor of the University of Massachusetts Amherst. At the opening session, Dr. Scott explained with some poignancy that even as his university's top administrator—or perhaps *especially* as the top administrator—he had to be extremely circumspect about discussing spirituality in academic settings. The seminar operated quietly and was advertised only by word of mouth to protect faculty careers and reputations.

The Taboo extends even to research on the effects of meditation, yoga, and other spiritual practices. There has been an explosive growth in such investigation over the past several decades, but it has focused mostly on instrumental effects—such as improving health, work productivity, creativity, attentiveness, compassion, and the like—or the neural correlates of these effects within our brains. Only rarely is there mention of ego-transcendence, the central purpose for which these methods were devised.[19]

Then again, there are some indications that—as in the 1960s and '70s—the Taboo's strength may be softening somewhat. While still upholding the Taboo against adopting a post-egoic perspective, universities have gradually become more willing to integrate contemplative practice and the discussion of spirituality into classes. And in the 2010s, a small number of psychologists and neuroscientists started quietly defying the Taboo by taking up ego-transcendence as an *object of inquiry*. Some of this new research has even been published in peer-reviewed scientific journals (as was transpersonal research several decades earlier). Even so, virtually no scholars have turned it around and adopted a post-egoic perspective as a *tool of inquiry* for investigating psychology, history, or society generally.[20]

Today many US scientists and scholars express dismay with fundamentalist-Christian and Republican Party rejection of scientific ideas—such as evolutionary biology, human-induced climate change, or effective practices for pandemic control—or with their disparagement of intellect generally. They condemn this as close-minded and dangerous. At the same time, the bulk of the research community effectively denies the possibility of post-egoic psychospiritual development—a possibility that a substantial subset privately takes seriously. This violates the core scientific norms of openness and candor, forfeiting inquiry that could be key to understanding and benefiting modern societies.

Disciplinary Divisions and Knowledge Compartmentalization

One of the hallmarks of modernity is that knowledge is advanced via specialization. Subdisciplines have proliferated, while transdisciplinary research and interdisciplinary collaboration are celebrated in rhetoric more than practice. Professors are hired and promoted primarily based on their contributions to a single discipline.

Knowledge compartmentalization has proven extraordinarily productive. But it needn't have entailed downplaying interdisciplinary inquiry, and the skew toward disciplinary research has become part of the apparatus that masks the social causes and consequences of intense egoism. This is reflected in missed intellectual connections. Taking our own inquiry as a counterpoint:

- There is minimal tradition of developmental psychologists partnering with historians to see what each might be able to learn from the other (as exemplified in Chapter 8). For instance, according to a recent overview of developmental psychology, macrosocial forces influence "the nature of interaction within all other levels of the ecology of human development, yet . . . this level remains the most elusive and least studied aspect of the person ↔ context interaction."[21]
- The thesis that macrosocial forces influence psychological development (Chapter 6) has likewise not been married with sociologists' complementary insight that people's beliefs and behavior aggregate and fold back to influence the evolution of social structures (as depicted in Figure 6).[22]
- Transpersonal psychologists have rarely turned their insights toward trying to explain history or society from a post-egoic stance. By the same token, few historians or social theorists have paid attention to transpersonal psychology.[23]

The Taboo and the skew toward monodisciplinary research operate in tandem. For instance, the possibilities for integrating psychological development into early modern history shrink if post-egoic insights—such as the ego's reliance on self-deception to protect ego-sovereignty—are forbidden.

Taboo-compliant knowledge compartmentalization results in the odd phenomenon that modern societies allow post-egoic insights to flourish in designated spiritual spaces (such as meditation retreats, yoga studios, and the spirituality section of bookstores) and secular knowledge to flourish in others (e.g., academe and highbrow publications). Moreover, many people—such as spiritually inclined professors or intellectually inclined meditators—move freely between those two types of spaces. And yet while it is perfectly acceptable to interpret spiritual texts with the assistance of modern disciplinary knowledge (such as anthropology, psychology, or history), the converse maneuver—using psychological insights drawn from spirituality to inform modern disciplinary knowledge—is prohibited in conventional scholarship.

Disciplinary divisions are sustained in part because intellectual specialization has shown itself effective in advancing knowledge as well as a wealth-building, consumer-centric sociotechnical order. But compartmentalized knowing is also ego-protective, and it is consonant with the ego's resistance to the wholeness that might lead toward ego-transcendence.

THE DURYODHANA EFFECT

There is another type of masking that occurs not *despite* our modern prowess in knowledge making but *because* of it. Call it the Duryodhana effect. The ease with which the Pandavas see through the architectural illusions that fool Duryodhana deflects the *Mahabharata's* protagonists from considering that *they* might be the victims of other, subtler illusions. In the same way, the dazzling success of modern science in revealing secret after secret, from the hidden architecture of stem cells to that of distant galaxies, deflects us from imagining that we might be the victims of four centuries of fundamental self-deception concerning ourselves and our society.

Here's another example: Cosmopolitan, college-educated American liberals were dumbfounded by the spectacle of tens of millions of other Americans who could not see—or else would not admit—that President Donald Trump was a lying malignant narcissist who imperiled US democracy, disastrously botched management of the coronavirus pandemic, and decisively lost his campaign for reelection. And yet the sense of superiority that can accompany detecting a mass delusion also becomes just one more deflection from imaging that we—exactly like the Pandavas when laughing derisively at Duryodhana—might be the weavers of other subtler but also harmful self-deceptions.[24]

HOW KARL MARX HELPED SAVE CAPITALISM

Marx is renowned as a social theorist in part because he propounded a sophisticated theory of masking—in his case, of how social injustice is ideologically masked in capitalist societies. In Marxism, "ideology" denotes a false set of beliefs that arise out of an unjust system of social relations, camouflaging—and thus sustaining—the injustice. When in Chapter 7 I quoted from the passage in *The Communist Manifesto* that encapsulates the dislocation intrinsic to capitalism, I omitted the clauses italicized below:

> All fixed, fast-frozen relations, *with their train of ancient and venerable prejudices and opinions,* are swept away, all new-formed ones become antiquated before they can ossify. All that is solid melts into air, all that is holy is profaned, *and man is at last compelled to face with sober senses his real condition of life and his relations with his kind.*

In the italicized words Marx and Engels predicted that relentless dislocation would before long unmask all false understanding of our circumstances. This was not a crazy prediction, since early modern and industrial history had already included significant grassroots opposition to dislocation and injustice. Nonetheless, the prediction has proven overoptimistic. The two radical thinkers failed to anticipate that dislocation can produce new layers of perceptual and cognitive distortion.

As we previously noted, Marx also insisted that religion—including faith in a heavenly afterlife—can play only a regressive social role. He famously dubbed religion "the opium of the people." Again, this was not a crazy thought. Organized religion has often encouraged brutality or accommodation to oppression.[25]

But Marx's implication that religion can *only* function regressively has had unfortunate consequences, teaching succeeding generations of critical social theorists—including even many non-Marxists—to throw out the spiritual baby along with its polluted bathwater. (Some self-selection in career paths may be involved: among US academics, those who self-identify as "far left" are also those least likely to self-identify as spiritual or religious.) Marxism's approach to *unmasking* capitalist social injustice has thus, ironically, contributed to *masking* any consideration of the possibility that modern psychological development might be ego-arrested (see again Figure 10).[26]

Psychospiritual stunting and social injustice are interdependent in complex ways, but neither can be collapsed conceptually into the other. On the one hand, social injustice contributes to the dislocation that distorts psychological development. At the same time, beliefs that are ego-protective fold back to exacerbate injustice. For instance, by obscuring the extent to which capitalism is harmful to everyone up and down the class spectrum, such beliefs weaken the case for transforming a system that, among other things, perpetuates inequality and injustice.

Chapter 12

WHEN THE NEED FOR
ILLUSION IS DEEP

The ego/world system

A great deal of intelligence can be invested in ignorance when the need for illusion is deep.
—Saul Bellow, *To Jerusalem and Back*

Chapter 11 exposes some of the beliefs that have concealed the global
economy's role in altering psychospiritual development. But the chapter reveals something more. If we consider the various ideas and social
processes that have prevented people from working out the conventional formulation of our theory over the past several centuries, *all* of
them are consonant with intensive ego-identification.

For instance, mainstream economic theory is the central scholarly
apparatus that teaches people to venerate the global market economy.
It is also riddled with assumptions characteristic of egoic psychology:
It promises that the market will satisfy preferences, thereby legitimating a system that makes enduring satisfaction psychologically unattainable (think of Yudhishthira imagining that amassing an empire
would fulfill rather than inflame his desires). It posits that people are
naturally egoistic, unaware that it is advancing a techno-economic system that tends to *make* people egoistic. It evaluates the world based
on a material metric of value and non-holistic reasoning, while making no allowance for psychological development . . . and certainly not
for the reality that the global economy adversely alters psychological
development.

Karl Marx propounded a critique of capitalism that likewise draws
upon a material metric of value; he criticized capitalism for its injustice
but applauded its prodigious productivity. He also denigrated religion

unconditionally, thereby deflecting generations of social theorists from mounting a critique along our lines.

And then there is the Taboo, a prohibition based on the supposition—reverentially upheld absent any empirical validation—that a post-egoic perspective is a fairy tale leading nowhere but down intellectual dead ends. Is it perhaps suspicious that: (a) the ego is desperate to perpetuate itself, including via self-deception; and (b) modern academia upholds a Taboo targeted precisely to prevent social research that might undo the deception?

One can explain some of these beliefs without invoking egoism as a contributing cause. For instance, left-of-center critics argue that mainstream economics legitimates the free market and obfuscates injustice in order to advance the interests of "the billionaire class" (in the terminology of US Senator Bernie Sanders). Then again, mainstream economists could have built a theory that legitimated capitalism without relying time and again on egoic premises and disregarding psychological development.

When several successive throws of the dice come up double sixes, that could be random chance. But when *every* throw comes up double sixes, it becomes more and more clear that the dice must be loaded. And when the same player keeps raking in all the winnings, one cannot easily escape the conclusion that the player has had a hand in loading the dice.

Just so, modern people believe all sorts of different things. But when, notwithstanding that diversity of thought, an evolving system of belief unerringly advances the ego's interest in sustaining its sovereignty—and not just for a little while but over centuries—it is reasonable to conclude that the ego has played a role in achieving that outcome.

Or consider the matter from another direction. Scholars recognize that:

- Dislocation can trigger addiction.
- Addiction is a developmental disorder.
- Addiction and insatiability are both forms of intense craving.
- The historical birth of mass consumerism—a token of insatiability—brought in its wake colossal demand for addictive drug foods.

These observations are not state secrets. And yet they have not been woven together to formulate our theory in even its less specific, conventional form—to wit, addiction and insatiability are twin symptoms of a dislocation-induced alteration in psychological development.

How can we account for this striking failure of scholarly imagination? Again, I am not asking why our theory hasn't been accepted—after all, it is new and hasn't been extensively vetted—but why it hasn't even been formulated.

The conventional variant of our theory has no answer. Neither, of course, does anyone else. (You can't expect people to explain what they don't know needs explaining.) In contrast, the transpersonal version of our theory can explain exactly why this has happened: the global techno-economic system promotes arrest in strong ego-identification, and the ego is adept at self-protective self-deception. As this chapter's epigraph puts it: "A great deal of intelligence can be invested in ignorance when the need for illusion is deep."[1]

Explanatory power is an important metric for assessing a theory's validity. By that measure, the power of a transpersonal perspective to *inspire* our foundational hypotheses (as in Chapters 6 and 8), and to *explain* what other theories cannot, makes a strong case for believing that the transpersonal version of our theory is true: we have failed to understand our psychosocial circumstances because we are blinded by the intensified egoism that those circumstances engender.

Figure 11 summarizes how the psychosocial dynamics in which we are enmeshed are self-camouflaged.

Social scientists have elucidated collective ego-defense mechanisms, such as group denial, through which the members of modern organizations cope with shared anxieties. The masking system generated by pervasive ego-sovereignty qualifies as such a mechanism. Except in our case the "organization" is modern civilization and there are no social scientists positioned to observe it from the outside.[2]

I can speculate a bit further: The transpersonal formulation of our theory can specify the agent (our egos) and motive (preservation of ego-sovereignty) that account for masking our psychosocial plight. It furthermore identifies various mechanisms through which our egos achieve this ego-protective knowledge regime (e.g., by acting based on a material metric of value and upholding the Taboo). But how do our egos ensure that people's diverse perceptions and beliefs consistently *aggregate* to preserve ego-sovereignty? One possibility is that our egos' terror of ego-transcendence animates an unconscious capability to procure this outcome.

For instance, perhaps the ego has a kind of subconscious sixth sense that steps in as needed to keep our psychosocial situation veiled. You can see such a mechanism operating on a small scale in the minds of meditators. Novice meditators quickly develop the ability, even if only fleeting, to turn attention inward and, with detachment, observe thoughts and feelings floating by. This represents a glimpse of ego-disidentification. Yet meditators commonly experience something else: inner resistance. When we try to set aside a time to meditate, suddenly a half dozen other activities—such as writing grocery lists or checking email—loom up as more pressing. Trying to abide in meditative

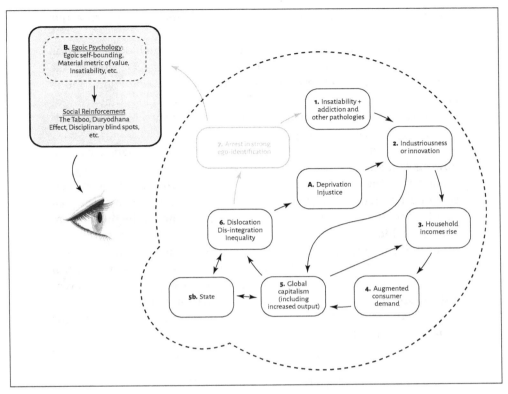

Figure 11. How Egoic Psychology Masks Modern Civilization's Dependence on Perpetuating Ego-Arrest. The material within the dashed circle reproduces Figure 10, adding shaded Box B and an eye outside of the circle looking in. Step 7 drops the language of the conventional formulation of our theory ("impaired psychological development") in favor of the more specific transpersonal formulation ("arrest in strong ego-identification").

The eye symbolizes the ego in its role as system observer. Box B lists aspects of egoic psychology and behavior that distort the ego's understanding of the system that it is observing. The arrow from Step 7 to Box B indicates that today's intensified egoic psychology is a product of dislocation-induced developmental arrest; both that arrow and Step 7 are faded out to indicate that the ego prevents itself from knowing this.

The figure depicts masking as the ego might prefer that we understand it, with the eye hovering outside the system, observing with detached impartiality. In reality the eye is stationed inside Step 7.

Note that Step 6 now includes "Dis-integration." Figure 10 omitted dis-integration because the figure addresses Euro-American psychosocial dynamics of the seventeenth to nineteenth centuries, and the dis-integrative device paradigm did not come aggressively into force until the early twentieth century. (See the section on "Stabilizing Insatiability" in Chapter 13, below.)

awareness, we are distracted by little itches or captivating thoughts. Any of these intrusions easily becomes more compelling than maintaining one's intention to meditate. We can infer that when people edge toward ego-disidentification, they experience anxiety. Without consciously understanding why, the ego responds with self-protective measures.

Perhaps a similar disquiet arises across a much wider canvas when there are ideas abroad that threaten the ego's safety. That unease could help animate offsetting maneuvers such as deflection, Taboo enforcement, or—more generally—tending to favor ideas that are ego-protective, while also ensuring that the *totality* of such maneuvers suffices to protect ego-sovereignty.

While this hypothetical "sixth-sense" mechanism *could* explain how egoism sustains an ego-protective knowledge regime, I can't be certain that the explanation is correct. For our immediate purposes, that doesn't matter. A social theory, such as ours, that can specify an agent, its motives, the ends that it achieves, and part of the mechanism through which those ends are accomplished can be deeply insightful even if in some respects the theory remains incomplete. That is, a theory that explains some important things but not everything is still a valuable theory. For instance, as it is our theory suffices to reveal hidden dimensions of our psychosocial situation (with more to come in Chapter 14), and it sets the stage for beginning to seek ways out (Chapters 16 and 17).[3]

LIFTING THE VEIL

If the social dynamics that secure ego-stabilization are so profoundly masked, how can it be possible to propound a theory that lifts the veil? We've had a decisive assist from the *Mahabharata*, a work composed by spiritual adepts long prior to the emergence of pervasive, dislocation-stabilized ego-sovereignty. Ordinarily, the epic's teachings remain invisible to people entrapped in Maya's Palace. However, through our structural decoding we have managed to craft corrective lenses enabling us to first read between the lines . . . and then turn around and see through the veil.

And in a sense, we're not alone. Even if no one has previously mustered a theory like ours, many people may have intuited something along similar lines. That could be what we're seeing in the case of people who experience modernity as spirit-crushing and soul-stifling, and who have responded by seeking more economically self-reliant and communitarian alternatives, often with a spiritual dimension.[4]

ARE WE AS HAPPY AS WE THINK?

Over the past several decades social scientists have ascertained that many people around the world assess themselves as being reasonably happy. This seems to contradict our contention that insatiability is omnipresent, because one would expect insatiability to manifest in chronic discontent. Or is it possible that modern people are in some manner "contentedly discontent"?[5]

We've already predicted the latter. For a consumer society to stay in business, most people must remain content ("happy") with pursuing the satisfaction of cravings that are never long appeased.

One way this may come about is when people simply assess their contentment inaccurately. "Endowed by their Creator with . . . [an] unalienable Right . . . [to] the pursuit of Happiness," according to the Declaration of Independence, Americans especially may have a hard time conceding themselves failures in that pursuit. In other words, people may sometimes unconsciously exaggerate their level of contentment in an effort to feel better about their lives. For such reasons, many scholars urge caution in taking self-reported happiness levels at face value. (Psychotherapists know that clients sometimes insist they're happy when there's convincing evidence otherwise—including that they came to therapy in the first place.)[6]

A study of forty-two thousand Australians sampled over an eight-year period found, rather remarkably, that experiencing moderate to severe depression produced little change in self-reported happiness: "Even quite strong negative feelings about the self can co-exist with normal or even high levels of SWB [subjective well-being]." It's fair to conclude that happiness surveys are not conveying the full reality of human experience when people suffering from significant depression judge themselves "happy."[7]

And yet it also seems a stretch too far to dismiss all self-reported contentment as outright mirage. The ego's masking talents, together with the *Mahabharata*'s teachings in the stage-specificity of knowledge, suggest another way to make sense of the possibility of being happily discontent: our perception and evaluation of our inner state is development-dependent. In particular, the ego's capacity for self-deception can produce a type of contentment that, from a post-egoic stance, appears superficial at best.

When the Pandavas become established in Maya's Palace, they regress into intensive egoism, which manifests in Yudhishthira as hubris, greed, and addiction. Yet had they been surveyed at the time, they would doubtless have rated their happiness as "ten" on a scale of one to ten, based on their success in fulfilling materialistic—i.e., egoic—values.

Yudhishthira's behavior while ego-bound betrays his underlying discontent. Had he truly been satisfied, he would never have wagered everything, even his family's and his own freedom, in a gambling match for trifling rewards—additional territory for which he had no need beyond a small-minded wish to further humiliate cousin Duryodhana.

This doesn't mean that Yudhishthira's happiness during this time was entirely fictitious. But he was happy and sovereign *only as judged by his internalized egoic standards.* Looking back from a more evolved stance, he realized that while gambling he had become bereft of inner sovereignty, equanimity, contentment, and moral clarity.

Likewise, both the survey instruments that social scientists use to assess happiness and the self-assessments of those surveyed measure happiness *in the way that the ego perceives and understands it.* This includes assessing contentment not in comparison with what it might be—e.g., if ego-identification softened—but in comparison with what one has experienced or observed in others. (E.g., "Am I 'content'? I guess so because I figure I'm as content as other people.") And ultimately the ego is content with discontent because that's infinitely preferable to the alternative: the prospect of relinquishing ego-sovereignty and entering the post-egoic range of psychospiritual growth.[8]

In contrast, post-egoic people, while often finding pleasure in what the world has to offer, are more apt to be directed toward self-realization and the well-being of others than to securing happiness in the ego's sense. In the post-egoic range, happiness is typically more settled, deep, and integrally ethical and altruistic, with energy no longer diverted to camouflaging or trying to placate unappeasable egoic emptiness. Hand the Dalai Lama a slice of pizza, and he'll savor it. But there is no intense craving, clinging, or anxiety, and there is more sensitivity to the downside of ego-driven consumerism.[9]

New York Times columnist David Brooks addresses these points when he characterizes moral maturation as a quest to summit two successive mountain peaks: "If the first mountain is about building up the ego and defining the self, the second is about shedding the ego and dissolving the self. If the first mountain is about acquisition, the second mountain is about contribution. . . . On the first mountain we shoot for happiness, but on the second mountain we are rewarded with joy. . . . On the second mountain you see that happiness is good, but joy is better."[10]

If someone had asked Yudhishthira if he was happier after leaving Maya's Palace, his answer would have varied over time. Immediately after the Kurukshetra War, he was beside himself with grief and remorse (*Mahabharata* Book 12); during those weeks he would not have reported happiness by any standard. Yet he never returned to Maya's Palace, literally or figuratively, even though while he lived there it was judged the most magnificent structure on earth. The implication: even under conditions of adversity and anguish, post-egoic people do not regret their ego-disidentification.

"Contentment with discontent" is another element in the ego's project of concealing the adverse consequences of its sovereignty.

ON EGO-ARREST AS A CAUSE OF SUFFERING

Chapter 6 summarized evidence that dislocation plays a role in distorting psychological development, thereby contributing to many mental and physical ailments. Now we have concluded that this distortion involves intense ego-identification. But what is the nature of that egoic "involvement"? Validation of the transpersonal formulation of our theory allows us to clarify that strong egoism is implicated in more than one pathway running from dislocation to disease.

Figure 12 shows that ego-arrest contributes directly to mental and follow-on physical pathologies (i.e., the arrow from Step 7 to Step 1). For instance, one might reasonably conjecture that addiction and anxiety are—at least in part—symptoms, respectively, of egoic emptiness and insecurity. And it is likely that ego-arrest is a contributing factor in many other developmentally based mental disorders. On the other hand, it's also clear that health disorders can issue from the stresses of dislocation, deprivation, and injustice, without the direct mediation of

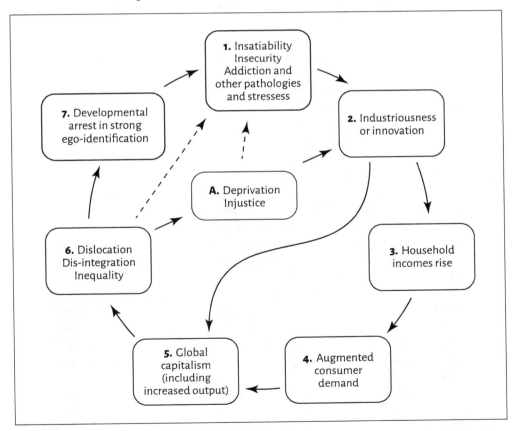

Figure 12. Ego-Arrested Development as a Cause of Mental and Physical Ailments. To reduce visual clutter, this figure omits several elements shown in Figure 11, including Step 5b (the State) and the arrow leading directly from Step 5 to Step 3.

intensified egoism (i.e., the new dashed arrows from Step 6 and Step A to Step 1). As simple proof: malnutrition contributes to disease in both modern and nonmodern societies (i.e., independent of the strength of ego-identification).[11]

But either way, in our day ego-arrest has become a factor in causing many instances of mental and physical disease. When it doesn't contribute directly to engendering these pathologies, it can do so indirectly through the insatiability and masking that are essential to sustaining a ceaselessly disruptive global techno-economy.

Moreover, as we observed in Chapter 7, dislocation is distressing in ways far beyond its role in stunting psychospiritual growth or inducing illness. For instance, when a business is forced to close, the resulting loss of jobs can take an enormous emotional toll, including on those forced to move elsewhere for employment, sometimes at reduced wages. Ego-arrest bears some responsibility for this and countless other forms of suffering caused by modern dislocation because, again, it is an essential component in driving the global economy (hence the addition of "Stresses" to Step 1 in Figure 12).

MAINSTREAM ECONOMIC THEORY REVISITED

Affirmation of the transpersonal formulation of our theory reveals additional ways in which mainstream economics contributes to camouflaging our psychosocial circumstances. For instance, from a post-egoic perspective, two linchpin economic values—"consumer sovereignty" and "consumer satisfaction"—are each impossibly self-contradictory: Sovereignty (i.e., self-command, moral autonomy) is exactly what a rational egoist lacks, and satisfaction is what it can never achieve. Think of Palace-bound Yudhishthira. To imagine organizing society around the objective of satisfying the wants of *Homo economicus*—the most ego-bound developmental incarnation of a human being—distracts from seeking the conditions under which people can flourish psychospiritually.

One can imagine an economist's comeback: "Look, if people crave that kind of self-actualization, nothing prevents them from allocating money and effort toward achieving it. Our free-market society offers ample opportunities to pursue growth-oriented psychotherapy, personal transformation through religious and spiritual exercises, and so on."

Our reply: "Yes, many people have such options. But the techno-economic landscape is structurally rigged to limit success. *The dice are loaded.*"

The *impulse* behind the concept of consumer sovereignty—to enable personal freedom and fulfillment—is worthy. But safeguarding consumer sovereignty has the contrary effect. When "the consumer" is elevated to sovereignty, command of the Palace has passed over into the ego's hands. Had it been advanced two thousand years ago, this is the theory that would have explained that living perpetually unsatisfied, enslaved, and deluded in Maya's Palace offers the best of all possible social arrangements.

Material measures of well-being, such as gross domestic product (GDP), are another economic contrivance that helps keep people content with their lot in the Palace. Growing numbers of scholars recognize that GDP is a flawed indicator. One concern is that GDP lumps together social goods and bads. For instance, when industrial pollution sickens people, the combined costs of medical treatment, funerals, burials, and environmental cleanup are folded into GDP as *positive* contributions. As a result, GDP perversely registers higher overall well-being.[12]

But the range of distortions is greater than critics have imagined. Consider the enormity of the misrepresentation in relying on GDP as an index of well-being when it fails to consider that some appreciable fraction of all modern psychological and physical affliction, as well as psychospiritual developmental distortion, can be attributed to routine market operation. Even worse, the latter distortion is not a remediable side effect; capitalism *requires* it in order so sustain insatiability.

In effect, whenever we hear that GDP has gone up—an outcome normally portrayed only in approving terms—a TV news commentator could reasonably interject: "You know, I'm not sure that's a signal to pop the champagne corks. Yes, GDP means jobs and financial return on investment. That's not nothing. But it also means that much more difficulty in growing psychologically or maturing spiritually, all the while sustaining another jump up in mental illness, emotional suffering and, from that, more cancer and all sorts of other terrible diseases. Wouldn't you think there'd be some way to provide for our daily bread without choking on the crust and wasting away from the empty calories and tainted ingredients?"

Under today's capitalism, economic development and psychospiritual development secretly diverge. GDP marches higher, while the prospect of human self-realization wanes. We saw an analogous divergence while the Pandavas were living in Maya's Palace: as they excelled in accumulating territory, wealth, and renown, their moral development was quietly regressing.[13]

CAPITALISM *DEPENDS* ON FRUSTRATING PSYCHOSPIRITUAL DEVELOPMENT

The conventional formulation of our theory exposes global capitalism as an engine of malady and discontent (Chapter 9). Now we know more.

The youthful Pandavas experience intensive ego-identification, but only temporarily. In contrast, today civilization sits mired in Maya's Palace, with most adults arrested in a strongly egoic psychological configuration (see Figure 13). Beyond this, we understand how this arrest has occurred. Capitalism cannot survive without perpetuating the psychospiritual distortion from which insatiability derives; this is a system optimized for *preventing* ego-transcendence.

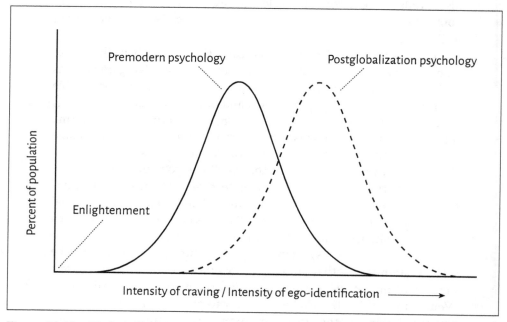

Figure 13. The Modern Shift in Trajectories of Psychological Development—Transpersonal Formulation. This figure re-renders Figure 7 from the standpoint of the transpersonal version of our theory. The shift in the distribution of craving under the influence of globalization (i.e., the bell curve's rightward shift) reflects intensifying ego-identification and, with it, an intensifying drive to perpetuate ego-sovereignty. The latter drive lies beneath the modern tendency to become developmentally arrested in intense ego-identification.

That means that whenever we seek solace, healing, or growth—perhaps through psychotherapy, psychiatric medicines, religion, or spiritual practice—we are swimming against a powerful countercurrent that together we regenerate in going about our daily lives.

This is not to imply that if we were, as a civilization, somehow to escape Maya's Palace, everyone would become spiritually enlightened. It would merely open the possibility of establishing a world in which the intensity of ego-identification is diminished, there is less suffering, and higher levels of psychospiritual attainment—and thus deeper satisfactions and greater moral maturity and discernment—would become more widely accessible.

Another consequence of intense ego-identification is chronic insecurity: egoic insatiability creates anxiety that one will never have enough or be enough. This fear can persist even among people whose material needs are reliably being met or whose social status is immense, because the fear is a creature of the rigid ego boundary that separates modern people from their world, establishing an existential emptiness. The resulting anxiety is then compounded by the ego's complementary fear that softening its boundary would mean annihilation. (Hence the addition of the word "Insecurity" in Step 1 of Figure 12, above.)

As evidence, consider this comparison: Anthropologists report that nomadic hunter-gatherers are typically confident that their needs will be met in virtue of their strong bonds with one another and with a natural world that they "perceive . . . and act with . . . as with a friend, a relative, a parent who shares resources with them." In contrast, a 2011 Boston College survey of 165 wealthy American households—families with an average net worth of $78 million—found that "most of them still do not consider themselves financially secure; for that, they say, they would require on average one-quarter more wealth than they currently possess." For perspective, a net worth of US $78 million puts one in the top 1/100 of 1 percent of wealth-holders worldwide.[14]

THE EGO/WORLD SYSTEM

Modern political-economic systems and populations stabilized in ego-identification are perfectly symbiotic. *The ego desperately* _wants_ *exactly what sustaining a capitalist global economy* _requires_: *perpetual and ubiquitous ego-sovereignty.* The ego contributes through its insatiability and capacity for self-deception. The modern techno-economy contributes through the dislocation that stabilizes strong ego-identification, unleashing energies—both psychological and external—subordinate to egoic purposes.

In effect, this means that the entire world has evolved into a gigantic machinery for sustaining ego-sovereignty; I call it the *ego/world system* (Figure 14). Ego-identified, we are optimized to misunderstand and perpetuate this system, not infrequently judging ourselves "happy" although enslaved to unquenchable emptiness, our suffering extensive and our deeper potentials never realized. Yudhishthira's temporary aberration is today's normal because Maya's Palace—a passing waystation for the Pandavas—has ballooned into Maya's Global Empire.

The dashed line snaking through the center of Figure 14 symbolizes the boundary that modern people experience between self and

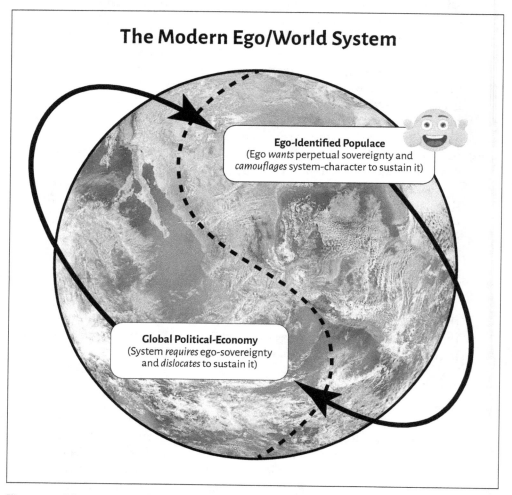

Figure 14. The Modern Ego/World System. The ego (symbolized by the happy emoji) most fervently *wants* what the modern political-economic and technological system *requires*: perpetual and ubiquitous ego-sovereignty. Egoic psychology and global macroforces coevolve to fulfill this joint imperative.

world. Living with chronic dislocation and pervasive dis-integration, it is as though the world is continuously *pushing us away*, joining us in hardening the ego boundary. In contrast, nomadic hunter-gatherers commonly know themselves to be *embraced* by the world—a world in which society, nature, and spirit are not distinct domains; one can imagine that this reassuring embrace softens the ego boundary. (For a cultural example suggesting such softening, see the discussion of the southern African Ju/'hoansi people in Chapter 13, below.)[15]

Chapter 13

MAYA'S GLOBAL EMPIRE

Charting ego-sovereignty through history and across cultures

If our civilization is optimized to sustain ego-sovereignty, to what extent does this distinguish us from other cultures and civilizations? Just as Chapter 10 clarified and refined the conventional formulation of our theory, now we'll do the same for the transpersonal formulation.

HIERARCHY AND INSATIABILITY IN PREMODERN EUROPE

For instance, how does our psychology differ from that of medieval Europeans? Generally, we lack the data and tools for assessing development in ages gone by. Nevertheless, there are some things we can say about premodern European psychology that further illuminate the dynamics of modern psychospiritual development.

Premodern Europe was no psychospiritual utopia; it was class-stratified, frequently oppressive to the masses of serfs and peasants, patriarchal and not uncommonly misogynist, and racked by internal wars. Widespread atrocities were committed in the name of religion during the Crusades and the Inquisition. On the other hand, there is evidence that many European peasants who worked for wages were functionally satiable and not prone to addiction. Thus, whatever their range of developmental attainments, generally such peasants were not arrested in intensive ego-identification.

An exploration of medieval European history does, nonetheless, uncover ample evidence of insatiability, including for sumptuous clothing, battle and glory, wealth, power, territory, and social stature. But this is predominantly among the nobility and the clergy. Pope Innocent III (1161–1216), for instance, seems to have known insatiability with some intimacy: "Desires are like a consuming fire which cannot be extinguished. . . . When man achieves what he desired he wants more and never stops longing for something else."[1]

In her acclaimed history of Western Europe in the fourteenth century, Barbara Tuchman paints a picture of an incessantly violent and greedy noble class. The clergy are often preoccupied with securing wealth and stature: "The [Franciscan] Order acquired lands and riches, built itself churches and cloisters, developed its own hierarchy—all the opposite of the founder's [i.e., St. Francis's] intent. . . . In some monastic orders the monks . . . wore jewels and fur-trimmed gowns, and employed servants who in wealthy convents sometimes outnumbered the members."[2]

Witnessing the opulence and hypocrisy of the papacy relocated from Rome to Avignon in France, the Italian scholar Petrarch wrote of cardinals ensconced in munificent quarters and regally enrobed as "rich, insolent and rapacious."[3]

Why might the nobility and clergy have been more prone to exhibit insatiable cravings than the peasant masses? Were they suffering from sustained dislocation? The *Mahabharata* suggests a different explanation. The Pandava brothers regress morally after partition, but Yudhishthira's character shift is distinctive. His unbounded acquisitiveness doesn't emerge immediately but some years later, coincident with assuming the throne within Maya's Palace of splendor. It's then that he conceives his colossal imperial ambitions which, as they near fulfillment, morph into uncontrollable greed and addiction. The lesser kings who witness Krishna's execution of King Shishupala are all arrogantly egoic, and ancient India recognized that kings were peculiarly prone to addiction—specifically to gambling, hunting, intoxicants, and sex.[4]

The parallel with late-medieval Europe is that in both cases stature in a social hierarchy can prove developmentally corrupting. In theory, the privileges of Europe's landed aristocracy and clergy were legitimated based on their commitment to upholding noble virtues on behalf of their entire society. But hierarchical stature can inflate egos and stabilize ego-sovereignty. Moreover, sometimes those who quest for hierarchical stature are motivated more by its perquisites than by any strong wish to embody its professed ideals. The late-medieval Church became a well-established route to wealth, with high offices available for purchase. This is not to say that there were no late-medieval clergy of genuine piety, humility, and integrity. Some were also mystics who engaged deeply in spiritual practice and attained to high spiritual levels. But these were not the norm.[5]

If we gaze further back in time, the slow, often-resisted shift from egalitarian nomadic forager societies to small and large settlements, chiefdoms, states, and empires—often by meandering, hybridized, or back-and-forth pathways—depended on achieving food surpluses that could support social stratification and hierarchical power. Elites concentrated their power and mobilized slaves, peasants, craftspeople, and armies in order to self-aggrandize. Indigenous experiential spiritualities morphed into patriarchal, priest-based religions that served to legitimate hierarchy. What we know of ancient history is consistent with the idea that hierarchy tends to strengthen and stabilize egoism among elites.[6]

While our knowledge of the inner lives of the lower social orders during Europe's medieval period is meager, one suspects that they may have been developmentally spread out, with most relatively unevolved but some more advanced. That's conceivable, since peasants, wage laborers, and artisans were neither embedded high in corrupting hierarchies nor subject to chronic dislocation. Moreover, there were techniques at large for supporting psychospiritual development. These included Christian spiritual exercises such as devotional prayer; various practices of mystical heretical sects; contemplative craft labor; polytheistic, animistic, and folk practices such as fertility rites and witchcraft; and spiritually oriented scholarly endeavors such as alchemy and astrology.[7]

On the other hand, sometimes the Church was leery of practices that could be psychospiritually effective, monitoring or persecuting practitioners on the de facto theory that the last thing needed was people who could speak from experience to the limitations of religious dogma or criticize clerical hypocrisy. Religious historian Bernard McGinn writes of the accomplished French mystic Marguerite Porete, who was condemned by the Church in 1310, that "Marguerite is the first documented case of an execution for mystical heresy in Western Christianity. Unfortunately, it was not to be the last. Her death was not just an individual tragedy; it also provided critical ammunition for an ongoing struggle between the mystical and the institutional elements of Christianity that has continued almost down to the present day."[8]

It remains a question how comprehensively serfdom, patriarchy, slavery, and class or caste stratification dampened psychospiritual development among those subjugated. Oppression and exploitation are rarely favorable to self-realization. In the case of early modern and industrializing Britain, hierarchical privilege not only inflated elite egos but also empowered the upper classes to disrupt the village-based agrarian economy. Moving forward I will use the term "hierarchy" in reference to any system of inequality that is developmentally harmful to superiors or to inferiors (typically hierarchy is harmful to both).

But we can also say that compared with modern mass psychology, by and large premodern lower social orders in Europe do not appear to have exhibited insatiable acquisitiveness, insatiability-driven industriousness, or extensive propensity to addiction. On that basis, it is reasonable to surmise that they were less strongly ego-identified.

MODERN IMPLICATIONS

Insofar as stature in a social hierarchy can be another route to becoming trapped in Maya's Palace, this can augment our understanding of our modern psychosocial plight. Chronic dislocation and dis-integration driven by the device paradigm are two basic processes responsible for stabilizing most people in ego-sovereignty and insatiability. But capitalist political economies often sustain economic inequality and abound in hierarchical institutional forms, including in government, business, the military, and academe. Thus, many leaders may be further impaired as a result of working at the upper echelons of organizational pyramids and enjoying the fruits of socioeconomic privilege. For instance, there is evidence that Americans are generally becoming more narcissistic, but disproportionately so among people who are successful in business or wealthy. Studies have found that wealthy people are more likely than others to judge greed favorably, while less likely to uphold egalitarian values or to exhibit compassion and other prosocial behaviors. People in positions of power tend also to become more impulsive and selfish and less able to see the world from another's perspective.[9]

This complicates our overall situation, because it increases the likelihood that those with the most power to alter basic social arrangements have the most cause to be arrested in ego-sovereignty and the most incentive to perpetuate the hierarchies and dynamics that hinder all of us in our psychospiritual development.

The psychological influence of hierarchy may also help explain a phenomenon that I've often found perplexing: leaders who in their personal and civic lives can be morally commendable—loving family members, caring friends, civic-minded, and philanthropic—yet who are prepared at work to sacrifice higher moral considerations in pursuit of institutional or career objectives. In such cases there is an apparent lack of integration or stability in psychospiritual attainment—a lapse in moral autonomy—that results in many people acting *less* morally evolved at precisely the times when they have the *most* nominal power to make a constructive difference in the world. We saw a version of this in the *Mahabharata*: the Pandavas falter in moral development and integration just as Yudhishthira is poised to achieve recognition as the King of Kings.[10]

In this context "integration" indicates that various aspects of a person's psyche have grown functionally complementary, operating as a harmonious whole. Failure to accomplish this represents "incomplete integration." Integration or other developmental attainments can also be "unstable," lapsing under certain circumstances.

Psychological studies confirm anecdotal observations. Modern leaders who are tested for their responses to hypothetical moral dilemmas sometimes default, when confronted with real-world moral dilemmas at work, to lower levels of moral reasoning and behavior. Leaders often self-select and are trained and incentivized to behave this way, rising through established hierarchies only after demonstrating loyalty to institutional norms and objectives, even when that means compromising wider societal concerns and their own extra-workplace moral convictions. In one study, Fortune 500 executives admitted "overwhelmingly" to such behavior.[11]

Future US senator Elizabeth Warren relates that in 2009 Larry Summers, the director of the National Economic Council and former president of Harvard, advised her that "I could be an [Obama administration] insider or I could be an outsider. . . . Insiders . . . get lots of access and a chance to push their ideas. . . . But insiders also understand one unbreakable rule: *They don't criticize other insiders.*"[12]

There is no empirical basis for comparing modern moral development with that in times gone by. There is not even a consensus among psychologists about how to conceptualize or measure moral development. But if we judge by the ideal trajectory of moral development portrayed in the *Mahabharata*, a few observations are possible.[13]

In terms of morality, there are several ways in which modern people resemble the Pandavas while they are ensnared in Maya's Palace (*Mahabharata* Book/Stage 2). Recall that after their exile from the Palace, the Pandavas are decisively dis-identified from the ego-function. Thereafter their morality develops without further episodes of regression—i.e., they advance in comprehending their moral duties—and their actions are consistent with their moral judgments.*

In contrast, today there is typically no sharp break from ego-identification. Even as we mature, our moral sentiments must contend with a countervailing impulse to advance our narrow self-interests. This is especially so when our cravings are intense, or we are subject to egoic insecurities. Animated cartoons model this inner conflict when they show Spider-Man or Mickey Mouse torn between the counsel of an angel whispering into one ear and a devil inveigling into the other. As Kant put it, "Man feels in himself a powerful counterpoise against all commands of duty . . . this counterpoise is his needs and inclinations."[14]

---

* The Pandavas' deviations from conventional warrior ethics during the Kurukshetra War do not, in my view, refute the claims in this paragraph; see Chapter 18, below.

Aside from our persistent ego-identification—and in part because of it—our actions are not always consonant with our moral judgments, and our moral views and behavior can fluctuate contextually. We've already noted that there is tendency for morality to downshift within hierarchical organizations. This also occurs in the marketplace, with problematic social consequences. One of modernity's distinctive characteristics is that we move back and forth between a variety of social settings, often adopting different personas within each. However, with the commodification of more and more domains of experience, including the commercialization of cyberspace, our economic selves (concerned primarily with "getting the best deal for me") are evoked much more often than our morally more-evolved whole selves.[15]

Yet in at least one important respect most modern people grow beyond Yudhishthira at his worst, while suffering from his gambling addiction: many adults consider the interests of others—at least of some others and some of the time—and act altruistically, at least on occasion. That does not make us moral titans, but even slight consideration of others is beyond Yudhishthira's debased morality during the dice match. The most morally evolved among us not only do great good in the world, but also become influential exemplars for others. All this is hopeful, because it means that there are reserves of moral character and commitment upon which societies can draw for constructive transformation. And there is every reason to expect that under more favorable development circumstances, morality would advance.[16]

Moreover, contextual variation in moral propensity cuts two ways. Viewed pessimistically, it can mean that people default to lower levels of morality in certain important social contexts, such as their workplaces and in the marketplace. But under the right circumstances, they may also perform at higher-than-expected capacity. Robert Coles describes numerous times during the 1960s American Civil Rights Movement that he encountered Black or white children, growing up in stressful and culturally limited circumstances, who nonetheless responded to dire moral dilemmas with compassion and wisdom. Out in the street or confronting racial segregation in their schools, time and again "they acquitted themselves impressively in pursuit of significant ethical objectives." Perhaps Coles was observing youngsters provoked toward ethical maturity through immersion in a field of contending social perspectives that also included encounters with people of high moral character. Thus, contextual variability is a social liability we must reckon with, but also a resource that we may be able to harness in plotting Palatial escape routes.[17]

Furthermore, social context is not destiny. There are people who assume high leadership roles without compromising their moral compass.

EGOIC CULTURAL CONCURRENCES
IN EARLY MODERN EUROPE

As Chapter 10 noted, the developmental transition into insatiability in the early modern period often went hand in hand with relaxing cultural norms that had previously curbed consumption. In contrast, Émile Durkheim presumed that modern market economies rupture cultures of restraint, unleashing insatiability without altering psychological development. However, a variety of perceptual, reasoning, behavioral, and value shifts occurred during the early modern period that are—like mass insatiability, addiction, and masking—consistent with a turn toward more intensive ego-identification. The mere dissolution of traditional norms cannot explain these shifts.

For instance, English political thinkers such as Thomas Hobbes (1588–1679) and John Locke (1632–1704) reconceived society as the outgrowth of a contractual agreement among "atomized" individuals—people who have no innate social bonds and who are motivated solely by self-interest. It seems plausible that this influential, radical act of reimagination—which most non-modern people would find both incomprehensible and abhorrent—may have reflected the modern turn toward stronger egoic self-bounding.[18]

For many Europeans, the seventeenth and eighteenth centuries were when God withdrew from active involvement in the world. As in the case of Krishna's absence during Yudhishthira's dice match, egoic self-bounding can make people feel isolated, cut off—including from divinity.[19]

Meanwhile, Europeans in many walks and stations of life became more concerned with privacy—less often bathing communally, beginning to acquire their own eating utensils and beds and, when they could afford it, building houses with more differentiated internal spaces, including distinct sleeping chambers. A new preoccupation with privacy could both mirror and reinforce the feeling of separateness that derives from strong ego boundaries.[20]

Historians associate the early modern era with the ascendance of a scientific perspective in which the observer stands apart from the object under investigation—in effect, adopting a view *of* the world rather than *from within* the world. This, again, appears consistent with sharpening the egoic boundary between self and other. At the same time, an organismic cosmos was reconceived as a machine (the "clockwork universe") that could be analyzed in terms of subsidiary material components—a fragmented and reductionist perspective that contrasts with the holism evident, for example, in traditional Chinese thought, among many indigenous cultures, or in the reasoning of Alexander Luria's peasant test subjects.[21]

God's withdrawal from a now-mechanistic universe contributed, in turn, to justifying Christian persecution of those still immersed in a world suffused with mystery and spirit: witches, heretical mystics, indigenous peoples, and so on. Marginalizing or murdering those whose spiritual orientations suggest that they may have been less intensely ego-identified could have become a contributing factor in fortifying the societal hegemony of ego-sovereignty.[22]

Beginning in the eighteenth century, European philosophers came to insist on a sharp analytic distinction between facts and values. This dichotomization gradually found expression in a broad societal division of labor, often with credentialed experts responsible for ascertaining "facts" while democratic deliberation or individuals' subjective preferences are assigned responsibility for rendering value judgments.[23]

The fact/value distinction could derive in part from modern egoism's sharp subject/object divide. Everything outside of the ego's self-defining boundary consists of "objects"—the vast realm of "not-me"—that become the domain of inquiry for scientific methods. On the interior of the ego boundary, one finds a "subject"—relatively opaque to objective outside scrutiny—that can declare and clarify its preferences or participate in determining social values. Functionally, the resulting social division of labor hinders the integrative knowing-and-doing that is consonant with post-egoism.

That ramped-up egoism *might* have contributed to all the preceding cultural shifts doesn't prove that it did. On the other hand, as in the case of masking, it doesn't seem particularly plausible that such a disparate range of phenomena—each one consistent with mass ego-sovereignty—occurred concurrently only by coincidence, and together with the eruption of mass addiction and consumer insatiability. Our theory provides an economical way to account for the concurrence of many phenomena, even explaining why it has proven difficult to formulate such a theory.

That said, psychological development is never the sole factor influencing belief and behavior. For instance, although intensive ego-identification fuels consumerism all across the earth, this has not erased cultural differences.[24]

PERCHANCE TO DREAM

Might the historical transition to intensive ego-identification have involved brain change? There is some pertinent indirect evidence. Psychiatrist Iain McGilchrist infers from changes in art, literature, and urban landscapes that industrialization was associated with a shift toward increasing functional dominance of the analytic left-brain hemisphere over the more intuitive, holistic, and empathic right hemisphere. This is consistent with the contrast between the holistic mental landscape found among various non-modern cultures and the analytic reductionism exhibited, for instance, by mainstream economists when they evaluate externalities.[25]

Researchers have also determined that premodern Europeans exhibited markedly different sleep patterns than their modern successors. Generally, they went to bed not long after sunset, but then they awoke for several hours in the middle of the night before falling back asleep. While awake during the tranquil wee hours, they might lie in bed in a state of meditative contemplation, converse quietly, make love, pray, or get up and work in the dark or by candle or firelight.

Among people exhibiting this sleep pattern, the intervening awake time is often notably peaceful. One modern scientist describes it as a mildly altered state of consciousness with brain-wave patterns resembling those of meditators. This may be related to altered hormonal secretions, including elevated prolactin levels—the same chemical that stimulates nursing mothers' lactation.[26]

The transition to slumbering steadily through the night occurred during the early modern period, initially in urban upper classes that had the first access to new artificial light sources, such as whale-oil and coal-gas lamps—and who not incidentally drank the most drowsiness-dispelling tea and coffee—then spreading into the lower classes and the countryside. Historian A. Roger Ekirch proposes that premodern humans had more undisturbed time during the middle of the night to ponder their dreams from the preceding first sleep interval, and thus they were more intimately familiar with their unconscious minds and inner world. Minimally dependent on artificial lighting, their bodies functioned more in tune with natural cycles of daylight and darkness. Spending more awake time in the dark, they relied more than we do on their nonvisual senses of sound, smell, and touch; this included navigating outdoors based on the rhythms of the moon and stellar constellations, indicating a more sensuous and knowing relationship with the natural world. These forebears were also more liable to experience a night world filled with spirits, mystery, and magic—an outer counterpart to their greater familiarity with the inner world of dreams, feelings, and quiet rumination.[27]

One might even speculate that Freud and other psychologists discovered the unconscious when they did—rather than some other genius pulling it off centuries earlier—because it had only recently come into existence as a domain so sharply cut off from waking awareness, inferable only indirectly (e.g., from nighttime dreams). In earlier times, what we now know as the "unconscious" certainly existed; evidence of some of its content has been passed down to us in myths, such as the *Mahabharata.* But perhaps it was experienced as a more accessible "semi-unconscious" with which people were routinely acquainted (the "Forest"). Joseph Campbell reached a similar conclusion based on his studies of the social function of myths, writing in 1949 that in his day, "The lines of communication between the conscious and unconscious zone of the human psyche have all been cut."[28]

That is speculative, but the more assured insight is that there is indirect evidence that alterations in brain functioning occurred during the transition into the modern era. How this might relate to other changes in psychological development, including intensified ego-identification, remains to be determined. Perhaps, for instance, the psychological repercussions of artificial lighting—a less intimate relationship with nighttime nature and the world of spirit—amount to another component of ego-intensifying dislocation.

STABILIZING INSATIABILITY: THE US EXAMPLE

Once mass insatiability is established in a society, why is there never reversion to functional satiability? The basic story is simple: techno-economic dislocation fuels egoic or deprivation-driven craving, leading to behavior that feeds back to extend dislocation. But the specifics are complex and variable.

Let's consider US history as an example. In the nineteenth century, workers began to agitate for a shorter workweek. In many cases their aim was simply to have time off from a regimented and punishing work routine. But some workers aspired to engage in cultivating their minds, artistic expression, and other uplifting activities. In the words of a famous labor-union protest song penned in 1911:

> No more the drudge and idler,
> Ten that toil where one reposes,
> But the sharing of life's glories:
> Bread and roses! Bread and roses!

Does this indicate a drift back toward a preference for leisure over consumption (i.e., toward functional satiability)?[29]

The question is more complicated than it appears. With the advent of industrial work regimes, US workdays lengthened and became increasingly intensive. The concept of nonaristocratic "leisure" emerged as an antithesis.

Modern leisure differs from premodern leisureliness in many ways. Time off from work is typically no longer experienced as unhurriedly expansive but as a scarce commodity. As far back as 1748, Benjamin Franklin advised that "time is money"—a maxim that would have been unintelligible in a premodern culture. A second difference is that leisure becomes a time apart, sharply distinct from a workday that often affords little opportunity for leisurely paced effort. A third is that time not occupied with work is often underlain by a disposition toward restlessness and boredom. There is a need to be occupied doing or thinking something, arguably indicative of the discontented emptiness intrinsic to tight ego-identification. In contrast, among non-dislocated people in the developing or indigenous worlds one finds that when a task is completed, there is more often a capacity to abide in calm not-doing or else to engage in activities that are unhurried and reflect no urgency to escape an idleness that would be disagreeable.[30]

Thus, in seeking a shorter workweek, some US workers may have been expressing a soul-yearning for self-realization. But others were, in effect, choosing to make space within their consumption baskets for a newly minted scarce commodity—leisure. Moreover, often their objective was time off combined with higher wages. That way they could indulge in consumption along with other noneconomic activities. This is different from peasant-style contentment with subsistence.

Many American employers resisted these new preferences until it became evident that leisure was distinctive among scarce commodities in affording workers the opportunity to function *as consumers* of goods and services.[31]

With the advent of mass production, a new anxiety emerged among businessmen that economic output could race ahead of consumer demand. Might consumers, after all, prove satiable? The new practice of scientifically informed advertising arose in the 1920s and '30s to address this worry.[32]

However, once one considers the coevolution of psychospiritual development with economic and technological forces, it appears that a modern market society's capacity to sustain insatiability was greater than anyone understood. For instance, this was the same period when new background infrastructures—paved highways, gas mains, municipal water and sewage systems, and electrification—were enabling a great expansion in the dislocating device paradigm. The paradigm unfolded in the lives of the affluent first, and the Great Depression put a damper on the pace at which it diffused, but gradually households were flooded with new mass-produced gadgets and appliances, ranging from gas cookstoves and bathtubs with hot running water to automobiles, electric irons, vacuum cleaners, refrigerators, washing machines, telephones, radios, and much besides.[33]

From roughly the 1920s forward, just when businesses were turning to modern advertising to stimulate consumer demand, the device paradigm was contributing covertly to the same result by boosting dislocation and egoic emptiness. This happens in multiple ways: the *social process* of mass producing and distributing devices boosts market-driven dislocation, while their subsequent *use* amplifies dislocation via the device paradigm's powers of dis-integration.

With time, television and internet-connected personal computers have taken turns advancing the frontiers of dislocation. Robert Putnam, in *Bowling Alone*, fingers the time invested in watching television as a significant culprit in explaining the declining cohesiveness and vibrancy of US civil society. These electronic contrivances have also become vehicles for disseminating advertising. Magic indeed! People pay to acquire devices—which, as always, are intrinsically dislocating—that also function as media that businesses co-opt to stimulate further buying . . . which also compounds economic dynamism and thus dislocation. Thus, dislocation-induced and advertising-induced insatiability became seamlessly integrated.[34]

More recently, mobile telecommunication has elevated this integration to a formerly unimaginable level. Now we pay for devices that amplify our dislocation, monitor and communicate our behavior to firms such as Google and Facebook, allow businesses to niche-advertise based on our device-revealed personal interests, and then "empower" us to make impulse purchases from these very same devices from any location at any time, stimulating still more dislocation. Had science-fiction writers of yore dared fantasize such a thing, they would have been dismissed as paranoid conspiracy theorists.[35]

The device paradigm also joins hands with the market in dismantling familial and local cooperative interdependence, forcing people to purchase still more devices to meet their basic needs (a positive feedback loop). For instance, 1950s glossy magazine ads notwithstanding, suburban moms did not covet shiny new washing machines simply so that they could one-up their neighbors; they also *needed* new labor-saving devices so that they could do alone what was accomplished formerly via a cooperative household division of labor. Likewise, today people may gravitate toward online communities by default because television and the internet have piled on top of earlier devices to eviscerate access to richly satisfying face-to-face social worlds. Consumerism can thus express material and social needs as well as ego-based emotional deficits—all of which are often intertwined and, in any case, appreciably artifacts of dislocation.

If the United States is any indication, the modern system of market-friendly governments, competitive markets, and accompanying technologies is impressively capable of innovating to perpetuate itself, including by generating macrosocial conditions that suffice to sustain strong ego-identification. There is no need to postulate an overarching demonic intelligence to explain this outcome. System perpetuation is achieved quite unknowingly by ego-identified people responding to market opportunities and constraints: Seeking to gratify our insistent cravings, we stabilize ego-sovereignty through market-driven dislocation. Seeking convenience and efficiency (as defined under the device paradigm), we evolve infrastructures and devices that hinder psycho-spiritual self-realization via dis-integration.

According to the late social theorist Michel Foucault, capitalism depends on an intricate network of ideas and internalized behaviors through which people are transformed into compliant citizens and industrious workers. In the variation that we have been working out, capitalism reengineers *psychospiritual development* to produce compliant, industrious, *endemically insecure, and insatiable* masses of human beings.[36]

In 1930, at the beginning of the Great Depression, British economist John Maynard Keynes looked beyond the prevailing societal pessimism to predict that within a hundred years the "economic problem" would be solved. Output would suffice to meet all basic needs, and the social challenge moving forward would be to learn to how to make constructive use of our time outside of work. Keynes's expectations have not been fulfilled. Economic growth has actually exceeded his hopes, but economic striving has not diminished correspondingly. There may be multiple explanations for this—including, assuredly, inequality in how the fruits of economic growth are distributed. But there is an overlooked factor: Keynes did not consider the possibility that techno-economic dynamism contributes to instilling unappeasable craving—an interdependence that can account for the seeming paradox that today it is common to experience more discontent, insecurity, and scarcity than do many tribal groups that have subsisted on vastly less material wealth.[37]

IS INTENSE EGOISM A NECESSARY PRECURSOR OR A HINDRANCE TO EGO-TRANSCENDENCE?

The life stories of saints such as Teresa of Avila and Sri Ramakrishna Paramahamsa suggest that it's not necessary to experience intense ego-identification to pass into the post-egoic developmental range. If so, is intense egoism primarily a *hindrance* to ego-transcendence? That is what we might expect, in part because stronger ego-identification translates into amplified fear of—and hence resistance to—ego-transcendence.[38]

Consider the ethnography of a tribal people such as the southern African Ju/'hoansi (pronounced "zhun-twasi"). Sometimes known as bushmen or !Kung (the exclamation point represents a tongue-clicking sound), these are the people caricatured in *The Gods Must Be Crazy* movies of the 1980s. We'll look at them as they were known to anthropologists in the 1960s.

A core Ju/'hoan ("zhun-twa") practice was a ritual called a *!kia*-healing dance, which took place once or twice a week from dusk to dawn. A tribe's women formed a clapping-and-song circle around a campfire; the men—and sometimes a woman or two—danced around the outside of the circle. The *!kia* dance released an internal energy called *n/um* that rose up a singing or dancing *n/um* master's spine. The *!kia* state involved a strong experience of transcendence. About one-half of adult men and one-third of adult women were able to go into the *!kia* state. Those who didn't contributed by creating the social context in which *!kia* healing could occur.

Anthropologist Richard Katz explains that the *!kia* dance performed many simultaneous functions: "It is the !Kung's [Ju/'hoansi's] primary expression of a religious existence and a cosmological perspective. It provides healing and protection, being a magicomedical mode of coping with illnesses and misfortune. The *!kia* at the dance also increases social cohesion and solidarity. It allows for individual and communal release of hostility. Finally, the dance alters the consciousness of many members of this community."[39]

Children watching the dance absorbed knowledge of how to *!kia*. Thus, the dance was also an education in transcendence. Some *!kia* dancers encountered God; others communicated directly with the ghosts of tribal ancestors. Hence the dance integrated the tribe with the spirit world. Any tribe member was welcome to undertake the arduous effort to become a *n/um* master. But *n/um* was never used primarily for personal benefit. *N/um* masters were healers, offering services to other people and to the tribe as a whole. In that sense the dance also taught non-selfishness and compassion.

It isn't obvious that any of the Ju/'hoansi passed through a period of insatiability or insecurity that would indicate strong ego-identification. Yet many Ju/'hoan adults learned to experience transcendence on a regular basis, converse with gods or deceased ancestors, and use their mastery of *n/um* energy exclusively for altruistic purposes. Also, the Ju/'hoansi experienced entering the *!kia* state as a kind of death, the pain and terror of which they had to surmount to become *n/um* masters. Across cultures, ego-transcendence commonly involves confronting the fear of death. All of this might indicate a degree of post-egoism without having ever been strongly egoic.

How is that possible? Traditionally the Ju/'hoansi benefited from circumstances that our theory predicts would be developmentally advantageous. They shared strong spiritual beliefs and integrative practices, and their society was neither hierarchically stratified nor overwhelmed by dislocation. (At least, not until the 1980s, when intensifying dislocation resulted in alcohol abuse becoming a problem.)[40]

Compared with modern people, indigenous groups that are egalitarian and non-dislocated are apt to be less intensely ego-identified and on that score less discontent and insecure. But they may also have easier entrée to the post-egoic developmental range. This improved accessibility could reflect favorable psychology (e.g., with softer ego-identification, greater ability to tolerate the fear that ego-transcendence excites), culture (e.g., open access to practices—such as the *!kia* dance—that support ego-transcendence, coupled with minimal mobilization of collective self-deception to protect ego-sovereignty), and political-economic circumstances (e.g., not being enmeshed in a global system optimized in every way to instill and sustain ego-sovereignty).[41]

But rather than episodically accessing the post-egoic range, are the members of such a society merely mired in childlike fantasy? One might think so if the evident purpose of the *!kia* dance were to alleviate fear of uncontrollable forces through ineffectual magical incantations (a strategy not unknown in modern electoral politics). But the Ju/'hoansi's socially guided mobilization of *n/um* energy produced a range of beneficial outcomes, more resembling confident enactment of interdependence and agency than powerlessness.

It is also common to suppose that tribal peoples are poorly individuated—so closely identified with the collective that there is no opportunity for individual self-realization. But this isn't necessarily true. The Ju/'hoansi were noteworthy for honoring individual differences and creativity. Dorothy Lee's ethnographic observations of a variety of tribal groups found that they afforded high opportunity for children to develop personal autonomy, self-respect, and individuality.[42]

Tribal societies also vary in the extent to which their altruism is limited to members of their own social world. We normally consider a society's morality less evolved when it is parochial in this way. On the other hand, one factor that may historically have limited parochialism among tribal groups is that many were involved in exchanges with other cultures and thus might conceivably have developed capacities in cross-cultural perspective-taking. Regarding the experiences of English colonists who were adopted into American Indian tribes (Chapter 10, above), historian James Axtell reports that many "soon discovered that the English had no monopoly on virtue and that in many ways the Indians were morally superior to the English, more Christian than the Christians."[43]

Skeptics may dismiss these reflections as "romanticizing the primitive." But the evidence we've reviewed derives not from wishful thinking but from studies by social scientists who are expert in these cultures.

INTENSIFYING EGOISM AS A
GLOBAL PHENOMENON

The dislocation, insatiability, and addiction that signal the emergence of intensive egoism in early modern Europe were aspects of a longer-term process in which widening swaths of the earth were becoming knit together into a global market economy.

Consider China. By the seventeenth century, China's traditional local subsistence agriculture coexisted with networks of regional and national markets for grain, textiles, books, and artisanal goods. China also functioned as an important node in intra-Asian and world commerce. Historian Kenneth Pomeranz has advanced the provocative thesis that significant areas of eighteenth-century China were sufficiently industrious, scientifically and technically capable, commercialized, and institutionally evolved to have matched Western Europe in economic growth had they not confronted natural-resource constraints that proved insuperable.[44]

Pomeranz's argument remains controversial. But productive capabilities aside, were the Chinese equally *motivated* toward expanding their consumption—that is, were they comparably insatiable? For instance, during this century, the Chinese produced sugar and tea, but they consumed less per person than the English, even though for the English these were much more expensive long-distance imports. This, along with their prodigious alcohol consumption, could indicate a greater susceptibility to addiction in the English.[45]

Moreover, China was far less urbanized and more socially stable than Britain, which in comparison was citifying at a blazing pace. Chinese peasants retained their land tenure; there was nothing analogous to the British land enclosures and nationwide destruction of village economies stretching out over more than a century. Also, Chinese officials' fear of dislocation and unrest provoked periodic measures to restrict trade with other nations. Overall, then, in China there would have been less dislocation-driven stimulation toward insatiable craving and addiction.[46]

On the other hand, the Chinese took to growing and consuming tobacco with great gusto soon after Europeans introduced it from the Americas in the late 1500s. One historian hazards a rough guess that by the eighteenth century there may have been enough tobacco under cultivation that many Chinese across all social strata would have been able to smoke a daily "pipeful or two." That would be within the ballpark of tobacco use in northwest Europe at the time.

Chinese physicians who wrote of tobacco believed that it could be beneficial to health under some circumstances, but they understood that long-term smoking could lead to disease, including lung disease and death. Referring to it as the "herb of longing," they also knew that smokers' cravings were often nagging and persistent. Moreover, periodic attempts to ban smoking failed. These are indications of addiction.[47]

Seventeenth- and eighteenth-century northwestern Europe developed a distinctive taste for novel goods and changing fashions in clothing, and anecdotes reveal that there were parallel propensities in China's most economically dynamic areas, although their extent is not well documented. For instance, one Chinese scholar remarked in the 1570s on a striking new passion for innovation in clothing: "Young dandies in the villages say that even silk gauze isn't good enough and lust for Suzhou embroideries. . . . Long skirts and wide collars, broad belts and narrow pleats—they change without warning." But unlike in Europe, no moral argument emanated out from the Chinese intelligentsia in favor of a consumer economy. Instead, consumerism and novelty were countered by an elite preference for cultural refinement and antique treasures, which were fixed in supply and thus not a force pulling toward higher economic output and further dislocation. Historians judge the passion for novelty across the classes a defining attribute of the eighteenth-century English turn toward insatiable consumption.[48]

In the ensuing century, a compounding factor contributed to Britain's relative economic vigor and to addictive craving among the Chinese: opium. From the 1600s forward, Britons adapted to dislocation and insatiability by consuming drug foods that enhanced their productivity—addictive stimulants like coffee, tea, and sugar. But in the nineteenth century Britain developed a problem: the British were addicted to Chinese tea, but the Chinese displayed little interest in anything that Britain offered to trade in return.

As their treasury drained away, the British settled on the ingenious idea to offset the cost of tea with Chinese purchases of opium cultivated in British-ruled India. The Chinese were now more deeply susceptible to addiction as a result of experiencing dislocation in multiple forms, including the conjunction of flood, famine, the most destructive civil war in world history (the Taiping Rebellion of 1851 to 1864, in which an estimated twenty to thirty million Chinese died), and the British imposition of opium imports and "free trade" via two Opium Wars (1839–1842 and 1856–1860). During British parliamentary debate leading into the first Opium War, the thirty-year-old future prime minister William Gladstone—whose younger sister Helen was addicted to medically prescribed opium—railed that "a war more unjust in its origin, a war calculated in its progress to cover this country with a permanent disgrace, I do not know."

By 1859, per capita opium imports flowing into China were nearly ten times higher than those entering Britain. Twenty years later Chinese per capita opium use had more than tripled; a quarter century later it had more than doubled again. Opium was previously used in

China in moderation and unproblematically, mostly as a medicine. In contrast, by the end of the nineteenth century somewhere between 3 and 10 percent of China's population had succumbed to addiction. But opium use was not evenly distributed; over 25 percent of adult males had become addicted.

The prevalence of opium addiction was especially high among Chinese men in what would have been their most productive years, sapping their energy, shortening their lives, and siphoning away most of their income. This compounded dislocation, but it also debilitated the Chinese emperor's army, corrupted the Chinese bureaucracy, and addled the mind of the young Xianfeng Emperor (reigned 1850–1861). Thus, whereas drug-food consumption stimulated British productivity, opium that the British imported into China illegally and later by force had the opposite effect.[49]

Chinese history suggests that the early modern forces generating intensive egoism were not restricted to Europe. As China, America, and other societies became integrated into the emerging global economy, addiction and consumer insatiability followed (although the extent of the latter—e.g., in China—is not always clear). But the process wasn't uniform. Britain's integration into the world economy leaped ahead of the pack, positioning the nation to become a dominant political-economic and military actor in shaping eighteenth- and nineteenth-century globalization. Along the way, British, Dutch, and other European nations' projects of overseas colonization shifted many domestic economies across Asia and Africa into reverse gear, sometimes deepening prior oppression, sometimes creating immiseration where it had not previously existed.[50]

Did Britain rise to global preeminence partly because of newly intensified cravings for wealth and consumption? That is possible. For instance, in the eighteenth century the British government took steps to encourage productivity-enhancing private-sector innovation, including the imposition of tariffs and bans on many types of imported fabrics. This established a protected domestic market for British-manufactured textiles, encouraging invention and entrepreneurialism by increasing their expected financial return. However, these policies could only work because of the insatiability of British consumers and capitalist innovators. Restricting imports into a market that exhibited limited consumer demand—that is, no dislocation-driven insatiability—would have provided none of the necessary stimulus to innovate. Inexhaustible British yearning for fashionable clothing at affordable prices drove British organizational and technological innovation among profit-oriented industrialists.[51]

The problem with this argument is that data on consumption—and hence the evidence for intensive ego-identification—is much better developed for Europe than Asia. Thus, while there are some supporting indications, it is hard to be confident in the judgment that during this time the British desire for consumer goods and drug foods was more extensive and intense than that in China.

A more assured conclusion is that capitalism would not have expanded as rapidly all across the globe had it not surreptitiously contributed to altering trajectories of psychospiritual development, thereby stimulating mass cravings for the wares newly on offer.

EGO-SOVEREIGNTY IN EARLIER CIVILIZATIONS?

There were many civilizations that engaged in long-distance trade prior to the sixteenth century. Some exhibited an enthusiasm for consumption that extended beyond the elite, as well as popular involvement—often in therapeutic or ritual religious contexts—with a variety of mind-altering substances, such as hallucinogens, opium, cannabis, and alcohol.[52]

For instance, beginning in the third century BC, it seems that many Roman women and men drank ample quantities of wine—or perhaps most did (the data is sparse). One scholar guesses that average daily wine consumption by adult males in the Roman Empire was "probably noticeably greater than half a litre, but it is uncertain how much greater." A half-liter of wine would be two and a half modern glasses of wine; in comparison, today on average French adults drink one and a half glasses per day. However, the Romans diluted their wine with water, the amounts they drank are disputed, and, while there was some habitual drunkenness, its extent is unknown.[53]

Still, why did the Romans drink so much? Ancient Rome traded heavily across its vast empire and beyond, had a well-monetized economy with sophisticated financial arrangements, was urbanized for its day, and even mass-produced some household goods, such as metal lamps, serving dishes, and utensils. Then again, Roman wealth was unevenly distributed: a small, elite group lived sumptuously, the bulk of the population was poor, and the number of those in between is unknown. So, did the Romans' social and economic arrangements—coupled with imperial conquest and rule—engender chronic dislocation and intense egoism? Or was non-elite consumption in the Roman world—whatever its extent—excited by cultural factors alone, with no underlying alteration in psychospiritual development? That would represent an inversion of Durkheim's supposition that the cultures of non-dislocated people invariably operated to repress their impulse to want more.[54]

This raises a more general issue. We've noted that shifts in trajectories of psychological development invariably go hand in hand with cultural changes. But the converse need not be true; doubtless there are countless cases in which as a culture evolves—perhaps adopting a new clothing style or modifying religious rituals—trajectories of psychospiritual development remain stable. Furthermore, it would not be surprising if occasionally a new cultural trait accidentally *mimics* a trait that could, under other circumstances, arise because of altered psychological development. Hence the possibility that Roman wine consumption might have represented a cultural innovation that had nothing to do with intensified egoic craving.[55]

This poses an explanatory challenge: When we observe cultural traits that *might* reflect intense egoism, how can we know if they are that *in fact*? One answer is that psychological development involves all aspects of people's mental life, including how they perceive, reason, feel, and behave. This means that when there is a society-wide shift in trajectories of psychological development, we would expect it to be expressed in many ways, not just one or two. As a result, one measure of whether a shift toward greater ego-sovereignty has occurred would be the *concurrence* of many phenomena that are *each* consonant with intense egoism (just as we've argued in the case of masking).

A follow-on challenge is that the further back we look in history, the more the evidence available to us tends to become patchy. For instance, in early modern Britain we've found a concurrence of steady dislocation, elite and middle-class consumerism, robust consumption of a wide range of drug foods among people of all classes, indications of extensive addiction, masking of what was psychospiritually afoot, and various cultural shifts—such as a greater concern with privacy—that are consistent with ego-sovereignty. In contrast, in the case of ancient societies it is typically difficult to ascertain whether there might have been comparable concurrences.

This challenge arises, for instance, with respect to ancient Athens, along the Silk Roads that traversed from Asia to the Mediterranean Sea, and in cultures of conquest and plunder, such as the Vikings and Mongols in Eurasia and the Spanish conquistadors in the Americas. All these cultures involved acquisitiveness (an outward behavior), which might indicate insatiability (an inner psychological disposition that can reflect strong egoism). But there is much about complex premodern civilizations that we don't know, especially concerning their non-elite members.[56]

That said, if there were cases in which masses of people consumed exuberantly (that is, more than just on festive occasions), throughout history it was common for the bulk of populations to live within relatively self-reliant, local subsistence economies. For instance, the fabled Chinese Silk Roads were often no more than dirt tracks and footpaths. The volume of goods carried overland across large distances was small, and the region's villagers lived mostly off the land with minimal access to exotic imported wares. There was some long-distance transport of tea—including tea carried by horse from China into Tibet—but drug foods do not figure prominently in Silk Road trade records compared with goods such as silk, furs, spices, and gemstones.[57]

At stake in addressing such matters is whether the transition into intense ego-identification on a mass basis is uniquely a phenomenon of the modern era. Or were there times further back in history when something similar occurred, subsequently reversing when the stimulating social conditions subsided? If so, was dislocation a driving force in this dynamic, and what does that teach us about the types of dislocation that suffice to drive a shift toward mass ego-sovereignty as well as the possibilities for reversing that shift? Answers to such questions could helpfully inform our understanding of our own situation, including the prospects for social-structural change that supports psychospiritual growth.[58]

Still, we already know that premodern long-distance trade was never as extensive or fast-paced as trade in today's global economy; there was no constantly churning and swiftly shape-shifting intercontinental division of labor; and the variety of goods available did not continuously turn over and expand to anywhere near the extent that it does today. Thus, our task remains to elucidate the modern evolutionary interdependence of macrosocial forces and trajectories of psychospiritual development—a dynamic that shapes the flux of our life experiences, the kind of people we can become, and our possibilities for evolving a world more conducive to human well-being and fulfillment.

This is particularly a concern for our era, because only the modern period has unleashed mass insatiability and widespread addiction, together with deep dislocation—unremitting "creative destruction" in the words of Schumpeter, "uninterrupted disturbance of all social conditions" to Marx and Engels—on a sustained global basis.

Chapter 14

PERILS OF PLANET EGO

Egoism and the human prospect

Besides the infirmities and stresses that people suffer individually because of intense ego-identification, there are adverse *collective* consequences. For instance, mental and physical afflictions that derive from dislocation and ego-arrest combine into follow-on social costs. Among these are:

- The family stress, dysfunction, trauma, or abuse that can result from one member's addiction or other mental disorders
- Further family distress resulting from ensuing physical illnesses
- Developmental harm to children from this familial dysfunction and distress
- Impaired learning at school that can be attributed to stress at home
- Treatment and counseling costs
- Elevated health-insurance costs
- Government taxation and expenditures to improve public health
- Family economic misfortune
- Diminished workplace creativity and productivity society-wide
- Homelessness
- Neighborhood disorder or decline
- Crime related to addiction, family dysfunction, and neighborhood decline, and the related costs of policing, judicial administration, imprisonment, and rehabilitation
- Gun sales stimulated by the fear of that crime, sometimes resulting in accidental shootings, gun suicides (twenty-three thousand in the US in 2016), homicides committed during flashes of anger, or easy access to lethal means by people who are antisocial or mentally deranged[1]

Dislocation-driven ego-arrest is not solely responsible for any of these social harms, but it contributes. Worse, most of these harms, such as family dysfunction or crime, fold back to amplify dislocation (and thus ego-identification), completing a socially destructive feedback loop.

A further collective consequence of mass egoism—and a centerpiece of our inquiry—is that our civilization has secretly devolved into a vast apparatus for limiting psychospiritual self-realization. That is a developmental loss for each affected individual. But it also increases societies' vulnerability to morally immature or antisocial behavior and, conversely, reduces societal contributions from people who might otherwise become more morally evolved, prosocially creative, and morally exemplary for others.

Well, as far as collective consequences go, that's all pretty bad.

But could it get worse?

MACROSCALE PROBLEMS AND PERILS

We've seen a powerful historical example of how egoic psychology produced macrosocial harm of the highest order: in early modern Europe, consumer demand for addictive drug foods provided a major impetus for developing the North Atlantic slave trade and slave plantations across the Americas, including for growing coffee in Brazil, tobacco in Virginia and North Carolina, and sugar throughout the Caribbean.

Let's turn to some of the macrochallenges with which humanity is contending today:

- **Poverty and Injustice:** struggles to surmount poverty and racial, gender, ethnic, and other kinds of injustice and to advance democratic self-determination
- **Unsustainability:** resource scarcity and environmental degradation, including the danger of catastrophic climate change
- **Mass Violence:** civil unrest and wars in the developing world, international nuclear weapons proliferation and the potential for nuclear war, and the specter of terrorists wielding weapons of mass destruction (and of costly and problematic countermeasures, including protracted military engagements, bloated homeland-security bureaucracies, and transgressions of civil rights and liberties), etc.
- **Refugee Crises:** mass population migrations prompted by the preceding kinds of social or ecological upheavals
- **Political Dysfunction:** political polarization, legislative paralysis, political corruption, or authoritarianism

- **Pandemics:** As I was writing this book, the COVID-19 pandemic erupted, causing illness, death, and economic havoc worldwide.

Several of these challenges represent significant threats to the human prospect, perhaps even jeopardizing our survival as a civilization or species. Mass ego-sovereignty fuels these grand challenges through two basic modes:

- **Mode A.** Exhibiting socially problematic psychological propensities such as ego-constrained morality, insecurity, insatiability, and denial
- **Mode B.** Sustaining techno-economic forces that, in turn, sustain ego-sovereignty

Mode A is not the stuff of front-page headlines. It is hardly news that selfishness, fear, acquisitiveness, and denial contribute to social problems.

But Mode B is a different matter. The modern system of ego-sovereignty depends on sustaining a dislocating and dis-integrating techno-economy. Yet *these same social structures and forces also contribute to establishing the great macrochallenges and crises confronting humanity*, such as social injustice, war, terrorism, and climate change.* This is depicted in Figure 15.[2]

Social forces and feedback loops of the kinds that are shown inside Figure 15's dotted rectangle and discussed in its caption are widely recognized. However, egoic masking prevents people from understanding that the same social dynamics that generate macrochallenges *also* stabilize ego-sovereignty.[3]

Mode B confronts the system of ego-sovereignty with a fundamental dilemma. On the one hand, our egos are desperate to perpetuate their sovereignty. On the other hand, the macrosocial conditions through which our egos fulfill this soul-stifling ambition—i.e., dislocation, inequality, and the device paradigm—also contribute to enormous suffering (augmenting the prevalence of addiction, depression, heart disease, cancer, family dysfunction, and so on). Worse, they have become powerful contributing causes in generating macrochallenges that harm overall societal well-being, even threatening modern

---

* The term "social structure" refers to the background features that help create or regulate patterns of human interaction. Familiar examples include laws, dominant political and economic institutions, and technological systems and complexes. All these are enduring social products that shape, but do not fully determine, social behavior.

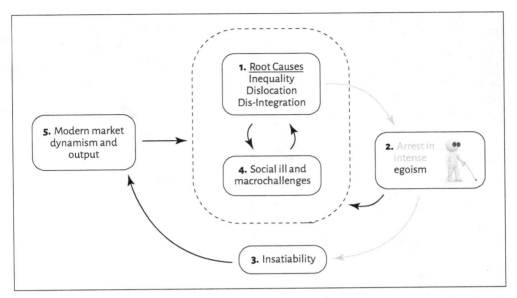

Figure 15. Egoism, Macrochallenges, and Root Causes. Root causes of intense egoism (Box 1) contribute to generating social ills and macrochallenges, as indicated by the arrow from Box 1 to Box 4. Macroscale social problems can also fold back to amplify the root causes (as indicated by the return arrow from Box 4 back to Box 1). For instance, climate change and refugee crises (Box 4) contribute to dislocation (Box 1). The dotted rectangle indicates that there is substantial interaction and overlap of this kind between Boxes 1 and 4.

Meanwhile, egoic masking (symbolized by the blind man) prevents us from knowing that the dislocation, inequality, and dis-integrative forces that help cause macrochallenges *also* sustain mass ego-sovereignty (Box 2). The latter engenders the insatiability (Box 3) that is essential to capitalism (Box 5), while also contributing directly to many social problems small and large (i.e., Mode A—indicated here by the arrow from Box 2 to the dotted rectangle). However, masking leads us to misconstrue intense ego-identification and insatiability as innate rather than socially induced (symbolized by the arrows and text that are faded out).

Note: "Inequality" in Box 1 includes hierarchy (i.e., inequality in organizational power and status) in addition to economic inequality.

civilization and possibly human survival. The latter prospect is as terrifying to the ego as that of being dethroned (see Figure 16).

There is no conclusive solution to this dilemma; it's too deep for that. Instead, without consciously understanding the overarching objective that it is fulfilling (i.e., to prevent ego-transcendence), the ego has evolved a de facto coping strategy:

- **Mode C.** In the face of social ills and threats, *striving always to sustain a system of social conditions* (including hierarchy, dislocation, dis-integration via the device paradigm, masking, and perhaps others not yet invented) *that secretly suffice to stabilize ego-sovereignty.*

Figure 16. The Ego's Existential Dilemma. The dynamics of the ego/world system in effect leave the ego perched precariously atop a double-sided precipice: as dislocation or the other root causes of ego-sovereignty ramp up ("Excess Dislocation"), societal harms and perils mount. But dialing back on those root causes would jeopardize ego-sovereignty—an outcome that the ego equates with death ("Insufficient Dislocation"). From the ego's standpoint, it's "Dead if you damp down on dislocation, and dead if you don't."

The Mode C stipulation is fulfilled through several complementary mechanisms, as shown in Figure 17:

- **Popular Buy-In to the Status Quo:** Egoic traits such as insatiability and a material metric of value boost popular enthusiasm for the cornucopia of goods and wealth produced by market economies (hence the happy emoji inside Box 5). This, in turn, builds tolerance of the inequality, dislocation, and disintegration that are integral to modern capitalism. Egoic self-deception contributes to the popular embrace of capitalism by sustaining the popular expectation that markets will provide a level of satisfaction that somehow never quite materializes.
- **Elite Self-Interest:** By perpetuating significant social disparities (Box 1), capitalism also establishes powerful elites who are

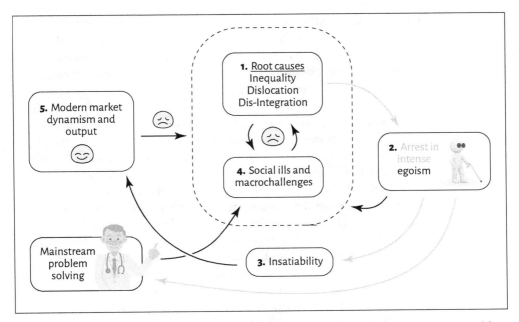

Figure 17. The Mode C Stipulation in Action. This figure adds "Mainstream problem solving" into Figure 15. In compliance with stipulation C, mainstream approaches prioritize managing social ills and challenges (Box 4) over addressing the root causes of ego-sovereignty (Box 1).

invested in sustaining the social system that secures their privileges. For instance, political conservatives often lean toward downplaying the ill effects of capitalism. Liberals are more apt to acknowledge capitalism's downside (symbolized by the sad emojis). But appreciative also of capitalism's merits, liberals tend to focus on addressing downstream problems (Box 4) more than root causes (Box 1). This is symbolized by the symptom-treating doctor. Mainstream problem-solving is exemplified in policies—such as those championed by Bill and Hillary Clinton—that embrace globalization and job automation (Box 5), while seeking to compensate for dislocation by retraining displaced workers for jobs in high tech. This fulfills the Mode C stipulation to manage social problems without jeopardizing the forces that stabilize ego-sovereignty.[4]

- **Egoic Masking:** Masking reinforces the preference for symptomatic problem-solving by obscuring the extent of harm for which the root causes are responsible (as indicated by the new faded-out arrow running from Box 2 into "Mainstream Problem-Solving"). The unrecognized harm includes stunted psychospiritual growth (Box 2), which also becomes a hidden factor in engendering many mental, physical, and social ills (a healthy portion of Box 4).

Unfortunately, the Mode C stipulation is cost-inefficient, not reliably effective, and increasingly dangerous. The basic reason is that even if a macrochallenge is successfully resolved, the stipulation leaves intact ego-perpetuating conditions that become factors in generating further macrochallenges. For instance:

- **Macrochallenge:** Capitalism confronted two existential threats during the twentieth century: the world communist movement (born in reaction to capitalism) and then, during the ensuing Cold War, the danger of global thermonuclear annihilation.[5]
- **Partial Resolution:** The United States and its allies managed to contain communist expansion until the Soviet Empire collapsed under the weight of its own unfulfilled promises. That, together with negotiated reductions in nuclear-weapon stockpiles, reduced the likelihood of nuclear war, although the danger has not been eliminated. Today nine nations are estimated to retain about thirteen thousand nuclear warheads.
- **Mode C Compliance:** The demise of the communist challenge to capitalism has allowed techno-economic forces requisite to sustaining ego-sovereignty to accelerate and deepen around the world.
- **New Macrochallenges:** Hyper-dislocation in the wake of internet-turbocharged globalization is a significant factor in: (a) driving the worldwide prevalence of addiction, depression, obesity, heart disease, and so forth; and (b) accelerating the expansion of slum-ridden megacities, domestic jobs lost to automation and offshoring, deepening inequalities in wealth and power, political polarization and dysfunction, authoritarian populism, extremism and terrorism, and overall a growing mismatch between the capacities of political systems and the challenges that they are summoned to resolve—including climate change and the danger of a renewed nuclear-arms race. Sober analysts judge that the latter two represent existential threats to human civilization.[6]

Globalization is not solely responsible for any of the preceding macrochallenges, but it is a factor in all of them. For instance, international terrorism and authoritarian populism are complex phenomena with causes that vary and that are not always well understood, but intense dislocation associated with a corporate-driven globalizing economy is commonly identified as among the contributing social conditions.[7]

Resolutions of macrochallenges that leave ego-sustaining social forces in place tend to generate new, sometimes worse macrochallenges. That's because egoic acquisitiveness combined with market incentives is expansive, always striving to reach into new territories and evolve new modalities of dislocation in pursuit of power, wealth, and the satiation of insatiable wants. This expands the macrosocial forces that, besides propagating intensive egoism, also contribute to engendering further macrochallenges as a byproduct.

KICK-THE-CAN AS A PLAN

The Mode C "solution" to managing the macro-dilemma that confronts ego-sovereignty (Figure 16) is about the same as becoming hopelessly addicted to a perverse game of kick-the-can: We spend all day kicking cans of explosives down the road only to keep stumbling upon more cans loaded with worse explosives. Sometimes a group of players pauses to defuse one of the cans, but this never seems to keep up with the appearance of new ones.

Meanwhile, playing the game secretly *sustains our compulsion to play* and *drives the appearance of new explosive canisters*, while also *rendering us oblivious* to these perverse psychosocial dynamics and to the option of exiting the game.

This kick-the-can game is, of course, insane. Armed with our insights into the machinations of Maya's Empire, we know this. But we also understand why, from the ego's standpoint, it all makes sense: the game sustains ego-sovereignty, while we try not to die individually or collapse as a civilization in the process.

The "terrible, unimaginable" other option—well, that's how the ego would assess it—is to get to work evolving soul-friendly alternatives to structural inequality, dislocation, and dis-integration (in effect, retiring the Mode C stipulation). That would start to shrink the big macrochallenges, limit the emergence of new ones, reduce the prevalence of pathological suffering, and weaken the conditions that perpetuate ego-sovereignty.

Win-win big time for our planet, bodies, psyches, and souls. But the last of these is exactly the outcome that the ego wants at all costs to avoid.

SECRET OPPORTUNITIES FOR SYSTEM TRANSFORMATION

Is the global system of ego-stabilization so flawlessly assembled that our situation is hopeless? Not necessarily.

Let's take the politics of climate change as an example. Here are some ways that egoic psychology (Mode A) and the structural forces with which it is interdependent (Mode B) contribute to environmental degradation, including climate change:

- Modern techno-economies are prone to disrupt ecological processes through resource depletion, pollution, and environmental alteration and degradation. This is, among other things, socially dislocating.
- This dislocation helps stabilize ego-sovereignty. Egoic psychology—including consumer insatiability and the lust for wealth and influence—contributes, in turn, to sustaining the system of dislocation and dis-integration, including its environmental dimensions. This establishes a destructive feedback loop running between egoism and environmental degradation.
- The sharp psychological boundary intrinsic to intense egoism distances people emotionally from the natural world and its primordial sacredness, creating fertile ground for environmentally destructive behavior. Think of Arjuna destroying the Khandava Forest.[8]
- Economic disembedding, globalization, and the device paradigm contribute to dismantling locally self-reliant economies. This diminishes capacities for local self-determination, including the capacity to dampen dislocation or limit externally imposed ecological harm. It also increases environmentally harmful long-distance transportation.
- By concealing the extent of social harm for which markets bear responsibility, egoic masking contributes to a preference for market-based solutions to redressing environmental externalities. This establishes another perverse feedback loop—that is, enrolling the cause of a problem as its solution—that helps perpetuate ecologically harmful egoism and dislocation.

Mainstream proposals for limiting climate change tend to center on three policy approaches: (a) discourage greenhouse-gas emissions with carbon taxes; (b) establish a market in which businesses can trade government-capped rights to emit greenhouse gases (this is called a "cap-and-trade" policy); or (c) implement programs that directly encourage reduced emissions (e.g., subsidies for adopting renewable energy technologies or regulatory limits on greenhouse-gas emissions). Many economists and environmental organizations favor the first option as the most efficient and effective—that is, when it is politically feasible.

Climate-change deniers, of course, oppose all three options, as do many greenhouse-gas-emitting corporations and politicians beholden to them. But notice that of the preceding ways in which egoism contributes to climate change, these mainstream policy approaches grasp and address *only the first*. That's not a promising basis for resolving a challenge that involves many psychosocial pathways to environmental harm.

However, there is another strain of environmental thought that disputes the conviction that these three approaches suffice; I'll call it "structure-critical environmentalism." As a representative of this alternative genre of environmentalism, consider Naomi Klein's best-selling book *This Changes Everything: Capitalism vs. the Climate*. Klein faults mainstream environmental policy for failing to challenge a techno-economic system that, left to its own devices, is assured to unleash assaults on the earth's ecosystems faster than we can ever implement effective policy responses. In effect, she is arguing that it's difficult to keep dodging bullets when the act of dodging is firing off ever-denser bullet volleys. Here, Klein is explicitly considering several of the items in our list, albeit without grasping the social-structural contingency of the egoism that fuels them.[9]

Klein furthermore observes that modern capitalism is not only environmentally unsustainable but also unjust and socially dislocating. The latter defects are bad in themselves, but in addition they compound our inability to address our environmental predicament. For instance, injustice becomes an impediment to sustainability when dominant actors in causing climate change are little inclined to contemplate structural solutions that would involve lessening their wealth and power.

Klein's proposed alternative is to complement carbon taxes with structural changes that can advance social justice while simultaneously achieving greater environmental sustainability. Her suggestions include:

> To demand the rebuilding and reviving of local economies; to reclaim our democracies from corrosive corporate influence; to block harmful new free trade deals and rewrite old ones; to invest in starving public infrastructure like mass transit and affordable housing; to take back ownership of essential services like energy and water; to remake our sick agricultural system into something much healthier; to open borders to migrants whose displacement is linked to climate impacts; to finally respect Indigenous land rights— all of which would help to end grotesque levels of inequality within our nations and between them.[10]

From our perspective, prescriptions such as Klein's are tantalizing, at first perplexingly so. Each of her recommendations moves in the direction of (a) improving sustainability, and either (b) reducing injustice and inequality, or (c) evolving a less dislocating, democratically re-embedded economy. These ambitions are entirely consistent with our understanding of conditions conducive to healthy psychospiritual development. How does this come about, given that Klein's concerns are with ecology, democracy, and justice, but not psychospiritual development?

Look at Figure 18, which adds "Social Movements for Structural Transformation" to Figure 17. Klein's structure-critical analysis recognizes that capitalism (Box 5) sustains social forces and harms that include dislocation, inequality, and injustice (Box 1), as well as environmental harm (Box 4). But in accordance with our culture generally, she doesn't perceive developmental arrest in strong ego-identification (Box 2) and all the harm that flows from it.

Klein's prescriptions are inadvertently conducive to psychospiritual development because the Box 1 social forces that she wishes to subdue are the same forces that intensify and stabilize ego-sovereignty.

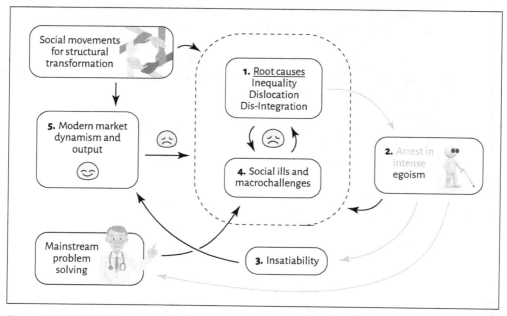

Figure 18. Social Movements for Structural Transformation. This figure introduces transformational social movements (upper left) into Figure 17. The distinction between problem-solving and transformational orientations is not always sharp. Most structural transformers also support ameliorative measures to reduce suffering. Conversely (and as Karl Polanyi observed), laissez-faire economies are innately self-destructive, which compels mainstream support for dampening dislocation at least enough to avert social and economic collapse.

This has several important implications.

The first is that Klein and other structure-critical environmentalists are selling themselves short. Their prescriptions for saving the planet would contribute to destabilizing ego-sovereignty and lessening all of its ancillary suffering. This would also bring about more environmental improvement than they anticipate, because egoic psychology contributes to environmentally destructive behavior. In practice it would take time to see any significant mass improvement in psychospiritual development, but it is moving in the right direction.

Second, structure-critical environmentalists understand that in speaking to the concerns of both environmental and social-justice movements, their analyses offer a basis for assembling broader coalitions for structural transformation. However, because these proposals can help realize a more extensive range of benefits than their proponents understand—including opportunities for psychospiritual growth and lessening all the ills to which intense egoism contributes—the potential for assembling muscular alliances is even greater than movement strategists recognize.

Better yet, what is true of structure-critical environmentalism holds for the proposals of many other progressive social movements. Any movement that targets reducing dislocation, dis-integration, or hierarchy as ends in themselves—or as means toward other worthy ends—is also helping to soften the forces that stabilize ego-identification. This can, for example, be true of structurally oriented peace, democracy, trade-union, or social-justice movements.

It can sometimes be true of conservative social movements as well. For instance, respecting cultural traditions and devolving power from central governments to localities can limit dislocation. But only if that does not mean perpetuating injustice or denying a market economy's potential to cause other types of harm.

The inadvertent convergence of many social-movement strategies toward evolving a more soul-friendly assemblage of social structures is reason to become more optimistic for our future as humans living on a beautiful, fragile, and fraught planet.

Pausing for a few sighs of relief might be appropriate.

Chapter 15

NOW WE KNOW IT

Our theory in its complete form

Naomi Klein's *This Changes Everything* became a bestseller, and many of the prescriptions advanced by structure-critical environmentalists subsequently found expression in proposed US legislation for a "Green New Deal." The world's governments, multinational corporations, and hedge-fund managers did not swiftly fall into line, however. Reacting to the accord on climate change negotiated by 195 nations in December 2015, which she conceded was politically groundbreaking, Klein nonetheless compared it to a dieter vowing to eat four hamburgers a day instead of five.[1]

So long as the ego's purposes and wiles remain so brilliantly self-camouflaged, structure-critical proposals that buck the Mode C stipulation face a steep uphill battle. Ego-protective Mode C strategies for addressing macrochallenges have powerful tailwinds at their back. For instance:

- **Egoic masking prevents anyone from understanding** the destructive psychosocial dynamics in which we are complicit (as depicted in Figure 15).
- Many persons of power and wealth—**especially while system-blinded** to the harm that they and their descendants too suffer within Maya's Empire—**perceive** an interest in perpetuating the hierarchies and social forces that sustain their privileges.
- Even political liberals who support environmental protection, racial and social equality, and so on may nonetheless **unwittingly** comply with Mode C if, all the same, they resist deeper structural transformation of our techno-economic order. Some do so based on **perceived** self-interest. Others are acting altruistically but—**incognizant** of the extent of social costs and

perils in which the ego/world system is implicated—resist system transformation on pragmatic grounds, such as reasoning that "Band-Aid remedies are good enough and all that's politically feasible."[2]

- Conversely, those who are the most structurally disadvantaged are **equally blind** to the destructive psychosocial dynamics of Maya's Empire, while also impaired in their ability to combat injustice, deprivation, dislocation, and other macrochallenges in virtue of bearing the greater brunt of those ills.
- Some of those harmed and disadvantaged are, **via masking and egoic psychology**—such as **ego-protective denial**—inspired to defend the system responsible for their distress.
- Some elites are skillful in promulgating **self-serving misrepresentations and framings,** as encapsulated in a truth-telling joke: "A banker, a worker, and an immigrant sit down at a table with 20 donuts. The banker takes 19 donuts and warns the worker, '**Watch out**, the immigrant is going to take your donut.'"[3]

These are among the factors that are commonly arrayed against soul-friendly structural transformation. This is a letdown from the optimistic note we struck at the end of the preceding chapter (see Figure 19).

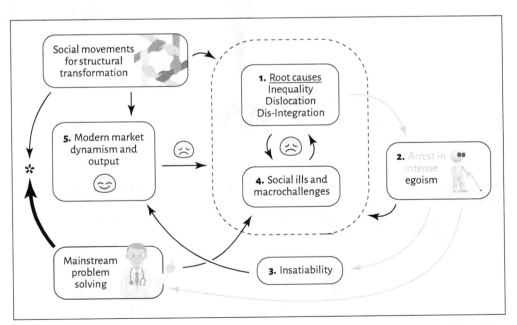

Figure 19. Mainstream Problem-Solving Versus Social Movements for Structural Transformation. The arrows to the left (marked with an asterisk) indicate that the balance of social forces often favors mainstream problem-solving (thicker arrow) over soul-friendly structural change (the opposing thinner arrow).

Except, now look again at the bolded words in the preceding bullet points. All the bolded text highlights egoic masking as prominent among the forces working against alleviating our plight. And the thing about egoic masking is that once it's revealed, the ego's secret superpower for preserving its sovereignty is no longer quite so super. (Remember, it doesn't take an invading army or Wonder Woman to expose the emperor's nakedness; just a truthful little kid.)

Unmasking reveals that the ordinary way in which we perceive our political, economic, and technological systems is skewed toward the ego's interest in sustaining ego-sovereignty (see Figure 20). Masking leads us to underestimate systemic harms, such as the stunting of psychospiritual growth and the personal and social ills that result. It also obscures problematic causal dynamics, such as capitalism's dependence on its capacity to instill mass insatiability and the psychospiritual consequences of our dis-integration from the worlds of community, nature, and spirit. By the same token, masking often leads us to exaggerate system benefits. For instance, it is common for people to overestimate the depth and duration of satisfaction that they will secure from their consumer purchases.

Figure 20. Ego-Skewed Social System Evaluation. Our egos rely on masking to tip the scales toward popular support for the structural status quo—a world in which chronic dislocation, dis-integration, and social and political inequality become the price people are willing to pay in return for economic growth and consumer goods.

The skewed assessment of system costs and benefits, as depicted symbolically in Figure 20, tilts the balance of social forces toward Mode C problem-solving rather than soul-friendly social-structural transformation.

But now let's imagine that unmasking were to gain cultural traction (Figure 21). Unmasking lends support to the argument that structural transformation can be more effective in preventing and addressing social ills—actually many social ills at once—than status quo problem-solving. It also reveals that structural reconfiguration can contribute to softening ego-identification and lessening the harms that flow from it.

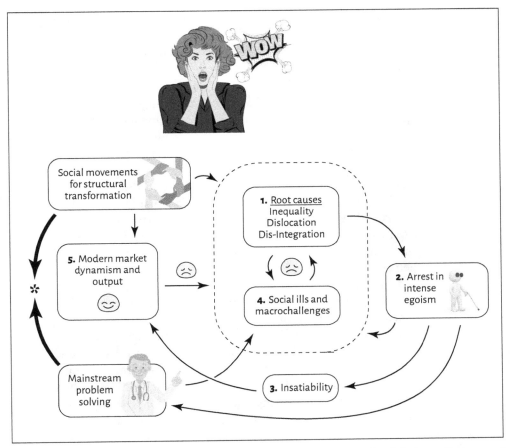

Figure 21. If Unmasking Gains Traction. . . . This figure drags the faded-out features of Figure 19 out into the light of day. By revealing the hidden dynamics of the ego/world system, unmasking has the potential to shift the balance of social forces so that they are more favorable to soul-friendly structural transformation (symbolized by showing the asterisked arrows as more equal).

Traditionally the most trenchant criticism of capitalism has been that it sustains economic disparities and injustice, benefiting *some at the expense of others*. But we have shown that there are also many respects in which capitalism works to the disadvantage of *everybody*. No one escapes increased vulnerability to psychospiritual stunting, psychological and physical harm, and ensuing societal macrochallenges. Our inquiry furthermore reveals that these two great ills of the ego/world system—injustice (harm to some) and irrationality (harm to all)—are interdependent. For instance, mass ego-stabilization (the irrationality) contributes to sustaining injustice via impaired morality, ego-serving distortions in reasoning, and Mode C compliance. Injustice, conversely, establishes privileged groups that are powerfully committed to preserving the ego/world system. By unmasking both the irrationality and how it is intertwined with injustice, our inquiry doubles and triples down on the moral case for system transformation.[4]

Unmasking has the potential to shift the balance of social forces toward soul-friendly structural change in several ways:

- As it becomes understood that structural change can help relax egoism and its ill effects, social-change movements will have an important new rationale supporting their side. This can lead to more success in recruiting members and assembling broader, more powerful coalitions.
- That recruitment can include reaching out to the millions of people seeking to advance their psychospiritual growth. All of them will have new skin in the game—new reasons to participate in social-change endeavors—once they learn the extent to which the modern world is arranged to counter the efficacy of their practices.
- Finally, some mainstream problem-solvers or problem-deniers are likely to weaken in their resolve or even become structural transformers. For example, many problem-solvers—including epidemiologists, public-health officials, social workers, and policy makers—know that dislocation contributes to disease and social disorder, but egoic masking prevents them from grasping the extent of social and psychospiritual harm. This biases their assessment of whether structural transformation is warranted or politically realistic. Second, some socially elite problem-solvers or problem-deniers (OK, not necessarily very many) will switch teams once they figure out that even today's nominal "winners" suffer from the camouflaged dynamics that unmasking reveals. There is precedent for this kind of pivot in the occasional person of great privilege who becomes sufficiently alarmed by environmental threats or economic inequality to join the effort for structural transformation.[5]

But if modern people are arrested in ego-identification, who is the "we" that could conceivably act on new insights into the mechanisms of ego-stabilization? Besides people who already favor structural transformation for other reasons, the "we" is our souls, long languishing under the ego's benighted rule but eager to resume their place on the Kurukshetra field of battle. As we noted in Chapter 13, pervasive ego-identification notwithstanding, in moral terms many modern adults already surpass Yudhishthira at his Palace-bound worst.

Unmasking doesn't guarantee that the world changes or does so without a fight. The ego/world system remains in place, here unmasked but not otherwise disarmed, and our egos are going to have their own ideas about all this. Still, it is not nothing to begin tearing aside centuries of camouflaging that has inhibited soul- and planet-friendly structural change.

CONSOLIDATING THE CORE ARGUMENT

We can now restate our core argument in its mature form:
Modern societies depend on:

- *Their ability—through chronic dislocation, dis-integration, and social hierarchies—to stabilize strong ego-identification and insatiability on a mass basis, thereby impeding access to the higher ranges of psychospiritual development; and*
- *Our egos' efficacy in camouflaging this ego/world system, including its role in engendering extensive personal suffering along with escalating threats to societal well-being and the human prospect.*

More succinctly we might say that: *People in the modern world have coevolved with a political-economic and technological system that depends on its secret ability to impede our psychospiritual growth.*

OBJECTIONS

One immediate criticism of this theory might be that it explains too much. How can one take seriously a theory that claims to elucidate undetected driving forces in modern history, expand our understanding of modern psychology, provide a novel basis for critiquing mainstream economics, help explain the intractability of societal macrochallenges, and so on? Talk about preposterous grandiosity!

Perhaps . . . but perhaps not. After all, wouldn't one expect a pervasive, self-camouflaging shift in psychological development to produce myriad social repercussions? Our theory of ego-arrested development is not a master key to explaining everything about modernity. Nevertheless, it fills in many gaps.

Moreover, there is another straightforward argument supporting our theory's general plausibility: Among psychologists it is widely accepted that macrosocial circumstances shape psychological development. But if any historical process could have been sufficiently momentous to have altered trajectories of psychological development, surely it would have been the profound social transformations involved in establishing global capitalism and afterward industrializing. And yet psychologists have not mustered evidence of such developmental changes. This suggests either that their widely accepted thesis is false . . . or that it has been hard to detect these psychological shifts because they are self-camouflaging.[6]

Of course, any new social theory warrants critical scrutiny. Invariably ours will require fixes, refinement, and reassessment. But care will be needed to distinguish valid criticism from the ego/world's talent for self-protective intellectual sleight of hand.

ON TRANSGRESSING THE TABOO

I would like to speak for just a moment to those who have shown me the kindness of reading this far despite harboring skepticism toward the scholarly utility of a post-egoic perspective.

Explanatory power is esteemed currency of the realm in academia. But much of our argument's explanatory power is specific to its trans-personal formulation. We can explain all that we can explain, and find hopeful new possibilities for social transformation, only because we have adopted a post-egoic perspective on psychological development. Perhaps this lends support to our supposition that there *is* such a thing as "post-egoism" and that it is fruitful to relax the Taboo against integrating a post-egoic perspective into scholarly inquiry.

After all, we know that adults understand many things that children are developmentally incapable of grasping. By analogy, it stands to reason that integrating a developmentally more evolved, post-egoic stance into research might reveal much about the world that we can never learn if we limit ourselves to knowledge-making practices that keep our egos secure in their comfort zone. Far from protecting us from some terrible unspecified danger, perhaps the Taboo prevents us from accessing untapped reservoirs of useful knowledge. (In this respect, the Taboo is akin to a terrifying ogre who—while only a figment of the townspeople's fevered imagination—nonetheless steals away the map to a real buried treasure.)

This doesn't imply that we should suspend our normal critical faculties. It merely means allowing research that is informed by a post-egoic stance to proceed and then subjecting it to the same processes of peer review that we apply to any other research.

If violating the Taboo against adopting a post-egoic perspective yields intellectual riches while promising commensurate social improvement, then which is it more sensible to sacrifice: intellectual riches and social betterment or a Taboo that serves no discernible con-structive purpose?

THE STATE OF CIVILIZATION

Many people sense that there is something seriously amiss with mod-ern civilization. We can do so much. We know so much. We have so much. And yet there is so much discontent, distrust, fearfulness, rage, and suffering. Besides injustice, discrimination, ecological heedless-ness, hatred, and brutality—these are not new in human history—there is also denial, disconnection, emotional depletion, and dysfunction. We have the power to destroy and too often use it, while lacking the wisdom to live lightly on the earth or to build societies in which people can find greater harmony and serenity and even soar.

A trope repeated widely for over a century has it that morality has failed to keep pace with techno-economic accomplishment. President Obama invoked it in Hiroshima, Japan, while memorializing the tens of millions of lives cut short during World War II: "Technological progress without an equivalent progress in human institutions can doom us. The scientific revolution that led to the splitting of an atom requires a moral revolution as well." The trope is well rehearsed, but it fails to grasp that our techno-economic prowess *inhibits* the moral development for which it pleads.[7]

If you've read this far, you understand when, why, and how our world wrapped itself in a new form of insanity. Previous societies were imperfect and not a few were, by modern standards, horrendous. But modernity is unique in binding vast masses of people into a psycho-logical configuration that is abnormally insecure, lacking, pathology-prone, dis-integrated, stunted, and self-deceiving—a configuration determined come what may to stay as it is forever. Even if "come what may" risks driving civilization over a cliff.

Actually, it's worse than that. This hasn't happened by accident or as the burden we must bear in order to achieve some worthy para-mount objective. No, we suffer unnecessarily and subject ourselves to mounting existential peril in fulfillment of the ego's overarching ambi-tion to *preclude* something of incalculable value—access to higher ranges of self-realization (Figure 22). This is insanity.

But now we know it.

Figure 22. The Hidden Madness of Modern Civilization. Damping down dislocation, dis-integration, and inequality would tend to reduce societal harms and perils. But from the ego's standpoint, this would also mean damping down the root causes of ego-sovereignty, an outcome that it equates with annihilation (Figure 16). In reality, relaxing ego-sovereignty will tend to reduce personal suffering and open new opportunities for psychospiritual self-realization (symbolized by the bird soaring free). The hidden madness of modern civilization is that, in effect, we risk A in order to *prevent* B.

The preceding sentence includes the words "in effect" because our psychosocial situation is an *outcome* of egoic psychology—e.g., insatiability, the fear of ego-transcendence and deference to the Taboo—without reflecting the ego's *conscious intent.* That is, we suffer and imperil ourselves without understanding that this serves our egos' paramount interest in preventing ego-transcendence. The absence of conscious intent is an aspect of the "hiddenness" of our civilization's madness.

Part III

HEALING THE WORLD

Chapter 16

LEARNING TO HEAL

A strategy for evolving soul-friendly structural ecologies

One thing that we now know about the modern world is that it has been crafted to make sure that we don't know too much. We haven't known that it is designed to hinder us from becoming our most morally evolved, wise, creative, and caring selves. That it can't sustain itself without subjecting us and those we love—billions, in fact—to unnecessary suffering and growing danger of calamity.

And no one can know exactly what to do about it. But there are ways to find out and get started.

VALUES AND VISION

Modernity is certainly not an unmitigated disaster. Establishing the ideals of peace, democracy, social justice, human rights, and environmental sustainability—even while their realization remains imperfect—stands high among our civilization's achievements. These ideals are also interdependent with evolving a world more hospitable to psychospiritual self-realization. In looking toward more soul-friendly social arrangements, we won't want to abandon the quest to fulfill these principles.

Among modernity's many other commendable features are widespread literacy, medical and technological advances, broadened opportunities for developing our talents, and so on. These too we'll want to preserve (well, selectively so in the case of technologies). But we need to become more discerning about our societies' psychospiritual dimensions. A first step would be to fold into the list of high social ideals the ethical principle that:[1]

> *We should seek to evolve equal and ample opportunities for realizing our psychospiritual potential.*

Practically speaking, that means establishing this social commitment:

> *We must undo the system of egoic masking; lessen dislocation, dis-integration, hierarchy, and inequality; and forestall any further innovations in impeding self-realization.*

How much "lessening" is needed? Enough to establish an ecology—that is, an evolving system—of social forces and structures that fulfills the preceding equal-opportunities principle.

I can't present a detailed blueprint of such a structural ecology. One reason is that we don't know enough. A second is that satisfactory structural ecologies will vary based on local circumstances and aspirations. Instead let's sketch a plausible *learning strategy* for evolving a civilization healthier to our bodies, minds, and souls, beginning with a sample action step.

LOCAL ECONOMIC SELF-RELIANCE AS TEACHABLE MOMENT

The emergence of a global economy in the sixteenth century initiated an accelerating process of subverting local subsistence economies. This subjected communities to distant social forces over which they had no influence, and it was among the reasons that Karl Polanyi characterized a disembedded market economy as a machine optimized for producing tumultuous dislocation. The goal of re-embedding the economy—including reviving local economies—must almost certainly figure in any strategy for supporting psychospiritual growth. This doesn't mean reverting to oppressive social systems, such as feudalism. The re-embedding we seek needs to uphold modern ideals such as democracy and justice.

Many organizations are already working toward this end. Operating under banners such as "Transition Towns," "Relocalization," or "Local Futures," their goals vary, ranging from nurturing economic development and job creation to buffering communities from macroeconomic shocks, reducing local dependence on the actions of distant corporate headquarters, advancing social justice and self-determination, building community and cultural vibrancy, transitioning away from reliance on dwindling fossil-fuel reserves, limiting the effects of climate change, or any combination of these.

While these groups' ambitions are diverse, their strategies converge in seeking a more locally and regionally self-reliant economy, including more local production for local consumption. Initiatives underway include:

- Community-scale wind, solar electricity, and biofuel production
- Energy conservation
- Community-supported agriculture and community gardens and greenhouses
- Local farmers' markets and craft bazaars
- Job retraining matched to local and regional employment opportunities

Self-reliance activities can also extend to measures such as:

- Worker- and community-owned businesses
- Locally governed water- and sewage-management systems, including water conservation, water recycling, and graywater reuse
- Manufacturing that uses regionally sourced and recycled materials
- Credit unions, local mutual funds, and other vehicles for local investment
- Local currencies, which can stimulate local commerce and encourage goods and services to circulate closer to home[2]

By diversifying local economic activity, self-reliance also builds resilience, stabilizing communities and reducing the likelihood that people will be forced to move away to find work.

Generally, a more locally self-reliant economy will pay lower wages than do elite jobs in today's cosmopolitan urban centers. But a drop in top-tier earnings would be a good thing for reducing inequality that is at once materially, ethically, and politically problematic. (As a benchmark, in 2017 the average annual *income*—not net worth—of the top twenty-five US hedge-fund managers was $672 million.) And participating in a more locally self-reliant economy provides many nonmonetary rewards, not the least of them psychospiritual.[3]

For our purposes we don't need to go further into specifics. The important point is that by dampening dislocation, a more locally and regionally self-reliant economy holds promise for improving our prospects for psychospiritual self-realization. Let's unpack the preceding sentence.

Shared Causes and Convergent Remedies

As we learned in Chapter 14, the social forces that sustain ego-sovereignty produce other, more obvious social harms and dangers. That is how it happens that groups working to address the structural causes of social and environmental problems—for instance, by increasing local self-reliance—are accidentally helping to evolve a structural ecology favorable to psychospiritual growth. There are many other examples of this type of soul-favorable strategic convergence. For instance, efforts to increase economic equality via progressive taxation, or to advance racial and gender justice, are reducing social hierarchy and thus contributing to the structural ecology we seek.

The upshot is that many action steps that appear promising for building a more psychospiritually supportive society are not original ideas. Ordinarily that would not be an occasion for an author to dance and celebrate, but in this case non-originality translates into practicality: we can join forces with existing social movements rather than confront the formidable task of building a stand-alone social movement from scratch.

LEARNING BY DOING

> You seem desirous of knowing what Progress
> we make here in improving our Governments.
> We are, I think, in the right Road of Improvement, for we are making Experiments.
> —Benjamin Franklin, 1786, in a letter
> to his English friend Jonathan Shipley

Is it premature to think about acting based on a social theory that has barely been vetted? Not necessarily. For one thing, it makes sense to consider actions that would be warranted *if* our theory were to survive critical scrutiny. But also, taking action is sometimes the best way to test and refine a social theory, in the process learning how to move ahead with constructive structural transformation.

As an analogy, suppose that you've studied the chemistry and physics of cooking in order to work out a theory of spaghetti. Your theory says that if you throw it up against the wall, a great cooked spaghetti noodle will stick lightly against the surface. One way to evaluate your theory is to encourage experts to assess the science that you drew upon in crafting the theory. This kind of critical scrutiny is always a good idea.

But there's a complementary evaluative strategy that bridges the potential gap between expert analysis and the real world: Taking inspiration from your theory, you cook up several batches of spaghetti and throw some of each against the wall. Maybe one does the best, but it's not perfect. If it slides down the wall, next time you add a bit less salt to the water or cook it a little longer. With each round of cooking and throwing, you're honing your spaghetti-making skills, while also gathering information that you can use to improve your theory. Or if your spaghetti remains mediocre no matter how many times you throw it against the wall, eventually you'll know that it's time to find a better theory. This is a trial-and-error learning procedure. And along the way you're getting to eat a lot of spaghetti, one of your favorite dishes.

Because it's more complex and involves weightier stakes, evaluating our ego/world theory requires a more multifaceted approach. But what we're seeking remains, at heart, a trial-and-error learn-by-doing approach.[4]

We can expect scholars of various kinds to weigh in on our theory, identifying its strengths and deficiencies. But expert critique has its limits. Experts sometimes succumb to groupthink or rely too uncritically on received wisdom. This may be especially true under the influence of the Taboo and our egos' other self-protective stratagems.

Moreover, we've been working out an alternative worldview—a new "paradigm" in the language of philosopher of science Thomas Kuhn in his seminal 1962 book, *The Structure of Scientific Revolutions*. When paradigms conflict, typically the proponents of each can point to inadequacies in the others. In such cases, the paradigm that prevails may not necessarily be truer—the criteria for ascertaining truth, such as whether it is legitimate to adopt a post-egoic perspective, can be part of what is being contested—but because it proves more useful.[5]

Assessing Our Theory Based on Its Usefulness

Our theory's explanatory power represents one kind of usefulness. But the theory will merit further approbation if it can inform actions that demonstrably improve people's lives. Easing distress, healing the world, making way for soul work, and so on. However, that poses a circularity dilemma: we need to undertake action steps to find out whether they were worth undertaking. One solution would be to focus at the outset on action-and-learning activities that are low cost and low risk. Using our earlier analogy, an example would be to boil up a few batches of spaghetti. That's low cost/low risk, especially if you were planning to eat spaghetti anyway.

When it comes to advancing psychospiritual development, the phenomenon of shared causes and convergent remedies ensures that there are many such low-risk/low-add-on-cost opportunities. For instance, it is well known that dislocation and deep inequalities contribute to a vast array of personal maladies, social woes, and macro-challenges. Hence remedying these structural conditions will result in enormous social benefit, independent of any improvement in psycho-spiritual self-realization.

Of course, there will be those who disagree. Some of them will be problem-deniers. Others will be mainstream problem-solvers who—even after devouring this book—judge the benefits accompanying dislocation and inequality to outweigh the social costs. But what matters is that there are already people and organizations hard at work pursuing structural transformations that can lessen the ills we've identified. Since they're already "making the spaghetti," there's little add-on cost or risk in tagging along to see what happens to psychospiritual development. The cost is low because *evaluating* a social initiative typically costs only a small fraction of what it costs to *undertake* it.

Research Questions and Methods

This is not to say that it will suffice to piggyback on the work of others. We also need to conduct research to refine concepts and measures of psychospiritual development and the social conditions that influence it. For instance, it would be helpful to discover if there are easily detectable markers, other than the prevalence of addiction, for drawing inferences about ego-identification and psychospiritual development across a population.[6]

At present we have no way of anticipating *how much* structural transformation must occur before psychospiritual benefits become discernible. But as new markers of psychospiritual growth are developed, it may become possible to ascertain that conditions favorable to psychospiritual growth are emerging based on leading-edge indicators, such as a drop in the incidence of mental illness or improvements in moral reasoning and caring.

Other examples of pertinent research questions include:

- What types of dislocation and inequality are most consequential for psychospiritual development?
- It will take social and techno-economic innovation to transform the ego/world system, but if it's too much, too fast, or the wrong kind it will compound dislocation. How can societies modulate innovation without exerting a heavy hand that inhibits innovations that are desirable?
- Returning to our sample action step: From the standpoint of supporting psychospiritual development, what is the right balance between local economic self-reliance and translocal economic interdependence?[7]

One type of research that can be low cost/low risk involves capitalizing on "natural experiments." Instead of undertaking scientifically controlled social experiments—which can be impractical or raise ethical concerns—compare societies as we find them to see if variations in the extent of dislocation, dis-integration, and hierarchy correlate with variations in psychospiritual development. For instance, how do dislocation and psychospiritual growth compare between Toulouse, Tallahassee, and Taipei?

One place to start is by seeking out communities and cultures that exhibit structural ecologies that our theory predicts might be favorable to psychospiritual growth. These can be societies from the past or present. For instance, there are more than two hundred Old Order Amish settlements in the United States and Canada; as of 2017, their population exceeded three hundred thousand. The Amish have long experience in innovating selectively to maintain stable community bonds, integrative practices (such as using horses for farm work and local transportation), and partially self-reliant economies within an encompassing sea of dislocation. What can we learn from them about how their practices influence mental health and psychospiritual development? Studies that have assessed their mental health have mostly been limited to the several dozen settlements in Lancaster County, Pennsylvania. But the findings are encouraging; they report markedly lower levels of anxiety, depression, bipolar disorder, and general mental distress among the Amish than in the surrounding non-Amish populations.[8]

Another type of natural experiment would compare structural ecologies and psychospiritual outcomes cross-nationally. For instance, compared with the United States, many Western European nations, especially in Scandinavia, have more extensive welfare-state protections, more equal access to higher education, less economic inequality, and sometimes more workplace democracy. Do Western Europeans experience somewhat less dislocation, even while integrated in the global market economy? If so, does that result in less-intensive ego-identification and better mental health? And is it possible that less intense ego-identification contributes to a virtuous cycle in which there is greater willingness to support welfare-state programs that mitigate the effects of dislocation? Epidemiologists have already discovered that disorders such as addiction, depression, and anxiety are more prevalent in English-speaking high-income nations—including the laissez-faire-oriented US and UK—than in high-income nations in continental Europe and Asia.[9]

Our theory doesn't lead us to expect that Amish or Scandinavian people would necessarily be highly evolved spiritually, but they might be less intensely egoic than people who live in more dislocated social worlds. We would also anticipate that when people who live in less dislocating circumstances engage in practices designed to support psychospiritual growth, they will tend to experience greater improvement than other populations who undertake the same practices. Natural experiments can be an effective way to test such predictions.

Who Will Do the Research?

In light of the Taboo against integrating a post-egoic perspective into scholarship, who might undertake the research needed to evaluate our theory or to translate it into societally transformative action? Or who might want to explore other ways of integrating post-egoic insights into research—for instance, by working to invent psychospiritually inclusive disciplines of history, economics, and public-policy analysis? Perhaps some of the tens if not hundreds of thousands of researchers worldwide who have felt constrained to honor a taboo that disrespects their spiritual identities and experiences. Thousands of these scholars are already networked via organizations such as the international Mind and Life Institute.[10]

For those tempted, there are additional draws: any who dare venture toward these forbidden trees of knowledge will find them laden with low-hanging fruit. Thanks to the Taboo, almost nobody's been picking in this garden for a long time. Also, as more researchers are emboldened to defy the Taboo, it will surely soften.

Learning and Social Change By, With, and For the People

Research by credentialed experts is needed, but it has limitations. One is that in certain respects *everyone* is an expert with a distinctive perspective and useful knowledge that is otherwise unobtainable. Research practices that integrate layperson and community wisdom go by such names as community-based participatory research (CBPR), participatory action research (PAR), and participatory technology assessment (pTA). Combining learning with social change, these methods can powerfully complement expert knowledge systems.[11]

For example, let's suppose that there are groups in your area trying to improve local economic self-reliance (as there probably are). Taking into consideration local values and circumstances, which approaches show the most promise? How can your community best combine and augment social-change initiatives so that there is overall movement toward a more soul-friendly local structural ecology?

Participatory research methods are perfect for addressing these kinds of questions. In the participatory action research model, community members and credentialed experts collaborate in undertaking community-driven social transformation; along the way they are learning together and strengthening community ties. The experts' assignment is to assist, not drive, the process. There are networks of practitioners engaged in CBPR, PAR, and pTA around the world. Expanding these into a more robust participatory-learning infrastructure is desirable for many reasons independent of psychospiritual development, and the expense can be covered with only a modest reallocation of existing research expenditures.[12]

For our purposes, some advantages of these research methods are:

- Community participation in framing and answering questions helps ensure that research serves community needs. Not shackled by the Taboo against a post-egoic perspective, lay participants can fortify the resolve of their expert collaborators to disregard it.
- Communities are repositories of common-sense, indigenous, local, and historical knowledges, all of which will be necessary to evolving structural ecologies adapted to local cultures and concerns.
- Participatory methods broaden access to knowledge-building, which is a self-realizing activity. Children and teens can join in during school hours or outside of the classroom.
- When it brings a diverse range of people together to understand and transform their own community, participatory action research *becomes* an integrative practice.
- When a PAR project is undertaken for other reasons—perhaps in order to uplift impoverished communities or to reduce greenhouse-gas emissions—within which evolving a soul-sustaining structural ecology is introduced as a supplementary consideration, then it satisfies a low-add-on cost/low-risk criterion.

BOOTSTRAPPING: CAN EGO-IDENTIFIED PEOPLE REACH SOUL-SUPPORTIVE DECISIONS?

Research can inform practical decisions, but only democratic deliberation can decide legitimately what to do in light of the knowledge at hand. However, our egos will predictably strive to subvert attempts to undo their sovereignty. Are there circumstances under which our souls might nonetheless gain an upper hand?[13]

Unmasking the ego/world system is one step in the soul's favor. We've also surmised that the strength of ego-identification can vary contextually. In the marketplace or within hierarchically structured settings, we may not be at our best. But perhaps we can extend the range of settings in which we do better.

Elevating Psychospiritual Performance

A citizen-deliberation process known as a "consensus conference" exemplifies the possibility of eliciting higher psychospiritual performance. Invented in Denmark in the 1980s, processes of this kind have now been used hundreds of times around the world, including dozens of times in the United States and on several occasions transnationally.

In the original Danish model, the first step was to assemble a panel of twelve to fifteen laypeople charged with the task of informing a contentious and complex parliamentary decision. The panelists were selected randomly to represent the Danish population and situated in a group educative process designed to offset initial knowledge disparities. Anyone with expertise or a direct stake in the pending decision was excluded from the panel. The panelists' deliberations were professionally facilitated to ensure that each person was comfortable speaking and that no one dominated. To protect against procedural bias, a steering committee composed of an ideologically balanced group of topic experts and stakeholder representatives oversaw all stages of project execution.

After participating in two preparatory weekends, the lay panelists took public testimony from competing experts and stakeholders for a day and then cross-examined them on the following day. Afterward the lay panelists deliberated privately for a third day, writing a report with their factual findings and policy recommendations that they delivered the next morning at a national press conference in the Danish Parliament building.[14]

A consensus conference offers decision-makers and the public a unique window into the informed views of everyday citizens. In 2011 the Oregon state legislature enacted a law stipulating that the final report from such a citizens' panel must be distributed to all voters before they head to the polls to decide statewide ballot initiatives. Independent evaluators have found that the process helpfully informs voter decisions and that its influence is increasing. The Oregon process has also been pilot-tested in Arizona, California, Colorado, and Massachusetts.[15]

Various design features distinguish a consensus conference from better-known forms of democratic deliberation, such as New England town meetings, committees of stakeholder representatives, or courtroom juries. And while a consensus-conference panel may reach conclusions that tilt ideologically in one direction or another, well-structured egalitarian deliberation has historically precluded ill-considered reactionary outcomes.[16]

A consensus conference embeds the affirming expectation that any citizen can contribute to complicated policy decisions. The participants are treated with respect and receive strong educational and procedural support, and their report is widely circulated. As a result, they tend to rise to the occasion. Well-structured democratic deliberative processes appear to elicit people's higher, more morally evolved personas.[17]

Beyond this boost to individuals' psychological performance, a consensus conference elicits high-quality *collective* judgment. Imagine a room with a balanced and diverse cross section of everyday people, contextually encouraged to be their most evolved selves and immersed in a neutrally facilitated process that reduces power and knowledge disparities. Under these circumstances, parochial or self-interested perspectives tend to offset one another. The group synthesizes them or puts them to the side, concentrating on points on which they find themselves able to reach some agreement. The judgments that emerge reflect a creative and mature representation of the common good.

I saw this in action as a co-organizer of the first US emulation of a Danish-style consensus conference in April 1997. The lay panel was drawn from the greater Boston area and asked to address the topic "Telecommunications and the Future of Democracy." Selected by random telephone calls and supplementary targeted recruitment to be broadly representative of the area's population, the panelists included an auto mechanic, the business manager of a high-tech firm, a retired teacher/farmer/nurse, and an industrial engineer. There was also an arts administrator, a recent inner-city high-school graduate, a consultant, an unemployed social worker, a writer/actress, and a homeless-shelter resident. Eight of the fifteen panelists were women, five were people of color, and the panelists' life stages ranged from teenager through elder.

After absorbing expert testimony, the lay panelists crafted a judicious public-interest agenda that transcended their immediate self-interest. For instance, among the expert and stakeholder perspectives that they heard were several parochial claims about how Boston or Massachusetts could capitalize on strategic advantages to compete economically against other regions. Yet although the panel was drawn exclusively from the greater Boston area, and never instructed by the organizers in the ethical perspective they should adopt, no portion of their concluding report was Boston-centric. They wrote, for example, that "As information goes global . . . the United States has a responsibility to set an example of integrity in content. We are concerned about maintaining a free flow of information while not taking advantage of other countries through exploitative commercialism."

Two decades before Russian agents created bogus social-media accounts to try to sway the 2016 US presidential election, and before the eruption of public outrage with corporate harvesting of online personal data, the Boston lay panelists wrote:

> We are concerned about misinformation on the
> Internet. . . . Data and information integrity is a ques-
> tion of reputation and "record" built up over time. We
> encourage the development of "seals of approval" for
> accurate and trustworthy Web sites. . . .
>
> Business interests, profit motives and market
> forces too often dictate public policy to the exclusion
> of the interests of the people. . . . The new technology
> creates an even greater risk of the abuse of power. . . .
> We believe there is a need for legislation to prevent
> access to an individual's private, personal data files
> and other computer data without prior approval by
> the individual.[18]

Is it conceivable that when a deliberative process evokes everyone's
best currently available self and balances out particularity, it accidentally allows an approximation of the transpersonal to shine through?
In effect, this would be an instance of non-enlightened people participating in a process that elicits relatively enlightened collective
judgments. That could be what is happening when a lay panel reaches
unexpectedly astute, morally informed policy judgments.[19]

The example of the consensus conference suggests that it's possible
to craft contexts in which the odds go up that a soul perspective can
prevail. Perfection in reaching decisions faithful to a soul perspective
is not necessary. If we get it right some of the time, that's better than
never. And each time we get it right, that improves the odds for doing
better the next time.[20]

THE PATH AHEAD

We've sketched basic elements in a low-add-on-cost, low-risk, trial-
and-error strategy for transforming the ego/world system into a more
soulful home for humans. The hope is that growing numbers of people will, in effect, embrace a new strategic stipulation in place of ego-
protective Mode C (see Chapter 14). Let's call it Mode S, with "S"
standing for "soul-friendly":

- **Mode S.** When addressing social ills or aspirations, favoring
  strategies that contribute to evolving an ecology of social structures that supports equal and ample opportunities for psychospiritual self-realization.

The Mode S stipulation addresses the limitation that today's strategies for social-structural transformation are only accidentally and

haphazardly oriented toward evolving a soul-friendly social order. In effect, the Mode S stipulation elaborates the Golden Rule to reflect an understanding of the evolutionary interdependence between social structures and trajectories of psychospiritual development. Moreover, in contrast to the fragmented analysis that is intrinsic to contemporary economic theory—in which, for example, externalities are assessed in isolation from one another—Mode S is holistic, considering how the totality of social activities produces structural results.

There are precedents that demonstrate that it is feasible to analyze and adjust structural ecologies. Contemporary societies already pull it off for advancing environmental, economic, national security, social justice, and other objectives. For instance, we have learned how to assess overall environmental quality and to adopt policies for improvement.

In the remainder of this chapter, we'll consider additional local-level action steps that are plausible candidates for Mode S trial-and-error testing. The objective is just to lay out some "for instances" suitable for consideration. The actions that we'll explore are skewed toward ones that organized groups are already pursuing for reasons of their own; this makes these actions relatively practicable. However, societies will certainly want to explore alternative routes to establishing soul-friendly structural ecologies.

But first a caveat. The following prescriptions do not derive from a judgment that consumption is inherently bad. Our complaint here is not with consumption per se, but with the disruption in psychospiritual development that can drive it and the harms that can result. Beyond that, we need to be concerned that consumption feeds back to perpetuate dislocation. This includes consumption over which we have little choice as individuals, such as product packaging or the need to own an automobile when public transportation is inaccessible.

Of course, there are sound *non*-psychospiritual reasons to be concerned about consumption, such as adverse environmental effects. But that wanders astray from our mission. Although, as we've noted, efforts to protect the environment and to support psychospiritual growth can often be complementary.

Reviving Local Community Life

Stable place-based communities are vital to psychospiritual development. As psychologist Robert Kegan puts it: "Serial communities are much in vogue these days, but we might consider at what price we elect them. Long-term relationships and life in a community of considerable duration may be essential . . . to the human coherence of our lives," including to knowing ourselves and being known by others in our fullness.[21]

Other social scientists have documented the heavy toll that thinned-out community relationships have taken on child development, family well-being, public health, and the viability of democratic governance.[22]

Those concerned with the erosion of community life have proposed many sensible remedies, such as boosting investment in civic and cultural organizations, combating suburban sprawl, enlivening public spaces, subsidizing affordable housing within affluent neighborhoods, reviving informal mutual-aid practices, and devolving power from national and state governments to localities (which is a good idea, so long as it's done without compromising social justice). Reclaiming land, social services, and certain business activities from privatization can contribute to community building, while also taking a step toward lessening the commodification of daily life. Proponents have called this "reclaiming the commons" in homage to popular resistance to the English land enclosures of earlier centuries.[23]

While the growth of the internet has fostered connection over huge distances, it is unlikely that online communities can substitute for loss of the old-fashioned kind. Symptoms of dislocation, including addictive relationships with our electronic devices, have continued to escalate during the years that use of the internet and mobile telecommunications devices has soared. In 2018 an average American adult spent more than eleven hours a day using electronic media. Silicon Valley entrepreneurs are among those who think we've gone too far in allowing electronic screens to take over our lives, and they're proving it by putting limits on their own children's access. One CEO told the *New York Times* that "On the scale between candy and crack cocaine," kids' screened devices are "closer to crack cocaine."[24]

Proposals for helping people untether from their devices are multiplying, although, so far, most attention is on adverse impacts to individuals rather than on communities and civil society. We need technical design modifications and social policies that can hold the presence of electronic media in our lives sufficiently in check that place-based social worlds are able to thrive. Theaters, cafés, and restaurants take a step in this direction when they restrict cell phone use.[25]

There is a rich modern history of experimenting with more communitarian and locally self-reliant ways of organizing social life. There are also strong countervailing social forces, such as the pressure to survive market competition and the corrosive effect of the device paradigm. The need to identify and skillfully navigate these contrary forces offers fertile ground for participatory action research.

Many people working to weave together stronger communities are doing so for reasons unrelated to psychospiritual development. Their agendas present another low-add-on-cost/low-risk opportunity for evaluating and advancing structural conditions favorable to psycho-spiritual growth.

Integrative Practices

A further promising antidote to ego-sovereignty would be to restore a healthier balance between devices and integrative practices. There are many conceivable approaches. Walking and bicycling are integrative activities. By encouraging co-location of residences, businesses, and cultural venues that are linked by safe, aesthetic walkways and bike paths, cities expand opportunities for people to exert their bodies and interact with one another in new ways. Other integrative activities include organizing community sports teams, community garden plots, baking bread or making yogurt at home, hunting and fishing, open-mic music and poetry gatherings, book clubs, and regularly scheduled block parties and neighborhood potluck meals.[26]

Moving toward a more diversified local economy creates opportunities for increasing reliance on integrative practices at work, including in craft production and the arts, compassionate caring for others, and low- and intermediate-mechanization agriculture and manufacturing. All these offer the potential to combine psychological and bodily intelligence, and to work in convivial collaboration with others.[27]

Artisanal work often involves working with hand tools and natural materials. The fruits of this labor can be tailored to the needs of those who will use them—people the craftsperson can know personally. This can counter a market economy's tendency toward transactional and commodified relationships, while increasing satisfaction, meaning, and dignity in work. Craft work persists in many economic domains, including parts of the construction trades, small-scale and sustainable farming, cooking, hairstyling, the arts, and custom clothing and furniture businesses. It could be extended to many more.[28]

Ideally, a more locally self-reliant economy would offer everyone opportunities to parcel a reasonably remunerated, humane-duration workweek flexibly between artisanal and other kinds of work. This work would be as integrative as is practicable and desired, with burdens, pleasures, and social responsibilities shared equitably. Work that is stultifying or over-arduous as a full-time occupation can be rewarding if it's part time and collaborative. With internet facilitation, scheduling challenges can become manageable. Career diversification would also provide protection against ever becoming fully unemployed.[29]

Work regimes of this sort will not come about through the grace of God or the magic of the marketplace, but only as a result of social policy. Today's struggling artists who barely get by driving long hours for Uber are not reasonably remunerated, working humane hours, or benefiting from the equitable sharing of burdens. One approach would be to add a surcharge—proportionate to their hidden social costs—to products and services that are produced non-integratively, using the proceeds to boost the income earned from integrative work practices and to subsidize the cost of their products.[30]

Absent such subsidy, integratively generated goods and services are typically more expensive than those mass produced, sometimes greatly so. But that is in large measure because we gauge "expense" without considering the soulfulness of the product and the production experience and the many social costs associated with a dislocating and dis-integrating global economy. Moreover, engaging in work that is soulful tends to create a taste for enjoying the fruits of others' soulful work, which can alter the composition of economic demand, incentivizing market reorganization and dynamics that are less ego-stabilizing. As Marx put it in one of his youthful Romantic moods, "Supposing that we had produced in a human manner. . . . In that case our products would be like so many mirrors out of which our essences shone."[31]

One indication that such ideas might resonate is that many people are not wildly enthusiastic about current work arrangements. According to a recent large-scale survey of the American workforce, only 38 percent of workers report that they are "very satisfied" with the meaningfulness of their jobs. Moreover, the COVID-19 pandemic has created unanticipated opportunities to creatively re-envision how work is organized.[32]

Crucially, integrative work of all kinds—"caring, craft, and cultural" occupations, in the elegant phrasing of economist Tim Jackson—exhibits *low* labor productivity. In conventional GDP-obsessed economic thought, that is a bad thing. But we can turn it around: Low labor productivity means that there must be more jobs in order to sustain comparable economic output. The result is that by transitioning toward more integrative practices, consumerism and GDP growth could decline without sacrificing employment (and, again, while improving the quality of work and life).[33]

There is no need to envision *eliminating* all devices. Rather, the concern is that psychospiritual growth suffers when we become over-reliant on devices and are thus insufficiently integrated with one another, stable communities, and the natural or spirit worlds.

Our theory proposes that integrative practices are vital in sustaining psychospiritual development. But they're great for other reasons too. Walking and bicycling are health-boosting and environmentally friendly. Many people enjoy craft work and gardening so much that they do them for fun in their spare time. As we learned in Chapter 7, Albert Borgmann contends that sacrificing some ease and convenience in return for integrative activity produces strong psychological and cultural satisfactions. To the extent that people experience immediate satisfactions when they pursue integrative activities, this presents another low-add-on-cost/low-risk opportunity for testing our theory of psychospiritual development.

By weaving people into deeper relations with one another and the natural world, integrative practices can potentially lead to recovering a sense of nature—including, possibly, all of the cosmos—as sacred. This can be another portal to softening ego boundaries. It could also nurture the emergence of new kinds of pluralistic spiritual cultures.[34]

The question of how far to go in replacing devices with integrative practices is partly a matter of personal preferences. But there are also social considerations. The device paradigm seduces us with convenience while concealing the full price, including faraway environmental harm and the dislocating shallowness of life in the foreground. Some devices, such as televisions and smartphones, lend themselves to addictive use. Sometimes devices insinuate themselves into our lives as necessities by eroding away integrative alternatives. The challenge for public policy is to determine when the harms that accompany the device paradigm rise to a level that warrants offsetting incentives in support of integrative practices.

Relocalizing Infrastructures

The device paradigm will weaken naturally if communities revive integrative practices and relocalize infrastructures in pursuit of greater local self-reliance. Localized infrastructures, such as community-scale renewable-energy and water-management systems, have the further advantage that they enhance opportunities for democratic self-governance, which can be favorable to psychospiritual self-realization.[35]

It is possible to relocalize infrastructures in ways that contribute to psychosocial reintegration to a greater or lesser extent. For instance, urban small-plot or rooftop gardens can build community cohesiveness and help reintegrate people experientially into the natural world and its rhythms. In contrast, high-tech, high-rise indoor farming under artificial lights is less psychosocially integrative. But compared with today's more remote, gigantic-scale agribusiness infrastructures, for-profit indoor farming can nonetheless secure certain psychospiritual benefits, such as greater opportunity for people to experience their interdependencies, as well as increased urban-area agricultural self-reliance.[36]

Transportation and telecommunications infrastructures intrinsically include a translocal function. From our perspective the challenge is to reform them so that advancing psychospiritual development rises in priority. That might mean ensuring that these infrastructures are:

- Locally owned and governed when that is practicable;

- Designed first and foremost to support intercultural under-standing, democratic self-determination, and other civic pur-poses; and
- Not a hindrance to place-based community life and the dem-ocratically desired degree of local and regional economic self-reliance.

As an example, well-designed public transit can often foster more extensive social interaction than reliance on private automobiles.

Limiting Hierarchy and Social Stratification

A certain amount of hierarchical organization is justified on admin-istrative efficiency grounds or in instances when hierarchy serves the developmental interest of subordinates, as in effective school settings. But sometimes hierarchy results in ego-inflation among leaders, orga-nizational pyramids that are perpetuated more for the benefit of elites than for efficiency, and reduced opportunity for creativity and self-determination among subordinates.[37]

Antidotes that can be implemented locally include flattening hier-archies when possible, rotating leadership, worker self-management, worker and community representation in organizational decision-making, and diffusing activities into fluidly evolving social and insti-tutional networks (provided that the latter are in some reasonable manner egalitarian and democratically coordinated, representative, and accountable). Organizations can also put more effort into selecting leaders who are not prone to ego-inflation and who will be attentive to the developmental needs of those affected by their decisions.[38]

Localities can in addition contribute to leveling opportunities for self-realization through progressive local taxation, robust social-support services, redressing injustice and discrimination, and provid-ing equality, breadth, and wholeness in educational opportunities.

Cosmopolitan Localism

Place-based community life is a virtue, but living too insularly can be stifling and compromise personal growth. Learning to see the world from a variety of perspectives is a core element in moral development. Parochialism can also impair learning and sharing that are beneficial to translocal political coordination, desirable economic and institu-tional innovation, intercultural understanding, and peace and security.

Today mass literacy, television, and movies make it difficult for anyone not to learn something about a wider world. Yet knowing "about" other places and cultures is not the same as experiential know-ing and developing bonds of affinity. Contemporary parochialism arises substantially from self-sorting, through which many of us gravitate to places and virtual worlds in which we rarely engage with people outside our cultural comfort zone. An obvious way that communities can counter this is by encouraging local cultural diversity and mutual respect and by creating opportunities for people of different backgrounds to develop personal relationships.[39]

Chapter 17

MAKING CIVILIZATION
SAFE FOR THE SOUL

Nonlocal action steps and concluding reflections

A virtue in the action steps that we have considered is that communities can get started on them now using resources at hand and without permission from distant power centers. But local initiatives won't suffice to counter all the macroforces that hinder psychospiritual development.

MACROSTEPS SUPPORTING
PSYCHOSPIRITUAL GROWTH

It would be naive to envision that macrolevel changes to diminish the sway of ego-sovereignty can be implemented quickly. It took several centuries to work our way into our psychosocial predicament, and it's unrealistic to imagine transforming our civilization positively except piecemeal over decades. Efforts at local transformation, besides being essential, can build social capacity for tackling macrolevel change.[1]

As in the case of local actions, translocal initiatives that might prove conducive to psychospiritual development are already being sought for other sound reasons. Hence, folding in psychospiritual development as a supplementary consideration can, once again, be a low-add-on-cost, low-risk proposition. We'll quickly consider a few illustrative examples.

Economic and Political Equality

Great inequality is ego-inflating to those favored, while stressful and disempowering to those disfavored. People of low income and no wealth, or who suffer discrimination, can be especially vulnerable to dislocation and have less opportunity for self-realization. Great inequality compromises democracy, which is needed to counter dislocation and represents an important terrain for self-actualization.

Mechanisms for reducing inequality are easy to specify and difficult to implement, in part because inequality empowers those who are favored to perpetuate their advantages. Of course, the favored are also susceptible to the ills that accompany ego-arrest, though people of great privilege may not be predisposed to see it that way. However, any softening in their resistance can only be helpful. Meanwhile, unmasking the ego/world system will tend to strengthen social movements pressing for greater equality.[2]

Examples of remedies include:

- Progressive taxes on income and wealth, using part of the proceeds to pay for health insurance, income support, and other social well-being services
- Strong legal support for trade unions and collective bargaining
- Robust restrictions on the influence of wealth in political campaigns and lobbying
- Corporate charter reform to require: managerial consideration of the common good (i.e., beyond merely advancing shareholder interests); worker and community representation on corporate boards of directors; or other measures in support of workplace democracy
- Expansion of antitrust law to consider adverse effects of corporate size on democracy and psychospiritual growth[3]

Receptivity to such ideas has grown dramatically in recent years in response to deeper awareness of the toll that inequality takes on the fabric of social life. Social safety nets and economic redistribution are complementary: people are more likely to accept some lowering of the economic ceiling when it is coupled with raising the floor.

Reforming Global Trade Systems

Many laws and policies have been optimized to facilitate global commerce. This boosts dislocation, subverts localized economies, and disrupts local cultures, thus deepening hindrances to psychospiritual growth.

The entire international trade and development regime—including the General Agreement on Tariffs and Trade, the North American Free Trade Agreement, the International Monetary Fund, and so on—needs to become democratically governed, including being insulated from corporate dominance, and reformed to preserve local economies. Instead of "free trade" we need mutually beneficial trade that is attentive to adverse repercussions of the ego/world system.[4]

Translocal internet commerce and national-chain and big-box store sales ought to be taxed sufficiently to protect local economies. Some of the revenue can be rebated to communities to subsidize the financial viability of integrative practices, vibrant public spaces and civic life, and other measures that are favorable to psychospiritual development.[5]

A tax on translocal advertising would reduce the commercial colonization of our lives while generating useful revenue. Taxes on internet commerce and advertising would additionally help rebalance cyberspace toward civic, research, and educational uses. That goal sounds fanciful—until we remember that the internet was largely restricted to these uses until the mid-1990s.[6]

World Peace and Relocalized Economies

Some peace researchers contend that international commerce builds mutual interests that reduce the likelihood of war. As Steven Pinker puts it, a government's power to initiate war is "constrained by stakeholders who control the means of production and who might oppose a disruption of international trade that's bad for business." Is there a tragic trade-off between local self-reliance—which is important to reducing dislocation—and world peace?[7]

Probably not.

First, it is possible to pursue local economic self-reliance without adopting national-level protectionist policies. The two are not tightly coupled and are often antithetical. Protectionism has frequently been integral to national modernization projects that included concerted efforts to undermine local economic self-reliance. And if executed clumsily, protectionism can also lead to retaliation, exacerbating dislocation. For instance, the Trump administration's willy-nilly imposition of tariffs on foreign goods quickly resulted in tit-for-tat tariffs on American goods, including by the European Union, Mexico, China, Russia, and Turkey.[8]

Second, we've recommended establishing a measure of economic self-reliance at the local level, but not absolute self-sufficiency. There will necessarily be an appreciable residue of translocal commerce, including international components.

Third, if international commerce can sometimes conduce to peace, it needn't take the form of contemporary trade regimes. Trade that is equitable, environmentally sustainable, democratically governed, and not unduly dislocating can contribute to peace regimes that place the broad human interest ahead of power and profit.[9]

Finally, peace can continue to be advanced by many means other than economic interdependence, including diplomacy, military deterrence, intercultural exchanges that build mutual understanding and trust, nonviolent civil resistance, and United Nations–style peacekeeping.[10]

Strong Democracy

Democratic practices falling into the domain that political theorist Benjamin Barber calls "strong democracy" have particular potential to support psychospiritual development. Strong democracy seeks equality among citizens in political influence and affords extensive opportunities for political participation.[11]

Strong democracy can function as a foundational mechanism for re-embedding the techno-economy in a way that fulfills modern ideals of social justice. Combining political equality with balance among multiple points of view, strong democracy is also an integrative practice that can elicit less egoic decisions and foster moral development. Danish-style consensus conferences (discussed in Chapter 16) are an example of strong democratic practice.

The practicability of extending popular democratic deliberation even into complex international issues has begun to be demonstrated via processes such as World Wide Views, developed by the nonprofit Danish Board of Technology Foundation. World Wide Views, described as "a global citizen consultation," recruits from fifty up to one hundred or more demographically representative citizens from a single nation to assemble on the same day as counterparts in many other nations. The groups deliberate on a pending global-policy issue and formulate judgments that inform international policymaking. For example, World Wide Views on Climate and Energy took place on June 6, 2015, in collaboration with the secretariat of the United Nations Framework Convention on Climate Change. More than ten thousand citizens participated at ninety-seven sites in seventy-six nations; afterward their views were presented to decision-makers involved in a series of international climate-policy negotiations. There are also promising examples of bottom-up approaches to global governance that cut across single issues, such as the annual World Social Forum gatherings and the Global Parliament of Mayors.[12]

Democratic theorists of many stripes favor the "subsidiarity principle," which says that political decision-making should be delegated down to the lowest level of governance competent to address an issue under consideration, subject to the constraint that there can be no violation of fundamental civil rights and liberties. That, again, is a way to ensure that decision processes are widely accessible and that their results are adapted to local concerns and not unduly dislocating, and in those ways support psychospiritual growth.[13]

Many of the limits to decentralizing decision-making are not inalterable facts of nature. For instance, translocal economic integration, large-scale background infrastructures, and far-ranging ecological impacts cannot be managed effectively from the local level. But these limiting conditions can also be modified or reversed. Our prior prescriptions for moving in the direction of relocalizing economies and reviving integrative practices can put meat back on the bones of subsidiarity.[14]

Automating jobs, including via robotics and artificial intelligence, exemplifies a process that, if left to the vagaries of market forces, can pose a challenge to strong democracy, unleashing massive new waves of job loss, exacerbating economic inequality, and extending the dis-integrative device paradigm. But there are also ways to imagine automation playing a constructive social role. An example might be encouraging innovation that eliminates jobs that are especially dangerous, while discouraging automation that displaces desirable integrative practices. There may also be a compelling social interest in relying on automation to make certain important goods and services—such as steel, medications, or solar panels—widely and affordably available. Economic policies can be crafted to encourage the judicious integration of automation into democratically managed local and regional firms rather than as a prop to multinational corporations.

Policy innovation will be needed to create a context in which localities can participate in making such choices. For instance, automated and robotic production could be taxed at a rate that suffices to keep it from foreclosing local opportunities to adopt integrative alternatives. This would amount to an extension of the taxes on translocal commerce that we considered earlier.[15]

Innovation in Mode S

Many of the action steps we've already discussed go far, implicitly, toward bringing technologies and organizational structures into compliance with Mode S. But this will also entail reorganizing and democratizing research systems in order to evolve technologies and organizational structures that are consistent with strong democracy and provide ample options for relocalization and integrative practice.[16]

Environmental Sustainability

Chapter 14 covered much of what needs to be said about environmental sustainability. Mainstream approaches to addressing environmental challenges most often rely on scientific and economic analysis to inform top-down government regulations or adjustments in market incentives (such as carbon taxes). Whether or not this approach to achieving sustainability can suffice—a point that some environmentalists dispute—it is psychospiritually problematic for several reasons:

- It leaves much of techno-economic dynamism intact, thus inadvertently sustaining the egoic emptiness that underlies modern consumerism and wealth accumulation.
- It shows no preference for local solutions over reliance on experientially remote infrastructures, such as nuclear power, agribusiness, and a heavily globalized market economy.
- It does little to reintegrate people experientially into nature, thus forfeiting a psychospiritually significant opportunity to recover a sense of belonging within an embracing totality—a totality that many non-dislocated cultures have experienced as sacred.[17]

This does not mean that there is no role for scientific inquiry, trans-local democratic governance, and modified market incentives within a sustainable, less intensely egoic future. It is encouraging that many structure-critical environmentalists believe that greater local economic self-reliance, place-based community life, and democratic subsidiarity—all of which appear psychospiritually promising—are also favorable to achieving sustainability. The most thorough of their analyses affirm that sustainable, low-growth or no-growth economies—as might result from pursuing more locally self-reliant and integrative practices or, in the longer term, from less intense cravings—can also be viable and fair.[18]

SOUL-SUSTAINING STRUCTURAL ECOLOGIES

Each of the actions that we have considered on psychospiritual grounds has other points in its favor. This reduces the risk and add-on cost of giving them a try. Conversely, if confidence in our theory grows, that will boost enthusiasm for steps that until now haven't built enough momentum to achieve strong liftoff.

Moreover, there is another way in which our overall strategy is low risk: history suggests that it is much easier to *limit the intensity* of ego-identification than to *stably transcend* it. After all, there have been many civilizations in which the depth of egoism—e.g., the intensity of craving—appears to have been low compared with that in modern times, but there has never been a society in which a great many people became enlightened. Fortunately, realizing the easier objective (softening ego-identification) promises immediate benefits (e.g., reducing discontent, anxiety, selfishness, and susceptibility to many illnesses), while *also* improving access to the post-egoic developmental range.

None of our proposed action steps are individually sufficient to fulfill the Mode S stipulation to "support equal and ample opportunities for psychospiritual development." For that to happen, a diverse set of steps must gradually coalesce into social settings that are no longer optimized to hold people frozen in intense ego-identification. This will typically entail screening initiatives to ensure that they are not soul-adverse and combining and augmenting them as needed to achieve soul-friendly structural ecologies. This screening would amount to a middle way between the premodern presumption that innovation is socially dangerous, and the modern presumption that innovation is inherently desirable . . . and that disruptive innovation is best of all.

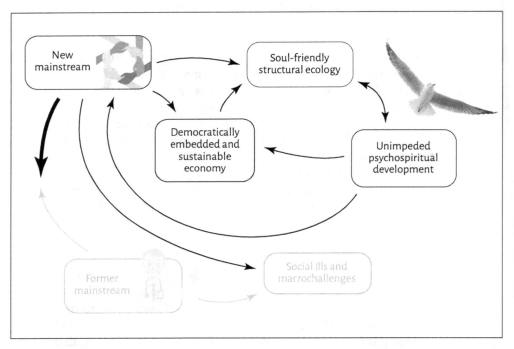

Figure 23. A Civilization Made Safe for the Soul. Figure 21 suggested how unmasking could improve the balance of forces between mainstream problem-solving and social movements for structural transformation. If the Mode S stipulation began to be fulfilled, the ego/world system would transform in the direction depicted symbolically in this diagram: efforts toward soul-friendly structural transformation morph into the new mainstream, the root causes of ego-arrest and many macrosocial ills (i.e., dislocation, dis-integration, and inequality) transmute into a Mode S–compliant structural ecology, macrochallenges become fewer and less intractable, and our psychospiritual growth is no longer structurally impeded (symbolized by the bird flying free). This depiction is not a prediction but an aspirational map, akin to the North Star in the nighttime sky that guided escaped Black slaves toward freedom.

This will involve social learning and democratic oversight, including the development of institutional capabilities for conducting Mode S assessments. There is precedent for this kind of evaluative process in broad-scope environmental-impact analyses and in government-sponsored technology assessments that incorporate participatory processes.[19]

We are not looking toward evolving any single "best" structural ecology. Many different complexes of social structures have shown themselves able to stabilize ego-sovereignty. By the same token, through experimentation people will discover diverse structural assemblages favorable to softening ego-identification. This will help techno-economic and institutional development become aligned with, rather than adverse to, psychospiritual development.

Even under ideal conditions, the odds are heavily against most people becoming enlightened sages. But we can evolve a world in which everyone has a chance to thrive beyond the tight, pathology-prone developmental confines that modernity has imposed (see Figure 23).

The notion that soul-friendly structural transformation might one day become mainstream may sound utterly fantastical . . . until you remember that it has happened before. Voting by women, equal rights for ethnic and racial minorities and people of diverse sexual identities, and environmental protection are all fringe ideas that went mainstream.

Spiritual Practice in an Age of Ego-Sovereignty

The opportunities for engaging in spiritual practice and other self-transformational activities have become vast in our time. Practices that were formerly inaccessible are now widely available. But ancient spiritual practices never anticipated a world custom-crafted to frustrate their efficacy. My expectation is that people who persevere will be more likely to progress once they are no longer striving against formidable counterforces.

Today contemplative practices are sometimes stripped of the ethical instruction that was originally integral to their purpose and efficacy. Our ancestors did not pursue these practices as physical exercise, to reduce stress and anxiety, or to sculpt more beautiful bodies. The objective was to advance psychospiritually. As is reflected in the *Mahabharata*, most traditional cultures concurred that ethical training is essential to psychospiritual self-realization, wisdom, and enhanced inclination to do good in the world.[20]

There are already many qualified spiritual teachers and millions of sincere students. Especially when the instruction encourages ethical social engagement, these practitioners can become a force for good, including soul-friendly structural transformation. But when spiritual practices are diluted or commercially corrupted so that they reinforce narcissistic self-involvement, both the practitioner and society are short-changed. Or when, for instance, corporations or the military introduce contemplative practices shorn of their ethical underpinning, there is danger of improving an organization's productivity while sidestepping ethical scrutiny of its methods and mission. Using meditation to become more serenely efficient at promoting consumerism, producing unhealthy processed foods, or deploying weapons that terrorize civilian populations is not progress.[21]

This concern is especially acute because the modern world differs from its predecessors in the extent to which people across the earth are interdependent, in our collective power to alter the world, and in how this power is distributed. It is more important than ever not only to reinstate the ethical component within spiritual practice but also to expand its scope geographically and temporally (i.e., commensurate with our interdependencies and influence) and qualitatively (i.e., to encompass Mode S). This includes among leaders, who for now hold disproportionate power to make—or to hinder others from making—a difference in the world and whose work environments often incentivize on-the-job moral regression. Spiritual seekers and teachers may also wish to consider expanding their ethical instruction and practice to include honoring the Mode S stipulation.

GETTING STARTED PERSONALLY

Are you inspired to do something practical? It shouldn't be hard to find a starting point that speaks to your situation and soul calling. Here are some possibilities:

Integrative Practice

Consider weaving some new integrative practices into your life—anything that deepens your involvement in community, nature, or the world of the sacred, or that facilitates integration of your body, mind, heart, and soul.

One goal might be to reduce your screen time. Life will get spacious. But if you're an addict like me, this will be a challenge, I know. Garden alone or communally, do some other work that involves your muscles or hands, play a team sport, take a yoga class, or bike to work with a friend or colleague. If you can, buy handmade or make things of your own. Barter and trade services. Learn to fix and repair. If circumstances permit and it's what you always secretly wanted, keep chickens or a goat, or heat your home with an eco-friendly woodstove using logs that you cut, split, or stack yourself. (I have some experience with heating by wood as an integrative practice: it works! I learned to handle an ax and splitting maul with skill. I felt closer to nature, I got to know neighbors who paused to chat as I worked outside, our family life and friendships deepened as we spent time together in front of the burning stove, and more.)[22]

I am not suggesting that we should forswear all devices. Try adopting one or two new integrative practices and see how it goes.

Other starting points can be oriented more toward social transformation:

- **Schmooze and Simmer.** Read and discuss this book with others. Be patient and see what unfolds.[23]
- **Social Action.** Look through the suggested action steps in this and the preceding chapter. Join an organization that is working on a step that you're drawn to. Over time, see if you can interest them in exploring how to adjust their agenda so that it is in better alignment with Mode S. Also, see if becoming attentive to psychospiritual development expands opportunities to recruit new members or build new alliances.
- **Engaged Spirituality.** Join a socially engaged religious or spiritual community. Again, be patient—but in time, see whether they might be receptive to tweaking their action agenda so that it is better aligned with Mode S.
- **Leadership.** If you happen to be a public intellectual, a recognized expert in your field of endeavor, or a leader in social-change activism or engaged spirituality, you may be well positioned to expand your mission to include fulfilling the Mode S stipulation.
- **Participatory Research.** Seek out a teacher at a nearby school or college who will join you in assembling a participatory action research project to evaluate some of the preceding kinds of initiatives from the standpoint of their implications for psychospiritual development.
- **Participatory or Post-egoic Research.** If you are a scholar or researcher, *be* the one that such a person finds. Or help evaluate or extend our theory. Or investigate how the ego/world system and egoic masking have affected research in your discipline or problem area. Get started on trying to work out what a post-egoic makeover of your research specialty might look like.

Receptivity to the Sacred

As you adopt new integrative practices or become involved in soul-friendly social action, you might want to be attentive to how your experience of life shifts. The wholeness that comes with deeper integration with other people and the natural world sometimes expands access to a sense of the sacred, nourishing the soul and supporting psychospiritual growth. If enough people awaken to this experience, it can inspire further action, establishing a virtuous cycle of personal and social transformation.[24]

Mode S as Karma Yoga

The *Bhagavad Gita* teaches that when we're not egoically attached to the outcome, our ethical actions become karma yoga. Seeking to fulfill the Mode S stipulation can fit the bill. When we integrate a commitment to advancing the Mode S stipulation into our lives, we are also engaged in our own soul work. This is especially so when we're doing it to help others and not only ourselves.[25]

QUESTIONS AND RESERVATIONS

Our inquiry has swept across a wide terrain, so let's briefly consider some potential concerns.

Personal Freedom?

Will a more democratically embedded economy destroy markets as a crucial domain of personal freedom? Our action proposals presume that there will still be competitive markets, and people will be able to take initiative and exercise choice within them. Yes, there will be societal oversight, as in some measure there is today. But there will be different market incentives, more democratically decided, and for better purposes than we've known.

On the other hand, the question may also betray a certain naivete concerning the current order. Our contemporary techno-economies are persistently dislocating, while according multinational corporations and people of great wealth disproportionate power to adjust the rules of the game to their purposes. In the case of the United States, look at who wins and who loses in the tax code, in international trade agreements, and in the aftermath of the 2008 global financial crisis. Across modern societies the distribution of actual freedom to influence our social circumstances is wildly unequal and meager for many.

In addition, the modern freedom of people across the socioeconomic spectrum to pursue "their" wants is exaggerated. The action steps that we have explored seek to support freedom from the limited autonomy intrinsic to strong ego-identification.

Modernity as Progress?

Related to the celebration of market freedom is the judgment of not a few that the experience of modernity has been overwhelmingly positive. For instance, some people celebrate the dizzying flux of modern life for delivering opportunities to escape constraining norms and identities. Political scientist Ronald Inglehart has amassed evidence showing that over the past several decades people who have grown up under conditions of modern economic affluence are more egalitarian, open to new ideas, tolerant of outgroups, and ecologically minded.[26]

But none of these perspectives consider our insights into the modern distortion of psychospiritual development. Our project is not to vilify modernity but to redress its shortcomings.

Inexorability?

Are modernization and global techno-economic dynamism inexorable and inalterable forces? *New York Times* columnist Thomas Friedman often writes this way, implying that our only options are to adapt artfully, resist futilely, or be steamrolled. Were this true, our project to heal modern civilization would be defeated from the start.[27]

But the premise is unsound. Human agency has altered the course of history from one evolutionary path to another time and again. Corporations fighting hard to adjust the terms of global trade to their advantage know this too. Our inquiry enlarges the scope for human agency by unmasking social dynamics that have—so long as they remained undetected—greatly diminished our power to comprehend and transform our circumstances . . . and ourselves.

Capitalism Versus Socialism?

Why has our critique of capitalism not led to a ringing endorsement of socialism? One answer is that the stark dichotomy between capitalism and socialism/communism stopped making sense a long time ago. There is no homogenous "capitalism" or "socialism." There are capitalisms, socialisms, hybrids, and political-economic options off that continuum. The capitalisms of contemporary France, Denmark, Brazil, India, and the United States are each different beasts. The communism of Stalin's Soviet Union has little in common with that of the economically vibrant Emilia-Romagna region of northern Italy or the caring and educative state of Kerala in southeastern India, or with the surprising hybridization of state communism and capitalism that has emerged in China.[28]

Moreover, the historical proposition that socialism is the only practical alternative to capitalism has been based on social-justice considerations that omit a fully fleshed-out psychospiritual critique. Seeking to support self-realization, we've proposed that societies need to become less incessantly disruptive and disease-inducing and more strongly democratic, egalitarian, relocalized, integrative, non-parochial, sustainable, and conducive to psychospiritual growth. So long as all those conditions are on their way to being fulfilled, it seems not so important whether the noun that follows is capitalism, socialism, communitarianism, or another term yet to be invented.

Killing the Goose That Lays Golden Eggs?

Will socially re-embedding the market destroy innovation, productivity, growth, and other important economic factors that contribute to well-being? As conventionally understood, none of these is necessarily a social good. Improved productivity or efficiency in stabilizing ego-arrest is not a good. Innovation that accelerates dislocation and dis-integration is not an unequivocal good. Our prescriptions aspire to incentivize innovation that sustains equal and ample opportunities for psychospiritual growth and that is, as a result, more conducive to overall well-being.

But if insatiability begins to diminish, won't people simply lose all motivation to innovate and be productive? This is an interesting question. We've seen that, historically, insatiability functioned as an essential stimulant to industrious effort, economic growth, and technological innovation. But now we are looking to transform the economy in a new direction that is less burdened with pathology and peril and that unshackles our psychospiritual potential. A techno-economy no longer optimized to sustain ego-sovereignty will deprioritize uber-disruptive and dis-integrative economic growth in favor of evolving a more just, sustainable, and soul-friendly civilization.

During the transition to such a world, insatiability will, of course, remain a force to be reckoned with. But action steps discussed earlier in Part III would begin to empower and incentivize people to work more soulfully than is typical today—that is, more creatively, joyously, purposefully, convivially, reverentially, or compassionately—serving the common good and flourishing. This kind of work orientation is not entirely hypothetical. Many of the world's most creative and morally exemplary people—including artists, inventors, healers, and peace-makers—have always been motivated in this way; they have led lives of deep meaning and purpose, and everyone has benefited.[29]

This would, in some measure, be moving toward what Keynes, writing in 1930, envisioned for humanity in 2030: a world in which "the economic problem" has been solved—everyone has the basic material necessities of life—and people can devote time to higher, even delightful purposes. (It's an entirely plausible scenario . . . but only, we now understand, if ego-identification softens so that "enough" is not an ever-receding goalpost. Inequality being what it is, today some of us truly need more, but many others can gain and give the most by needing to need less.) Our vision also aligns with that of economist Tim Jackson, who foresees a sustainable post-growth economy that is rich in "caring, craft, and cultural" occupations, and with the counsel of theologian Howard Thurman: "Don't ask what the world needs. Ask what makes you come alive, and go do it. Because what the world needs is people who have come alive."[30]

If this all sounds fanciful ("Real people aren't like that!"), pause and imagine yourself acting from egoic impulse ("I want! I need!"). Now, pause again, close your eyes, and think of fulfilling your soul's yearning.

Which feels more real and authentic?

We can evolve societies in which we assume the worst about ourselves (e.g., *Homo economicus*) or aspire to the best. Either can become a self-fulfilling prophecy, so which will we choose?

Economic Cost?

Can we afford it all? There's no way to predict the cost of achieving the type of structural ecologies that we have in mind. At the outset we don't even know what those ecologies are going to look like. And even if we did, conventional economic measures would be of little use, because they fail to take the interdependence of psychospiritual and techno-economic development into account.

However, even by conventional measures, we know that some of the actions that we envision will lower monetary costs. Reducing dislocation and inequality will lower the incidence of stress and mental and physical illness, with an accompanying reduction in healthcare costs. And any time that structural change is undertaken for non-psychospiritual reasons—such as to limit climate change or replace aging infrastructure—it can provide an opportunity, at little or no add-on cost, to include improved psychospiritual growth as one of the objectives.

Still, if structural change is undertaken unwisely or too abruptly, severe economic effects are possible, including harms visited upon groups that are already disadvantaged. Part of the purpose in proceeding gradually via trial-and-error learning is to ensure that structural change unfolds at an acceptable pace, fairly, and cost-effectively.

So can we afford to make our world friendlier to the soul? Perhaps the better question is: Can we afford not to?

LOOKING FORWARD

At the beginning of this book, I introduced our daughter, Lena, who around the time she turned six began posing difficult questions about why there is so much sorrow, unfairness, and meanness in the world. I wished I had answers. I wished even more that there was a way to help the world heal. But then one special spring evening Lena taught herself to see Earth from Venus, reminding me that sometimes a shift in perspective can open our eyes to new horizons of possibility.

The world that I envision will neither restore a mythic ideal past nor cast away everything that now exists. It will reestablish commendable features of some non-modern societies (notably, healthy integration within the realms of community, nature, and spirit), while still striving to fulfill high modern ideals (social justice, peace, democratic self-determination, and sustainability), and in those two ways opening space for new soul-friendly possibilities to emerge.

How likely is it that a world more hospitable to psychospiritual unfolding and less threatening to civilization will come into being? Given the ego/world's formidable capacity for self-preservation, under ordinary circumstances it would not be particularly likely.

But our circumstances are not ordinary.

For one thing, we have now exposed the protective cloak of invisibility in which Maya's Empire has wrapped itself for centuries. We understand as never before the high-stakes rigged game of dice that we have been seduced into playing . . . over and over again. This improves our odds of winning.

We also now know that if we perpetuate the macroforces that sustain the ego/world system, our civilization is going to continue down pathways of increasing stress and alienation, more unnecessary suffering from debilitating psychological and physical maladies, and deepening threats to the human prospect. And why? Only for the perverse purpose of blocking higher possibilities for human flourishing. This is a heads-we-all-lose, tails-nobody-wins wager.

As more people understand this, will they stand by and do nothing? Perhaps. But if we stand by, the world will not. The options are to either plot an escape from Maya's Empire or place bets on how long it will take before the ego/world collapses under the weight of its own increasing irrationality.

And even were we in no existential peril, evolving beyond the ego/world system would remain no less vital and urgent. There is no need for you, me, and billions of other people to experience suffering and stunting to the extent that we do. This is a tragedy overripe for remedy.

I began this book admitting to distress and perplexity about modern civilization. I remain distressed, but I've become less perplexed and more hopeful. Insatiably acquisitive and addicted Yudhishthira trapped in Maya's Palace—that's us. But it can be otherwise.

Epilogue

Chapter 18

A DOG AT HEAVEN'S GATE

The Pandavas' journey to wholeness

When we decrypted the *Mahabharata* in Part I, we focused on the saga's earliest books because they were the most useful for our purposes. Now it's time to tie up a few loose ends. In this final chapter, we will follow the Pandavas' journey to its end, deepening our understanding of the epic's developmental structure and meaning. This will also offer us a glimpse of psychospiritual possibilities that await us as we begin to work our way free from Maya's Empire. You might think of this as the dessert at the end of a feast.

IS THE *MAHABHARATA* SECRETLY A TANTRIC TEXT?

Look back at Figure 4 in Chapter 3, which models the *Mahabharata*'s subsurface structure as a double helix with a central column running up the center. Does the general form of that illustration strike any familiar chords? Consider Figure 24, which shows variants of images that you might see hanging on the wall in a modern yoga studio.

In Hinduism, spiritual awakening is sometimes represented as including the sequential activation of a series of psychic energy centers (chakras) that sit along a vertical line within the human body—elements in a system that is called the "subtle body." These chakras come alive when latent internal energy, known as kundalini, awakens at the base of the spine and travels upward along the spinal column. At the culmination of this process the uppermost chakra, located at the crown of the skull, may unfold—literally or metaphorically—in the form of a thousand-petaled lotus flower. In the words of a modern Indian guru, awakening the crown chakra "is the culmination of

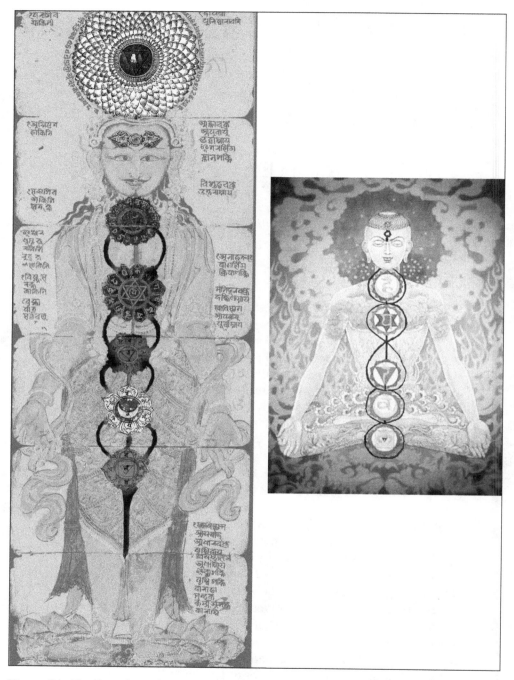

Figure 24. The Location of Major Chakras in the Human Body. The standing man is a seventeenth-century gouache painting from Nepal, depicting the major chakras (subtle energy centers) strung out along the body's core column and an ascending double helix of subtle energy channels. The seated man is a modern rendering of the same idea. (The standing man is from the collection of Prince Stanislas Klossowski de Rola and used with the Prince's permission. The seated man is used with the permission of the artist, Pieter Weltevrede.)

yoga, . . . total union and the unfolding of enlightenment." These ideas originated within an esoteric and often-secretive strain of Hinduism known as tantra.[1]

Both images in Figure 24 depict the path along which kundalini energy arises during a tantric spiritual awakening. Each figure shows seven chakras arrayed vertically and connected by three subtle energy channels—a central vertical channel and two adjacent serpentine channels. If we compare these images with Figure 4, it appears as though the *Mahabharata* exhibits an underlying structure corresponding to one traditional Hindu model of spiritual development. (While the reality of these phenomena is immaterial to our core argument, kundalini awakening is not simply a figment of the ancient tantric imagination. Thousands of modern Westerners have experienced kundalini awakenings, and the release of kundalini-type energy is known to other cultures. For instance, it bears resemblance to the upward flow of *n/um* energy described by the southern African Ju/'hoan people during their *!kia*-healing dance.)[2]

Could the visual similarity between Figures 4 and 24 be coincidental? Or might we even be imagining a patterning structure that isn't there? Yes, especially at first glance, either of those hypotheses is possible. The most obvious objection is that scholars are unaware of any written reference in Indian thought to a vertically ascending organization of the chakras prior to the eighth century AD, which is at least several centuries after the *Mahabharata*'s compilation in the form that we know it.[3]

On the other hand, spiritual ideas commonly circulated orally in antiquity long before being committed to writing (as, it is believed, did the *Mahabharata*). Thus the absence of preserved textual references to tantric concepts at the time of the *Mahabharata*'s composition is hardly proof that such ideas were unknown to the epic's authors. Besides, spiritual adepts—which the core authors seem clearly to have been—often experience or intuit phenomena out ahead of their culture's front edge. And because the *Mahabharata* became a foundational text in Indian civilization, it wouldn't be surprising if it correctly "anticipated" later ideas because it contributed to incubating them.

Moreover, it is a commonplace of many of the world's esoteric spiritual traditions, including medieval Hindu tantra, that there is a dynamic correspondence between the physiology of the human subtle body (the microcosm) and the spiritual structure of geographical landscapes or the entire cosmos (the macrocosm). In that respect, it is not startling to find an analogous micro/macro correspondence—in this case between the subtle body and the Pandavas' life story—encoded in the structure of the *Mahabharata*.[4]

Some modern Indian spiritual teachers contend, based on knowledge passed down orally through their religious lineages, that tantra traces back more than a millennium earlier than most scholars believe. Our structural decoding of the *Mahabharata* may represent textual evidence that supports this claim.[5]

WHY IS THE *BHAGAVAD GITA* PLACED IN *MAHABHARATA* BOOK 6?

Many scholars judge the *Bhagavad Gita* to be a relatively late addition to the *Mahabharata*, perhaps placed there during the first century AD. If so, why does this great revelation of Krishna's teachings appear in Book 6, immediately prior to the Kurukshetra War? It could as easily have been inserted elsewhere.[6]

The *Gita* has three major components: (a) Krishna's argument that Arjuna must fight to fulfill his duty as a warrior; (b) an introduction to three major spiritual paths (karma, bhakti, and jnana yoga); and (c) the disclosure of Krishna in his cosmic form. While it obviously makes sense to place component (a) just before the war, (b) and (c) might as reasonably have fit somewhere else in the story. For instance, long before—back in *Mahabharata* Book 3—Arjuna practiced arduous spiritual exercises and then lived for five years in the god Indra's heavenly palace. After all that, why on earth would he still need elementary spiritual teachings (component (b))?

But by bundling these three elements together, something further is being accomplished. For one thing, placing a dramatic spiritual dialogue just before the war is a tip-off that the impending battle— and perhaps by inference the entire *Mahabharata*—is an allegory of spiritual development. V. S. Sukthankar concurred in recognizing the *Gita* as "the real kernel of the Great Epic" and central in revealing the saga's allegorical meaning. "The *Gita* is in fact the heart's heart of the *Mahābhārata*."[7]

Still, if the *Gita* offers a key to interpreting the larger epic symbolically, why not offer this gift to readers at an earlier stage in the story? A tantric reading of the *Mahabharata* may provide an explanation.

Figure 4 depicts three logics that jointly encode the *Mahabharata*'s understanding of psychospiritual development: First, there is the surface story, through which, for instance, Arjuna undertakes intense spiritual exercises and acquires spiritual powers, while Yudhishthira is progressing morally. Second, there is the sequential awakening of subtle-body chakras (as encoded in the double-serpentine sequence of Apart and Together Stages). Finally, there is a progression through eighteen stages in psychospiritual self-realization.

These three logics inform one another. For instance, a deviation from the normal Apart/Together sequence alerted us to the possibility of developmental deviation during the Pandavas' residence in their new city of Indraprastha. But the three logics aren't tightly bound together temporally—each unfolds at its own pace over quite different time spans. The surface narrative stretches out over more than a dozen human generations. Chakra activation during a kundalini awakening can unfold over months, days, or even in a matter of seconds. The eighteen stages through which the soul reaches enlightenment typically extend over at least a decade but can also require a lifetime (as in Yudhishthira's case) or many human reincarnations.

Given these disparate timescales, naturally the three logics cannot roll out in temporal alignment. Together Stage 4, for example, doesn't take place in Book 4 but in Book 2. However, from a tantric perspective there *is* an instance in which these three logics fall into temporal alignment: exactly at the climactic moment of the *Bhagavad Gita*, when Krishna grants Arjuna the immortal eyesight needed to perceive the avatar in his cosmic form. This occurs at the beginning of the sixth Together Stage, which falls within the *Mahabharata*'s sixth book (again, see Figure 4).

Now let's turn to the surface narrative. Paramahansa Yogananda—a guru of considerable renown who played a key role in introducing Americans to Eastern spirituality in the 1920s—explains that to a *tantrika* (a practitioner of tantra), Krishna's gift of "immortal eyesight" represents the activation of a chakra that lies in the center of the forehead, as shown in Figure 24. Extant early tantric texts describe various numbers of chakras in the human body—five, six, seven, or even many more. Figure 4 suggests, however, that among all these possibilities, the *Mahabharata*'s core authors believed there were seven chakras (corresponding to the epic's seven Together Stages—the seventh occurring in Book 18, when Yudhishthira reencounters Duryodhana in heaven). Counting in that way, the forehead chakra would be the sixth.[8]

Thus, the *Bhagavad Gita*—a key to unlocking the epic's allegorical meaning—is positioned precisely where there is a temporal alignment: the *sixth* Together Stage (the commencement of the great war between the Pandavas and the Kauravas) occurs in the *Mahabharata*'s *sixth* book, which is also where the surface narrative describes the activation of Arjuna's *sixth* chakra. In structural terms, the *Bhagavad Gita*'s placement does not seem arbitrary.

That's not all. Adding together the numerical coordinates of this positioning (6 + 6 + 6) yields the *Mahabharata*'s favorite number: eighteen. Where better to situate the eighteen-chapter *Bhagavad Gita* within the eighteen-book *Mahabharata*'s story of eighteen armies battling for eighteen days? Lest this numerical wizardry sound far-fetched, historian of religion David Gordon White affirms that early Indian *tantrikas* were "obsessed" with the symbolic significance of numbers.[9]

Of course, all of this involves a certain measure of speculation on my part. Nonetheless, if—as is true in mathematics and the sciences—elegance counts in a theory's favor, then perhaps this explanation for the *Gita*'s positioning within the *Mahabharata* lends a bit more credence to our interpretation of the epic in terms of three interdependent developmental logics, one of which is transparently tantric.

WERE THE AUTHORS AWARE OF THEIR ACCOMPLISHMENT?

Did the *Mahabharata*'s composers understand the intricate structure encoded in their tale? It is hard to imagine that they didn't conceive the eighteen books to represent a progression in psychospiritual development. It also seems likely that they understood there to be a connection between a deviation in the Apart/Together pattern and a deviation in the Pandavas' characters. Overall, my suspicion is that having transcended the ego, the authors were likely to have experienced intuition as a steady bridge between their conscious and unconscious minds, enabling them to understand many complex matters intuitively without necessarily formulating them in explicit terms.

BUT WHY WERE THE *MAHABHARATA*'S DEEPER MEANINGS CONCEALED?

If the *Mahabharata*'s authors were aware of what they were doing, why didn't they make its deeper layers of meaning more accessible? One possibility is that spiritual texts are often circumspect in how much they wish to reveal to the uninitiated reader. Some spiritual traditions teach that intensive study of such texts can awaken spiritual powers that may prove counterproductive if bestowed upon someone not prepared to handle them. Think of Mickey Mouse in his comically disastrous debut as the sorcerer's apprentice in the 1940 Disney movie *Fantasia*.[10]

The surface story in a spiritual text may also be a diversion—a trick for slipping a hidden subtext past the ego's self-protective radar so that ego-subversive teachings can work upon the reader subconsciously. In this respect, the *Mahabharata* may have been written not merely to impart the *meaning* of subtle teachings, but to enable readers—through a kind of inner alchemy—to *experience the transformative power* of those teachings.[11]

Related to this, ancient spiritual texts were sometimes intended for use within living teacher-and-disciple communities. Deeper meanings were hidden so that a teacher could support students in making their own discoveries, transforming spiritually through their efforts. One indication that the *Mahabharata* is likely to have been used this way is that the story more or less says so. The initial nested recitation of the saga is presented not by its putative author, Vyasa, but—at his request—by his disciple Vaisampayana, who has studied the story closely under Vyasa's tutelage. Why would a great enlightened sage spend years teaching his most promising student to memorize and recite a vast epic unless the task was integral to a program of spiritual transformation?[12]

It is also possible that in times gone by at least a subset of the *Mahabharata*'s audiences would not have found its deeper meanings as difficult to intuit as we do. In our materialistic world it is natural to read Yudhishthira's ascent to the status of world emperor as a triumph. But for people living in ancient cultures that venerated spiritual development, it's conceivable that it would have been easier to catch the clues that the youthful Pandavas were experiencing ego-identification and -inflation.

There's another small textual clue that concealment of deeper truths was part of the authors' intent. The *Mahabharata* isn't widely celebrated as a bundle of laughs, but there may be a sly exception in the *Bhagavad Gita*. Krishna explains that the most accessible forms of yoga are bhakti (devotion) and karma (ethical action). In contrast, the path of jnana yoga (meditation and intense engagement with spiritual texts) demands more discipline and effort, and so it is for the few, not the many. The inside joke is that this admonition is conveyed within a popular epic that is likely also to have functioned secretly as a text for teachers and students of jnana yoga.

WHY ARE THERE THREE DEVELOPMENTAL LOGICS?

Some contemporary scientists of the mind have reached the conclusion that conventional objective research methods can never be sufficient, by themselves, to comprehend the mysteries of human consciousness. For instance, many subtle inner experiences are not detectable with scientific instruments. These scientists' solution is to integrate three complementary research modes: first-person experiential inquiry, second-person inquiry via dialogue, and conventional third-person (objective) research. Perhaps this offers a hint into what the *Mahabharata*'s three developmental logics represent in relation to the epic's psychospiritual mission:[13]

- **First Person:** The *Mahabharata*'s Apart/Together logic symbolizes what people experience when their chakras (subtle psychic energy centers that exist outside of the observable physical realm) are activated during a kundalini awakening. That is a first-person experiential perspective.

- **Second Person:** The *Mahabharata*'s surface narrative unfolds in the form of dialogues, representing an intersubjective second-person perspective in which one person (a "you") assists another's understanding. Dialogue is a way to learn to see from multiple perspectives, which plays a central role in moral development.

- **Third Person:** The *Mahabharata*'s eighteen books represent psychospiritual stages in the soul's awakening to its own true nature. In the ancient world, as in ours, trained outside observers can often detect developmental changes that are opaque to those experiencing them. That is a third-person objective perspective.

One might reasonably conjecture that the *Mahabharata*'s authors understood that spiritual development entails healing egoic fragmentation into wholeness. Integrating first-, second-, and third-person standpoints might have been one way to support spiritual students in achieving that wholeness.

WHY DO THE PANDAVAS DEVIATE ETHICALLY DURING THE WAR?

At several decisive moments during the Kurukshetra War, Krishna counsels the Pandavas to violate the conventional norms of warrior morality. In the most famous instance, he convinces Yudhishthira to demoralize the Kaurava commander, Drona, by telling the lie that Drona's son has died on the battlefield. Later, Krishna exhorts the Pandavas to dispatch Duryodhana with an unfair mace blow to the thigh (i.e., "below the belt").[14]

Readers often struggle to make sense of these breaches of ethical propriety. Did God incarnate on Earth for no higher purpose than weighing in, capriciously and ingloriously, on one side of an intratribal squabble? Or is the Kurukshetra War a metaphor for the decline of morality during humanity's degenerate Kali Yuga epoch? And for us: If the Pandavas backslide ethically on the battlefield, how is this consistent with interpreting the epic as a story of stages in psychospiritual self-realization?

If one reads the *Mahabharata* as a spiritual allegory, the explanation is not difficult. Krishna has incarnated to ensure that the soul succeeds in its developmental quest. Under ordinary circumstances and on the mundane plane, dharma can mean loyalty to kin and clan, performance of socially assigned obligations, or compliance with universal norms of ethical conduct. But the lesson of the Pandavas' supposed ethical lapses during the Kurukshetra War is that ultimately dharma is not a matter of complying with this or that conventional notion of morality. It is *knowing and doing the right thing.* Yudhishthira learns this lesson explicitly after the war, in Book 12.[15]

Under ordinary circumstances, conventional morality offers a reasonable approximation to the right worldly action. Complying assists us in behaving correctly and advancing psychospiritually. But on the inner terrain of the soul's struggle for liberation, the right action is that which is necessary to succeed. There the forces of egoism must be subdued. By this point the Pandavas know that Krishna is God, and Krishna has told them what they must do to win. In so doing, they are complying with Lord Krishna's final "most mysterious" teaching in the *Bhagavad Gita*, delivered immediately before the hostilities commence, that unconditional surrender to Krishna is beyond all the various conceptions of dharma:

> Listen to one more final word of mine that embodies the greatest mystery of all. . . . Keep your mind on me, honor me with your devotion and sacrifice, and you shall come to me. *Abandon all the Laws* [i.e., "all dharmas" (*sarvadharmān*)] and instead seek shelter with me alone. Be unconcerned, I shall set you free from all evils.[16]

This is not the cynical counsel to do whatever we find expedient. Nor is it a blanket instruction that the ends justify the means. It is saying that dharma means doing what is right, and in these few decisive moments on the inner terrain of developmental struggle, Krishna—arguably personifying supranormal intuition—has intervened to tell the Pandavas what that is.

HOW DOES THE JOURNEY END?

In the *Mahabharata*'s remaining books, any residual traces of egoism are worn down and the Pandavas gain true command of their kingdom (rather than the faux command of Book 2). Then they voluntarily renounce everything.

In keeping with its ascending spiral structure, prior episodes of the *Mahabharata* often repeat at a new, higher level of meaning. Near the end of the epic, a hunter accidentally slays Krishna (Book 16). Long before, during the dice match of Book 2, the Pandavas could no longer see Krishna because they had slipped into egoism. Now they can no longer see him because he has shed his mortal form. But a deeper message is that the Pandavas are at the threshold of transcending the dualism that allowed them to perceive Krishna as distinct from themselves. This time they can no longer see Krishna not because of a deficiency (i.e., their regression into egoism) but because they stand on the brink of knowing themselves as one with him (i.e., realizing their divinity).

Hindu mythology teaches that an avatar descends to earth when he's needed and departs when his task is complete. Here that's true, but with a twist. Throughout earlier portions of the *Mahabharata*, Krishna is there when the Pandavas need him, prodding them along their spiritual journey. Now he must die because otherwise he will become an obstruction. Up until this time the Pandavas' devotion to Krishna, a bhakti yoga practice, pulled them forward. Now it is the worldly attachment holding them back. Learning of Krishna's death, the Pandavas sink into despair. Soon after, counseled by the sage Vyasa, they renounce their kingdom and the world. Krishna's death is the acid that dissolves the emotional bonds that are holding the Pandavas back from liberation.

As the five brothers and Draupadi make their final ascent on foot up through the Himalayas toward Indra's heaven, one by one they become exhausted and die, until only Yudhishthira is left to enter heaven by himself.

At the conclusion of Book 2, Yudhishthira surmounted the illusion of false sovereignty. Now with the death of his brothers and wife in Book 17, he surmounts any remaining illusion of fragmentation and multiplicity. Coming on the heels of Krishna's death (literally—Krishna dies because of an arrow shot into his heel), this is a further stage in transcending dualism.[17]

Book 17, like Books 16 and 18, is abnormally succinct. Their voyage of spiritual development is nearly done. As the Pandavas set out on their final journey, a stray dog trails along. Many animals are revered in Hindu mythology—sacred cows and snakes, the elephant-headed Ganesh, the beloved monkey god Hanuman, and so on. But dogs receive little love. When I was living in Varanasi, most of the dogs I saw were emaciated and homeless, roaming through the streets and treated with disregard or, as commonly, with contempt or casual cruelty.

Nearing the gateway to heaven, Yudhishthira is greeted by Lord Indra, who tells him that he may enter, "But lose the dog." Out of compassion, Yudhishthira refuses. It would be wrong to abandon a helpless creature, even one as culturally impure as a dog. This is not a failure of renunciation. Yudhishthira has no long history with this dog; it is not "his" dog. It is merely a creature that will die if forsaken.[18]

During the Khandava fire, an ego-inflated Arjuna butchers thousands of innocent animals without hesitation. Now on the threshold of triumph, Yudhishthira is prepared to sacrifice the Pandavas' lifelong quest for liberation on behalf of a stray mutt.

Also apropos is one of the first episodes in Book 1 of the *Mahabharata*, which is set forward in time and introduces several grown great-grandsons of Arjuna who gratuitously abuse a stray dog. Reproached by the dog's mother for having failed to intervene, their brother, King Janamejaya, shows remorse. Janamejaya is also the person within the *Mahabharata* who hears the epic recited in the presence of its author, Vyasa. Contrasted with Yudhishthira's culminating readiness to sacrifice his liberation for the sake of a dog, the Pandavas' great-grandsons are not living in strong alignment with dharma (specifically with the dharmic duty of compassion). Yet Janamejaya's remorse and wish to know the *Mahabharata* indicate that throughout the epic we are witnessing the simultaneous spiritual education of *two* dharma kings: Yudhishthira, who lives the story, and his great-grandnephew Janamejaya, who learns by hearing it.

Krishna's death in *Mahabharata* Book 16 signals the Pandavas' impending transcendence of the bhakti path of devotion, which depends on maintaining a dualistic separation between oneself and God. Early in the *Bhagavad Gita*, Krishna also taught karma yoga—selfless ethical action without attachment to the results—as a path of liberation. Yudhishthira's readiness now to renounce even the fruits of renunciation signifies completion of the path of karma yoga.

Standing at the threshold of heaven, Yudhishthira refuses to forsake his canine fellow voyager. The dog wags his tail and transmutes into the God of Dharma, Yudhishthira's true father. This was a final test of Yudhishthira's selflessness and commitment to dharma, and he passes. He is able to enter heaven.

This episode is doubly noteworthy. It's a fine teaching in renunciation and compassion. But it can also be read as a teaching in tantra. Ordinary nondualistic Hinduism teaches that the world is illusory; only a person's soul—which is one with God—is real. Tantric philosophy differs in acknowledging the world as real. But there is, as in conventional nondual Hinduism, an illusion of separateness. The world is real, but it is not separate from divinity . . . nor are we. In this strand of tantra, God, people, and the world are one.[19]

And that is an essential point in the story of Yudhishthira and the dog. The conventionally despised hound merits—and from Yudhishthira receives—the same sacred regard as anything else. And in receiving that sacred regard, the dog reveals its divine form. Pure tantra.

Importantly, it is at this moment that the *Mahabharata*'s triple logics, by attaining their respective highest stages simultaneously, coincide temporally one more time—the only such instance after the *Bhagavad Gita*: upon entering heaven, Yudhishthira finds each of his

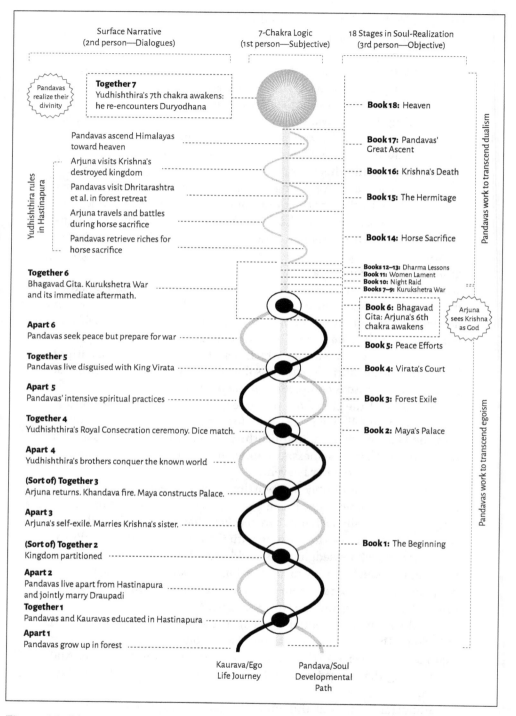

Surface Narrative
(2nd person—Dialogues)

7-Chakra Logic
(1st person—Subjective)

18 Stages in Soul-Realization
(3rd person—Objective)

Pandavas realize their divinity

Together 7
Yudhishthira's 7th chakra awakens: he re-encounters Duryodhana

Book 18: Heaven

Pandavas ascend Himalayas toward heaven

Book 17: Pandavas' Great Ascent

Arjuna visits Krishna's destroyed kingdom

Book 16: Krishna's Death

Yudhishthira rules in Hastinapura

Pandavas visit Dhritarashtra et al. in forest retreat

Book 15: The Hermitage

Arjuna travels and battles during horse sacrifice

Pandavas retrieve riches for horse sacrifice

Book 14: Horse Sacrifice

Together 6
Bhagavad Gita. Kurukshetra War and its immediate aftermath.

Books 12–13: Dharma Lessons
Book 11: Women Lament
Book 10: Night Raid
Books 7–9: Kurukshetra War

Book 6: Bhagavad Gita: Arjuna's 6th chakra awakens

Arjuna sees Krishna as God

Apart 6
Pandavas seek peace but prepare for war

Book 5: Peace Efforts

Together 5
Pandavas live disguised with King Virata

Book 4: Virata's Court

Apart 5
Pandavas' intensive spiritual practices

Book 3: Forest Exile

Together 4
Yudhishthira's Royal Consecration ceremony. Dice match.

Book 2: Maya's Palace

Apart 4
Yudhishthira's brothers conquer the known world

(Sort of) Together 3
Arjuna returns. Khandava fire. Maya constructs Palace.

Apart 3
Arjuna's self-exile. Marries Krishna's sister.

(Sort of) Together 2
Kingdom partitioned

Book 1: The Beginning

Apart 2
Pandavas live apart from Hastinapura and jointly marry Draupadi

Together 1
Pandavas and Kauravas educated in Hastinapura

Apart 1
Pandavas grow up in forest

Kaurava/Ego
Life Journey

Pandava/Soul
Developmental
Path

Pandavas work to transcend dualism

Pandavas work to transcend egoism

Figure 25. Diagramming the Entire *Mahabharata*'s Structure. This diagram integrates the *Mahabharata*'s three developmental logics. The seven points where the two counter-spirals intersect depict a kundalini ascent through the chakras. The central vertical column is demarcated into eighteen stages in psychospiritual development. Corresponding events in the surface narrative are indicated along the left side of the figure, as they were before in Figure 4.

The two moments when the three logics come into temporal alignment are noted inside sawtooth circles. For completeness, the figure also shows several additional, spiraling alternations between the Forest and the Pandavas' home base that occur after the Kurukshetra War. Because the heroes have destroyed their Kaurava enemies, there is no more Kaurava counterspiral. The upper half of Figure 25 shows that the Pandavas' spiritual growth depends on combat with the Kauravas, but only up to a point. Once the Kauravas are killed or subdued, many steps remain.

The far-right side of the figure also indicates that from birth through the end of the Kurukshetra War, the Pandavas are working to transcend egoism (Books 1–9). From then on, they are working to transcend fragmentation and dualism (Books 10–18).

brothers "blazing with his own effulgence," while Draupadi sits alight in "solar splendor." These images echo earlier passages in the epic in which we learn that, upon death, yoga practitioners "penetrate the orb of the sun"—a concept that scholars link, in turn, with contemporaneous Indian texts in which dying spiritual adepts raise their consciousness up along their subtle body's central channel and then out the crown of the head, "piercing through the solar orb" to reach "*the highest station*"—i.e., enlightenment. (In tantra, this corresponds to activating the uppermost chakra—the final phase in a classical kundalini awakening.)[20]

This is also the moment of the Pandavas' *final lifetime passage* into a Together Stage (i.e., Yudhishthira's final encounter with Duryodhana). And this occurs in the concluding book of the *Mahabharata*, representing the *culminating eighteenth stage* of psychospiritual self-realization.

There is an additional instructive dimension to the story of Yudhishthira and the dog. Throughout the *Mahabharata*, Yudhishthira wants to do the right thing, but often he's unsure what that is. Both before and after acting, he deliberates at length with his brothers and Draupadi, sage counselors, or Krishna. But at the end of the *Mahabharata*, as he is offered his opportunity to step into heaven as one of the gods, Yudhishthira stands alone before Lord Indra. Indra has told him to abandon the inconsequential and impure dog outside heaven's gate, and there is no one else Yudhishthira can ask for advice. And yet he does not hesitate. He knows the right thing to do and he does it. This is a new, culminating stage in his development: perfection in moral intuition. During the Kurukshetra War, the Pandavas deviate from conventional morality by doing what God *tells* them is the right thing to do. In Book 18 Yudhishthira does the right thing *despite* what God tells him to do.[21]

WHY DO THE THREE LOGICS CONVERGE TWICE?

Each of the two times that the three logics come into temporal alignment, the Pandavas know God *as God*, experientially. The first time is at the climactic moment of the *Bhagavad Gita*. Krishna has just been instructing Arjuna in bhakti yoga—the spiritual path of devotion. Now he reveals the full fruits of that path: a vision of divinity in its transcendent glory. This is the pinnacle of devotion, a dualistic experience. Arjuna knows and loves God as God. But he does not know his own divinity; he doesn't know himself as God.

The second time there is a triple alignment, Krishna, Draupadi, and the four younger Pandava brothers have died (Books 16 and 17). Yudhishthira stands on the threshold of transcending dualism and fragmentation. In Book 18, upon realizing his own divine nature, he enters heaven. Perhaps the logics converge twice to reveal those two ways of knowing God as God: dualistically and unitively (i.e., nondualistically). See Figure 25.

HOW IS IT POSSIBLE FOR THE THREE LOGICS TO COME INTO TEMPORAL ALIGNMENT?

The *Mahabharata*'s triple logics exhibit incommensurate timescales. But as we've noted, there are two exceptions when the logics do line up temporally. In both cases, the Pandavas know God as God, the first time dualistically and the second time unitively. What do enlightened sages and spiritual scriptures all say about knowing God or becoming enlightened? That there's an awakening into eternity or immortality. When there is illumination, time collapses. When the Pandavas know God as God, the three logics integrate as their temporal incommensurability dissolves into a timeless now.

MORAL POSSIBILITIES

The Pandavas' trajectory of moral development runs through successive stages of comprehending dharma. Their initial loyalty to family and clan gives way gradually to more encompassing duties as members of the social order of warriors (that is part of Krishna's instruction to Arjuna during the *Bhagavad Gita*). Then, during and following the Kurukshetra War, Yudhishthira learns when it can be appropriate to make exceptions to the strictures of dharma based on contextual considerations, is taught his ethical duties as a king, and explores universal ethical principles such as non-harming (ahimsa) and doing "good to all creatures." Finally, he passes beyond all formulations of dharma and their exceptions—as well as the direct instructions of God—demonstrating instinctively correct moral judgment.[22]

This developmental progression is close to that described in a strain of modern moral theory, according to which a "budding ethical expert would learn at least some of the ethics of his community by following strict rules, would then go on to apply contextual maxims, and, in the highest stage, would leave rules and principles behind and develop more and more refined spontaneous ethical responses."[23]

During the Kurukshetra War, after the Pandavas have come to know Krishna as God, they are evolved to the point where they are prepared even to accept this god's counsel to violate conventional morality. This is a high stage in moral and spiritual development, transcending conventional dualistic notions of good and evil. But the highest stage is when Yudhishthira can see moral truth directly—on the spot, without any taint of egoic self-interest or external assistance.

Long ago, trapped in Maya's Palace, Yudhishthira saw with Duryodhana's eyes. Now he can enter heaven as one of the gods because he sees with God's eyes.

Acknowledgments

Transdisciplinary research is not possible without the generosity of friends and colleagues who read draft versions and do what they can to pry one loose from embarrassing mistakes. The saints and saviors who read my entire manuscript at various stages include Frédérique Apffel-Marglin, Annie Cheatham, Colleen Dunlavy, Penny Gill, Renee Hill, Sally Kempton, Susan Lilly, Richard D. Mann, Richard P. Mendelson, Lee Paddy, Scott Schang, Jeff Scheuer, Jishnu Shankar, Jonathan Stevens, Peter Sterling, and Rick Worthington, as well as the late Oliver Hill and G. Michael Black.

I never had a chance to thank Michael Black in person. In June 2013, a drunk driver struck and killed him as he was walking beside a road in Santa Rosa, California. When I entered Michael's house some weeks after, I found an early draft of this book open on his desk with his comments handwritten in the margins. Thanks, old friend.

I'm also deeply grateful to those who lent a critical eye to selected chapters: Daniel Barbezat, Lindy Biggs, Lisa Bornstein, Clair Brown, Joshua Cohen, B. N. Goswamy, Gary Herrigel, Ramaswamy Iyengar, Vijaya Nagarajan, Richard Norgaard, Elissa Parker, Robert Roeser, and Lena Sclove. Special kudos to Gerald Friedman, who was generous in spotlighting many inaccuracies in my initial attempt to fathom mysteries of epidemiology and economic history.

For reading suggestions and substantive critique I also thank Hank Berry, Douglas Brooks, Jane Crosthwaite, Ted Dreyfus, Jay Garfield, Ronen Goffer, Ian Gold, Al Kaszniak, Marilyn Knight-Mendelson, Diana Lipton, Nik Luka, Anne McCants, Al Miller, Lynn Morgan, Fred Moseley, Ajit Murti, Lee Perlman, Baba Harihar Ramji, Mahip Rathore, Dean Robinson, Paul Roud, Marcie Sclove, Keshov Sharma, Pamela Smith, Ervin Staub, Jim Trostle, Jim Wald, Simon Warwick-Smith, Lucas Wilson, Roger Zim, and John Zorn.

I benefited greatly from the discussion during invited talks and seminars organized for me by Lee Perlman at MIT, Lynn Morgan at Mount Holyoke College, and Lisa Bornstein at McGill University.

I also had the good fortune to share the camaraderie of the online Reenchanting Scholarship and the World seminar.

Doubtless grave errors remain, but there would have been untold more but for the efforts of all these large-hearted souls.

Susan Lee Cohen of Riverside Literary Agency offered great wisdom in how to strengthen, structure, and style my argument. Karavelle Press assembled an outstanding team to bring this project to fruition: Dave Valencia, Katie Myers, Paul Barrett, Christina Henry de Tessan, and others at Girl Friday Productions assisted superbly in the arcane arts of production and marketing. Dan Crissman provided excellent editorial guidance, Mary Bellino proved herself a line editor and fact- and quote-checker extraordinaire, Elizabeth Cameron attended to the fine points of spelling and grammar, and Steve Kent and Rachel Aydt assisted skillfully and strategically with publicity.

Among the many others who assisted with acts of kindness are Teri Akin, Robert M. Alter, Andrew Bellak, Emily Benedek, Greg Bleier, Cynthia Brubaker, Swami Chidananda, Frank Darmstadt, Richie Davidson, Carolyn Douglas, Jamie Elkin, Deborah Frieze, Chellis Glendinning, Daniel Goleman, Glen Gollogly, Susan Griffin, Joel Gurin, Hazel Henderson, Carol Horton, Steve Howland, Ruthie Hunter, Jon Kabat-Zinn, Lynn Koerbel, David Korten, Fran Korten, Addie Lancaster, Melissa Lane, Aaron Lansky, Anna Lappé, Frances Moore Lappé, David M. Levy, Francis Levy, Linda Loewenthal, Jerry Mander, Nina Mankin, Jane Mayer, Stephanie Mills, Ajit Murti, Jacob Needleman, Mark Nickerson, Anne C. Petersen, Michael Peyser, Linda Roghaar, Howard Sapper, Michael Shuman, Rene Theberge, Susan Theberge, Dick Tofel, Diane Turner, Ani Tuzman, Bruce Wilcox, and Arthur Zajonc. David Patten deserves special mention for assuring me, as we chatted amiably outside a restaurant in Ubud, Bali, in 2003, that the *Mahabharata* is every bit as much a spiritual text as is its short *Bhagavad Gita* section.

I cherish our grown daughter Lena's astonishing integrity, wisdom, wit, and readiness to ponder with me the meaning of life (including on Venus). Lena has also taught me much about social justice and spirituality. My wife, Marcie Sclove, lived and breathed every stage of this project along with me. She helped me navigate thorny stages in the argument, advised me on how to say things more simply, supported me during periods of struggle and setback, held me in her wisdom, and showered me with love throughout the long, solitary journey from initial inspiration to printed page.

Writing this book has felt like striving to fulfill a kind of life assignment. It's a lucky thing to receive a life's assignment and luckier still to be able to complete it. I'm grateful for the alchemical adventure that unfolded.

Thank you. Thank you to one and all.

Guide to Important Sanskrit Words, Place Names, and *Mahabharata* Characters

Note: When Sanskrit is rendered in English, the letter *a* is pronounced "uh" (as in "cut"), while the letter *ā*, with a horizontal line, is pronounced "ah" (as in "cot"). When consonants such as *b*, *d*, or *k* are followed by an *h* (as in dharma), they are aspirated. If you put your hand in front of your mouth as you say the first syllable in dharma (i.e., *dhar-*), you should feel a puff of air against your hand. Stress marks (') indicate a syllable that receives emphasis when a word is pronounced.

SANSKRIT WORD OR PLACE
(PRONUNCIATION) MEANING

ahimsā (uh-him'-sah) nonviolence or non-harming

Bhagavad Gitā (bhug'-uh-vuhd-gee'-tah) celebrated spiritual discourse in the *Mahabharata*, Book 6

bhakti (bhuk'-tee) devotion

Brāhmin (brah'-min) Hinduism's priestly caste

chakras (chuh'-kruhz) spiritual energy centers in the body

dharma (dhar'-muh) moral duty and law

Hastināpura (huh-stee-nah'-pur-ruh) capital of the Kuru kingdom

Indraprastha (in-druh'-pruhs-tuh) capital of the Pandavas' Khandava Kingdom

jnāna (nyah'-nuh) wisdom

karma (kar'-muh) law of moral cause and effect

karma yoga (kar'-muh yoh'-guh) spiritual practice of detached ethical action in the world

Kurukshetra (koo-roo-kshay'-truh) site of *Mahabharata*'s great battle

Khāndava (khan'-duh-vuh) forest that becomes Pandavas' kingdom after partition

kundalini (koon-duh-lee'-nee) spiritual energy

Rājasuya (rah-juh-soo'-yuh) Royal Consecration ritual

Rakshasa (rock-shuh'-suh) man-eating giant

Mahābhārata (muh-hah-bhah'-ruh-tuh) monumental epic poem of ancient India

māyā (mah'-yah) illusion

tantra (tuhn-truh) esoteric strand within Hinduism

Vedas [adjective *Vedic*] (vay'-duhz) Hindu ritual texts that predate the *Mahabharata*'s composition

yoga (yoh'-guh) spiritual practice

MAHABHARATA CHARACTER (PRONUNCIATION) FAMILY POSITION

Agni (uhg'-nee) the fire god

Arjuna (ar'-juh-nuh) greatest warrior of the Pandavas

Bhima (bhi'-muh) strongest of the Pandava brothers

Bhishma (bhi'-shmuh) revered Kuru elder

Brahmā (bruh'-mah) the god of creation

Dhritarāshtra (dhri-tuh-rah'-shtruh) blind king, father of the Kauravas

Draupadi (drou'-puh-dee) joint wife of the five Pandavas

Drona (droh'-nuh) Pandavas' and Kauravas' teacher

Duryodhana (dur-yoh'-dhuh-nuh) leader of the Kauravas

Dushālā (doo-shah'-lah) sister of the one hundred Kaurava brothers

Indra (in'-druh) king of the gods

Janamejaya (jah-nuh-may'-jay-uh) a great-grandson of Arjuna

Jarāsamdha (juh-rah'-sum-dhuh) rival to Yudhishthira as King of Kings

Kauravas (kow'-ruh-vuhz) Pandavas' 101 cousins and rivals

Krishna (krish'-nuh) Pandavas' ally and God incarnate

Kurus (koo'-rooz) joint Pandava-Kaurava clan

Mayā (muh-yah') demon who builds Pandava palace after partition

Pāndavas (pahn'-duh-vuhz) five brothers—heroes of the *Mahabharata*

Shakuni (shah-koo'-nee) Kauravas' uncle, dicing trickster

Shishupāla (shih-shoo-pah'-luh) king who insults Krishna

Takshaka (tuhk'-shuh-kuh) snake of the Khandava Forest

Vidura (vih-duhr'-ruh) the Pandavas' benign uncle

Virāta (vih-rah'-tuh) king with whom Pandavas live during their thirteenth year of exile

Vyāsa (vyah'-suh) enlightened sage, Kurus' grandfather, and *Mahabharata* author

Yudhishthira (yoo-dhih'-shtih-ruh) eldest and leader of the Pandavas

Notes

When I cite a work more than once, I present it initially in complete form (author, full title, publisher, date, etc.) and subsequently in abbreviated form (author and shortened title only). The selected bibliography includes all the works that I cite more than once; you can use it to find complete citations without the need to search through prior endnotes.

CHAPTER 1: SEEING EARTH FROM VENUS

1   Joseph Campbell, *The Hero with a Thousand Faces*, Bollingen Series XVII, 3rd ed. (Novato, CA: New World Library, 2008), esp. pp. 196–205.

2   Bruno Bettelheim, *The Uses of Enchantment: The Meaning and Importance of Fairy Tales* (New York: Alfred A. Knopf, 1976).

3   John Brockington, *The Sanskrit Epics* (Leiden: Brill, 1998), p. 517.

4   Emerson quoted in Barbara Stoler Miller, trans., *The "Bhagavad-Gita": Krishna's Counsel in Time of War* (New York: Bantam, 1986), p. 147.

5   *The Writings of Henry David Thoreau*, vol. 2, *Walden* (Boston, 1897), p. 459.

6   Evan I. Schwartz, *Finding Oz: How L. Frank Baum Discovered the Great American Story* (Boston: Houghton Mifflin Harcourt, 2009), pp. 209–11, 232–41, 276, 280–82.

7   Shilpa Jamkhandikar, "'Avatar' May Be Subconsciously Linked to India – Cameron," 15 March 2010, https://in.reuters.com/article/bollywoodNews/idINIndia-46916320100315; Nyay Bhushan, "James Cameron Offers 3D Expertise to India," *Hollywood Reporter*, 11 Dec. 2010.

8   Recollection of lines from the *Bhagavad Gita*: Robert Jungk, *Brighter Than a Thousand Suns: A Personal History of the Atomic Scientists* (New York: Harcourt, Brace & World, 1958), p. 201.

9   James A. Hijiya, "The *Gita* of J. Robert Oppenheimer," *Proceedings of the American Philosophical Society*, vol. 144, no. 2 (June 2000),

pp. 123–67. After the war, Oppenheimer continued to feel justified in having directed the atomic bomb project, which the US government undertook out of fear that Nazi Germany might develop the bomb first. But he came to regret the destruction of Hiroshima and Nagasaki, especially when he learned to doubt their military necessity. See Kai Bird and Martin J. Sherwin, *American Prometheus: The Triumph and Tragedy of J. Robert Oppenheimer* (New York: Vintage, 2006), pp. 320, 324, 348–49, 389, 560, 578.

10   Asawin Suebsaeng, "Steve Bannon's Long Love Affair with War," *Daily Beast*, 31 Jan. 2017.

CHAPTER 2: THE WAR WITHIN

1   J. A. B. van Buitenen, trans. and ed., *The Bhagavadgītā in the Mahābhārata* (Chicago: Univ. of Chicago Press, 1981), pp. 71–123, 143; quote is from p. 115.

2   Summary based on J. A. B. van Buitenen, trans. and ed., *The Mahābhārata*, vol. 1, *Book 1: The Book of the Beginning* (Chicago: Univ. of Chicago Press, 1973); and *The Mahābhārata*, vol. 2, *Book 2: The Book of the Assembly Hall; Book 3: The Book of the Forest* (Chicago: Univ. of Chicago Press, 1975). Hereafter cited as van Buitenen, *MBh*, vol. 1 and *MBh*, vol. 2.

3   Van Buitenen, *Bhagavadgītā*, p. 123.

4   Juan Mascaro, trans., *The Bhagavad Gita: Translated from the Sanskrit with an Introduction* (Harmondsworth: Penguin, 1962), p. 22.

5   Quoted in Paul Friedrich, *The "Gita" Within Walden* (Albany: State Univ. of New York Press, 2008), p. 140.

6   For a summary of scholarly interpretations of the *Mahabharata*, see Brockington, *The Sanskrit Epics*, chaps. 3–5; Aditya Adarkar, "The 'Mahābhārata' and Its Universe: New Approaches to the All-Encompassing Epic," *History of Religions*, vol. 47, no. 4 (May 2008), pp. 304–19.

7   V. S. Sukthankar, *On the Meaning of the "Mahābhārata"* (Bombay: Asiatic Society of Bombay, 1957), pp. 100–101. On pp. 101–2 Sukthankar indicates that the *Gita*'s symbolic spiritual correspondences offer a key to unlocking the allegorical meaning of the entire *Mahabharata*. Julian Woods, in *Destiny and Human Initiative in the "Mahabharata" Destiny* (Albany: State Univ. of New York Press, 2001), is one modern scholar who has taken Sukthankar's interpretive suggestions seriously.

8   Adyashanti, a contemporary spiritual teacher, characterizes the post-egoic developmental range as the period of "spiritual awakening," which is "very different from having a mystical experience. Mystical experiences are beautiful. They are in many ways the highest and

most pleasurable experiences that a 'me' can have. . . . Mystical experiences can change the structure of the egoic self to a radical degree, and often in very positive ways. . . . But when we are talking about spiritual awakening, we are . . . talking about awakening *from* the 'me.'" From Adyashanti, *The End of Your World: Uncensored Straight Talk on the Nature of Enlightenment* (Boulder: Sounds True, 2010), pp. 18–19, emphasis in the original.

There is no established, uniform terminology for discussing such matters. For instance, while I will use "ego-transcendence" to refer to the post-egoic developmental range, others use the terms "ego-transcendence" or "self-transcendence" to refer to fleeting episodes of ego-dissolution or mystical transport that may occur while someone remains developmentally ego-identified. See, for example, Adam Hanley, Yoshio Nakamura, and Eric L. Garland, "The Nondual Awareness Dimensional Assessment (NADA): New Tools to Assess Nondual Traits and States of Consciousness Occurring Within and Beyond the Context of Meditation," *Psychological Assessment*, vol. 30, no. 12 (Dec. 2018), pp. 1625–39.

9   For an overview, see Harris L. Friedman and Glenn Hartelius eds., *The Wiley-Blackwell Handbook of Transpersonal Psychology* (Malden, MA: John Wiley & Sons, 2015). Some contemporary Western philosophers and cognitive scientists concur that the notion that people are psychologically distinct is oversimplified if not illusory: see Edwin Hutchins, "How a Cockpit Remembers Its Speed," *Cognitive Science*, vol. 19 (1995), pp. 265–88; Andy Clark and David Chalmers, "The Extended Mind," *Analysis*, vol. 58, no. 1 (Jan. 1998), pp. 7–19.

10 Modern scientists of consciousness often regard psychological boundedness and the related experience of subject/object dualism as essential to ego-identification. See, for example, Hanley et al., "The Nondual Awareness Dimensional Assessment," pp. 2, 15; Paul J. Mills, Christine Tara Petersen, Meredith A. Pung, et al., "Change in Sense of Nondual Awareness and Spiritual Awakening in Response to a Multidimensional Well-Being Program," *Journal of Alternative and Complementary Medicine*, vol. 24, no. 4 (April 2018), pp. 343–51.

11 Robert Coles, *The Spiritual Life of Children* (Boston: Houghton Mifflin, 1990); Lisa Miller, *The Spiritual Child: The New Science on Parenting for Health and Lifelong Thriving* (New York: St. Martin's Press, 2015).

CHAPTER 3: THE STORY BENEATH THE STORY

1   Aniela Jaffé, ed., *C. G. Jung: Word and Image*, Bollingen Series XCVII: 2 (Princeton: Princeton Univ. Press, 1979), pp. 227–29.

2   Sukthankar, *On the Meaning of the "Mahābhārata,"* pp. 109, 97; see also pp. 92–93, 98, 117.

3   Van Buitenen, *MBh*, vol. 1, pp. 300–01.

4   Van Buitenen, *MBh*, vol. 2, pp. 178.

5   There are psychodynamic and neuroscientific bases for interpreting partition in terms of flawed integration. See, for example, Miller, *Spiritual Child*, pp. 213–23, 266–67, 298–315; Iain McGilchrist, *The Master and His Emissary: The Divided Brain and the Making of the Western World* (New Haven: Yale Univ. Press, 2010).

6   Arjuna quote: van Buitenen, *MBh*, vol. 2, p. 77.

7   Carl Jung, M.-L. von Franz, and John Freeman, eds., *Man and His Symbols* (Garden City, NY: Doubleday and Company, 1964), pp. 177–95. It's not entirely fortuitous that the *Mahabharata* foreshadows Jungian ideas; Jung's theories reflect his deep study of ancient religious myths.

8   For a modern conceptualization of psychospiritual development along analogous twinned-spiral lines, see Michael Washburn, *The Ego and the Dynamic Ground: A Transpersonal Theory of Human Development*, 2nd ed. (Albany: State Univ. of New York, 1995), chap. 1. For a recent attempt to integrate the evolution of the soul into developmental psychology, see Elizabeth Marie Teklinski, "A Matter of Heart and Soul: Towards an Integral Psychology Framework for Postconventional Development" (PhD diss., California Institute of Integral Studies, 2016), https://pqdtopen.proquest.com/pubnum /10117900.html.

9   J. A. B. van Buitenen, trans. and ed., *The Mahābhārata*, Vol. 3, *Book 4: The Book of Virata; Book 5: The Book of the Effort* (Chicago: Univ. of Chicago Press, 1978), pp. 141–42. Hereafter cited as van Buitenen, *MBh*, vol. 3.

10   Daniel P. Brown, "The Stages of Meditation in Cross-Cultural Perspective," in *Transformations of Consciousness: Conventional and Contemplative Perspectives on Development*, by Ken Wilber, Jack Engler, Daniel P. Brown, et al. (Boston: Shambhala, 1986), pp. 219–82; quote is from pp. 223–24, emphasis added.

11   Common cultural well: Edwin F. Bryant, *The Yoga Sūtras of Patañjali: A New Edition, Translation, and Commentary* (New York: North Point Press, 2009), pp. xxiii–xxv. Brockington, *The Sanskrit Epics*, p. 2, notes that most *south* Indian manuscript versions of the *Mahabharata* are divided into 24 books. But he also observes (p. 155) that the *Mahabharata*'s final three short books were probably "treated as separate books only at a very late date, in order to produce the significant number 18 for the total of the books." This underscores that, for those versions of the *Mahabharata* that are divided into eighteen books, the number eighteen holds important symbolic significance. For discussion of the *Mahabharata*'s later books and

further evidence confirming that the saga's books correspond to developmental stages, see Chapter 18, below.

12 Ken Wilber, *Integral Psychology: Consciousness, Spirit, Psychology, Therapy* (Boston and London: Shambhala, 2000), pp. 209–11; Harris Friedman, Stanley Krippner, Linda Riebel, and Chad Johnson, "Transpersonal and Other Models of Spiritual Development," *International Journal of Transpersonal Studies*, vol. 29, no. 1 (2010), pp. 79–94.

CHAPTER 4: THE PALACE OF ILLUSION

1 Van Buitenen, *MBh*, vol. 2, pp. 39–54.

2 Van Buitenen, *MBh*, vol. 2, pp. 4–6, 11, 20–21, 27–30.

3 On the customary *rajasuya*, see Johannes Cornelis Heesterman, *The Ancient Indian Royal Consecration: The Rājasūya Described According to the Yajus Texts and Annotated* ('s—Gravenhage: Mouton & Co., 1957), pp. 142–57.

4 Brockington, *The Sanskrit Epics*, p. 245; Julian Woods, *Destiny and Human Initiative in the "Mahābhārata."* The notion that human behavior that *appears* to be causally determined (in this case, by Krishna) may coexist with a realm of freedom that operates beyond the domain of appearances was essential to Kant's philosophical project. See, for example, Immanuel Kant, "Preface to the Second Edition," in *Critique of Pure Reason*, trans. Norman Kemp Smith (New York: St Martin's Press, 1965), pp. 17–37. Chapter 18, below, suggests that rather than determining earthly outcomes for his own inscrutable reasons, Krishna has incarnated to support the Pandavas' moral and spiritual self-realization—in effect, their quest to *become* free.

Yet another interpretation of the dice match regards it as a ritual mechanism for redistributing wealth. See Brockington, *The Sanskrit Epics*, pp. 53, 187–88; J. C. Heesterman, *The Inner Conflict of Tradition: Essays in Indian Ritual, Kinship, and Society* (Chicago: Univ. of Chicago Press, 1985), pp. 148–49. But this, again, is not an entirely satisfactory explanation. Redistributing wealth is one thing but losing self-composure and wagering everything—even one's kingship and freedom—is something quite different.

5 Van Buitenen, *MBh*, vol. 2, pp. 287, emphasis in the original.

6 Van Buitenen, *MBh*, vol. 2, pp. 290–91. There are prior indications that Yudhishthira is acting under the sway of addiction and other base emotions, e.g., pp. 138–40, 145.

7 Adam W. Hanley and Eric L. Garland, "Mindfulness Training Disrupts Pavlovian Conditioning," *Physiology & Behavior*, vol. 204 (15 May 2019), pp. 151–54, present evidence pertinent to understanding

egoism as involving conditioned wants and automated responses. As Buddhists would put it, the ego or "I" is "only a combination of ever-changing physical and mental forces or energies" (Walpola Rahula, *What the Buddha Taught*, rev. ed. [New York: Grove Press, 1974], p. 20).

8   Immanuel Kant, *Foundations of the Metaphysics of Morals*, trans. Lewis White Beck (Indianapolis: Bobbs-Merrill, 1959).

9   See also Alasdair MacIntyre, *After Virtue* (Notre Dame: Univ. of Notre Dame Press, 1981), chaps. 5, 12–18.

10   On emptiness and lack, see David R. Loy, *A Buddhist History of the West: Studies in Lack* (Albany: State Univ. of New York Press, 2002). Regarding modern scientific studies of some of the personal and social benefits of ego-dissolution, see Raphaël Millière, Robin L. Carhart-Harris, Leor Roseman, et al., "Psychedelics, Meditation, and Self-Consciousness," *Frontiers in Psychology*, vol. 9 (Sept. 2018), article no. 1475, esp. pp. 19–21. On post-egoic intuitive knowing see, for example, Arthur J. Deikman, *The Observing Self: Mysticism and Psychotherapy* (Boston: Beacon Press, 1982), chap. 5.

11   Thich Nhat Hanh, *No Death, No Fear* (New York: Riverhead Books, 2002), pp. 12–13.

12   The Pandavas are intellectually aware of Krishna's divinity by Book 3 (see van Buitenen, *MBh*, vol. 2, pp. 246–49), but this knowledge only becomes certain and experiential later, during the *Bhagavad Gita*. For instance, in Book 3 Draupadi casts doubt on Krishna's omnipotence based on his failure to prevent her humiliation during the dice match.

13   Van Buitenen, *MBh*, vol. 1, pp. 417–18.

14   Van Buitenen, *MBh*, vol. 2, p. 26; Bhishma quote is from p. 95.

15   Van Buitenen, *MBh*, vol. 2, p. 155, emphasis added.

CHAPTER 5: MAYA'S ARTS OF DECEPTION

1   Deborah Layton, *Seductive Poison: A Jonestown Survivor's Story of Life and Death in the People's Temple* (New York: Anchor Books, 1999).

2   Phebe Cramer, *Protecting the Self: Defense Mechanisms in Action* (New York: Guilford Press, 2006).

3   Idries Shah, *World Tales* (New York and London: Harcourt Brace Jovanovich, 1979), pp. 254–57. Shah hints elsewhere that he interpreted the story as an allegory of the ego's faux sovereignty: "It is not always a question of the Emperor having no clothes on. Sometimes it is, 'Is that an Emperor at all?'" Idries Shah, *Reflections*, 2nd ed. (London: Octagon, 1969), p. 146. Versions of this fable have circulated in many cultures. Shah's version is based on a fourteenth-

century Spanish telling of the tale (which is based, in turn, on the Moorish version): Prince Don Juan Manuel, *Count Lucanor; or, The Fifty Pleasant Stories of Patronio*, trans. James York (New York and London, 1889), pp. 52–58.

4   The quote is from Shah, *World Tales*, p. 256.

5   Van Buitenen, *MBh*, vol. 2, pp. 91–104; quotes are from pp. 103–4.

6   Van Buitenen, *MBh*, vol. 2, pp. 35–39, 52–60; quote is from p. 39. Later, Krishna, too, approves Yudhishthira's imperial aspirations. But this is Krishna as perceived by an egoic Yudhishthira. We know because here Krishna—unlike an omnipotent avatar—purports to live in fear of a human king, Jarasamdha, who has driven Krishna from his homeland.

7   Van Buitenen, *MBh*, vol. 2, p. 6, emphasis in the original.

8   Alf Hiltebeitel, *Rethinking the "Mahābhārata": A Reader's Guide to the Education of the Dharma King* (Chicago: Univ. of Chicago Press, 2001), pp. 92–104.

9   On nuanced differences in adult versus child psychology see, for example, Alison Gopnik, *The Philosophical Baby: What Children's Minds Tell Us About Truth, Love, and the Meaning of Life* (New York: Farrar, Straus and Giroux, 2009).

10   Wilber, *Integral Psychology*, p. 18 and see also p. 98; Chellis Glendinning, *My Name Is Chellis and I'm in Recovery from Western Civilization* (Gabriola Island: New Catalyst Books, 1994), p. 5.

11   Robert Kegan, "Epistemology, Fourth Order Consciousness, and the Subject-Object Relationship," *What Is Enlightenment?*, no. 22 (Fall/Winter, 2002), pp. 143–54, emphasis in the original; James Côté, *Arrested Adulthood: The Changing Nature of Maturity and Identity* (New York: New York Univ. Press, 2000).

12   Washburn, *Ego and the Dynamic Ground*, p. 117, emphasis in the original.

13   Brown, "Stages of Meditation," p. 271. I am familiar with Brown's more recent thought through an interview that I conducted with him on Jan. 6, 2012. See also Brown's "Pointing Out the Great Way" website, https://pointingoutway.org/meditations; and the transcript of an interview he gave on May 20, 2020, https://deconstructingyourself.com/awakening-and-the-path-of-liberation-full-transcript.html. Enlightenment is not the only conceivable ideal culmination to psychospiritual self-realization; see, for example, Christopher M. Bache's musings concerning collective awakening and cosmic evolution in *LSD and the Mind of the Universe: Diamonds from Heaven* (Rochester: Park Street Press, 2019), pp. 21, 75–76, 135–41, 194–95, 201, 256.

14   Michael Lifshitz, Michiel van Elk, and T. C. Luhrmann, "Absorption and Spiritual Experience: A Review of Evidence and Potential

Mechanisms," *Consciousness and Cognition*, vol. 73 (Aug. 2019), article no. 102760, p. 1.

CHAPTER 6: A PROCESSION OF ADDICTS

1   Bruce K. Alexander, *The Globalization of Addiction: A Study in Poverty of the Spirit* (Oxford: Oxford Univ. Press, 2008). Statistics drawn or calculated from: Rose A. Rudd, Puja Seth, Felicita David, and Lawrence Scholl, "Increases in Drug and Opioid-Involved Overdose Deaths – United States, 2010–2015," *Morbidity and Mortality Weekly Report*, vol. 65, nos. 50–51 (30 Dec. 2016), pp. 1445–52; Josh Katz, "Drug Deaths in America Are Rising Faster Than Ever," *New York Times*, 5 June 2017; F. B. Ahmad, L. M. Rosen, and P. Sutton, "Provisional Drug Overdose Death Counts," National Center for Health Statistics, 2021, https://www.cdc.gov/nchs/nvss/vsrr/drug-overdose-data.htm; "Overdose Death Rates," National Institute on Drug Abuse, 10 March 2020, https://www.drugabuse.gov/related-topics/trends-statistics/overdose-death-rates; Harvey A. Whiteford, Louisa Degenhardt, Jürgen Rehm, et al., "Global Burden of Disease Attributable to Mental and Substance Use Disorders: Findings from the Global Burden of Disease Study 2010," *Lancet*, vol. 382, no. 9904 (9 Nov. 2013), pp. 1575–86, esp. p. 1582.

2   National Institute on Drug Abuse, "Trends & Statistics," https://www.drugabuse.gov/related-topics/trends-statistics (accessed 22 Aug. 2016); Council of Economic Advisers, *The Underestimated Cost of the Opioid Crisis*, Nov. 2017, https://www.hsdl.org/?view&did=806029.

3   Alexander, *Globalization of Addiction*, e.g., chap. 10 and pp. 1, 12; Steve Sussman, Nadra Lisha, and Mark Griffiths, "Prevalence of the Addictions: A Problem of the Majority or the Minority?," *Evaluation & the Health Professions*, vol. 34, no. 1 (March 2011), pp. 3–56; Gabor Maté, *In the Realm of Hungry Ghosts: Close Encounters with Addiction* (Berkeley: North Atlantic Books, 2010), p. 414.

4   Maté, *In the Realm of Hungry Ghosts*, pp. 142, 146–47.

5   Alexander, *Globalization of Addiction*, pp. 62–63, emphasis in the original.

6   On chronic versus traumatic stress: Peggy A. Thoits, "Stress and Health: Major Findings and Policy Implications," *Journal of Health and Social Behavior*, vol. 51, no. 1 supplement (Nov. 2010), pp. S41–S53, esp. p. S43.

7   Alexander, *Globalization of Addiction*, pp. 64, 205. Quote is from Bruce K. Alexander, "The Roots of Addiction in Free Market Society" (unpublished manuscript; Vancouver: Canadian Center for Policy

Alternatives, April 2001), http://www.brucekalexander.com/pdf/roots_addiction_2001.pdf, pp. 13–14.

8   Alexander, *Globalization of Addiction*, pp. 62, 141–43.

9   Alexander, *Globalization of Addiction*, p. 67. See also Urie Bronfenbrenner, *The Ecology of Human Development: Experiments by Nature and Design* (Cambridge: Harvard Univ. Press, 1979), pp. 266–75.

10   Alexander, *Globalization of Addiction*, pp. 65, 92; Erik H. Erikson, *Childhood and Society* (New York: W. W. Norton, 1986), pp. 61, 80–84, 93–94, 238, 248–49, 252, 257, 260–63.

11   Erik H. Erikson, "Growth and Crises of the Healthy Personality" (1950), in *Identity and the Life Cycle* (New York: W. W. Norton, 1980), pp. 64–65; Robert A. Zucker, Brian M. Hicks, and Mary M. Heitzeg, "Alcohol Use and the Alcohol Use Disorders Over the Life Course: A Cross-Level Developmental Review" in *Developmental Psychopathology*, vol. 3, *Maladaptation and Psychopathology*, ed. Dante Cicchetti, 3rd ed. (Hoboken: John Wiley & Sons, 2016), pp. 793–832.

12   E.g., Côté, *Arrested Adulthood*; Bronfenbrenner, *Ecology of Human Development*, pp. 272–75; Urie Bronfenbrenner, Peter McClelland, Elaine Wethington, et al., *The State of Americans: This Generation and the Next* (New York: The Free Press, 1996); Robert H. Bradley and Robert F. Corwyn, "Socioeconomic Status and Child Development," *Annual Review of Psychology*, vol. 53 (Feb. 2002), pp. 371–99; Sally Grantham-McGregor, Yin Bun Cheung, Santiago Cueto, et al., "Developmental Potential in the First 5 Years for Children in Developing Countries," *Lancet*, vol. 369, no. 9555 (6–12 Jan. 2007), pp. 60–70; Robert Kegan, *The Evolving Self: Problem and Process in Human Development* (Cambridge: Harvard Univ. Press, 1982), e.g., p. 116; Maté, *In the Realm of Hungry Ghosts*, part 4.

13   For modern psychological hints that addiction is often symptomatic of a failure to develop past strong ego-identification see Miller, *Spiritual Child*, pp. 3, 37–38, 43, 58–59, 71–78, 208–09, 221, 226–30, 308–15, 318.

14   Regarding evidence for the reality of post-egoism: There are many self-reports and qualitative observational reports about those who are believed to have stably transcended ego-identification or attained enlightenment. For scientific evidence see, for example, Jake H. Davis and David R. Vago, "Can Enlightenment Be Traced to Specific Neural Correlates, Cognition, or Behavior? No, and (a Qualified) Yes," *Frontiers in Psychology*, vol. 4 (Nov. 2013), article no. 870; Ulf Winter, Pierre LeVan, Tilmann L. Borghardt, et al., "Content-Free Awareness: EEG-fcMRI Correlates of Consciousness *as Such* in an Expert Meditator," *Frontiers in Psychology*, vol. 10 (Feb. 2020), article no. 3064. However, personally, I don't find the attainment of content-free

mental awareness the most significant aspect of enlightenment. I am more interested in the transcendence of suffering, becoming selflessly compassionate and dedicated to helping others or society as a whole, and developing an enhanced intuitive ability to know how to help.

15   Psychologists have debated the possibility of specifying—or, for that matter, of *not* specifying—an ideal direction or endpoint for development. See, for example, Urie Bronfenbrenner, Frank Kessel, William Kessen, and Sheldon White, "Toward a Critical Social History of Developmental Psychology," *American Psychologist*, vol. 41, no. 11 (Nov. 1986), pp. 1218–30; Barbara Rogoff, *The Cultural Nature of Human Development* (Oxford: Oxford Univ. Press, 2003), pp. 18–24.

Throughout this book I will use terms such as developmental "impairment," "distortion," and "disruption" interchangeably in order to denote developmental trends that cause unnecessary suffering or that interfere with people's ability to flourish. My assumptions are that it is desirable to: (a) suffer less; (b) become less psychologically constrained in how we want to direct our energies and realize our potentials; and also (c) understand more about our history and our social circumstances. Throughout Part II we will be exploring whether post-egoic insights into psychological development can advance objective (c). If this strategy proves successful that will, in turn, enhance the plausibility of post-egoic insights more generally, including the claim that softening ego-identification and improving access to the post-egoic range of development can: (a) reduce our personal and collective suffering; and (b) expand our freedom (that is, freedom from being guided and constrained by untamed egoic impulses).

I will use adjectives such as "impeded," "stunted," or "arrested" to denote development that has slowed or come to a halt. Our particular focus will be on ego-identification that is sufficiently intense that it obstructs movement into the post-egoic developmental range.

16   See, for example, Alexander, *Globalization of Addiction*, pp. 162, 230–33, 241–64, 339, 347; Chanokruthai Choenarom, Reg Arthur Williams, and Bonnie M. Hagerty, "The Role of Sense of Belonging and Social Support on Stress and Depression in Individuals with Depression," *Archives of Psychiatric Nursing*, vol. 19, no. 1 (Feb. 2005), pp. 18–29; Maté, *In the Realm of Hungry Ghosts*, chap. 26 and pp. 236–37, 264; Vivek H. Murthy, *Together: The Healing Power of Human Connection in a Sometimes Lonely World* (New York: HarperCollins, 2020); Robert Jay Lifton, *The Protean Self: Human Resilience in an Age of Fragmentation* (New York: Basic Books, 1993), chaps. 9–10; Robert D. Putnam, *Bowling Alone: The Collapse and Revival of American Community* (New York: Simon & Schuster, 2000), sect. 4.

17   *Depression and Other Common Mental Disorders: Global Health Estimates* (Geneva: World Health Organization, 2017), pp. 5, 8, and 13; S. E. Gilman, I. Kawachi, G. M. Fitzmaurice and S. L. Buka, "Socio-Economic Status, Family Disruption and Residential Stability in Childhood: Relation to Onset, Recurrence and Remission of Major Depression," *Psychological Medicine*, vol. 33 (2003), pp. 1341–55; Brandon H. Hidaka, "Depression as a Disease of Modernity: Explanations for Increasing Prevalence," *Journal of Affective Disorders*, vol. 140, no. 3 (Nov. 2012), pp. 205–14; Johann Hari, *Lost Connections: Uncovering the Real Causes of Depression—and the Unexpected Solutions* (New York: Bloomsbury, 2018); A. W. Geiger and Leslie Davis, "A Growing Number of American Teenagers— Particularly Girls—Are Facing Depression," Pew Research Center, 12 July 2019, https://pewrsr.ch/2xCxEmP.

18   Maté, *In the Realm of Hungry Ghosts*, pp. 438–42 (on ADHD); Jean M. Twenge, "The Age of Anxiety? Birth Cohort Change in Anxiety and Neuroticism, 1952–1993," *Journal of Personality and Social Psychology*, vol. 79, no. 6 (2000), pp. 1007–21; Eva Jane-Llopis and Irina Matytsina, "Mental Health and Alcohol, Drugs and Tobacco: A Review of the Comorbidity Between Mental Disorders and the Use of Alcohol, Tobacco and Illicit Drugs," *Drug and Alcohol Review*, vol. 25, no. 6 (Nov. 2006), pp. 515–36.

19   Deborah M. Stone, Thomas R. Simon, Katherine A. Fowler, et al., "Vital Signs: Trends in State Suicide Rates – United States, 1999– 2016 and Circumstances Contributing to Suicide – 27 States, 2015," *Morbidity and Mortality Weekly Report*, vol. 67, no. 22 (8 June 2018), pp. 617–24; Clay Routledge, "Suicides Have Increased. Is This an Existential Crisis?," *New York Times*, 23 June 2018; Sally C. Curtin and Melonie Heron, "Death Rates Due to Suicide and Homicide Among Persons Aged 10–24: United States, 2000–2017," *National Center for Health Statistics Data Brief*, no. 352 (Oct. 2019); Anne Case and Angus Deaton, *Deaths of Despair and the Future of Capitalism* (Princeton: Princeton Univ. Press, 2020).

20   Jean M. Twenge, Brittany Gentile, C. Nathan DeWall, et al., "Birth Cohort Increases in Psychopathology Among Young Americans, 1938–2007: A Cross-Temporal Meta-Analysis of the MMPI," *Clinical Psychology Review*, vol. 30, no. 2 (March 2010), pp. 145–54; quote is from p. 152.

21   A. H. Weinberger, M. Gbedemah, A. M. Martinez, et al., "Trends in Depression Prevalence in the USA from 2005 to 2015: Widening Disparities in Vulnerable Groups," *Psychological Medicine*, vol. 48, no. 8 (June 2018), pp. 1308–15 (includes citations to pertinent European studies); Jean M. Twenge, A. Bell Cooper, Thomas E. Joiner, et al., "Age, Period, and Cohort Trends in Mood Disorder Indicators and Suicide-Related Outcomes in a Nationally

Representative Dataset, 2005–2017," *Journal of Abnormal Psychology*, vol. 128, no. 3 (2019), pp. 185–99; Jingjin Shao, Dan Li, Dajun Zhang, et al., "Birth Cohort Changes in the Depressive Symptoms of Chinese Older Adults: A Cross-Temporal Meta-Analysis," *International Journal of Geriatric Psychiatry*, vol. 28, no. 11 (Nov. 2013), pp. 1101–08.

Amanda J. Baxter, Kate M. Scott, Alize J. Ferrari, et al., "Challenging the Myth of an 'Epidemic' of Common Mental Disorders: Trends in the Global Prevalence of Anxiety and Depression between 1990 and 2010," *Depression and Anxiety*, vol. 31, no. 6 (June 2014), pp. 506–16, concludes that there was no global increase in depression and anxiety from 1990 to 2010 that cannot be attributed to demographic changes, although subclinical psychological distress grew significantly during that period. On the other hand, Fiona J. Charlson, Amanda J. Baxter, Hui G. Cheng, et al., "The Burden of Mental, Neurological, and Substance Use Disorders in China and India: A Systematic Analysis of Community Representative Epidemiological Studies," *Lancet*, vol. 388, no. 10042 (23–29 July 2016), pp. 376–89, esp. p. 386, note large increases in the prevalence of the disorders that they studied that cannot be attributed solely to population growth and aging.

22   Darcia Narvaez, *Neurobiology and the Development of Human Morality: Evolution, Culture, and Wisdom* (New York: W. W. Norton & Co., 2014), chap. 2. McGilchrist, *Master and His Emissary*, pp. 393–98; Carl Ratner, *Macro Cultural Psychology: A Political Philosophy of Mind* (Oxford: Oxford Univ. Press, 2012), pp. 188–91 and Liah Greenfeld, *Mind, Modernity, Madness: The Impact of Culture on Human Experience* (Cambridge: Harvard Univ. Press, 2013) explore schizophrenia as a disease of modernity.

23   *18 Ways Smoking Affects Your Health*, http://smokefree.gov/health-effects, n.d.; Centers for Disease Control and Prevention, *Fact Sheets – Alcohol and Your Health*, n.d., https://www.cdc.gov/alcohol/fact-sheets/alcohol-use.htm. Websites accessed 18 Nov. 2015.

24   David A. Kessler, *The End of Overeating: Taking Control of the Insatiable American Appetite* (New York: Rodale, 2009); Ryan K. Masters, Eric N. Reither, Daniel A. Powers, et al., "The Impact of Obesity on US Mortality Levels: The Importance of Age and Cohort Factors in Population Estimates," *American Journal of Public Health*, vol. 103, no. 10 (Oct. 2013), pp. 1895–1901; Marie Ng, Tom Fleming, Margaret Robinson, et al., "Global, Regional, and National Prevalence of Overweight and Obesity in Children and Adults During 1980–2013: A Systematic Analysis for the Global Burden of Disease Study 2013," *Lancet*, vol. 384, no. 9945 (Aug. 2014), pp. 766–81. On whether fast food satisfies strict scientific criteria for addiction, see Andrea K. Garber and Robert H. Lustig, "Is Fast Food Addictive?,"

Current Drug Abuse Reviews, vol. 4, no. 3 (2011), pp. 146–62; Anahad O'Connor, "Unhealthy Foods Aren't Just Bad for You, They May Also Be Addictive," *New York Times*, 18 Feb. 2021.

25   Elizabeth Reisinger Walker, Robin E. McGee, and Benjamin G. Druss, "Mortality in Mental Disorders and Global Disease Burden Implications," *JAMA Psychiatry*, vol. 72, no. 4 (April 2015), pp. 334–41. On suicide: *Depression and Other Common Mental Disorders*, pp. 5, 14–15.

26   Robert D. Putnam, *Our Kids: The American Dream in Crisis* (New York: Simon & Schuster, 2015); Michelle Alexander, *The New Jim Crow: Mass Incarceration in the Age of Colorblindness* (New York: The New Press, 2010); Tim Rhodes, "Risk Environments and Drug Harms: A Social Science for Harm Reduction Approach," *International Journal of Drug Policy*, vol. 20 (2009), pp. 193–201, esp. p 196. Statistics calculated from *Behavioral Health Barometer: United States, 2015*, HHS Publication No. SMA-16-Baro-2015 (Rockville, MD: Substance Abuse and Mental Health Services Administration, 2015), p. 13–14.

27   "Serious Mental Illness (SMI) Among U.S. Adults," National Institute of Mental Health, n.d., http://www.nimh.nih.gov/health/statistics/ prevalence/serious-mental-illness-smi-among-us-adults.shtml (accessed 11 March 2019); Weinberger et al., "Trends in Depression Prevalence in the USA from 2005 to 2015," pp. 1310, 1312; Ronald C. Kessler and Evelyn J. Bromet, "The Epidemiology of Depression Across Cultures," *Annual Review of Public Health*, vol. 34 (2013), pp. 119–38.

28   *Behavioral Health Barometer: United States, 2014*, HHS Publication No. SMA—15—4895 (Rockville, MD: Substance Abuse and Mental Health Services Administration, 2015), p. 11; Richard G. Wilkinson and Kate E. Pickett, "Income Inequality and Population Health: A Review and Explanation of the Evidence," *Social Science & Medicine*, vol. 62, no. 7 (April 2006), pp. 1768–84, esp. p. 1778; Cynthia L. Ogden, Molly M. Lamb, Margaret D. Carroll, and Katherine M. Flegal, "Obesity and Socioeconomic Status in Adults: United States, 2005–2008," National Center for Health Statistics, Data Brief no. 50, Dec. 2010, pp. 1–2. On social disconnection as adverse to health, independent of class and race: Putnam, *Bowling Alone*, pp. 328–32. On race-based unequal access to treatment see, for example, Hector M. González, Thomas W. Croghan, Brady T. West, et al., "Antidepressant Use Among Blacks and Whites in the United States," *Psychiatric Services*, vol. 59, no. 10 (Oct. 2008), pp. 1131–38.

29   Suniya S. Luthar, "The Culture of Affluence: Psychological Costs of Material Wealth," *Child Development*, vol. 74, no. 6 (Dec. 2003), pp. 1581–93; Miller, *The Spiritual Child*, part 2.

30   On addiction or related afflictions among people of great privilege, see Alexander, *Globalization of Addiction*, pp. 12–13, 40, 62, 114–19,

190, 223, 252, 355, 364. On narcissism: Jean M. Twenge, Sara Konrath, Joshua D. Foster, et al., "Egos Inflating Over Time: A Cross-Temporal Meta-Analysis of the Narcissistic Personality Inventory," *Journal of Personality*, vol. 76, no. 4 (Aug. 2008), pp. 875–901; Paul K. Piff, "Wealth and the Inflated Self: Class, Entitlement, and Narcissism," *Personality and Social Psychology Bulletin*, vol. 41, no. 1 (Jan. 2014), pp. 34–43; Côté, *Arrested Adulthood*, pp. 92–97, 115, 130, 191–95. Work statistics: James Surowiecki, "The Cult of Overwork," *New Yorker*, 27 Jan. 2014, p. 23.

31   Steven Sussman, "Workaholism: A Review," *Journal of Addiction Research & Therapy*, vol. S6 (2012), pp. 1–10; Seth A. Rosenthal and Todd L. Pittinsky, "Narcissistic Leadership," *Leadership Quarterly*, vol. 17, no. 6 (Dec. 2006), pp. 617–33.

32   L. Alan Sroufe, Byron Egeland, Elizabeth A. Carlson, and W. Andrew Collins, *The Development of the Person: The Minnesota Study of Risk and Adaptation from Birth to Adulthood* (New York: Guilford Press, 2009), chaps. 11–13; Narvaez, *Neurobiology*, chaps. 2–3, 6; Andrew S. Garner, Jack P. Shonkoff, Benjamin S. Siegel, et al., "Early Childhood Adversity, Toxic Stress, and the Role of the Pediatrician: Translating Developmental Science into Lifelong Health," *Pediatrics*, vol. 129, no. 1 (Jan. 2012), pp. e224–e231. Quote is from L. Alan Sroufe, "The Concept of Development in Developmental Psychopathology," *Child Development Perspectives*, vol. 3, no. 3 (Dec. 2009), pp. 178–83, on p. 181. "Roughly 40 percent": Katie A. McLaughlin, "Future Directions in Childhood Adversity and Youth Psychopathology," *Journal of Clinical Child & Adolescent Psychology*, vol. 45, no. 3 (2016), pp. 361–82, esp. p. 362; Ronald C. Kessler, Katie A. McLaughlin, Jennifer Greif Green, et al., "Childhood Adversities and Adult Psychopathology in the WHO World Mental Health Surveys," *British Journal of Psychiatry*, vol. 197, no. 5 (Nov. 2010), pp. 378–85, esp. p. 379.

33   Miller, *Spiritual Child*, chap. 10 and p. 326; Washburn, *Ego and the Dynamic Ground*, chaps. 4, 7–8; Kegan, *Evolving Self*, pp. 44, 82, 130, 193–97; Evelyn Bromet, Laura Helena Andrade, Irving Hwang, et al., "Cross-National Epidemiology of DSM-IV Major Depressive Episode," *BMC Medicine*, vol. 9, no. 90 (2011), p. 6; Stephanie L. Burcusa and William G. Iacono, "Risk for Recurrence in Depression," *Clinical Psychology Review*, vol. 27, no. 8 (Dec. 2007), pp. 959–85; Benedict Carey and Robert Gebeloff, "Many People Taking Antidepressants Discover They Cannot Quit," *New York Times*, 7 April 2018.

34   On public health: David M. Cutler, "The Role of Public Health Improvements in Health Advances: The Twentieth-Century United States," *Demography*, vol. 42, no. 1 (Feb. 2005), pp. 1–22; David Cutler, Angus Deaton, and Adriana Llera-Muney, "The Determinants of Mortality," *Journal of Economic Perspectives*, vol. 20, no. 3 (Summer 2006), pp. 97–120.

35   On modern mental illnesses as ego-pathologies see, for example, Washburn, *Ego and the Dynamic Ground*, pp. 104–5, 111–17. Miller, *Spiritual Child*, esp. chaps. 2, 8, 10, presents neuroscientific, epidemiological, and clinical psychological evidence consistent with this thesis; her orientation is spiritual but not specifically transpersonal.

36   Michael Pollan, *How to Change Your Mind: What the New Science of Psychedelics Teaches Us About Consciousness, Dying, Addiction, Depression, and Transcendence* (New York: Penguin, 2018), esp. chaps 1, 5, 6; D. E. Nichols, M. W. Johnson, and C. D. Nichols, "Psychedelics as Medicines: An Emerging New Paradigm," *Clinical Pharmacology & Therapeutics*, vol. 101, no. 2 (Feb. 2017), pp. 209–19; Jacob S. Aday, Cayla M. Mitzkovitz, Emily K. Bloesch, et al., "Long-Term Effects of Psychedelic Drugs: A Systematic Review," *Neuroscience and Biobehavioral Reviews*, vol. 113 (June 2020), pp. 179–89.

37   Millière et al., "Psychedelics, Meditation, and Self-Consciousness," delineate distinctions between the effects of psychedelics versus spiritual practices, in both the short and long run. David B. Yaden and Roland R. Griffiths, "The Subjective Effects of Psychedelics Are Necessary for Their Enduring Therapeutic Effects," *ACS Pharmacology & Translational Science*, vol. 4, no. 2 (9 April 2021), pp. 568–72, propose that psychedelics' therapeutic benefits derive not only from their biochemical effects in the brain but also from a patient's subjective experiences during treatment, such as ego dissolution or various spiritual phenomena.

CHAPTER 7: UNINTERRUPTED DISTURBANCE

1   Ken Morrison, *Marx, Durkheim, Weber: Formations of Modern Social Thought* (London: Sage, 1995), pp. 120–51, 163–88.

2   Joseph A. Schumpeter, *Capitalism, Socialism and Democracy*, 3rd ed. (New York: Harper & Row, 1950), chap. 7. On job loss and replacement: "Business Employment Dynamics Summary," US Dept. of Labor, Bureau of Labor Statistics, 29 April 2020, https://www.bls .gov/news.release/cewbd.nr0.htm; and Claire Cain Miller, "As Robots Grow Smarter, American Workers Struggle to Keep Up," *New York Times*, 16 Dec. 2014. On emotional pain: Nick Powdthavee, *The Happiness Equation: The Surprising Economics of Our Most Valuable Asset* (London: Icon Books, 2010), at Kindle locations 1522–61; Farah Stockman, *American Made: What Happens to People When Work Disappears* (New York: Random House, 2021). "Paradoxically . . . eroded": Deepak Lal, *Unintended Consequences: The Impact of Factor Endowments, Culture, and Politics on Long-Run Economic Performance* (Cambridge: MIT Press, 1998), p. 69.

3   On elite attitudes toward innovation, see Daron Acemoglu and James A. Robinson, *Why Nations Fail: The Origins of Power, Prosperity, and Poverty* (New York: Currency, 2012).

4   Karl Polanyi, *The Great Transformation: The Political and Economic Origins of Our Time* (Boston: Beacon Press, 1957), p. 73.

5   David McLellan, ed., *Karl Marx: Selected Writings* (Oxford: Oxford Univ. Press, 1977), p. 224.

6   The concern that modern life has grown bereft of meaning has been widely expressed. Classic statements include Max Weber's "Science as a Vocation," in H. H. Gerth and C. Wright Mills, trans. and ed., *From Max Weber: Essays in Sociology* (New York: Oxford Univ. Press, 1946), pp. 129–56; Herbert Marcuse, *One-Dimensional Man: Studies in the Ideology of Advanced Industrial Society* (Boston: Beacon Press, 1964); Peter L. Berger, Brigitte Berger, and Hansfried Kellner, *The Homeless Mind: Modernization and Consciousness* (New York: Pelican, 1974).

7   On the number of Americans who moved: Putnam, *Bowling Alone*, p. 204. For an update, listen to Jed Kolko, interview by Audie Cornish, *All Things Considered*, NPR, 4 Aug. 2017, https://www.npr.org/2017/08/04/541675186.

8   Michael J. Sandel, *What Money Can't Buy: The Moral Limits of Markets* (New York: Farrar, Straus and Giroux, 2012).

9   Kant, *Foundations of the Metaphysics of Morals,* p. 53, emphasis in original.

10   Stephen A. Marglin, *The Dismal Science: How Thinking Like an Economist Undermines Community* (Cambridge: Harvard Univ. Press, 2008), chaps. 1–2.

11   Institute for the Study of Diplomacy Working Group, *New Challenges to Human Security: Environmental Change and Human Mobility* (Washington, DC: Institute for the Study of Diplomacy, April 2017); Katharine Mach, Caroline M. Kraan, W. Neil Adger, et al., "Climate Changes as a Risk Factor for Armed Conflict," *Nature*, vol. 571 (11 July 2019), pp. 193–97.

12   Edward E. Baptist, *The Half Has Never Been Told: Slavery and the Making of American Capitalism* (New York: Basic Books, 2014); Sven Beckert, *Empire of Cotton: A Global History* (New York: Vintage, 2015), pp. 35–38, 52, 60–61, 84, 98–135, 147; Douglas A. Blackmon, *Slavery by Another Name: The Re-enslavement of Black Americans from the Civil War to World War II* (New York: Anchor Books, 2009); Alexander, *New Jim Crow*; Isabel Wilkerson, *Caste: The Origins of Our Discontents* (New York: Random House, 2020).

13   On the mental health challenges experienced by migrants, see Dinesh Bhugra and Susham Gupta, eds., *Migration and Mental Health* (Cambridge: Cambridge Univ. Press, 2011), sects. 1 and 2.

14 "New Cigna Study Reveals Loneliness at Epidemic Levels in America," News Release, 1 May 2018, https://www.cigna.com /newsroom/news-releases/2018/new-cigna-study-reveals -loneliness-at-epidemic-levels-in-america.

15 M. Roberts, "Modernity, Mental Illness and the Crisis of Meaning," *Journal of Psychiatric and Mental Health Nursing*, vol. 14, no. 3 (May 2007), pp. 277–81.

16 Richard E. Sclove, *Democracy and Technology* (New York: Guilford Press, 1995), chap. 2.

17 Alvin Toffler, *Future Shock* (New York: Bantam, 1970), esp. chap. 16.

18 Albert Borgmann, *Technology and the Character of Contemporary Life* (Chicago: Univ. of Chicago Press, 1984), chaps. 8–11. Borgmann uses the term "thing" rather than "integrative practice." I prefer the latter because its meaning is more self-evident.

19 Re adverse psychological repercussions: Routledge, "Suicides Have Increased. Is This an Existential Crisis?"; Hari, *Lost Connections*, part 2.

20 See, for example, Andrea Faber Taylor and Frances E. Kuo, "Is Contact with Nature Important for Healthy Child Development? State of the Evidence," in *Children and Their Environments: Learning, Using and Designing Spaces*, ed. Christopher Spencer and Mark Blades (Cambridge: Cambridge Univ. Press, 2006), pp. 124–40; Andrea Faber Taylor and Frances E. Kuo, "Could Exposure to Everyday Green Spaces Help Treat ADHD? Evidence from Children's Play Settings," *Applied Psychology: Health and Well-Being*, vol. 3, no. 3 (2011), pp. 281–303; Howard Frumkin, Gregory N. Bratman, Sara Jo Breslow, et al., "Nature Contact and Human Health: A Research Agenda," *Environmental Health Perspectives*, vol. 125, no. 7 (July 2017); Louise Chawla, "Benefits of Nature Contact for Children," *Journal of Planning Literature*, vol. 30, no. 4 (2015), pp. 433–52; Susan L. Prescott and Alan C. Logan, "Transforming Life: A Broad View of the Developmental Origins of Health and Disease Concept from an Ecological Justice Perspective," *International Journal of Environmental Research and Public Health*, vol. 13, no. 11 (Nov. 2016); Darcia Narvaez, "Getting Back on Track to Being Human," *Interdisciplinary Journal of Partnership Studies*, vol. 4, no. 1 (Winter 2017), article 5; John S. Hutton, Jonathan Dudley, Tzipi Horowitz-Kraus, et al., "Associations Between Screen-Based Media Use and Brain White Matter Integrity in Preschool-Aged Children," *JAMA Pediatrics* vol. 174, no. 1 (Jan. 2020). Jean M. Twenge, Brian H. Spitzberg, and W. Keith Campbell, "Less In-Person Social Interaction with Peers Among U.S. Adolescents in the 21st Century and Links to Loneliness," *Journal of Social and Personal Relationships*, vol. 36, no. 6 (2019), pp. 1892–1913, esp. p. 1908, point to digital media use as a cause of loneliness and follow-on mental disorders; but we know from Chapter 6 that such disorders are often developmental.

21   The story and quotes that follow are drawn from A. R. Luria, *Cognitive Development: Its Cultural and Social Foundation*, trans. Martin Lopez-Morillas and Lynn Solotaroff, ed. Michael Cole (Cambridge: Harvard Univ. Press, 1976), pp. 60–63. On the general problem of cross-cultural testing that reflects hidden cultural biases see, for example, Rogoff, *The Cultural Nature of Human Development*, chaps. 1, 2, and 7.

22   Abraham Maslow, *Toward a Psychology of Being*, 2nd ed. (New York: Van Nostrand Reinhold, 1968), pp. 75–78, 99; Michael Basseches, "The Development of Dialectical Thinking as an Approach to Integration," *Integral Review*, vol. 1 (2005), pp. 47–63. See also Richard E. Nisbett, Kaiping Peng, Incheol Choi, and Ara Norenzayan, "Culture and Systems of Thought: Holistic Versus Analytic Cognition," *Psychological Review*, vol. 108, no. 2, (2001), pp. 291–310, esp. pp. 300–02.

23   On modern psychology's historically atypical non-holism see, for example, McGilchrist, *Master and His Emissary*.

24   See, for example, Ratner, *Macro Cultural Psychology*, pp. 189–91.

25   Erazim Kohák, *The Embers and the Stars: A Philosophical Inquiry into the Moral Sense of Nature* (Chicago: Univ. of Chicago Press, 1984), pp. 3–26, 107–08, 179–204. On spirituality as humanly innate and beginning at birth, see Miller, *Spiritual Child*.

26   See also Frédérique Apffel-Marglin, "Western Modernity and the Fate of Anima Mundi: Its Murder and Transformation into a Postmaterial Ecospirituality," in *Contemporary Voices from Anima Mundi: A Reappraisal*, ed. Frédérique Apffel-Marglin and Stefano Varese (New York: Peter Lang, 2020), pp. 17–44; John V. Davis, "Ecopsychology, Transpersonal Psychology, and Nonduality," *International Journal of Transpersonal Studies*, vol. 30, nos. 1–2 (2011), pp. 89–100.

27   Information in this section is drawn from Sherry Turkle, *Alone Together: Why We Expect More from Technology and Less from Each Other* (New York: Basic Books, 2011), pp. 153–302.

28   Richard E. Sclove, "Cybersobriety: How a Commercially Driven Internet Threatens the Foundations of Democratic Self-Governance and What to Do About It," in *Community Practice in the Network Society: Local Action/Global Interaction*, ed. Peter Day and Douglas Schuler (London and New York: Routledge, 2004), pp. 36–51, esp. pp. 43–47, http://richardsclove.com/publications.

29   John P. Robinson and Geoffrey Godbey, *Time for Life: The Surprising Ways Americans Use Their Time* (University Park: Pennsylvania State Univ. Press, 1997), p. 39.

30   On depression and suicide, see Ariel Shensa, César G. Escobar-Viera, Jaime E. Sidani, et al., "Problematic Social Media Use and Depressive Symptoms Among U.S. Young Adults: A Nationally-Representative Study," *Social Science & Medicine*, vol. 182 (June 2017), pp. 150–57;

Jean M. Twenge, Thomas E. Joiner, Megan L. Rogers, and Gabrielle N. Martin, "Increases in Depressive Symptoms, Suicide-Related Outcomes, and Suicide Rates Among U.S. Adolescents After 2010 and Links to Increased New Media Screen Time," *Clinical Psychological Science*, vol. 6, no. 1 (2018), pp. 3–17, quoted statistic on pp. 9–10; Jean M. Twenge, "More Time on Technology, Less Happiness?: Associations Between Digital-Media Use and Psychological Well-Being," *Current Directions in Psychological Science*, vol. 28, no. 4 (2019), pp. 372–79; Jean M. Twenge, Jonathan Haidt, Andrew B. Blake, et al., "Worldwide Increases in Adolescent Loneliness," *Journal of Adolescence*, published online ahead of print, 20 July 2021. Sherry Turkle's *The Second Self: Computers and the Human Spirit* (New York: Simon & Schuster, 1984) showed that computerized toys and games can alter children's psychological development; at the time she was sanguine about the results.

CHAPTER 8: THE WANTS OF MANKIND

1   C. Robert Cloninger, "The Science of Well-Being," *World Psychiatry*, vol. 5, no. 2 (June 2006), pp. 71–76; esp. pp. 71–72. See also Daniel Vigo, Graham Thornicroft, and Rifat Atun, "Estimating the True Global Burden of Mental Illness," *Lancet Psychiatry*, vol. 3, no. 2 (Feb. 2016), pp. 171–78.

2   Nurit Bird-David, Allen Abramson, Jon Altman, et al., "Beyond 'The Original Affluent Society': A Culturalist Reformulation [and Comments and Reply]," *Current Anthropology*, vol. 33, no. 1 (Feb. 1992), pp. 25–47, esp. pp. 25–26; quote is from p. 30 (ellipses in original), and sources for the internal quotes are Karen L. Endicott, "Batek Negrito Sex Roles: Behaviour and Ideology," in *Proceedings of the Second International Conference on Hunting and Gathering Societies* (Quebec: Université Laval, 1980), p. 650 ("view work as a burden"), and John A. Hart, "From Subsistence to Market: A Case Study of the Mbuti Net Hunters," *Human Ecology* vol. 6, no. 3 (1978), p. 337 ("The overall pace").

3   Among historians, the definition of the word "peasant" remains imprecise; see, for example, J. V. Beckett, "The Peasant in England: A Case of Terminological Confusion," *Agricultural History Review*, vol. 32, no. 2 (1984), pp. 113–23. Here I use it to designate the lower social orders that worked the land, including, for example, wage laborers, tenant farmers, and small landowners. But even these categories can be ambiguous. For instance, some smallholders worked for wages seasonally or part-time.

On consumption by English peasants: Christopher Dyer, *Everyday Life in Medieval England* (London: Hambledon and

London, 2000), chaps. 1 and 4; Christopher Dyer, *An Age of Transition?: Economy and Society in England in the Later Middle Ages* (Oxford: Clarendon Press, 2005), chap. 4; Frank Trentmann, *Empire of Things: How We Became a World of Consumers, from the Fifteenth Century to the Twenty-First* (New York: Harper, 2016), p. 58. On reducing hours of work as wage rates climbed: John Hatcher, "England in the Aftermath of the Black Death," *Past and Present*, no. 144 (Aug. 1994), pp. 3–35, esp. pp. 11, 14, 27–28; Juliet B. Schor, *The Overworked American: The Unexpected Decline of Leisure* (New York: Basic Books, 1992), pp. 43–48; Dyer, *Everyday Life*, pp. 179, 186–89; Jan de Vries, *The Industrious Revolution: Consumer Behavior and the Household Economy, 1650 to the Present* (Cambridge: Cambridge Univ. Press, 2008), pp. 87–92; David Routt, "The Economic Impact of the Black Death," *EH.Net Encyclopedia*, ed. Robert Whaples, 20 July 2008, http://eh.net/encyclopedia/the-economicimpact-of-the-black-death; Mark Koyama, "The Transformation of Labor Supply in the Pre-industrial World," *Journal of Economic Behavior & Organization*, vol. 81, no. 2 (Feb. 2012), pp. 505–23, esp. pp. 505–07; Joseph Henrich, *The WEIRDest People in the World: How the West Became Psychologically Peculiar and Particularly Prosperous* (New York: Farrar, Straus and Giroux, 2020), pp. 367–71. In *The Overworked American*, Schor observes (p. 46) that the work of medieval peasants was leisurely paced in part because their caloric intake was too low to sustain anything more; however, when their nutrition improved after the Black Death, many English peasants worked even *less*.

While concurring that many English peasants opted to increase their leisure time, Christopher Dyer has shown that an upper tier among them—typically this would be small landowners—appreciably expanded their earnings and consumption, including by purchasing discretionary items such as fashionable clothing, linen sheets, tablecloths, and pewterware. See his *Everyday Life*, chap. 9, and *An Age of Transition?*, pp. 137–49, 232–38; as well as Phillipp R. Schofield, *Peasants and Historians: Debating the Medieval English Peasantry* (Manchester: Manchester Univ. Press, 2016), pp. 228–29. Also, some English peasants' earnings were sufficient that they were able to increase their consumption along with their leisure; see Hatcher, "England in the Aftermath," pp. 17, 31, 33. The fact that some English peasants used increased income to make novel consumer purchases shows that the different choices made by other peasants (e.g., to work and consume less than they might have) cannot be explained simply by a dearth of alluring consumer goods.

For the late-medieval period, more is known about the economic circumstances of the peasantry in England than elsewhere; for a sense of geographic variations in the economic aftereffects of the Black

Death, see Samuel Cohn, "After the Black Death: Labour Legislation and Attitudes Towards Labour in Late-Medieval Western Europe," *Economic History Review*, vol. 60, no. 3 (Aug. 2007), pp. 457–85.

4   Emmanuel Le Roy Ladurie, *Montaillou: The Promised Land of Error*, trans. Barbara Bray (New York: George Braziller, 1978). Quoted sentences from pp. 278, 339, 354–55; see also pp. 120–35. The peasant accounts were obtained by an agent of the Inquisition, Bishop Jacques Fournier, who later became Pope Benedict XII.

5   As in the case of the term "peasant" (see note 3, above), the definition of the "middling sort" is not precise. See, for example, H. R. French, "The Search for the 'Middle Sort of People' in England, 1600–1800," *Historical Journal*, vol. 43, no. 1 (March 2000), pp. 277–93.

Dyer, *An Age of Transition?*, makes a convincing case that England's transformation into a consumer society did not occur out of the blue, but instead unfolded gradually and unevenly across prior centuries. However, the breadth of people who qualified as consumers, and the range of goods available, expanded notably beginning in the seventeenth century. As Trentmann writes in *Empire of Things*: "It was in the north-west of Europe, in the Netherlands and Britain, that a more dynamic, innovative culture of consumption came to take hold in the seventeenth and eighteenth centuries. . . . The exponential rise in stuff went hand in hand with a rise in novelty, variety and availability, and this was connected to a more general openness to the world of goods and its contribution to the individual self, to social order and economic development" (p. 53).

6   James Steuart, *An Inquiry into the Principles of Political Oeconomy* (Dublin, 1770), pp. 38, 59.

7   Benjamin Franklin, "Remarks Concerning the Savages of North America," 1784, http://franklinpapers.org/framedVolumes.jsp at link "unpub. 1784–85."

8   De Vries, *The Industrious Revolution*, pp. 47–55, 87–97; on the inadequacy of standard emulation theory, see also Trentmann, *Empire of Things*, pp. 73–74; Beverly Lemire, *Global Trade and the Transformation of Consumer Cultures: The Material World Remade, c. 1500–1820* (Cambridge: Cambridge Univ. Press, 2018), pp. 112–13.

9   See Rudi Matthee, *The Pursuit of Pleasure: Drugs and Stimulants in Iranian History, 1500–1900* (Princeton: Princeton Univ. Press, 2005), p. 7; Jan de Vries, "Between Purchasing Power and the World of Goods: Understanding the Household Economy in Early Modern Europe," in *Consumption and the World of Goods*, ed. John Brewer and Roy Porter (London and New York: Routledge, 1994), pp. 85–132, esp. p. 117; Trentmann, *Empire of Things*, pp. 49–53 (quote is from p. 4).

10   For de Vries's various arguments, see his *Industrious Revolution*, chap. 2 and p. 149.

11   Colin Campbell, *The Romantic Ethic and the Spirit of Modern Consumerism*, 3rd ed. (Great Britain: Alcuin Academics, 2005), chaps. 2–4; Colin Campbell, "On Understanding Modern Consumerism and Misunderstanding the Romantic Ethic Thesis: A Reply to Boden and Williams," *Sociology*, vol. 37, no. 4 (Nov. 2003), pp. 791–97, esp. p. 796.

12   Quote is from Bird-David et al., "Beyond 'The Original Affluent Society,'" p. 31.

13   Tony Waters, *The Persistence of Subsistence Agriculture: Life Beneath the Level of the Marketplace* (Lanham, MD: Lexington Books, 2007), explores the cultural orientation that underlies subsistence societies, but his book doesn't consider the possible role of psychological development in evolving that orientation.

14   Justin Fox, "Telling Us to Go Shopping," *Time*, 19 Jan. 2009.

15   E.g., Benjamin Kline Hunnicutt, *Free Time: The Forgotten American Dream* (Philadelphia: Temple Univ. Press, 2013), chap. 6; John Kenneth Galbraith, *The Affluent Society* (Boston: Houghton Mifflin, 1998), chaps. 10–13.

16   Richard W. Pollay, "The Distorted Mirror: Reflections on the Unintended Consequences of Advertising," *Advertising & Society Review*, vol. 1, no. 1 (2000), pp. 18–36; Campbell, *Romantic Ethic*, p. 21.

17   Fernand Braudel, *Afterthoughts on Material Civilization and Capitalism*, trans. Patricia Ranum (Baltimore: Johns Hopkins Univ. Press, 1979), p. 11; Sidney W. Mintz, "The Changing Roles of Food in the Study of Consumption," in Brewer and Porter, *Consumption and the World of Goods*, p. 271. "Not an aberration": Kenneth Pomeranz and Steven Topik, *The World That Trade Created: Society, Culture, and the World Economy 1400 to the Present*, 2nd ed. (Armonk, NY: M. E. Sharpe, 2006), pp. 72, 75. Cocoa (also known as cacao or chocolate) was intermediate in cultural and economic significance compared with the other globally traded drug foods; see, for example, Kathryn E. Sampeck and Jonathan Thayn, "Translating Tastes: A Cartography of Chocolate Colonialism," in *Substance and Seduction: Ingested Commodities in Early Modern Mesoamerica*, ed. Stacey Schwartzkopf and Kathryn E. Sampeck (Austin: Univ. of Texas Press, 2017), pp. 72–99.

18   See, for example, Michael Dietler, "Alcohol: Anthropological/ Archaeological Perspectives," *Annual Review of Anthropology*, vol. 35 (2006), pp. 229–49.

19   On the importance of the drug foods in world trade: Pomeranz and Topik, *World That Trade Created*, pp. 77–78.

20 Carole Shammas, "Changes in English and Anglo-American Consumption from 1550 to 1800," in Brewer and Porter, *Consumption and the World of Goods*, p. 179; de Vries, *Industrious Revolution*, pp. 164, 173.

21 Shammas, "Changes in English and Anglo-American Consumption," pp. 183–84; Kenneth Pomeranz, *The Great Divergence: China, Europe, and the Making of the Modern World Economy* (Princeton: Princeton Univ. Press, 2000), p. 117; Pomeranz and Topik, *World That Trade Created*, p. 78; de Vries, *Industrious Revolution*, p. 160. Pomeranz's estimate for annual English tea consumption in 1800 is one pound per person; Shammas estimates two pounds by taking smuggled tea into account.

22 Shammas, "Changes in English and Anglo-American Consumption," pp. 181–83; Sidney W. Mintz, *Sweetness and Power: The Place of Sugar in Modern History* (New York: Penguin, 1985), pp. 116, 143; Pomeranz, *The Great Divergence*, p. 118; de Vries, *Industrious Revolution*, p. 160. If England evidenced an outsized taste for tea and sugar, the comparably market-oriented Netherlands did the same for coffee and tobacco. According to de Vries (p. 158), in the 1780s the Dutch smoked roughly five times as much per person as other continental Europeans, while drinking nearly seven times as much coffee.

23 On the gradual transition from ale to beer see, for example, Milan Pajic, "'Ale for an Englishman Is a Natural Drink': The Dutch and the Origins of Beer Brewing in Late Medieval England," *Journal of Medieval History*, vol. 45, no. 3, pp. 285–300. A similar progression from low- to high-alcohol-content beverages unfolded elsewhere in the world during the early modern period; see, for example, Stacey Schwartzkopf, "Alcohol and Commodity Succession in Colonial Maya Guatemala: From Mead to Aguardiente," in Schwartzkopf and Sampeck, *Substance and Seduction*, pp. 55–71.

24 Gin layered upon beer: Jessica Warner, Minghao Her, Gerhard Gmel, and Jürgen Rehm, "Can Legislation Prevent Debauchery?: Mother Gin and Public Health in 18th-Century England," *American Journal of Public Health*, vol. 91, no. 3 (March 2001), pp. 375–84, esp. p. 381. John Burnett, *Liquid Pleasures: A Social History of Drinks in Modern Britain* (London: Routledge, 1999), p. 164; de Vries, *Industrious Revolution*, p. 165.

25 E.g., Anne E. C. McCants, "Poor Consumers as Global Consumers: The Diffusion of Tea and Coffee Drinking in the Eighteenth Century," *Economic History Review*, vol. 61, no. S1 (Aug. 2008), pp. 172–200; Mintz, "Changing Roles of Food," pp. 263–67.

26 Evelyn S. Welch, *Shopping in the Renaissance: Consumer Cultures in Italy, 1400–1600* (New Haven: Yale Univ. Press, 2009), although the conclusions one can draw remain limited by the fact that much more is known about upper than lower social orders.

27   Daron Acemoglu, Simon Johnson, and James Robinson, "The Rise of Europe: Atlantic Trade, Institutional Change, and Economic Growth," *American Economic Review*, vol. 95, no. 3 (June 2005), pp. 546–79; Beckert, *Empire of Cotton*, chap. 2; Peter Linebaugh and Marcus Rediker, *The Many-Headed Hydra: Sailors, Slaves, Commoners, and the Hidden History of the Revolutionary Atlantic* (Boston: Beacon Press, 2013), chaps. 1–2 ("1,000 villages" is on p. 17).

28   Acemoglu and Robinson, *Why Nations Fail*, chap. 7. British Civil War casualty figures: Stephen Mortlock, "Death and Disease in the English Civil War," *Biomedical Scientist*, 1 June 2017, www.thebio medicalscientist.net/science/death-and-disease-english-civil-war.

29   E. P. Thompson, *Customs in Common: Studies in Traditional Popular Culture* (New York: The New Press, 1993), chap. 3; Polanyi, *The Great Transformation*; Linebaugh and Rediker, *Many-Headed Hydra*.

30   Dror Wahrman, *The Making of the Modern Sense of Self: Identity and Culture in Eighteenth-Century England* (New Haven: Yale Univ. Press, 2006), esp. chaps. 4–5, 7; quote is from p. 208. Charles Taylor, *Sources of the Self: The Making of Modern Identity* (Cambridge: Harvard Univ. Press, 1989), provides a more general treatment of modern transformations in the concept and experience of selfhood, but—unlike Wahrman—he is primarily looking through the eyes of intellectuals rather than at selfhood as experienced in daily life by those living it.

31   Addiction definition: Daniel Kardefelt-Winther, Alexandre Heeren, Adriano Schimmenti, et al., "How Can We Conceptualize Behavioural Addiction Without Pathologizing Common Behaviours?," *Addiction*, vol. 112, no. 10 (Oct. 2017), pp. 1709–15; the definition is on p. 1710. See also Steve Sussman and Alan N. Sussman, "Considering the Definition of Addiction," *International Journal of Environmental Research and Public Health*, vol. 8, no. 10 (2011), pp. 4025–38. Alexander, *Globalization of Addiction*, chap. 2, esp. p. 29.

32   On tea: "One of the many things that the English did in the eighteenth century that enhanced their health was to get addicted to tea."—Joel Mokyr, *The Enlightened Economy: An Economic History of Britain 1700–1850* (New Haven, Yale Univ. Press, 2010), p. 294. Pomeranz and Topik, *World That Trade Created*, pp. 72–78, write of early modern European "addiction" to coffee, tea, cocoa, tobacco, and sugar.

     Tea actually did become unhealthy under some circumstances. Tea brewed in boiled water was always preferable to impure water, but it became detrimental when workers' nutrition declined as result of substituting tea for moderate consumption of beer. See Mintz, *Sweetness and Power*, p. 117; and A. E. Dingle, "Drink and Working-Class Living Standards in Britain, 1870–1914," *Economic History Review*, vol. 25, no. 4 (Nov. 1972), pp. 608–22, esp. p. 613.

33   On caffeine and sugar: Deborah S. Hasin, Charles P. O'Brien, Marc
      Auriacombe, et al., "DSM-5 Criteria for Substance Use Disorders:
      Recommendations and Rationale," *American Journal of Psychiatry*,
      vol. 170, no. 8 (Aug 2013), pp. 834–51, esp. p. 843 on caffeine; Garber
      and Lustig, "Is Fast Food Addictive?"

34   Quoted in Tanya Pollard, "The Pleasures and Perils of Smoking in
      Early Modern England," in *Smoke: A Global History of Smoking*, ed.
      Sander L. Gilman and Zhou Xun (London: Reaktion Books, 2004), p.
      43; I have modernized the spelling.

35   Gin: Warner et al., "Can Legislation Prevent Debauchery?," pp.
      375–84. Tea and tobacco: Shammas, "Changes in English and Anglo-
      American Consumption," pp. 179–84.

36   Koyama, "Transformation of Labor Supply," p. 518.

37   Alcoholic liver disease: Mervyn London, "History of Addiction: A UK
      Perspective," *American Journal on Addictions*, vol. 14, no. 2 (2005),
      pp. 97–105. London mortality: Mokyr, *Enlightened Economy*, pp. 295,
      465. For further evidence that excess alcohol consumption contrib-
      uted to ill health and death, see Peter Razzell and Christine Spence,
      "The Hazards of Wealth: Adult Mortality in Pre-Twentieth-Century
      England," *Social History of Medicine*, vol. 19, no. 3 (Dec. 2006), pp.
      381–405; and Burnett, *Liquid Pleasures*, pp. 164–65. Note, however,
      that Razzell and Spence probably understate the extent of drug-food
      consumption in the lower classes; e.g., see Ernest L. Abel, "The Gin
      Epidemic: Much Ado About What?," *Alcohol & Alcoholism*, vol. 36,
      no. 5 (Sept. 2001), pp. 401–5. Infant mortality in London climbed
      sharply during the first half of the eighteenth century, but the causes
      are not certain; see Peter Razzell and Christine Spence, "The History
      of Infant, Child and Adult Mortality in London, 1550–1850," *London
      Journal*, vol. 32, no. 3 (Nov. 2007), pp. 271–92.

38   Shammas, "Changes in English and Anglo-American Consumption,"
      pp. 180–81, determines that eighteenth-century tobacco imports
      were enough to supply about a pipeful a day to all English adults. But
      since few women smoked, we can conclude that on average men were
      smoking nearly twice that amount. And since not all men smoked,
      and some men smoked much less than others (often because they
      couldn't afford it), we can infer that many other smokers were indulg-
      ing in several pipefuls daily. On evidence that this smoking harmed
      health, see Razzell and Spence, "Hazards of Wealth." Pipes and cig-
      arettes: A. Tevrdal and K. Bjarveit, "Health Consequences of Pipe
      Versus Cigarette Smoking," *Tobacco Control*, vol. 20, no. 2 (March
      2011). Lemire, *Global Trade and the Transformation of Consumer
      Cultures*, pp. 192, 223–30, 246, calls use of tobacco as a disciplinary
      tool "coercive consumption."

39   Virginia Berridge, "Fenland Opium Eating in the Nineteenth Century,"
      British Journal of Addiction, vol. 72, no. 3 (March 1977), pp. 275–84

(quote is from p. 280); Anthony S. Wohl, *Endangered Lives: Public Health in Victorian Britain* (Cambridge: Harvard Univ. Press, 1983), pp. 34–35; Michael Obladen, "Lethal Lullabies: A History of Opium Use in Infants," *Journal of Human Lactation*, vol. 32, no. 1 (2016), pp. 75–85; Alfred W. McCoy, "Opium History, 1858 to 1940," n.d., https://web.archive.org/web/20070404134938/http://www.a1b2c3.com/drugs/opi010.htm (accessed 6 April 2019). Opium import data: London, "History of Addiction," p. 98.

40   Friedrich Engels, *The Condition of the Working-Class in England in 1844*, trans. Florence Kelley Wischnewetzky (London, 1892), chap. 5; quote is from p. 127, and see pp. 104–5 on laudanum. *Works of Charles Dickens*, vol. 11, *Sketches by Boz* (London, 1866), pp. 173–74.

41   The quote is from Alexander, *Globalization of Addiction*, p. 29, emphasis added.

CHAPTER 9: MAYA'S MODERN ARCHITECTURE

1   For a neurobiological take on the developmental psychology of unbounded acquisitiveness, see Narvaez, *Neurobiology*, pp. 147–50.

2   On English factory workers: E. P. Thompson, "Time, Work Discipline, and Industrial Capitalism," *Past and Present*, no. 38 (Dec. 1967), pp. 56–97. On the other hand, some early industrial work-shirking laborers drank heavily during their time off, suggesting the possibility of dislocation-induced alcohol abuse.

      On ale as a regulated dietary staple (discussed in the caption to Figure 7) see, for example, Shami Ghosh, review of *Medieval Market Morality: Life, Law and Ethics in the English Marketplace*, by James Davis, *Reviews in History*, Review Number 1246, 3 May 2012; Pajic, "'Ale for an Englishman Is a Natural Drink,'" pp. 285–86, 288–89.

3   Emile Durkheim, *Suicide: A Study in Sociology*, trans. John A. Spaulding and George Simpson (1897, New York: Free Press, 1951), p. 247. See also Ryan Gunderson, "Anomie's Eastern Origins: The Buddha's Indirect Influence on Durkheim's Understanding of Desire and Suffering," *European Journal of Social Theory*, vol. 19, no. 3 (Aug. 2016), pp. 355–73.

CHAPTER 10: IN THE SWEETNESS OF OUR REPOSE

1   On regional variation in late-medieval English peasants' access to non-subsistence consumption goods see, for example, Jo Sear, "Consumption and Trade in East Anglian Market Towns and Their Hinterlands in the Later Middle Ages," Paper given to the Medieval

Economic and Social History Seminar, University of Cambridge, 27 May 2015, esp. pp. 20–23, https://cambridge.academia.edu/JoSear.

2 The Varanasi rickshaw-wallahs that I knew were subject to opposing dislocating and integrative forces. Among the latter were extensive reliance on integrative practices at work and in domestic life, embedding in robust familial and social networks, and a culture steeped in religious spirituality. Symptomatic of the former was some wallahs' consumption of substances with addictive potential, including tobacco, alcohol, and paan (a popular chewed product that contains betel leaf).

3 Howard Zinn, *A People's History of the United States* (New York: Harper Colophon, 1980), p. 53. See also James Axtell, *The European and the Indian: Essays in the Ethnohistory of Colonial North America* (Oxford: Oxford Univ. Press, 1982), chap. 7, including p. 171, which affirms Zinn's observation; and Linebaugh and Rediker, *Many-Headed Hydra*, pp. 24, 32–35, 138–39.

4 J. Hector St. John de Crèvecoeur, *Letters from an American Farmer* (New York: Duffield and Company, 1908), p. 305.

5 Axtell, *European and the Indian*, p. 206. One might reasonably ask why if, in developmental terms, whites were strongly ego-identified, they became more contented and functionally satiable after assimilation into American Indian society? Recall what happened to Yudhishthira after exile: knocked off his imperial pedestal and back in the Forest—i.e., once his circumstances shifted—he resumed his path of psychospiritual growth. It's plausible that the same thing happened to whites after they left their dislocated and intensely egoic world and were welcomed into non-dislocated egalitarian native societies..

6 Chrestien Le Clerq, *Gaspesian: With the Customs and Religion of the Gaspesian Indians*, trans. William F. Ganong (Toronto: The Champlain Society, 1910), pp. 104–06; the original French text was published in Paris in 1691. See also Linebaugh and Rediker, *Many-Headed Hydra*, p. 265, for similar sentiments expressed in the eighteenth century by Mosquito Indians of Nicaragua.

7 Quoted in Axtell, *European and the Indian*, p. 170, emphasis in the original.

8 See four chapters in Peter C. Mancall and James H. Merrell, eds., *American Encounters: Natives and Newcomers from European Contact to Indian Removal* (New York: Routledge, 2000): Neal Salisbury, "The Indians' Old World: Native Americans and the Coming of Europeans," pp. 3–25; Cornelius J. Jaenen, "Amerindian Views of French Culture in the Seventeenth Century," pp. 68–95; Christopher L. Miller and George R. Hamell, "A New Perspective on Indian-White Contact: Cultural Symbols and Colonial Trade," pp. 176–93; and Daniel H. Usnerm Jr., "The Frontier Exchange

Economy of the Lower Mississippi Valley in the Eighteenth Century," pp. 216–39. See also Bruce G. Trigger, "Early Native American Responses to European Contact: Romantic Versus Rationalistic Interpretations," *Journal of American History*, vol. 77, no. 4 (March 1991), pp. 1195–1215; Lemire, *Global Trade and the Transformation of Consumer Cultures*, pp. 56–64, 72–73, 191–93, 230–31.

Indians also traded for alcohol. For instance, native groups in eastern North America initially used alcohol ceremonially and as a means of accessing spiritually valued mental states. Later, as dislocation mounted—and as Bruce Alexander has taught us to expect—they became increasingly susceptible to socially destructive alcohol abuse. See Peter C. Mancall, "The Bewitching Tyranny of Custom: The Social Costs of Indian Drinking in Colonial America," in Mancall and Merrell, *American Encounters*, pp. 194–215.

9   R. C. Allen and J. L. Weisdorf, "Was There an 'Industrious Revolution' Before the Industrial Revolution? An Empirical Exercise for England, c. 1300–1830," *Economic History Review*, vol. 64, no. 3 (Aug. 2011), pp. 715–29.

10 Thompson, *Customs in Common*, chap. 3; E. P. Thompson, *The Making of the English Working Class* (Middlesex: Penguin, 1980), part 2; Eric Hobsbawm and George Rudé, *Captain Swing* (New York: W. W. Norton, 1975), part 1 and chap 15.

11 On the range of people oppressed and exploited, see Linebaugh and Rediker, *Many-Headed Hydra*.

12 On imperialism: Beckert, *Empire of Cotton*, pp. 129–31, 180–82, 224, 236–39, 267, 279–80, 296–97, 300–301, 304–5, 309, 313–14, 318, 323–24, 326, 333–35, 343, 357, 360, 368, 371, 420–21, 437; Acemoglu and Robinson, *Why Nations Fail*, chap. 9.

13 Anne E. C. McCants, "Exotic Goods, Popular Consumption, and the Standard of Living: Thinking About Globalization in the Early Modern World," *Journal of World History*, vol. 18, no. 4 (Dec. 2007), pp. 433–62; de Vries, *Industrious Revolution*, pp. 123n2, 149–54, 175–77.

14 Émile Durkheim, *On Suicide*, trans. Robin Buss (London: Penguin, 2006), pp. 269–82. On ambiguities in Durkheim's theory of insatiability, see Donald N. Levine, *The Flight from Ambiguity: Essays in Social and Cultural Theory* (Chicago: Univ. of Chicago Press, 1985), chap. 4; Finn Bowring, "The Individual and Society in Durkheim: Unpicking the Contradictions," *European Journal of Social Theory*, vol. 19, no. 1 (Feb. 2016), pp. 21–38.

15 E.g., Linebaugh and Rediker, *Many-Headed Hydra*, pp. 21, 33–35; Axtell, *European and the Indian*, p. 206.

16 Linebaugh and Rediker, *Many-Headed Hydra*, chaps. 2–4; Thompson, *Customs in Common*, chaps. 3–4, 6; Thompson, *Making of the English Working Class*, part 3; Hobsbawm and Rudé, *Captain Swing*.

17   Eugene D. Genovese, *From Rebellion to Revolution: Afro-American Slave Revolts in the Making of the Modern World* (Baton Rouge: Louisiana State Univ. Press, 1979); Linebaugh and Rediker, *Many-Headed Hydra*, chaps. 6–7.

18   Bronislaw Malinowski, *Argonauts of the Western Pacific* (Long Grove, IL: Waveland Press, 2013), esp. chaps. 2, 5–6, 12, 17.

19   On Trobriand holism, see Dorothy Lee, *Freedom and Culture* (Englewood Cliffs: Prentice-Hall, 1959), pp. 42–43, 89–120. Inés Hernández-Ávila, "Spirit Crossings: An Indigenous Cultural Perspective on Mortality, Death, and Dying," in Apfel-Marglin and Varese, *Contemporary Voices from Anima Mundi*, pp. 87–112, esp. pp. 95–96, contrasts indigenous cultures' "fluid dualities" with the sharp binary dualities that are characteristic of modern Western civilization.

20   Compare James Hillman, *The Soul's Code: In Search of Character and Calling* (New York: Warner Books, 1996); Matthew Fox, *The Reinvention of Work: A New Vision of Livelihood in Our Time* (New York: HarperCollins, 1994); David Brooks, *The Second Mountain: The Quest for a Moral Life* (New York: Random House, 2019), part 1.

CHAPTER 11: A BUTTERFLY DREAMING

1   Malinowski, *Argonauts*, p. 328.

2   On alchemy as a practice for advancing psychospiritual transformation, see Jaffé, *C. G. Jung*, pp. 96–109; Carl G. Jung, *Jung on Alchemy*, ed. Nathan Schwartz-Salant (Princeton: Princeton Univ. Press, 1995); and Mircea Eliade, *The Forge and the Crucible: The Origins and Structures of Alchemy*, trans. Stephen Corrin (Chicago: Univ. of Chicago Press, 1978).

3   Adam Smith, *The Theory of Moral Sentiments*, 6th ed., Vol. 1 (London, 1790), pp. 461–65.

4   Smith, *Theory of Moral Sentiments*, p. 466.

5   See, for example, Mark Pluciennik, "Archaeology, Anthropology, and Subsistence," *Journal of the Royal Anthropological Institute*, vol. 7, no. 4 (Dec. 2001), pp. 741–58; Rogoff, *The Cultural Nature of Human Development*, pp. 18–20.

6   See, for example, Georg Wilhelm Friedrich Hegel, *The Philosophy of History*, trans. J. Sibree (New York: Dover, 1956).

7   See, for example, John Ruskin's 1860 work, *"Unto This Last": Four Essays on the First Principles of Political Economy* (Lincoln: Univ. of Nebraska Press, 1967).

8   Johan Heilbron, Lars Magnusson, and Björn Wittrock, eds., *The Rise of the Social Sciences and the Formation of Modernity: Conceptual*

Change in Context, 1750–1850 (Dordrecht: Kluwer Academic, 1998). On normalizing and universalizing the familiar, see Joseph Henrich, Steven J. Heine, and Ara Norenzayan, "The Weirdest People in the World?," *Behavioral and Brain Sciences*, vol. 33, nos. 2–3 (June 2010), pp. 61–135.

9   On contradictions and fallacies: Sclove, *Democracy and Technology*, pp. 161–70; Bowles, "Endogenous Preferences"; and see the criticisms summarized in "Homo economicus," *Wikipedia*, last modified 14 Feb. 2021, https://en.wikipedia.org/wiki/Homo_economicus.

10   Others have taken steps toward articulating such a critique. We've noted that Durkheim argued that market-driven dislocation engenders the "constantly renewed torture" of insatiable craving and increases the incidence of suicide. Psychologists have found that dislocation can also interfere with psychological development, again causing mental disorders. Herbert Marcuse, John Kenneth Galbraith, and Juliet Schor are among those who have explored ways in which modern societies manufacture the discontent and cravings needed to keep the economy churning. See, for example, Galbraith, *The Affluent Society*; Marcuse, *One-Dimensional Man*; Juliet B. Schor, *The Overspent American: Why We Want What We Don't Need* (New York: Harper Perennial, 1998). Mainstream economics has been criticized from many other angles, often to devastating effect. However, our critique drives a nail deeper into the heart of the mainstream's central concern with satisfying people's preferences.

11   On the new turn in economics: Matthew Rabin, "A Perspective on Psychology and Economics," *European Economic Review*, vol. 46, nos. 4–5 (May 2002), pp. 657–85.

12   On internalizing norms as represented in behavioral economics see, for example, Elinor Ostrom, "Collective Action and the Evolution of Social Norms," *Journal of Economic Perspectives*, vol. 14, no. 3 (Summer 2000), pp. 137–58. On development as distinct from internalizing norms, see John C. Gibbs, *Moral Development and Reality: Beyond the Theories of Kohlberg, Hoffman, and Haidt*, 3rd ed. (Oxford: Oxford Univ. Press, 2014), p. 11 and chaps. 3–4 (quote is from p. 35, emphasis in the original); and also Narvaez, *Neurobiology*, p. 119: "Morality is integrated into one's being . . . instead of adopted as a separate, intellectual code of ethics." Writing from a transpersonal perspective, Cassandra Vieten, Tina Amorok, and Marilyn Mandala Schlitz write: "Altruism and compassion may arise as a natural consequence of experiences of interconnection and oneness . . . and a resulting shift in the sense of self and self in relationship to others" ("I to We: The Role of Consciousness Transformation in Compassion and Altruism," *Zygon*, vol. 41, no. 4 [Dec. 2006], pp. 915–31, esp. p. 930).

13   E.g., Gerald Marwell and Ruth E. Ames, "Economists Free Ride, Does Anyone Else?," *Journal of Public Economics*, vol. 15, no. 3 (1981), pp. 295–310.

14   The Taboo is so strongly policed that it is rare even to find it discussed. See, however, Riyad Ahmed Shahjahan, "Spirituality in the Academy: Reclaiming from the Margins and Evoking a Transformative Way of Knowing the World," *International Journal of Qualitative Studies in Education*, vol. 18, no. 6 (Nov.–Dec. 2005), pp. 685–711; Jeffrey J. Kripal, *The Flip: Epiphanies of Mind and the Future of Knowledge* (New York: Bellevue Literary Press, 2019), chap. 1; Angela Voss and Simon Wilson, eds., *Re-enchanting the Academy* (Auckland and Seattle: Rubedo Press, 2017).

15   Cassandra Vieten, Helané Wahbeh, B. Rael Cahn, et al., "Future Directions in Meditation Research: Recommendations for Expanding the Field of Contemplative Science," *PLoS ONE*, vol. 13, no. 11 (2018), https://doi.org/10.1371/journal.pone.0205740, p. 21.

16   On the denigration of indigenous knowledge, see Apffel-Marglin, "Western Modernity"; Riyad A. Shahjahan and Kimberly A. Haverkos, "Revealing the Secular Fence of Knowledge: Towards Reimagining Spiritual Ways of Knowing and Being in the Academy," in *Indigenous Philosophies and Critical Education: A Reader*, ed. George. J. Sefa Dei (New York: Peter Lang, 2011), pp. 367–85. The modern criminalization of psilocybin and other drugs that induce mystical experiences could also be interpreted as a reflection of the impulse to protect ego-sovereignty; compare Robert Forte, ed., *Entheogens and the Future of Religion* (Rochester: Park Street Press, 2012).

17   Charles T. Tart, ed., *Transpersonal Psychologies* (London: Routledge & Kegan Paul, 1975); Charles T. Tart, "States of Consciousness and State-Specific Sciences," *Science*, vol. 176, no. 4040 (16 June 1972), pp. 1203–10; Constance Holden, "Altered States of Consciousness: Mind Researchers Meet to Discuss Exploration and Mapping of 'Inner Space,'" *Science*, vol. 179, no. 4077 (9 March 1973), pp. 982–83; Scott D. Churchill, "Humanistic Psychology as 'The Other': The Marginalization of Dissident Voices Within Academic Institutions," *Journal of Theoretical and Philosophical Psychology*, vol. 17, no. 2 (Fall 1997), pp. 137–49; David N. Elkins, "Why Humanistic Psychology Lost Its Power and Influence in American Psychology: Implications for Advancing Humanistic Psychology," *Journal of Humanistic Psychology*, vol. 49, no. 3 (July 2009), pp. 267–91.

18   Jennifer A. Lindholm, Helen S. Astin, and Alexander W. Astin, "Spirituality and the Professoriate: A National Study of Faculty Beliefs, Attitudes, and Behaviors," Higher Education Research Institute, Univ. of California, Los Angeles (2005), p. 3, http://spirituality.ucla.edu/docs/results/faculty/spirit_professoriate.pdf.

19 Matthieu Ricard, Antoine Lutz, and Richard J. Davidson, "Mind of the Meditator," *Scientific American*, vol. 311, no. 5 (Nov. 2014), pp. 38–45. On the exponential growth in scientific studies of contemplative practices, see the diagram of "'Mindfulness' Journal Articles Published by Year: 1980–2020" assembled by the American Mindfulness Research Association, https://goamra.org/Library (accessed 25 July 2021). On the challenge of conducting research on meditation without being perceived as "flakey" or "lunatic fringe," see Jon Kabat-Zinn, "Some Reflections on the Origins of MBSR, Skillful Means, and the Trouble with Maps," *Contemporary Buddhism*, vol. 12, no. 1 (May 2011), pp. 281–306; and Vieten et al., "Future Directions in Meditation Research," pp. 1–3, 21.

20 On recent openness to spirituality, see Arthur W. Chickering, Jon C. Dalton, and Liesa Stamm, eds., *Encouraging Authenticity and Spirituality in Higher Education* (San Francisco: John Wiley & Sons, 2006); Daniel P. Barbezat and Mirabai Bush, *Contemplative Practices in Higher Education: Powerful Methods to Transform Teaching and Learning* (San Francisco: Jossey-Bass, 2014); Michael D. Waggoner, "Spirituality in Contemporary Higher Education," *Journal of College & Character*, vol. 17, no. 3 (Aug. 2016), pp. 147–56. On the recent emergence of research into post-egoic psychology, see Vieten et al., "Future Directions in Meditation Research," pp. 3–4; and for examples see Mills et al., "Change in Sense of Nondual Awareness and Spiritual Awakening"; Zoran Josipovic, "Neural Correlates of Nondual Awareness in Meditation," *Annals of the New York Academy of Sciences*, vol. 1307, no. 1 (Jan. 2014), pp. 9–18.; Davis and Vago, "Can Enlightenment Be Traced to Specific Neural Correlates, Cognition, or Behavior?"; Hanley et al., "The Nondual Awareness Dimensional Assessment"; and Yaden et al., "The Varieties of Self-Transcendent Experience."

21 On the lack of cross-fertilization between psychologists and historians, see Michael Muthukrishna, Joseph Henrich, and Edward Slingerland, "Psychology as a Historical Science," *Annual Reviews of Psychology*, vol. 72 (Jan. 2021), pp. 717–49. Ratner, *Macro Cultural Psychology*, is a rare counterinstance. The quote is from Richard M. Lerner, Rachel M. Hershberg, Lacey J. Hilliard, and Sara K. Johnson, "Concepts and Theories of Human Development," in *Developmental Science: An Advanced Textbook*, ed. Marc H. Bornstein and Michael E. Lamb, 7th ed. (New York: Psychology Press, 2015), p. 23.

22 The sociological perspective is exemplified in Anthony Giddens's influential *The Constitution of Society: Outline of the Theory of Structuration* (Berkeley: Univ. of California Press, 1984).

23 As rare counterexamples, see Theodore Roszak, *Where the Wasteland Ends: Politics and Transcendence in Postindustrial Society* (Garden City: Anchor Books, 1973); Elena Mustakova-Possardt and

Julie Oxenberg, "Toward Cultivating Socially Responsible Global Consciousness," in *Toward a Socially Responsible Psychology for a Global Era*, ed. Elena Mustakova-Possardt, Mikhail Lyubansky, Michael Basseches, and Julie Oxenberg (New York: Springer, 2014), pp. 121–47; Loy, *A Buddhist History of the West*; David R. Loy, *The Great Awakening: A Buddhist Social Theory* (Boston: Wisdom Publications, 2003).

24 Adam Grant analyzes this type of superiority complex in *Think Again: The Power of Knowing What You Don't Know* (New York: Viking, 2021).

25 The quote is from Karl Marx, *Critique of Hegel's "Philosophy of Right,"* trans. Joseph O'Malley (Cambridge: Cambridge Univ. Press, 1977), p. 131. See also N. Lobkowicz, "Karl Marx's Attitude Toward Religion," *The Review of Politics*, vol. 26, no. 3 (July 1964), pp. 319–52.

26 "Far-left" academics: Jennifer A. Lindholm, *The Quest for Meaning and Wholeness: Spiritual and Religious Connections in the Lives of College Faculty* (San Francisco: Jossey-Bass, 2014), pp. 50–52.

CHAPTER 12: WHEN THE NEED FOR ILLUSION IS DEEP

1 Saul Bellow, *To Jerusalem and Back: A Personal Account* (New York: Penguin, 1998), p. 127.

2 See, for example, Andrew D. Brown, "Narcissism, Identity, and Legitimacy," *The Academy of Management Review*, vol. 22, no. 3 (July 1997), pp. 643–86. On denial operating at the societal level, see Stanley Cohen, *States of Denial: Knowing About Atrocities and Suffering* (Cambridge: Polity Press, 2001); Eviatar Zerubavel, *The Elephant in the Room: Silence and Denial in Everyday Life* (Oxford: Oxford Univ. Press, 2006).

3 On the value of an incomplete social theory see, for example, G. A. Cohen, *Karl Marx's Theory of History: A Defense* (Princeton: Princeton Univ. Press, 1978), chap. 9. However, our theory—which specifies not an only an agent's (i.e., the ego's) interests but also its motives and various mechanisms through which it achieves its ends—is more fully fleshed out than the functional explanations that Cohen discusses.

4 For examples, see the Boston Ujima Project, https://www.ujimaboston.com; and *Yes!* magazine, https://www.yesmagazine.org. For historical examples see Ian Tod and Michael Wheeler, *Utopia* (New York: Harmony Books, 1978); and two books by Dolores Hayden: *Seven American Utopias: The Architecture of Communitarian Socialism, 1790–1975* (Cambridge: MIT Press, 1976) and *The Grand*

Domestic Revolution: A History of Feminist Designs for American Homes, Neighborhoods, and Cities (Cambridge: MIT Press, 1982).

5   On happiness studies see, for example, John F. Helliwell, Haifang Huang, and Shun Wang, "The Geography of World Happiness," in *World Happiness Report 2015*, ed. John F. Helliwell, Richard Layard, and Jeffrey Sachs (New York: Sustainable Development Solutions Network, 2015), pp. 29–34.

6   On judgments that reflect an unconscious interest in sustaining a flattering self-image see, for example, David Dunning, "A Newer Look: Motivated Social Cognition and the Schematic Representation of Social Concepts," *Psychological Inquiry*, vol. 10, no. 1 (1999), pp. 1–11.

7   Robert A. Cummins, "Subjective Wellbeing, Homeostatically Protected Mood and Depression: A Synthesis," *Journal of Happiness Studies*, vol. 11, no. 1 (March 2010), pp. 1–17, esp. pp. 1–3, 9, 13–14; quote is from p. 14. Cummins ranks depression on a scale that ranges from no depression ("normal") to "moderate," "severe," and then "extreme" depression.

8   On the Western individualistic bias that is unconsciously embedded in happiness studies, including how this contrasts with Eastern religious critiques of ego-identification, see John Chambers Christopher and Sarah Hickinbottom, "Positive Psychology, Ethnocentrism, and the Disguised Ideology of Individualism," *Theory and Psychology*, vol. 18, no. 5 (Oct. 2008), pp. 563–89, esp. pp. 568–69. For a wide-ranging assessment of cultural bias in studies of happiness and subjective well-being, see Roland Littlewood, "State-of-Science Review—SR–X5: Comparative Cultural Perspectives in Wellbeing," Foresight Project, UK Government Office for Science, Sept. 2008. On the ego's happiness with emotional pain, and even a certain drive to enhance such pain in the service of perpetuating ego-identification, see the discussion of the "pain-body" in Eckhart Tolle, *The Power of Now: A Guide to Spiritual Enlightenment* (Novato, CA: New World Library, 1999).

   As one indication that modern people are assessing their contentment in comparative terms, and not always accurately: Most people in developed countries rank their happiness as "above average"— which is a statistical impossibility. In one study of 2,300 middle-aged twins born in Minnesota and judged otherwise representative of Minnesotans overall, 86 percent imagined themselves to be in the top 35 percent in terms of contentment. But statistically, only 35 percent can actually have been in the top 35 percent, so at least 51 percent (i.e., 86 – 35 percent) were wrong. On Minnesota, see David Lykken and Auke Tellegen, "Happiness Is a Stochastic Phenomenon," *Psychological Science*, vol. 7, no. 3 (May 1996), pp. 186–89, esp. p. 186; and, more generally, see Bruce Headey and Alex Wearing,

"The Sense of Relative Superiority—Central to Well-Being," *Social Indicators Research*, vol. 20, no. 5 (Oct. 1988), pp. 497–516.

9   On post-egoic happiness, see, for example, Matthieu Ricard, *Happiness*, trans. Jesse Browner (New York: Little, Brown and Co., 2006). Related considerations are addressed in studies concerned with the Aristotelian concept of *eudaimonia*, but without considering the possibility of a post-egoic developmental range; see, for example, Carol D. Ryff and Burton H. Singer, "Know Thyself and Become What You Are: A Eudaimonic Approach to Psychological Well-Being," *Journal of Happiness Studies*, vol. 9, no. 1 (Jan. 2008), pp. 13–39. Contemporary Buddhist reflections on consumption and desire are also pertinent; see, for example, Mark Epstein, *Open to Desire: Embracing a Lust for Life* (New York: Gotham Books, 2005); Allan Hunt Badiner, ed., *Mindfulness in the Marketplace: Compassionate Responses to Consumerism* (Berkeley: Parallax Press, 2002); Stephanie Kaza, *Hooked!: Buddhist Writings on Greed, Desire, and the Urge to Consume* (Boston: Shambhala, 2005). Or watch: "Dalai Lama Starts Eating Pizza During Interview," YouTube video, 7:18, broadcast by Canberra TV, posted 26 June 2018, https://www.youtube.com/watch?v=qE7tck1QZoE, starting at 4:46.

10 David Brooks, "The Moral Peril of Meritocracy," *New York Times*, 6 April 2019.

11 As noted at the end of Chapter 6, one preliminary indication that ego-identification factors into multiple mental illnesses is the fact that psychedelics-induced ego dissolution is showing itself effective as a treatment. See also Yaden and Griffiths, "The Subjective Effects of Psychedelics Are Necessary for Their Enduring Therapeutic Effects." On malnutrition and disease in premodern times see, for example, Sharon DeWitte and Philip Slavin, "Between Famine and Death: England on the Eve of the Black Death—Evidence from Paleoepidemiology and Manorial Accounts," *Journal of Interdisciplinary History*, vol. 44, no. 1 (Summer 2013), pp. 37–60.

12 Joseph E. Stiglitz, Amartya Sen, and Jean-Paul Fitoussi, *Report by the Commission on the Measurement of Economic Performance and Social Progress* (2009), https://www.insee.fr/en/statistiques/fichier/2662494/stiglitz-rapport-anglais.pdf; Ed Diener and Martin E. P. Seligman, "Beyond Money: Toward an Economy of Well-Being," *Psychological Science in the Public Interest*, vol. 5, no. 1 (July 2004), pp. 1–31, esp. pp. 20–25.

13 The possibility that economic and psychological development might secretly diverge flies beneath the radar even of Amartya Sen's admirably egalitarian and humanistic *Development as Freedom* (New York: Anchor Books, 1999).

14 Hunter-gatherers: Bird-David et al., "Beyond 'The Original Affluent Society,'" pp. 29–31, 41–42 (quote from p. 31). Wealthy families:

Graeme Wood, "Secret Fears of the Super-Rich," *The Atlantic*, April 2011; 120 of the 165 families said that their net worth was at least $25 million and two reported that they were billionaires. Wealth-rank data calculated from *Global Wealth Report 2015* (Zurich: Credit Suisse Research, 2015), p. 26. For further discussion of the psychology of abundance, scarcity, security, and insecurity in non-modern versus modern societies, see John H. Bodley, *Anthropology and Contemporary Human Problems*, 6th ed. (Lanham, MD: Altamira, 2012), chaps 1–2, 4, 6–7; and Monica L. Smith, ed., *Abundance: The Archaeology of Plenitude* (Boulder: Univ. Press of Colorado, 2017). Note, however, that the evidence in Smith's book does not obviously provide support for her casual conclusion that, just as in modern times, all non-modern cultures—even going back to the Paleolithic—experienced "a relationship to material culture in which 'too much is not enough'" (Smith, p. 16).

15   On hunter-gatherers, see Bird-David et al., "Beyond 'The Original Affluent Society,'" pp. 29–30, 42. For similar observations regarding indigenous cultures more generally, see Frédérique Apffel-Marglin, *Subversive Spiritualities: How Rituals Enact the World* (Oxford: Oxford Univ. Press, 2011).

CHAPTER 13: MAYA'S GLOBAL EMPIRE

1   Pope Innocent III, "On the Misery of Man," in Bernard Murchland, ed. and trans., *Two Views of Man* (New York: Ungar, 1966), p. 35.

2   Barbara Tuchman, *A Distant Mirror: The Calamitous 14th Century* (New York: Ballantine Books, 1978), pp. xix–48; quote is from p. 31.

3   Tuchman, *A Distant Mirror*, p. 28.

4   Van Buitenen, *MBh*, vol. 2, p. 145; and Wendy Doniger, *The Hindus: An Alternative History* (New York: Penguin, 2009), pp. 320–21 and, on propensities to debilitating addiction among India's emperors during the later Mughal period, pp. 539–44, 567.

5   Tuchman, *Distant Mirror*, pp. 25–32. On hierarchical stature unleashing insatiable desires, see also Durkheim, *On Suicide*, pp. 276–78.

6   On the ancient history of hierarchy as conventionally understood: Kent Flannery and Joyce Marcus, *The Creation of Inequality: How Our Prehistoric Ancestors Set the Stage for Monarchy, Slavery, and Empire* (Cambridge: Harvard Univ. Press, 2014), part 1; Stephen K. Sanderson, *Social Transformations: A General Theory of Historical Development* (Lanham, MD: Rowman & Littlefield, 1999), chaps. 2–4; Bodley, *Anthropology*, chaps. 2, 4, 6. On meandering and hybridized pathways: David Graeber and David Wengrow, The Dawn

of Everything: *A New History of Humanity* (New York: Farrar, Straus and Giroux, 2021).

7   E.g., Jennifer Hillman Elizabeth Tingle, *Soul Travel: Spiritual Journeys in Late Medieval and Early Modern Europe* (Oxford: Peter Lang, 2019); Carlo Ginzburg, *Ecstasies: Deciphering the Witches' Sabbath*, trans. Raymond Rosenthal (Chicago: Univ. of Chicago Press, 2004); Hans Peter Duerr, *Dreamtime: Concerning the Boundary Between Wilderness and Civilization*, trans. Felicitas Goodman (Oxford: Basil Blackwell, 1985); D. M. Dooling, ed., *A Way of Working* (Garden City: Anchor Books, 1979).

8   Bernard McGinn, *The Flowering of Mysticism: Men and Women in the New Mysticism, 1200–1350* (New York: Crossroad, 1998), pp. 244–45.

9   On narcissism: Piff, "Wealth and the Inflated Self"; Côté, *Arrested Adulthood*, pp. 191–95. On prosocial behavior: Paul K. Piff, Daniel M. Stancato, Stéphane Côté, et al., "Higher Social Class Predicts Increased Unethical Behavior," *Proceedings of the National Academy of Sciences*, vol. 109, no. 11 (13 March 2012), pp. 4086–91; Paul K. Piff, Michael W. Kraus., Stéphane Côté, et al., "Having Less, Giving More: The Influence of Social Class on Prosocial Behavior," *Journal of Personality and Social Psychology*, vol. 99, no. 5 (Nov. 2010), pp. 771–84; Benjamin I. Page, Jason Seawright, and Matthew J. Lacombe, "What Billionaires Want: The Secret Influence of America's 100 Richest," *Guardian*, 31 Oct. 2018. On pathologies of power: Dacher Keltner, *The Power Paradox: How We Gain and Lose Influence* (New York: Penguin, 2016), chap 4.

10   On factors at play in modern organizations, see Linda K. Trevino, Gary R. Weaver, and Scott J. Reynolds, "Behavioral Ethics in Organizations: A Review," *Journal of Management*, vol. 32, no. 6 (Dec. 2006), pp. 951–90; Tim Kasser, Steve Cohn, Allen D. Kanner, and Richard M. Ryan, "Some Costs of American Corporate Capitalism: A Psychological Exploration of Value and Goal Conflicts," *Psychological Inquiry*, vol. 18, no. 1 (2007), pp. 1–22.

11   On moral backsliding, see Linda Klebe Trevino, "Moral Reasoning and Business Ethics: Implications for Research, Education, and Management," *Journal of Business Ethics*, vol. 11, nos. 5–6 (May 1992), pp. 445–59, esp. pp. 450, 456; Robin Stanley Snell, "Complementing Kohlberg: Mapping the Ethical Reasoning Used by Managers for Their Own Dilemma Cases," *Human Relations*, vol. 49, no. 1 (Jan. 1996), pp. 23–49, esp. pp. 44–46; Anne Applebaum, "History Will Judge the Complicit: Why Have Republican Leaders Abandoned Their Principles in Support of an Immoral and Dangerous President?," *Atlantic*, July/Aug. 2020. Fortune 500 executives: Linda Klebe Trevino, "Ethical Decision Making in Organizations: A Person-Situation Interactionist Model," *Academy of Management*

Review, vol. 11, no. 3 (1986), pp. 601–17, esp. p. 602. On inconsistency between moral reasoning and action, see Stephen Thoma, "Moral Judgments and Moral Action," in *Moral Development in the Professions: Psychology and Applied Ethics*, ed. James R. Rest and Darcia Narvaez (Hillsdale: Lawrence Erlbaum Associates, 1994), pp. 199–211. On inconsistency between empathic feelings and moral behavior, see Gibbs, *Moral Development and Reality*, chap. 5.

12   Elizabeth Warren, *A Fighting Chance* (New York: Metropolitan Books, 2014), p. 106, emphasis in the original.

13   On the diversity of modern theories of moral development, see Melanie Killen and Judith G. Smetana, eds., *Handbook of Moral Development*, 2nd ed. (New York: Psychology Press, 2014); Beverly Garrigan, Anna L. R. Adlam, and Peter E. Langdon, "Moral Decision-Making and Moral Development: Toward an Integrative Framework," *Developmental Review*, vol. 49 (Sept. 2018), pp. 80–100, esp. pp. 80–85.

14   Kant, *Foundations of the Metaphysics of Morals*, p. 21. See also Gibbs, *Moral Development and Reality*, pp. 14, 100, 130–31, 246.

15   The moral corrosiveness of modern markets is addressed in Kasser et al., "Some Costs of American Corporate Capitalism"; and Samuel Bowles, "Endogenous Preferences: The Cultural Consequences of Markets and Other Economic Institutions," *Journal of Economic Literature*, vol. 36 (March 1998), pp. 75–111, esp. pp. 88–89, 92, 99, 104; and debated in Jagdish Bhagwati, John Gray, Garry Kasparov, et al., *Does the Free Market Corrode Moral Character?* (West Conshohocken, PA: John Templeton Foundation, Autumn 2008). I extend these concerns to cyberspace in Sclove, "Cybersobriety," pp. 44–45.

16   See, for example, John C. Gibbs, Karen S. Basinger, Rebecca L. Grime, and John R. Snarey, "Moral Judgment Development across Cultures: Revisiting Kohlberg's Universality Claims," *Developmental Review*, vol. 27, no. 4 (Dec. 2007), pp. 443–500. On moral exemplars, see Anne Colby and William Damon, *Some Do Care: Contemporary Lives of Moral Commitment* (New York: Free Press, 1992); and Philip Hallie, *Lest Innocent Blood Be Shed: The Story of the Village of Le Chambon and How Goodness Happened There* (New York: Harper Colophon, 1979).

17   Robert Coles, *The Moral Life of Children* (Boston: Houghton Mifflin Co., 1986), p. 25; Elena Mustakova-Possardt, Mikhail Lyubansky, Michael Basseches, and Julie Oxenberg, eds., *Toward a Socially Responsible Psychology for a Global Era* (New York: Springer, 2014), pp. 136–41, 256, 264.

18   C. B. Macpherson, *The Political Theory of Possessive Individualism: Hobbes to Locke* (Oxford: Oxford Univ. Press, 1962).

19   Marcel Gauchet, *The Disenchantment of the World: A Political History of Religion*, trans. Oscar Burge (Princeton: Princeton Univ. Press, 1997); Charles Taylor, *A Secular Age* (Cambridge: Belknap Press of Harvard Univ. Press, 2007).

20   De Vries, *Industrious Revolution*, pp. 126–27; Fernand Braudel, *The Structures of Everyday Life: The Limits of the Possible*, trans. Siân Reynolds (New York: Harper & Row, 1981), pp. 308–9, 329–30; Dyer, *An Age of Transition?*, p. 53; Yi-Fu Tuan, *Segmented Worlds and Self: Group Life and Individual Consciousness* (Minneapolis: Univ. of Minnesota Press, 1982), chap. 4; Norbert Elias, *The History of Manners*, trans. Edmund Jephcott (New York: Pantheon, 1978), chap. 2. Elias begins his story among the European nobility of the Middle Ages, but these were people who, from our standpoint, were under the influence of their hierarchical stature and thus in the social vanguard of stabilizing in ego-sovereignty.

21   Carolyn Merchant, *The Death of Nature: Women, Ecology, and the Scientific Revolution* (San Francisco: Harper & Row, 1980); Robert D. Romanyshyn, *Technology as Symptom and Dream* (London: Routledge, 1989), chaps. 2 and 3. Nisbett et al., "Culture and Systems of Thought," postulate that social and economic organization can account for a culture's predilection for holistic versus analytic thought, but they don't explore the possibility that psycho-spiritual development can be a mediating factor.

22   Apffel-Marglin, "Western Modernity"; Shahjahan and Haverkos, "Revealing the Secular Fence of Knowledge"; Silvia Federici, *Caliban and the Witch: Women, the Body and Primitive Accumulation* (Brooklyn: Autonomedia, 2004).

23   Hilary Putnam, *The Collapse of the Fact/Value Dichotomy and Other Essays* (Cambridge: Harvard Univ. Press, 2004).

24   For instance, on culture as an enduring historical force, see Ronald Inglehart and Wayne E. Baker, "Modernization, Cultural Change, and the Persistence of Traditional Values," *American Sociological Review*, vol. 65, no. 1 (Feb. 2000), pp. 19–51.

25   McGilchrist, *Master and His Emissary*, pp. 386–438. See also Henrich, *The WEIRDest People in the World*, pp. 3–17, 52–55.

26   Natalie Angier, "Modern Life Suppresses an Ancient Body Rhythm," *New York Times*, 14 March 1995.

27   A. Roger Ekirch, *At Day's Close: Night in Times Past* (New York: W. W. Norton, 2006), esp. pp. 123–46, 300–39.

28   Lancelot Law Whyte, *The Unconscious Before Freud* (New York: Doubleday Anchor, 1962); Campbell, *Hero with a Thousand Faces*, p. 334.

29   Hunnicutt, *Free Time*, pp. 6–7 and chap. 2.

30   Compare Mihaly Csikszentmihalyi and Judith LeFevre, "Optimal Experience in Work and Leisure," *Journal of Personality and Social*

Psychology, vol. 56, no. 5 (1989), pp. 815–22; Henrich, *The WEIRDest People in the World*, pp. 360–67. On complexities in understanding time in various cultures and historical periods see, for example, Paul D. Glennie and Nigel Thrift, "Reworking E. P. Thompson's 'Time, Work-Discipline and Industrial Capitalism,'" *Time & Society*, vol. 5, no. 3 (Oct. 1996), pp. 275–99.

31   Hunnicutt, *Free Time*, pp. 113–15; Trentmann, *Empire of Things*, chap. 10.

32   Roland Marchand, *Advertising the American Dream: Making Way for Modernity, 1920–1940* (Berkeley: Univ. of California Press, 1985).

33   Ruth Schwartz Cowan, *More Work for Mother: The Ironies of Household Technology from the Open Hearth to the Microwave* (New York: Basic Books, 1983), p. 87 and chaps. 6–7.

34   Putnam, *Bowling Alone*, pp. 283–84.

35   Shoshana Zuboff, *The Age of Surveillance Capitalism: The Fight for a Human Future at the New Frontier of Power* (New York: Hachette Book Group, 2019).

36   Paul Rabinow, ed., *The Foucault Reader* (New York: Pantheon, 1984), pp. 169–256.

37   Lorenzo Pecchi and Gustavo Piga, eds., *Revisiting Keynes: Economic Possibilities for Our Grandchildren* (Cambridge: MIT Press, 2008).

38   On Teresa of Avila: Carol Lee Flinders, *Enduring Grace: Living Portraits of Seven Women Mystics* (San Francisco: HarperCollins, 1993), pp. 155–90. On Ramakrishna: Swami Saradananda, *Sri Ramakrishna: The Great Master*, 5th ed. (Madras: Sri Ramakrishna Math, 1978), vol. 1, parts 1–2.

39   Richard Katz, "Education for Transcendence: !Kia-Healing with the Kalahari !Kung," in *Kalahari Hunter-Gatherers: Studies of the !Kung San and Their Neighbors*, ed. Richard B. Lee and Irven DeVore (Cambridge: Harvard Univ. Press, 1976), pp. 279–301; quote is from p. 286.

40   On recent tribulations of the Ju/'hoansi, see Robert K. Hitchcock, "The Plight of the Kalahari San: Hunter-Gatherers in a Globalized World," *Journal of Anthropological Research*, vol. 76, no. 2 (Summer 2020), pp. 164–84; James Suzman, *Affluence Without Abundance: The Disappearing World of the Bushmen* (New York: Bloomsbury, 2017), part 3. Narvaez, *Neurobiology*, argues that traditional hunter-gathering societies are superior to modern ones in providing social conditions that support healthy psychological and moral development (she makes this claim explicitly on pp. 28–30, but accumulates evidence gradually throughout the book).

41   Functional satiability, low incidence of addiction, and ethnographic observations support the notion that many non-dislocated indigenous peoples have been relatively content and secure. Attempts to compare contentment *quantitatively* across cultures ranging from

traditional indigenous to postindustrial are rare and limited in what they can conclude. For instance, Tov and Diener, "Culture and Well-Being," in *Handbook of Cultural Psychology*, ed. Shinobu Kitayama and Dov Cohen (New York: Guilford, 2007), pp. 691–713, esp. p. 694, report that quantitative measures of subjective life satisfaction among contemporary Inughuit (traditional Arctic-region hunters) and African Maasai (traditional African pastoralists) differs little from that of the very richest Americans. But they also observe that "Not all comparisons of SWB [subjective well-being] are meaning-ful. . . . Comparisons are possible, [but] they should only be made with due care to take into account the unique factors present in various societies" which are "best captured by specific descriptions of the local culture" (p. 695). Critiques of such quantitative comparisons abound. See for example, Christopher and Hickinbottom, "Positive Psychology, Ethnocentrism, and the Disguised Ideology of Individualism"; Littlewood, "State-of-Science Review—SR–X5: Comparative Cultural Perspectives in Wellbeing"; and Nicholas Hill, Svend Brinkmann, and Anders Petersen, *Critical Happiness Studies* (London: Routledge, 2020).

42 Richard Katz, Megan Biesele, and Verna St. Denis, *Healing Makes Our Hearts Happy: Spirituality & Cultural Transformation Among the Kalahari Ju/'hoansi* (Rochester: Inner Traditions, 1997), pp. 20–26, 57, 59, 74, 105, 119; Dorothy Lee, *Valuing the Self: What We Can Learn from Other Cultures* (Englewood Cliffs: Prentice-Hall, 1976).

43 On cross-cultural perspective-taking, see John R. Snarey, "Cross-Cultural Universality of Social-Moral Development: A Critical Review of Kohlbergian Research," *Psychological Bulletin*, vol. 97, no. 2 (March 1985), pp. 202–32, esp. p. 227. Joseph Henrich, Robert Boyd, Samuel Bowles, et al., "'Economic Man' in Cross-Cultural Perspective: Behavioral Experiments in 15 Small-Scale Societies," *Behavioral and Brain Sciences*, vol. 28, no. 6 (Dec. 2005), pp. 795–855, report that altruism increases with a small society's involvement in market exchanges. However, the societies that they studied were not deeply integrated into the disruptive global economy. Quote is from Axtell, *European and the Indian*, p. 203.

44 Pomeranz, *Great Divergence*; Loren Brandt, Debin Ma, and Thomas G. Rawski, "From Divergence to Convergence: Re-evaluating the History Behind China's Economic Boom," *Journal of Economic Literature*, vol. 52, no. 1 (March 2014), pp. 45–123, esp. pp. 50–59.

45 See Chapter 8, above; and Pomeranz, *Great Divergence*, pp. 116–24.

46 On urbanization: Robert Brenner and Christopher Isett, "England's Divergence from China's Yangzi Delta: Property Relations, Microeconomics, and Patterns of Development," *Journal of Asian Studies*, vol. 61, no. 2 (May 2002), 609–62, esp. pp. 632–36, 654.

47 Carol Benedict, *Golden-Silk Smoke: A History of Tobacco in China, 1550–2010* (Berkeley: Univ. of California Press, 2011), pp. 50, 72–74, 100–02, 251; quotes in this and previous paragraph from pp. 74, 101.

48 Pomeranz, *Great Divergence*, pp. 35, 92–96, 117–18, 121–23, 152–54; Campbell, *Romantic Ethic*, pp. 22, 37, 63, 89, 93–94, 158–59, 201; Trentmann, *Empire of Things*, pp. 43–77 (quote is from p. 47).

49 On the history of China's encounter with opium: Alexander, *Globalization of Addiction*, pp. 130–31; W. Travis Hanes III and Frank Sanello, *The Opium Wars: The Addiction of One Empire and the Corruption of Another* (New York: Barnes & Noble, 2005), pp. 20–21, 25, 34, 163–67, 171, 220, 294–95 (Gladstone quote p. 79); Pomeranz and Topik, *World That Trade Created*, pp. 79, 90–93.

I've derived opium statistics from the following sources: British opium imports in 1859: London, "History of Addiction," p. 98. Chinese opium imports in 1859: Hanes and Sanello, *Opium Wars*, p. 293. Chinese opium imports in 1879: 6,700 tons according to Jack Patrick Hayes, "The Opium Wars in China" (2018), https://asiapacificcurriculum.ca/learning-module/opium-wars-china; and 7,350 tons according to Hanes and Sanello, *Opium Wars*, p. 293; I have conservatively rounded down to 6,500 tons. Chinese domestic opium production in 1880: *2008 World Drug Report* (Vienna: United Nations Office on Drugs and Crime, 2008), p. 176. Chinese opium consumption in 1906: Lin Lu, Yuxia Fang, and Xi Wang, "Drug Abuse in China: Past, Present and Future," *Cellular and Molecular Biology*, vol. 28, no. 4 (June 2008), pp. 479–90 (statistics on p. 481). Following "Opium Trade," *Encyclopedia Britannica*, https://www.britannica.com/topic/opium-trade (accessed 10 June 2020), I assume an average of 140 pounds of opium per chest. The number of Chinese addicts in 1900 was 40 million according to Pomeranz and Topik, *World That Trade Created*, p. 92; and 13.5 million, including 27 percent of adult males, according to Lu et al., "Drug Abuse in China," p. 481.

50 Beckert, *Empire of Cotton*, chaps. 9–12; Acemoglu and Robinson, *Why Nations Fail*, chap. 9; Prasannan Parthasarathi, *Why Europe Grew Rich and Asia Did Not: Global Economic Divergence, 1600–1850* (Cambridge: Cambridge Univ. Press, 2011), pp. 78–80 and part 3.

51 Parthasarathi, *Why Europe Grew Rich*, part 2.

52 On long-distance trade see, for example, Justin Jennings, *Globalizations and the Ancient World* (Cambridge: Cambridge Univ. Press, 2014); Shadreck Chirikure, "Land and Sea Links: 1500 Years of Connectivity Between Southern Africa and the Indian Ocean Rim Regions, AD 700 to 1700," *African Archaeological Review*, vol. 31, no. 4 (Dec. 2014), pp. 705–24. On trade and mass consumption see, for example, Timothy Brook, *The Confusions of Pleasure: Commerce and Culture in Ming China* (Berkeley: Univ. of California Press, 1999) pp. 1–152. On mind-altering substances:

Richard Davenport-Hines, *The Pursuit of Oblivion: A Global History of Narcotics, 1500–2000* (London: Weidenfield & Nicholson, 2001), chap. 1; Marlene Dobkin de Rios and Charles S. Grob, "Ritual Uses of Psychoactive Drugs," in *Encyclopedia of Psychopharmacology*, ed. Ian P. Stolerman (Berlin: Springer, 2010), https://doi.org/10.1007/978-3-540-68706-1_50; Michael Winkelman, ed., "Special Issue on Psychedelics in History and World Religions," *Journal of Psychedelic Studies*, vol. 3, no. 2 (June 2019).

53   On the limited available data concerning wine consumption in the ancient Roman world, and the contrasting ways in which it is interpreted, see Shaun Anthony Mudd, "Constructive Drinking in the Roman Empire" (PhD diss., Univ. of Exeter, 2015), pp. 11–33, 43–51, https://core.ac.uk/download/pdf/43095602.pdf; quote is from p. 48. Contemporary French wine consumption calculated from Hannah Ritchie and Max Roser, "Alcohol Consumption," *Our World in Data* (Nov. 2019), https://ourworldindata.org/alcohol-consumption.

54   Peter Temin, *The Roman Market Economy* (Princeton: Princeton Univ. Press, 2013), chap. 11; Claire Holleran, *Shopping in Ancient Rome: The Retail Trade in the Late Republic and the Principate* (Oxford: Oxford Univ. Press, 2012), esp. pp. 39–43, 61, 194–202, 231–32; Melissa Ratliff, "Globalization, Consumerism and the Ancient Roman Economy: A Preliminary Look at Bronze and Iron Production and Consumption," *Theoretical Roman Archeology Journal* (2010), pp. 32–46, online at http://doi.org/10.16995/TRAC2010_32_46; and two chapters in Martin Pitts and Miguel John Versluys, eds., *Globalisation and the Roman World: World History, Connectivity and Material Culture* (Cambridge: Cambridge Univ. Press, 2016): Neville Morley, "Globalisation and the Roman Economy," pp. 49–68; and Martin Pitts, "Globalisation, Circulation, and Mass Consumption in the Roman World," pp. 69–98. On cultural factors in the Romans' enthusiasm for wine, see Mudd, "Constructive Drinking," chaps. 2–3.

55   Germane to these issues is Robert Kegan, *In Over Our Heads: The Mental Demands of Modern Life* (Cambridge: Harvard Univ. Press, 1994), which addresses ways in which modern adult psychological development has fallen out of step with institutional and cultural change.

56   On ancient Athens, see James Davidson. "Citizen Consumers: The Athenian Democracy and the Origins of Western Consumption," in *The Oxford Handbook of the History of Consumption*, ed. Frank Trentmann (Oxford: Oxford Univ. Press, 2013), pp. 23–46. On the silk roads, see Peter Frankopan, *The Silk Roads: A New History of the World* (New York: Vintage, 2015), chaps. 1, 6, 7, 9–10; S. Frederick Starr, *Lost Enlightenment: Central Asia's Golden Age from the Arab Conquest to Tamerlane* (Princeton: Princeton Univ. Press, 2013), chap. 2.

As marauders and empire builders the Mongols were acquisitive by any standard, but success brought new challenges. Alcohol consumption among the Mongols shot up "when they grew estranged from their nomadic way of life and took to greater idleness" (Matthee, *Pursuit of Pleasure*, p. 42). Perhaps after a lifetime on the march conquering the known universe, putting down roots could prove dislocating in its own way.

57   See especially Valerie Hansen, *The Silk Road: A New History* (Oxford: Oxford Univ. Press, 2012); and secondarily Susan Whitfield, *Life Along the Silk Road*, 2nd ed. (Oakland: Univ. of California Press, 2015); and Yang Fuquan, "The 'Ancient Tea and Horse Caravan Road,' the 'Silk Road' of Southwest China," *Silk Road Journal*, vol. 2, no. 1 (June 2004), pp. 29–33. On the prevalence of locally self-reliant subsistence economies in premodern times—and in much of the world long afterwards—see Waters, *The Persistence of Subsistence Agriculture*, esp. pp. 55, 226.

58   On the possibility that ancient urbanizing civilizations sometimes experienced periods of chronic dislocation, see Jennings, *Globalizations*, esp. p. 55.

CHAPTER 14: PERILS OF PLANET EGO

1   National Center for Health Statistics, Centers for Disease Control and Prevention, "Suicide and Self-Inflicted Injury," 30 May 2016, https://www.cdc.gov/nchs/fastats/suicide.htm.

2   I say more about social structures, including technologies as a type of social structure, in Sclove, *Democracy and Technology*, pp. 11–24, 35–37.

3   On the follow-on social consequences of climate change (mentioned in the caption to Figure 15) see, for example, Institute for the Study of Diplomacy Working Group, *New Challenges to Human Security*; and Caitlin E. Werrell and Francesco Femia, eds., *Epicenters of Climate and Security: The New Geostrategic Landscape of the Anthropocene* (Washington, DC: The Center for Climate and Security, June 2017).

4   On capitalism and inequality, see Thomas Piketty, *Capital in the Twenty-First Century*, trans. Arthur Goldhammer (Cambridge: Belknap Press of Harvard Univ. Press, 2014).

5   Fascism could arguably count as a third existential threat. However, fascism was most directly a threat to world peace, political freedom, human rights, and the very existence of Jews and other regime-vilified peoples. European fascism greatly modified capitalism but did not aspire to abolish it.

6   On turbo-charged globalization see, for example, Arvind Subramanian and Martin Kessler, "The Hyperglobalization of Trade

and Its Future," Working Paper Series (Washington, DC: Peterson Institute for International Economics, 2013). On the expansion of slum areas in cities see, for example, United Nations Department of Economic and Social Affairs, Statistics Division, "Make Cities and Human Settlements Inclusive, Safe, Resilient and Sustainable," https://unstats.un.org/sdgs/report/2019/goal-11 (accessed 18 Oct. 2021). On a renewed nuclear-arms race: Michael Krepon, "The New Age of Nuclear Confrontation Will Not End Well," *New York Times*, 3 March 2019. On other impending threats to world order: Michael Mandelbaum, *The Rise and Fall of Peace on Earth* (Oxford: Oxford Univ. Press, 2019). On existential threats: Science and Security Board, "2020 Doomsday Clock Statement," *Bulletin of the Atomic Scientists*, 23 Jan. 2020.

7   See also Ronald Inglehart, "The Age of Insecurity: Can Democracy Save Itself?," *Foreign Affairs*, vol. 97, no. 3 (May/June 2018), pp. 20–28.

8   Apffel-Marglin, *Subversive Spiritualities*, chaps. 2–3; Glendinning, *My Name Is Chellis and I'm in Recovery from Western Civilization*; Charles Eisenstein, *The Ascent of Humanity: Civilization and the Human Sense of Self* (Berkeley: North Atlantic Books, 2013), esp. chap. 2; Theodore Roszak, Mary E. Gomes, and Allen D. Kanner, eds. *Ecopsychology: Restoring the Earth, Healing the Mind* (San Francisco: Sierra Club Books, 1995); Davis, "Ecopsychology, Transpersonal Psychology, and Nonduality." Glendinning understands that the experience of separateness is partly a matter of distorted psychological development.

9   Naomi Klein, *This Changes Everything: Capitalism vs. the Climate* (New York: Simon & Schuster, 2014). Scholarly works that are similar in orientation include James Gustave Speth, *America the Possible: Manifesto for a New Economy* (New Haven: Yale Univ. Press, 2012); and Tim Jackson, *Prosperity Without Growth*, 2nd ed. (London: Routledge, 2017).

10   Klein, *This Changes Everything*, p. 7.

CHAPTER 15: NOW WE KNOW IT

1   "Recognizing the Duty of the Federal Government to Create a Green New Deal," H. Res. 109, 109th Congress (7 Feb. 2020); Owen Bennett, "Paris Climate Summit Was Like Agreeing to Cut Down from Five Burgers a Day to Just Four, Says Naomi Klein," *Huffington Post UK*, 14 Dec. 2015.

2   Compare Anand Giridharadas, *Winners Take All: The Elite Charade of Changing the World* (New York: Alfred A. Knopf, 2018).

3   Michael Lerner, "Psychopathology in the 2016 Election," *Tikkun*, vol. 31, no. 4 (Fall 2016), pp. 5–16; Yochai Benkler, Robert Faris, Hal

Roberts, and Ethan Zuckerman, "Breitbart-Led Right-Wing Media Ecosystem Altered Broader Media Agenda," *Columbia Journalism Review*, 3 March 2017, https://www.cjr.org/analysis/breitbart-media-trump-harvard-study.php.

4 There have been other moral bases, independent of distorted psychological development, for criticizing capitalism, including that it empties life of meaning, crushes the human spirit, dissolves bonds of communal affinity, or is inescapably destructive to the environment. See, for example, Tim Rogan, *The Moral Economists: R. H. Tawney, Karl Polanyi, E. P. Thompson, and the Critique of Capitalism* (Princeton: Princeton Univ. Press, 2017).

5 See, for example, Patricia Cohen, "A Message from the Billionaire's Club: Tax Us," *New York Times*, 24 June 2019.

6 Urie Bronfenbrenner's *Ecology of Human Development*, published in 1979, lays out the argument for macroconditioning of psychological development. The book's 53,000 Google Scholar citations attest to its enduring influence. On the paucity of historical evidence: Lerner et al., "Concepts and Theories of Human Development," p. 23. McGilchrist, *Master and His Emissary*, is able to infer historical shifts in the functional balance between people's left and right brains, and he correlates some of these with concurrent changes in cultural belief, but he builds no explanation of why these changes came about.

7 "Text of President Obama's Speech in Hiroshima, Japan," *New York Times*, 27 May 2016.

CHAPTER 16: LEARNING TO HEAL

1 On selectivity with respect to technologies see, for example, the sections on "Integrative Practices" and "Relocalizing Infrastructures" in this chapter and the section on "Innovation in Mode S" in Chapter 17.

2 See the websites of the Transition Town Movement (https://transitionnetwork.org); Local Futures (https://www.localfutures.org); Business Alliance for Local Living Economies (BALLE, https://bealocalist.org); *Yes!* magazine (https://www.yesmagazine.org/); the Post Carbon Institute (https://www.postcarbon.org); the New Economy Coalition (http://neweconomy.net); the Schumacher Society for a New Economics (https://centerforneweconomics.org); Beautiful Solutions (https://solutions.thischangeseverything.org); the Institute for Local Self-Reliance (https://ilsr.org); books on community economics by Michael H. Shuman (http://michaelhshuman.com); David Bollier and Silke Helfrich, eds., *The Wealth of the Commons: A World Beyond Market & State* (Amherst, MA: Levellers Press, 2012); Jonathan F. P. Rose, *The Well-Tempered City: What Modern Science, Ancient Civilizations, and Human Nature*

Teach Us About the Future of Urban Life (New York: Harper Wave, 2016), parts 2–3.

3   Nathan Vardi, "The 25 Highest-Earning Hedge Fund Managers and Traders," *Forbes*, 17 April 2018; Piketty, *Capital*, chaps. 14–15. The following year was a tough one: the average hedge fund lost 4 percent. Even so, in 2018 the average paycheck of the top twenty hedge-fund managers and traders topped half a billion dollars. See Nathan Vardi and Antoine Gara, "The 25 Highest-Earning Hedge Fund Managers and Traders," *Forbes*, 20 March 2019.

Then again, hedge-fund managers don't sit at the summit of the wealth pyramid. In 2020 the top twenty-five US hedge-fund managers held a *combined* net worth of $185 billion—a tidy sum, but less than the *personal* net worth of tech moguls Elon Musk ($292 billion) and Jeff Bezos ($195 billion) as of October 2021. See Jonathan Ponciano, "The Richest Hedge Fund Managers on the 2020 Forbes 400 List," *Forbes*, 8 Sept. 2020.

As another benchmark: In 1965, US corporate chief executive officers (CEOs) took home, on average, twenty times as much money as a typical worker. By 1985, CEO compensation was sixty-one times higher than that of workers; in 2019, it was *320* times higher. See Lawrence Mishel and Jori Kandra, "CEO Compensation Surged 14% in 2019 to $21.3 Million," *Economic Policy Institute*, 18 Aug. 2020, https://files.epi.org/pdf/204513.pdf.

4   For more on trial-and-error social learning see, for example, Otto Scharmer and Katrin Kaufer, *Leading from the Emerging Future: From Ego-System to Eco-System Economies* (San Francisco: Berrett-Koehler, 2013), pp. 18–25, 113–15, 127, and chaps. 6–8.

5   Thomas S. Kuhn, *The Structure of Scientific Revolutions*, 2nd ed. (Chicago: Univ. of Chicago Press, 1970).

6   For examples of research that improves concepts and measures of psychospiritual development, albeit without attention to the influence of macrosocial structures, see Ken Wilber, Jack Engler, Daniel P. Brown, et al., *Transformations of Consciousness: Conventional and Contemplative Perspectives on Development* (Boston: Shambhala, 1986), chaps. 6–8; Lisa Miller, ed., *The Oxford Handbook of Psychology and Spirituality* (Oxford: Oxford Univ. Press, 2012); Davis and Vago, "Can Enlightenment Be Traced to Specific Neural Correlates, Cognition, or Behavior?"; Hanley et al., "The Nondual Awareness Dimensional Assessment"; Millière et al., "Psychedelics, Meditation, and Self-Consciousness"; Steve Taylor, "Two Modes of Sudden Spiritual Awakening?: Ego-Dissolution and Explosive Energetic Awakening," *International Journal of Transpersonal Studies*, vol. 37, no. 2 (2018), pp. 131–43.

7   For food for thought along these lines, see Charles Heying, "Portland's
      Artisan Economy: Beyond the Myth of Romantic Localism," *Hedgehog
      Review*, vol. 18, no. 1 (Spring 2016), pp. 68–73.

8   Jared Diamond and James A. Robinson, eds., *Natural Experiments of
      History* (Cambridge: Belknap Press of Harvard Univ. Press, 2010). Amish
      statistics: "Amish," *Encyclopedia Britannica*, https://www.britannica
      .com/topic/Amish (accessed 8 July 2021); "Amish Population Change
      1992–2017," Young Center for Anabaptist and Pietist Studies,
      Elizabethtown   College,   https://groups.etown.edu/amishstudies
      /files/2017/08/Population_Change_1992-2017.pdf. On the Old Order
      Amish generally: Marc A. Olshan, "Modernity, the Folk Society, and
      the Old Order Amish: An Alternative Interpretation," *Rural Sociology*,
      vol. 46, no. 2 (Summer 1981), pp. 297–309; Donald M. Kraybill, Karen
      M. Johnson-Weiner, and Steven M. Nolt, *The Amish* (Baltimore: Johns
      Hopkins Univ. Press, 2013). On Amish mental health see, for example,
      Berwood Yost, Scottie Thompson, Kirk Miller, and Christina Abbott,
      "Physical and Mental Health Conditions in Five Plain Communities,"
      paper presented at the Young Center International Conference,
      Elizabethtown College, Elizabethtown, PA, June 2016, https://www
      .fandm.edu/uploads/files/819715467984575136-physical-and
      -mental-health-conditions-in-five-plain-communities.pdf;   Kirk
      Miller, Berwood Yost, Christina Abbott, et al., "Health Needs
      Assessment of Plain Populations in Lancaster County, Pennsylvania,"
      Journal of Community Health, vol. 42, no. 1 (Feb. 2017), pp. 35–42.

9   Zachary Steel, Claire Marnane, Changiz Iranpour, et al., "The Global
      Prevalence of Common Mental Disorders: A Systematic Review and
      Meta-Analysis 1980–2013," *International Journal of Epidemiology*,
      vol. 43, no. 2 (April 2014), pp. 476–93.

10   See the websites of the Mind and Life Institute (https://www
      .mindandlife.org) and the Center for Contemplative Mind in Society
      (http://www.contemplativemind.org).

11   On limitations of expert analysis, see Richard Sclove, *Reinventing
      Technology Assessment: A 21st Century Model* (Washington, DC:
      Woodrow Wilson International Center for Scholars, April 2010),
      pp. 10–17, 24–29, 49–54, http://richardsclove.com/publications.
      See also Matthias Stevens, Michalis Vitos, Julia Altenbuchner, et al.,
      "Taking Participatory Citizen Science to Extremes," *IEEE Pervasive
      Computing*, vol. 13, no. 2 (April–June 2014), pp. 20–29.

12   Kerry J. Strand, Nicholas Cutforth, Randy Stoecker, et al.,
      *Community-Based Research and Higher Education: Principles and
      Practices* (San Francisco: Jossey-Bass, 2007); *Gateways: International
      Journal of Community Research and Engagement* (https://epress.
      lib.uts.edu.au/journals/index.php/ijcre); Budd L. Hall and Rajesh
      Tandon, "Participatory Research: Where Have We Been, Where Are
      We Going?—A Dialogue," *Research for All*, vol. 1, no. 2 (2017), pp.

365-74. On costs and resource reallocation, see Richard E. Sclove, Madeleine L. Scammell, and Breena Holland, *Community-Based Research in the United States: An Introductory Reconnaissance, Including Twelve Organizational Case Studies and Comparison with the Dutch Science Shops and the Mainstream American Research System* (Amherst, MA: The Loka Institute, 1998), esp. pp. iv–vi, 96–109, http://richardsclove.com/publications. See also the websites of the international Living Knowledge network (https://www.livingknowledge.org), and the Expert and Citizens Assessment of Science and Technology (ECAST) network (https://ecastnetwork.org).

13   On deliberative democracy generally, see John S. Dryzek, André Bächtiger, Simone Chambers, et al., "The Crisis of Democracy and the Science of Deliberation," *Science*, vol. 363, no. 6432 (15 March 2019), pp. 1144–46.

14   Richard Sclove, "Town Meetings on Technology: Consensus Conferences as Democratic Participation," in *Science, Technology & Democracy*, ed. Daniel Lee Kleinman (Albany: State Univ. of New York Press, 2000), pp. 33–48, http://richardsclove.com/publications.

15   Sclove, *Reinventing Technology Assessment*, pp. 5–9, 15, 17, 24–30, 34–36, 42–54. Scholarly evaluations of the Oregon process are compiled at http://sites.psu.edu/citizensinitiativereview/publications. Information on the other US states that have pilot-tested the Oregon process is at https://healthydemocracy.org/cir.

16   On the contrast between a consensus conference and a committee of stakeholder representatives, see Sclove, *Reinventing Technology Assessment*, p. 17.

17   To witness the intelligence, dignity, and eloquence exhibited by lay panelists, see the fifteen-minute video of a 2006 Boston-area consensus conference, available via http://www.biomonitoring06.org.

18   Sclove, "Town Meetings on Technology," pp. 39–44. Quotes are from "Consensus Statement of the Citizens' Panel on Telecommunications and the Future of Democracy," 4 April 1997, http://loka.org/USResults.html.

19   See Sclove, *Reinventing Technology Assessment*, pp. 49–54.

20   For other examples of promising contexts, see Scharmer and Kaufer, *Leading from the Emerging Future*, pp. 16, 23–25, 179–90. A deliberative method known as a "citizens' assembly" exhibits many of the same features as a consensus conference, but it includes more participants (typically 50–200); see "Citizens' Assembly," *Wikipedia*, last modified 27 June 2021, https://en.wikipedia.org/wiki/Citizens_assembly.

21   Kegan, *Evolving Self*, p. 218; and see also pp. 121, 208, 243–45, 260–62.

22   E.g., Putnam, *Our Kids*.

23   See, for example, Robert D. Putnam and Lewis Feldstein, *Better Together: Restoring the American Community* (New York: Simon

& Schuster, 2004); Andres Duany, Elizabeth Plater-Zyberk, and Jeff Speck, *Suburban Nation: The Rise of Sprawl and the Decline of the American Dream* (New York: Farrar, Straus and Giroux, 2010); Yuval Levin, *The Fractured Republic: Renewing America's Social Contract in the Age of Individualism* (New York: Basic Books, 2016); Eric Klinenberg, *Palaces for the People: How Social Infrastructure Can Help Fight Inequality, Polarization, and the Decline of Civic Life* (New York: Broadway Books, 2018); Rose, *The Well-Tempered City*, part 4; Bollier and Helfrich, eds., *The Wealth of the Commons*; and the Project for Public Spaces (https://www.pps.org) and the US Cohousing Association (http://www.cohousing.org). On the English land enclosures, see Chapters 8 and 10, above.

24   Twenge et al., "Less In-Person Social Interaction"; Jean M. Twenge, "The Sad State of Happiness in the United States and the Role of Digital Media," in *World Happiness Report 2019*, ed. John F. Helliwell, Richard Layard, and Jeffrey D. Sachs (New York: Sustainable Development Solutions Network, 2019), pp. 86–95. In *Alone Together*, Sherry Turkle chides herself for having previously judged online groups functionally equivalent to face-to-face communities: "I spoke too quickly. I used the word 'community' for [an online] world of weak ties. Communities are constituted by physical proximity, shared concerns, real consequences, and common responsibilities" (p. 239). On hours of electronic media usage: Nielsen Company, *The Total Audience Report – Q1 2018*. The CEO is Chris Anderson, quoted in Nellie Bowles, "A Dark Consensus About Screens and Kids Begins to Emerge in Silicon Valley," *New York Times*, 26 Oct. 2018; see also Nellie Bowles, "Human Contact Is Now a Luxury Good," *New York Times*, 23 March 2019.

25   One of the many remedial ideas being floated: Tara Bahrampour, "This Simple Solution to Smartphone Addiction Is Now Used in Over 600 U.S. Schools," *Washington Post*, 5 Feb. 2018. See also Adam Alter, *Irresistible: The Rise of Addictive Technology and the Business of Keeping Us Hooked* (New York: Penguin Press, 2017), part 3; Melissa G. Hunt, Rachel Marx, Courtney Lipson, and Jordyn Young, "No More FOMO: Limiting Social Media Decreases Loneliness and Depression," *Journal of Social and Clinical Psychology*, vol. 37, no. 10 (2018), pp. 751–68.

26   For inspiring visions of how to make New York City more friendly to pedestrians, bicycles, and outdoor socializing, see Farhad Manjoo, "I've Seen a Future Without Cars, and It's Amazing," *New York Times*, 9 July 2020; and Robert Freudenberg, Ellis Calvin, Kate Slevin, et al., *The Five Borough Bikeway: Critical Infrastructure Connecting New York City* (New York: Regional Planning Association, June 2020).

27   On the inner spirit of craft work, see Dooling, *Way of Working*; Carla Needleman, *The Work of Craft: An Inquiry into the Nature of Crafts*

and Craftsmanship (London: Arkana, 1986); Sōetsu Yanagi, adapted by Bernard Leach, *The Unknown Craftsman: A Japanese Insight into Beauty* (New York: Kodansha, 1978); Mary Caroline Richards, *Centering in Pottery, Poetry, and the Person* (Middletown: Wesleyan Univ. Press, 1964), chaps. 1–2.

28   On the practicality of making craft and other integrative practices more prominent in economic life, see Juliet B. Schor, *Plenitude: The New Economics of Wealth* (New York: Penguin, 2010), pp. 123–27; Matthew B. Crawford, *Shop Class as Soulcraft: An Inquiry into the Value of Work* (New York: Penguin, 2010); Matthew B. Crawford, *The Case for Working with Your Hands, or Why Office Work Is Bad for Us and Fixing Things Feels Good* (New York: Penguin Viking, 2011); Tim Wu, "That Flour You Bought Could Be the Future of the U.S. Economy," *New York Times*, 24 July 2020; and Heying, "Portland's Artisan Economy." Heying's essay also points toward the need to explore what is gained and lost if local artisanal activities are integrated into the global economy.

29   Ideas along these lines have a long pedigree. For instance, from the nineteenth century: A. L. Morton, ed., *Political Writings of William Morris* (New York: International Publishers, 1973); and Peter Kropotkin, *Fields, Factories and Workshops Tomorrow*, ed. Colin Ward (London: Freedom Press, 1985). More recently: Romesh Diwan and Mark Lutz, eds., *Essays in Gandhian Economics* (New York: Intermediate Technology Development Group, 1987); Carmen Sirianni, "Self-Management of Time: A Democratic Alternative," *Socialist Review*, vol. 18, no. 4 (Oct.–Dec. 1988), pp. 5–56; Fox, *Reinvention of Work*. On popular participation in creative and/or intellectual work, see Adrian Smith and Andy Stirling, *Grassroots Innovation and Democracy*, STEPS Working Paper 89 (Brighton: STEPS Centre, 2016); Sclove, *Democracy and Technology*, chap. 11.

30   David Streitfeld, "He Has Driven for Uber Since 2012. He Makes About $40,000 a Year," *New York Times*, 12 April 2019; Anne Helen Petersen, "Are You Sure You Want to Go Back to the Office?: The Future of Work Is Flexibility," *New York Times*, 23 Dec. 2020.

31   Karl Marx, "On James Mill," in McLellan, *Karl Marx*, pp. 121–22. Even without subsidy, craft production can sometimes compete successfully against the corporate economy. See, for example, Wu, "That Flour You Bought Could Be the Future of the U.S. Economy."

32   Society for Human Resource Management, "2017 Employee Job Satisfaction and Engagement: The Doors of Opportunity Are Open," https://www.shrm.org/hr-today/trends-and-forecasting/research-and-surveys/pages/2017-job-satisfaction-and-engagement-doors-of-opportunity-are-open.aspx. On the yearning for more pleasurable and meaningful work, see also Justin M. Berg, Adam M. Grant, and Victoria J. Johnson, "When Callings Are Calling: Crafting Work

and Leisure in Pursuit of Unanswered Occupational Callings," *Organizational Science*, vol. 21, no. 5 (Sept.–Oct. 2010), pp. 973–94.

33   Jackson, *Prosperity Without Growth*, makes these points with considerable rigor. His objective is to reduce consumerism and GDP in order to achieve environmental sustainability; this reveals another strategic convergence with the mission of reducing structural hindrances to psychospiritual growth.

34   Apffel-Marglin, *Subversive Spiritualities*, provides food for thought along these lines.

35   See Chapter 17, below, and the discussion of infrastructural technology and democratic governance in Sclove, *Democracy and Technology*, chap. 7.

36   Ian Frazer, "High-Rise Greens: Growing Crops in the City, Without Soil or Natural Light," *New Yorker*, 9 Jan. 2017, pp. 52–59; Annette Kjellgren and Hanne Buhrkall, "A Comparison of the Restorative Effect of a Natural Environment with That of a Simulated Natural Environment," *Journal of Environmental Psychology*, vol. 30, no. 4 (Dec. 2010), pp. 464–72.

37   On morally legitimate hierarchy, see Sclove, *Democracy and Technology*, p. 62.

38   See also Scharmer and Kaufer, *Leading from the Emerging Future*, chaps. 6–7; and research studies involving inequality from the Connected Consumption and Connected Economy research project, https://www.bc.edu/bc-web/schools/mcas/departments/sociology/connected.html.

39   On conditions under which bonds of affinity may develop, see Thomas Edsall, "How Strong Is America's Multiracial Democracy," *New York Times*, 1 Sept. 2021. On online self-sorting, see Chris Bail, *Breaking the Social Media Prism: How to Make Our Platforms Less Polarizing* (Princeton: Princeton Univ. Press, 2021). On face-to-face alternatives, see Ervin Staub, *The Roots of Goodness and Resistance to Evil: Inclusive Caring, Moral Courage, Altruism Born of Suffering, Active Bystandership, and Heroism* (Oxford: Oxford Univ. Press, 2015), chaps. 20, 22; and the Braver Angels project (https://braverangels.org).

CHAPTER 17: MAKING CIVILIZATION
SAFE FOR THE SOUL

1   Anthony Flaccavento, *Building a Healthy Economy from the Bottom Up: Harnessing Real-World Experience for Transformative Change* (Lexington: Univ. of Kentucky Press, 2016), chaps. 5–7.

2   On the psychology of those greatly privileged see, for example, Page et al., "What Billionaires Want."

3   See, for example, Piketty, *Capital*, part 4; Lawrence H. Summers and Ed Balls, cochairs, *Report of the Commission on Inclusive Prosperity* (Washington, DC: Center for American Progress, Jan. 2015); Lawrence Mishel, "Unions, Inequality, and Faltering Middle-Class Wages," Economic Policy Institute, Issue Brief no. 342, 29 Aug. 2012; John Cavanagh and Jerry Mander, eds., *Alternatives to Economic Globalization: A Better World Is Possible*, 2nd ed. (San Francisco: Berrett-Koehler, 2004), chap. 9; Annie Lowery, *Give People Money: How a Universal Basic Income Would End Poverty, Revolutionize Work, and Remake the World* (New York: Crown, 2018); Tim Wu, *The Curse of Bigness: Antitrust in the New Gilded Age* (New York: Columbia Global Reports, 2018); and the Center for Responsive Politics (https://www.opensecrets.org).

4   Cavanagh and Mander, eds., *Alternatives to Economic Globalization*, chaps 3, 10. The COVID-19 pandemic quickly inspired critical reassessments of globalization by mainstream observers; see, for example, Neil Irwin, "It's the End of the World Economy as We Know It," *New York Times*, 16 April 2020; Roger Cohen, "No Return to the 'Old Dispensation,'" *New York Times*, 8 May 2020. Financial systems also need reinvention to reduce the frequency and depth of dislocating crises; see, for example, Jackson, *Prosperity Without Growth*, chaps. 8–10; and "FAQs on Financial Transaction Tax," Institute for Policy Studies, Jan. 2015, https://ips-dc.org/wp-content/uploads/2015/01/IPS_Financial_Transactions_FAQ-Jan_2015.pdf.

5   Compare Speth, *America the Possible*, pp. 140–41.

6   Sclove, "Cybersobriety," pp. 47–51.

7   Pinker, *Better Angels of Our Nature*, pp. 284–90, 341–42, 663–64; quote is from p. 287. The thesis that international trade promotes peace remains disputed; see, for instance, Katherine Barbieri, *The Liberal Illusion: Does Trade Promote Peace?* (Ann Arbor: Univ. of Michigan Press, 2002).

8   On protectionism and local self-reliance: J. Ann Tickner, *Self-Reliance Versus Power Politics: The American and Indian Experiences in Building Nation States* (New York: Columbia Univ. Press, 1987); Cavanagh and Mander, eds., *Alternatives to Economic Globalization*, chaps. 4–10. On Trump tariffs: Mary Amiti, Stephen J. Redding, and David E. Weinstein, "The Impact of the 2018 Tariffs on Prices and Welfare," *Journal of Economic Perspectives*, vol. 33, no. 4 (Fall 2019), pp. 187–210.

9   Cavanagh and Mander, eds., *Alternatives to Economic Globalization*, pp. 1–16, 271–332; Patrick Hiller, "Re-examining the Connection between Peace, Conflict and Trade," War Prevention Initiative, May 2015.

10   Joshua S. Goldstein, *Winning the War on War: The Decline of Armed Conflict Worldwide* (New York: Dutton, 2011); Craig Zelizer, ed.,

Integrated Peacebuilding: Innovative Approaches to Transforming Conflict (Boulder: Westview Press, 2013); Erica Chenoweth and Maria J. Stephan, *Why Civil Resistance Works: The Strategic Logic of Nonviolent Conflict* (New York: Columbia Univ. Press, 2013).

11   Benjamin Barber, *Strong Democracy: Participatory Politics for a New Age* (Berkeley: Univ. of California, 1984).

12   Bjørn Bedsted, Yves Mathieu, and Christian Leyrit, eds., *World Wide Views on Climate and Energy: Results Report* (Copenhagen: Danish Board of Technology Foundation, Missions Publiques, and the French National Commission for Public Debate, Sept. 2015); John S. Dryzek, Quinlan Bowman, Jonathan Pickering, et al., *Deliberative Global Governance* (Cambridge: Cambridge Univ. Press, 2019); Benjamin R. Barber, *If Mayors Ruled the World: Dysfunctional Nations, Rising Cities* (New Haven: Yale Univ. Press, 2013), chap. 12.

13   David Begg, Jacques Crémer, Jean-Pierre Danthine, et al., *Making Sense of Subsidiarity: How Much Centralization for Europe?* (Centre for Economic Policy Research, 1993); Mike Hais, Doug Ross, and Morley Winograd, *Healing American Democracy: Going Local* (Blue Zephyr, 2018).

14   See also Cavanagh and Mander, eds., *Alternatives to Economic Globalization*, esp. chap. 6.

15   Eduardo Porter, "Don't Fight the Robots. Tax Them," *New York Times*, 23 Feb. 2019.

16   Sclove, *Democracy and Technology*, esp. part 2 and chaps. 11–12; Sclove, *Reinventing Technology Assessment*. These works don't explicitly incorporate a post-egoic psychospiritual perspective, but their prescriptions are salient owing to the phenomenon of shared causes and convergent remedies. On the urgency of such matters, see Zuboff, *Age of Surveillance Capitalism*.

17   See, for example, Prescott and Logan, "Transforming Life"; Timothy B. Leduc, "Climates of Ontological Change: Past Wisdom in Current Binds," *Wiley Interdisciplinary Reviews: Climate Change*, vol. 5, no. 2 (March/April 2014), pp. 247–60; Wangari Maathai, *Replenishing the Earth: Spiritual Values for Healing Ourselves and the World* (New York: Doubleday, 2010); Thich Nhat Hanh, *Love Letter to the Earth* (Berkeley: Parallax Press, 2013).

18   See, for example, Speth, *America the Possible*, esp. pp. 73–87, 142–45; Jackson, *Prosperity Without Growth*.

19   For one example of an organizational model that could be adapted for this purpose, see Sclove, *Reinventing Technology Assessment*, esp. pp. 38–41, 46–49; and the US Expert and Citizen Assessment of Science and Technology (ECAST) network (https://ecastnetwork .org).

20   David Forbes, *Mindfulness and Its Discontents: Education, Self, and Social Transformation* (Nova Scotia: Fernwood Publishing, 2019);

Carol Horton and Rosanne Harvey, eds., *21st Century Yoga: Culture, Politics, and Practice* (Kleio Books, 2012); Barbara A. Holmes, *Joy Unspeakable: Contemplative Practices of the Black Church* (Minneapolis: Fortress Press, 2004), pp. 2–6, 21–23, 184–86.

21 On social engagement: Seil Oh and Natalia Sarkisian, "Spiritual Individualism or Engaged Spirituality: Social Implications of Holistic Spirituality Among Mind–Body–Spirit Practitioners," *Sociology of Religion*, vol. 73, no. 3 (1 Sept. 2012), pp. 299–322; Donald Rothenberg, *The Engaged Spiritual Life: A Buddhist Approach to Transforming Ourselves and the World* (Boston: Beacon Press, 2006). On dilution and corruption: Jeremy Carrette and Richard King, *Selling Spirituality: The Silent Takeover of Religion* (New York: Routledge, 2005); Ronald E. Purser, David Forbes and Adam Burke, eds., *Handbook of Mindfulness: Culture, Context, and Social Purpose* (Switzerland: Springer, 2016); Alice Hines, "Inside CorePower Yoga Teacher Training," *New York Times*, 6 April 2019.

22 On eco-friendly woodstoves see, for example, Rachel Kaufman, "How to Modernize the Wood Stove and Help Save the Planet," *Smithsonian*, 19 Jan 2016.

23 See Scharmer and Kaufer, *Leading from the Emerging Future*, esp. chap. 5.

24 On recovering a sense of the sacred, see Kohák, *Embers and the Stars*; Morris Berman, *The Reenchantment of the World* (Ithaca: Cornell Univ. Press, 1981); David Abram, *The Spell of the Sensuous: Perception and Language in a More-Than-Human World* (New York: Vintage Books, 1997). On how that sensibility supports psychospiritual development, see Miller, *Spiritual Child*. On the dialectics of psychospiritual and social transformations, see Mustakova-Possardt et al., eds., *Toward a Socially Responsible Psychology*.

25 Van Buitenen, *Bhagavadgītā*, chaps. 4–6.

26 See, for example, Pinker, *Better Angels of Our Nature*, or the more balanced treatments in Taylor, *Sources of the Self*; Lifton, *Protean Self*; and Ronald F. Inglehart, *Cultural Evolution: People's Motivations Are Changing and Reshaping the World* (Cambridge: Cambridge Univ. Press, 2018). On Pinker's one-sidedness see, for example, Alison Gopnik, "When Truth and Reason Are No Longer Enough," *Atlantic*, April 2018; other critiques include Ronald Aronson, "Pinker and Progress," *History and Theory*, vol. 52, no. 2 (May 2013), pp. 246–64; and Douglas P. Fry, ed., *War, Peace, and Human Nature: The Convergence of Evolutionary and Cultural Views* (Oxford: Oxford Univ. Press, 2015), pp. 15–20 and chaps. 7–8, 10–11. Inglehart's thesis has also not gone uncontested; see, for example, Ingolfur Blühdorn, "The Dialectic of Democracy: Modernization, Emancipation and the *Great Regression*," *Democratization*, vol. 27, no. 3 (2020), pp. 389–407; Michael Hout's review of Inglehart's *Modernization*

and Postmodernization in *Contemporary Sociology*, vol. 27, no. 2 (March 1998), pp. 190–92; and Michael J. Cripps, "Postmodernity in Advanced Societies," *Review of Politics*, vol. 60, no. 2 (Spring 1998), pp. 396–99. Inglehart's conclusions are also at odds with those of Piff, et al., "Higher Social Class Predicts Increased Unethical Behavior."

Inglehart also reaches back far before his survey data to contend that until modern times human values were always predominantly materialistic; see his "Evolutionary Modernization Theory: Why People's Motivations Are Changing," *Changing Societies & Personalities*, vol. 1, no. 2 (Sept. 2017), pp. 136–51, esp. pp. 138–39. Anthropological and historical evidence that we have reviewed suggests otherwise. Many non-modern people—including the southern African Ju/'hoansi, Trobriand Islanders, American Indians, and functionally satiable peasants—were, by Inglehart's definition, decidedly postmaterialistic in a number of respects.

27   E.g., Thomas L. Friedman, *The World Is Flat: A Brief History of the Twenty-First Century* (New York: Farrar, Straus and Giroux, 2006).

28   Peter A. Hall, "Varieties of Capitalism," in *Emerging Trends in the Social and Behavioral Sciences: An Interdisciplinary, Searchable, and Linkable Resource*, ed. Robert A. Scott and Marlis C. Buchmann (Wiley Online Library, 2015); Marisa Ferri and Timothy J. White, "Regionalism, Cooperation, and Economic Prosperity: Effective Autonomy in Emilia-Romagna," *Mediterranean Quarterly*, vol. 19, no. 5 (Summer 1999), pp. 89–106. On Kerala: Greg Jaffe and Vidhi Doshi, "One of the Few Places Where a Communist Can Still Dream," *Washington Post*, 27 Oct. 2017.

29   On empowering and incentivizing more soulful work, see the sections on "Integrative Practices" and "Limiting Hierarchy and Social Stratification," in Chapter 16 and on "Economic and Political Equality" in Chapter 17.

30   John Maynard Keynes, "Economic Possibilities for Our Grandchildren," in Pecchi and Piga, *Revisiting Keynes*, p. 21; Jackson, *Prosperity Without Growth*, chaps. 8 and 9—the quoted phrase appears on p. 149. Thurman's advice is widely quoted, including on the homepage of Boston University's Howard Thurman Center (www.bu.edu/thurman/about-us/about-the-htc), which suggests its authenticity. Keynes envisioned a fifteen-hour workweek and otherwise living lives of leisure. Personally, I find more inspiration in the vision of work becoming more soulful, which would soften or transcend the distinctions between work, leisure, social life, psychospiritual practice, and karma yoga, as is common in the indigenous world.

CHAPTER 18: A DOG AT HEAVEN'S GATE

1   The quote is from Swami Satyananda Saraswati, *Kundalini Tantra* (Munger, Bihar, India: Yoga Publications Trust, 2003), p. 190. In the modern West, tantra is associated primarily with esoteric sexual practices; this overlooks tantra's many other dimensions and forms. See, for example, David Gordon White, ed., *Tantra in Practice* (Princeton: Princeton Univ. Press, 2000); Hugh B. Urban, *Tantra: Sex, Secrecy, Politics, and Power in the Study of Religion* (Berkeley: Univ. of California Press, 2003); Pandit Rajmani Tigunait, *Tantra Unveiled: Seducing the Forces of Matter and Spirit* (Honesdale: Himalayan Institute Press, 2007). Tantra is also a strain within Buddhism and Jainism.

2   Regarding contemporary Western experiences of kundalini awakening see, for example, Bonnie Greenwell, *Energies of Transformation: A Guide to the Kundalini Process*, 2nd ed. (Saratoga, CA: Shakti River Press, 1995); Swami Durgananda, "To See the World Full of Saints: The History of Siddha Yoga as a Contemporary Movement," in Douglas Renfrew Brooks, Swami Durgananda, Paul E. Muller-Ortega, et al., *Meditation Revolution: A History and Theology of the Siddha Yoga Lineage* (South Fallsburg, NY: Agama Press, 1997), pp. 25–113; Gurumukh Kaur Khalsa, Andrew Newberg, Sivananda Rhada, et al., eds., *Kundalini Rising: Exploring the Energy of Awakening* (Boulder: Sounds True, 2009). See also the Author Interview at the back of this book.

We discussed the Ju/'hoansi *!kia*-healing dance in Chapter 13, above. For other cross-cultural examples of the release of a kundalini-type energy, see Lee Sannella, *The Kundalini Experience: Psychosis or Transcendence* (Lower Lake, CA: Integral Publishing, 1987), pp. 37–56.

3   David Gordon White, "Yoga, Brief History of an Idea," in *Yoga in Practice*, ed. David Gordon White (Princeton: Princeton Univ. Press, 2012), pp. 14–15.

4   David Gordon White, *The Alchemical Body: Siddha Traditions in Medieval India* (Chicago: Univ. of Chicago Press, 1996), pp. 12–29, 240–58, esp. pp. 245–47.

5   On the *Mahabharata*'s oral circulation: Brockington, *The Sanskrit Epics*, p. 28. As an example of a spiritual teacher speaking to the antiquity of tantra, see Saraswati, *Kundalini Tantra*, pp. 190–91. Alexis Sanderson, "The Śaiva Age: The Rise and Dominance of Śaivism During the Early Medieval Period," in *Genesis and Development of Tantrism*, ed. Shingo Einoo (Tokyo: Institute of Oriental Culture, Univ. of Tokyo, 2009), pp. 45, 129, pushes evidence for the origins of tantra back to the fifth century A.D., which is about a century after the *Mahabharata* as we know it was completed. Asko Parpola,

"Vāc as a Goddess of Victory in the Veda and Her Relation to Durgā,"
Zinbun, no. 34(2), 1999, pp. 101–43, finds evidence of proto-tan-
tric ideas running as far back as 2,000 B.C. Hugh B. Urban, "The
Torment of Secrecy: Ethical and Epistemological Problems in the
Study of Esoteric Traditions," *History of Religions*, vol. 37, no. 3 (Feb.
1998), pp. 209–48, discusses the challenge involved in acquiring reli-
able knowledge about tantra and other secretive religious sects. In
his book *Tantra*, Urban also writes: "The historical origins of the
vast body of traditions that we call tantra are today lost in a mire of
obscure Indian history and muddled scholarly conjecture. As Padoux
observes, 'the history of Tantrism is impossible to write' based on the
sheer poverty of data at present" (p. 23; the internal quote is from
André Padoux, "Tantrism: Hindu Tantrism," in *The Encyclopedia of
Religion*, ed. Mircea Eliade, vol. 14 [New York, 1987], p. 275).

6   *Bhagavad Gita* dating: Brockington, *The Sanskrit Epics*, pp. 145–
     48; Angelika Malinar, *The Bhagavadgītā: Doctrines and Contexts*
     (Cambridge: Cambridge Univ. Press, 2007), chap. 5. While noting
     that the *Gita* could have been inserted elsewhere, Van Buitenen,
     Bhagavadgītā, pp. 3–4, reasons that the logical position for a justifi-
     cation of Arjuna's duty to fight was just before the war begins. That's
     true, but it doesn't explain why the *Gita*'s various components were
     bundled together.

7   Sukthankar, *On the Meaning of the Mahābhārata*, pp. 115, 119.

8   Paramahansa Yogananda, *God Talks with Arjuna—The "Bhagavad
     Gita": Royal Science of God-Realization*, 2nd ed. (Los Angeles: Self-
     Realization Fellowship, 1999), p. 817. Today Yogananda is best known
     as the author of *Autobiography of a Yogi*. On various enumerations of
     the chakras see, for example, White, "Yoga, Brief History of an Idea,"
     p. 15; White, *The Alchemical Body*, p. 367, n. 95.
       After the Kauravas' defeat and the conclusion of the Kurukshetra
     War, there can be no more episodes of conflict between the Kauravas
     and the Pandavas, and hence no further Together Stages until
     Yudhishthira's reencounter with Duryodhana in heaven (Book 18).
     On the other hand, after the war the Pandavas continue to journey to
     and from their kingdom (see Figure 25, below). If one were to count
     those later journeys as additional Together/Apart episodes, then that
     would indicate that the *Mahabharata*'s authors believed that there
     were more than seven chakras. But even so, the spiritual center in the
     forehead would still be the sixth chakra.

9   White, *The Alchemical Body*, pp. 16–17.

10   See also Tigunait, *Tantra Unveiled*, pp. 13–16; David Gordon White,
     Kiss of the Yoginī: "Tantric Sex" in its South Asian Contexts (Chicago:
     Univ. of Chicago Press, 2003), pp. 157–59; Urban, *Tantra*; and, more
     generally, Ann Duncan, "Religion and Secrecy: A Bibliographic

Essay," *Journal of the American Academy of Religion*, vol. 74, no. 2 (June 2006), pp. 469–82.

11 Robert E. Ornstein, "Contemporary Sufism," in *Transpersonal Psychologies*, ed. Charles T. Tart (London: Routledge & Kegan Paul, 1975), pp. 353–88.

12 On decryption as a means to spiritual transformation see, for example, White, *Kiss of the Yoginī*, pp. 243–44.

13 Francisco J. Varela and Jonathan Shear, eds., *The View from Within: First-Person Approaches to the Study of Consciousness* (Bowling Green: Imprint Academic, 1999); Claire Petitmengin, "Describing One's Subjective Experience in the Second Person: An Interview Method for the Science of Consciousness," *Phenomenology and the Cognitive Sciences*, vol. 5 (2006), pp. 229–69; Richard J. Davidson and Alfred W. Kaszniak, "Conceptual and Methodological Issues in Research on Mindfulness and Meditation," *American Psychologist*, vol. 70, no. 7 (Oct. 2015), pp. 581–92.

14 Kisari Mohan Ganguli, trans., *The Mahabharata* (New Delhi: Munshiram Manoharlal Publishers, 2008), vol. 2, *Drona Parva*, sect. 191, pp. 444–46, and vol. 3, *Salya Parva*, sects. 30–34, 55–61, pp. 82–97, 150–69. See also vol. 2, *Bhishma Parva*, sect. 108, pp. 219–20, and vol. 3, *Karna Parva*, sects. 90–91, pp. 243–55.

15 See James L. Fitzgerald, trans. and ed., *The Mahābhārata*, vol. 7, *Book 11: The Book of the Women; Book 12: The Book of Peace, Part One* (Chicago: Univ. of Chicago Press, 2004), pp. 149, 152–63, 445, 499, 759 nn. 130.3 and 130.8.

16 Van Buitenen, *Bhagavadgītā*, pp. 142–45, with emphasis added.

17 Krishna's death from an arrow shot into his heel (Ganguli, *Mahabharata*, vol. 4, *Mausala Parva*, sect. 4, p. 8) is identical to the fate that befalls Achilles in some versions of the Trojan War saga, one of several similarities that may point to cultural transmission between ancient Greece and India.

18 "Lose the dog" is my loose translation. Ganguli, *Mahabharata*, vol. 4, *Mahaprasthanika Parva*, sect. 3, p. 5, translates Indra's command as "Do thou cast off this dog."

19 See, for example, Tigunait, *Tantra Unveiled*, pp. x, 11–12, 47–57.

20 "Effulgence" and "solar splendor": Ganguli, *Mahabharata*, vol. 4, *Swargarohanika Parva*, sect. 4, pp. 7–8. Other quotes: David Gordon White, "'Open' and 'Closed' Models of the Human Body in Indian Medical and Yogic Traditions," *Asian Medicine: Tradition and Modernity*, vol. 2, no. 1 (July 2006), pp. 1–13, esp. p. 7. Ajit Mookerjee, *Kundalini: The Arousal of the Inner Energy*, 3rd ed. (Rochester: Destiny Books, 1986), p. 39, equates Arjuna's vision of Krishna blazing like the "light of a thousand suns" (in the *Bhagavad Gita*) with awakening the chakra located at the top of the head; now, admitted into heaven, Yudhishthira reencounters Krishna blazing,

once again, in his cosmic form. Doniger, *The Hindus*, p. 282, interprets the Pandavas' entry into heaven without rebirth as implying that they attain *moksha* (liberation or enlightenment).

21   On intuition as the fruit of ego-transcendence see, for example, Deikman, *The Observing Self*, chap. 5.

22   On Yudhishthira's ethical instruction after the war, see Fitzgerald, "The Book of Peace, Part One," in *Mahābhārata*, vol. 7. The Pandavas' trajectory of moral development bears some interesting similarity to Lawrence Kohlberg's stage theory of moral development; see Kohlberg's *The Philosophy of Moral Development: Moral Stages and the Idea of Justice* (San Francisco: Harper & Row, 1981), pp. 311–72, 409–12.

23   Hubert L. Dreyfus and Stuart E. Dreyfus, "Towards a Phenomenology of Ethical Expertise," *Human Studies*, vol. 14, no. 4 (1991), pp. 229–50; quote is from pp. 236–37. See also David A. Pizarro and Paul Bloom, "The Intelligence of Moral Intuitions: Comment on Haidt (2001)," *Psychological Review*, vol. 110, no. 1 (Jan. 2003), pp. 193–96.

AUTHOR INTERVIEW: THE BACKSTORY

1   Children's versions that I've enjoyed are Namita Gokhale, *The Puffin "Mahabharata"* (New York: Penguin Group, 2009); and Anant Pai, ed., *Mahabharata* (Mumbai: India Book House, 2005)—a comic-book version published in three volumes.

2   On the Trobrianders, see Lee, *Freedom and Culture*, pp. 105–20.

3   Dorothy Walters, *Unmasking the Rose: A Record of a Kundalini Initiation* (Charlottesville, VA: Hampton Roads, 2002), pp. 17, 20–25, 57, 81, 166, 200–201.

Selected Bibliography

This bibliography includes works cited in the endnotes more than once.

Acemoglu, Daron, and James A. Robinson. *Why Nations Fail: The Origins of Power, Prosperity, and Poverty*. New York: Currency, 2012.

Alexander, Bruce K. *The Globalization of Addiction: A Study in Poverty of the Spirit*. Oxford: Oxford Univ. Press, 2008.

Alexander, Michelle. *The New Jim Crow: Mass Incarceration in the Age of Colorblindness*. New York: The New Press, 2010.

Apffel-Marglin, Frédérique. *Subversive Spiritualities: How Rituals Enact the World*. Oxford: Oxford Univ. Press, 2011.

Apffel-Marglin, Frédérique. "Western Modernity and the Fate of Anima Mundi: Its Murder and Transformation into a Postmaterial Ecospirituality." In Apffel-Marglin and Varese, *Contemporary Voices from Anima Mundi*, pp. 17–44.

Apffel-Marglin, Frédérique, and Stefano Varese, eds. *Contemporary Voices from Anima Mundi: A Reappraisal*. New York: Peter Lang, 2020.

Axtell, James. *The European and the Indian: Essays in the Ethnohistory of Colonial North America*. Oxford: Oxford Univ. Press, 1982.

Beckert, Sven. *Empire of Cotton: A Global History*. New York: Vintage, 2015.

Bird-David, Nurit, Allen Abramson, Jon Altman, et al. "Beyond 'The Original Affluent Society': A Culturalist Reformulation [and Comments and Reply]." *Current Anthropology*, vol. 33, no. 1 (Feb. 1992), pp. 25–47.

Bodley, John H. *Anthropology and Contemporary Human Problems*. 6th ed. Lanham, MD: Altamira, 2012.

Bollier, David, and Silke Helfrich, eds. *The Wealth of the Commons: A World Beyond Market & State*. Amherst, MA: Levellers Press, 2012.

Bowles, Samuel. "Endogenous Preferences: The Cultural Consequences of Markets and Other Economic Institutions." *Journal of Economic Literature*, vol. 36, no. 1 (March 1998), pp. 75–111.

Brewer, John, and Roy Porter, eds. *Consumption and the World of Goods*. London and New York: Routledge, 1994.

Brockington, John. *The Sanskrit Epics*. Leiden: Brill, 1998.

Bronfenbrenner, Urie. *The Ecology of Human Development: Experiments by Nature and Design*. Cambridge: Harvard Univ. Press, 1979.

Brown, Daniel P. "The Stages of Meditation in Cross-Cultural Perspective." In *Transformations of Consciousness: Conventional and Contemplative Perspectives on Development*. By Ken Wilber, Jack Engler, Daniel P. Brown, et al. Boston: Shambhala, 1986, pp. 219–82.

Burnett, John. *Liquid Pleasures: A Social History of Drinks in Modern Britain*. London: Routledge, 1999.

Campbell, Colin. *The Romantic Ethic and the Spirit of Modern Consumerism*. 3rd ed. Great Britain: Alcuin Academics, 2005.

Campbell, Joseph. *The Hero with a Thousand Faces*. Bollingen Series 17, 3rd ed. Novato, CA: New World Library, 2008.

Cavanagh, John, and Jerry Mander, eds. *Alternatives to Economic Globalization: A Better World Is Possible*. 2nd ed. San Francisco: Berrett-Koehler, 2004.

Christopher, John Chambers, and Sarah Hickinbottom. "Positive Psychology, Ethnocentrism, and the Disguised Ideology of Individualism." *Theory and Psychology*, vol. 18, no. 5 (Oct. 2008), pp. 563–89.

Côté, James. *Arrested Adulthood: The Changing Nature of Maturity and Identity*. New York: New York Univ. Press, 2000.

Davis, Jake H., and David R. Vago. "Can Enlightenment Be Traced to Specific Neural Correlates, Cognition, or Behavior? No, and (a Qualified) Yes." *Frontiers in Psychology*, vol. 4 (Nov. 2013), article no. 870.

Davis, John V. "Ecopsychology, Transpersonal Psychology, and Nonduality." *International Journal of Transpersonal Studies*, vol. 30, nos. 1–2 (2011), pp. 89–100.

Deikman, Arthur J. *The Observing Self: Mysticism and Psychotherapy*. Boston: Beacon Press, 1982.

Depression and Other Common Mental Disorders: Global Health Estimates. Geneva: World Health Organization, 2017.

de Vries, Jan. *The Industrious Revolution: Consumer Behavior and the Household Economy, 1650 to the Present*. Cambridge: Cambridge Univ. Press, 2008.

Doniger, Wendy. *The Hindus: An Alternative History*. New York: Penguin, 2009.

Dooling, D. M., ed. *A Way of Working.* Garden City: Anchor Books, 1979.

Durkheim, Émile. *On Suicide.* 1897. Translated by Robin Buss. London: Penguin, 2006.

Dyer, Christopher. *Everyday Life in Medieval England.* London: Hambledon and London, 2000.

Dyer, Christopher. *An Age of Transition?: Economy and Society in England in the Later Middle Ages.* Oxford: Clarendon Press, 2005.

Fitzgerald, James L., trans. and ed. *The Mahābhārata* Vol. 7, *Book 11— The Book of the Women, and Book 12—The Book of Peace, Part One.* Chicago: Univ. of Chicago Press, 2004.

Fox, Matthew. *The Reinvention of Work: A New Vision of Livelihood in Our Time.* New York: HarperCollins, 1994.

Galbraith, John Kenneth. *The Affluent Society.* 40th anniversary ed. Boston: Houghton Mifflin, 1998.

Ganguli, Kisari Mohan, trans. *The Mahabharata.* 5th ed. 4 vols. New Delhi: Munshiram Manoharlal Publishers, 2008. First published 1883–1896.

Garber, Andrea K., and Robert H. Lustig. "Is Fast Food Addictive?" *Current Drug Abuse Reviews*, vol. 4, no. 3 (2011), pp. 146–62.

Gibbs, John C. *Moral Development and Reality: Beyond the Theories of Kohlberg, Hoffman, and Haidt.* 3rd ed. Oxford: Oxford Univ. Press, 2014.

Glendinning, Chellis. *My Name Is Chellis and I'm in Recovery from Western Civilization.* Gabriola Island: New Catalyst Books, 1994.

Hanes III, W. Travis, and Frank Sanello. *The Opium Wars: The Addiction of One Empire and the Corruption of Another.* New York: Barnes & Noble, 2005.

Hanley, Adam, Yoshio Nakamura, and Eric L. Garland. "The Nondual Awareness Dimensional Assessment (NADA): New Tools to Assess Nondual Traits and States of Consciousness Occurring Within and Beyond the Context of Meditation." *Psychological Assessment*, vol. 30, no. 12 (Dec. 2018), pp. 1625–39.

Hari, Johann. *Lost Connections: Uncovering the Real Causes of Depression—and the Unexpected Solutions.* New York: Bloomsbury, 2018.

Hatcher, John. "England in the Aftermath of the Black Death." *Past and Present*, no. 144 (Aug. 1994), pp. 3–35.

Henrich, Joseph. *The WEIRDest People in the World: How the West Became Psychologically Peculiar and Particularly Prosperous.* New York: Farrar, Straus and Giroux, 2020.

Heying, Charles. "Portland's Artisan Economy: Beyond the Myth of Romantic Localism." *Hedgehog Review*, vol 18, no. 1 (Spring 2016), pp. 68–73.

Hobsbawm, Eric, and George Rudé. *Captain Swing*. New York: W. W. Norton, 1975.

Hunnicutt, Benjamin Kline. *Free Time: The Forgotten American Dream*. Philadelphia: Temple Univ. Press, 2013.

Inglehart, Ronald. "The Age of Insecurity: Can Democracy Save Itself?" *Foreign Affairs*, vol. 97, no. 3 (May/June 2018), pp. 20–28.

Institute for the Study of Diplomacy Working Group. *New Challenges to Human Security: Environmental Change and Human Mobility*. Washington, DC: Institute for the Study of Diplomacy, April 2017.

Jackson, Tim. *Prosperity Without Growth*. 2nd ed. London: Routledge, 2017.

Jaffé, Aniela, ed. *C. G. Jung: Word and Image*. Bollingen Series XCVII: 2. Princeton: Princeton Univ. Press, 1979.

Jennings, Justin. *Globalizations and the Ancient World*. Cambridge: Cambridge Univ. Press, 2014.

Kant, Immanuel. *Foundations of the Metaphysics of Morals*. 1785. Translated by Lewis White Beck. Indianapolis: Bobbs-Merrill, 1959.

Kasser, Tim, Steve Cohn, Allen D. Kanner, and Richard M. Ryan. "Some Costs of American Corporate Capitalism: A Psychological Exploration of Value and Goal Conflicts." *Psychological Inquiry*, vol. 18, no. 1 (2007), pp. 1–22.

Kegan, Robert. *The Evolving Self: Problem and Process in Human Development*. Cambridge: Harvard Univ. Press, 1982.

Klein, Naomi. *This Changes Everything: Capitalism vs. the Climate*. New York: Simon & Schuster, 2014.

Kohák, Erazim. *The Embers and the Stars: A Philosophical Inquiry into the Moral Sense of Nature*. Chicago: Univ. of Chicago Press, 1984.

Koyama, Mark. "The Transformation of Labor Supply in the Pre-industrial World." *Journal of Economic Behavior & Organization*, vol. 81, no. 2 (Feb. 2012), pp. 505–23.

Lee, Dorothy. *Freedom and Culture*. Englewood Cliffs: Prentice-Hall, 1959.

Lemire, Beverly. *Global Trade and the Transformation of Consumer Cultures: The Material World Remade, c.1500–1820*. Cambridge: Cambridge Univ. Press, 2018.

Lerner, Richard M., Rachel M. Hershberg, Lacey J. Hilliard, and Sara K. Johnson. "Concepts and Theories of Human Development." In *Developmental Science: An Advanced Textbook*. Edited by Marc H. Bornstein and Michael E. Lamb. 7th ed. New York: Psychology Press, 2015, pp. 3–41.

Lifton, Robert Jay. *The Protean Self: Human Resilience in an Age of Fragmentation*. New York: Basic Books, 1993.

Linebaugh, Peter, and Marcus Rediker. *The Many-Headed Hydra: Sailors, Slaves, Commoners, and the Hidden History of the Revolutionary Atlantic*. Boston: Beacon Press, 2013.

Littlewood, Roland. "State-of-Science Review—SR-X5: Comparative Cultural Perspectives in Wellbeing." Foresight Project, UK Government Office for Science, Sept. 2008.

London, Mervyn. "History of Addiction: A UK Perspective." *American Journal on Addictions*, vol. 14, no. 2 (2005), pp. 97–105.

Loy, David R. *A Buddhist History of the West: Studies in Lack*. Albany: State Univ. of New York Press, 2002.

Lu, Lin, Yuxia Fang, and Xi Wang. "Drug Abuse in China: Past, Present and Future." *Cellular and Molecular Biology*, vol. 28, no. 4 (June 2008), pp. 479–90.

Malinowski, Bronislaw. *Argonauts of the Western Pacific*. 1922. Reprint, Long Grove, IL: Waveland Press, 2013.

Mancall, Peter C., and James H. Merrell, eds. *American Encounters: Natives and Newcomers from European Contact to Indian Removal*. New York: Routledge, 2000.

Marcuse, Herbert. *One-Dimensional Man: Studies in the Ideology of Advanced Industrial Society*. Boston: Beacon Press, 1964.

Maté, Gabor. *In the Realm of Hungry Ghosts: Close Encounters with Addiction*. Berkeley: North Atlantic Books, 2010.

Matthee, Rudi. *The Pursuit of Pleasure: Drugs and Stimulants in Iranian History, 1500–1900*. Princeton: Princeton Univ. Press, 2005.

McGilchrist, Iain. *The Master and His Emissary: The Divided Brain and the Making of the Western World*. New Haven: Yale Univ. Press, 2010.

McLellan, David, ed. *Karl Marx: Selected Writings*. Oxford: Oxford Univ. Press, 1977.

Miller, Lisa. *The Spiritual Child: The New Science on Parenting for Health and Lifelong Thriving*. New York: St. Martin's Press, 2015.

Millière, Raphaël, Robin L. Carhart-Harris, Leor Roseman, et al. "Psychedelics, Meditation, and Self-Consciousness." *Frontiers in Psychology*, vol. 9 (Sept. 2018), article no. 1475.

Mills, Paul J., Christine Tara Petersen, Meredith A. Pung, et al. "Change in Sense of Nondual Awareness and Spiritual Awakening in Response to a Multidimensional Well-Being Program." *Journal of Alternative and Complementary Medicine*, vol. 24, no. 4 (April 2018), pp. 343–51.

Mintz, Sidney W. "The Changing Roles of Food in the Study of Consumption." In Brewer and Porter, *Consumption and the World of Goods*, pp. 261–73.

Mintz, Sidney W. *Sweetness and Power: The Place of Sugar in Modern History*. New York: Penguin, 1985.

Mokyr, Joel. *The Enlightened Economy: An Economic History of Britain 1700–1850*. New Haven, Yale Univ. Press, 2010.

Mudd, Shaun Anthony. "Constructive Drinking in the Roman Empire." PhD diss., Univ. of Exeter, 2015. https://core.ac.uk/download /pdf/43095602.pdf.

Mustakova-Possardt, Elena, Mikhail Lyubansky, Michael Basseches, and Julie Oxenberg, eds. *Toward a Socially Responsible Psychology for a Global Era*. New York: Springer, 2014.

Narvaez, Darcia. *Neurobiology and the Development of Human Morality: Evolution, Culture, and Wisdom*. New York: W. W. Norton, 2014.

Nisbett, Richard E., Kaiping Peng, Incheol Choi, and Ara Norenzayan. "Culture and Systems of Thought: Holistic Versus Analytic Cognition." *Psychological Review*, vol. 108, no. 2, (2001), pp. 291–310.

Page, Benjamin I., Jason Seawright, and Matthew J. Lacombe. "What Billionaires Want: The Secret Influence of America's 100 Richest." *The Guardian*, 31 Oct. 2018.

Pajic, Milan. "'Ale for an Englishman Is a Natural Drink': The Dutch and the Origins of Beer Brewing in Late Medieval England." *Journal of Medieval History*, vol. 45, no. 3, pp. 285–300.

Parthasarathi, Prasannan. *Why Europe Grew Rich and Asia Did Not: Global Economic Divergence, 1600–1850*. Cambridge: Cambridge Univ. Press, 2011.

Pecchi, Lorenzo, and Gustavo Piga, eds. *Revisiting Keynes: Economic Possibilities for Our Grandchildren*. Cambridge: MIT Press, 2008.

Piff, Paul K. "Wealth and the Inflated Self: Class, Entitlement, and Narcissism." *Personality and Social Psychology Bulletin*, vol. 41, no. 1 (Jan. 2014), pp. 34–43.

Piff, Paul K., Daniel M. Stancato, Stéphane Côté, et al. "Higher Social Class Predicts Increased Unethical Behavior." *Proceedings of the National Academy of Sciences*, vol. 109, no. 11 (13 March 2012), pp. 4086–91.

Piketty, Thomas. *Capital in the Twenty-First Century*. Translated by Arthur Goldhammer. Cambridge: Belknap Press of Harvard Univ. Press, 2014.

Pinker, Steven. *The Better Angels of Our Nature: Why Violence Has Declined*. New York: Penguin, 2011.

Polanyi, Karl. *The Great Transformation: The Political and Economic Origins of Our Time*. Boston: Beacon Press, 1957.

Pomeranz, Kenneth. *The Great Divergence: China, Europe, and the Making of the Modern World Economy*. Princeton: Princeton Univ. Press, 2000.

Pomeranz, Kenneth, and Steven Topik. *The World That Trade Created: Society, Culture, and the World Economy 1400 to the Present*. 2nd ed. Armonk, NY: M. E. Sharpe, 2006.

Prescott, Susan L., and Alan C. Logan. "Transforming Life: A Broad View of the Developmental Origins of Health and Disease Concept from an Ecological Justice Perspective." *International Journal of Environmental Research and Public Health*, vol. 13 (2016), article no. 1075.

Putnam, Robert D. *Bowling Alone: The Collapse and Revival of American Community*. New York: Simon & Schuster, 2000.

Putnam, Robert D. *Our Kids: The American Dream in Crisis*. New York: Simon & Schuster, 2015.

Ratner, Carl. *Macro Cultural Psychology: A Political Philosophy of Mind*. Oxford: Oxford Univ. Press, 2012.

Razzell, Peter, and Christine Spence. "The Hazards of Wealth: Adult Mortality in Pre-Twentieth-Century England." *Social History of Medicine*, vol. 19, no. 3 (Dec. 2006), pp. 381–405.

Rogoff, Barbara. *The Cultural Nature of Human Development*. Oxford: Oxford Univ. Press, 2003.

Rose, Jonathan F. P. *The Well-Tempered City: What Modern Science, Ancient Civilizations, and Human Nature Teach Us About the Future of Urban Life*. New York: Harper Wave, 2016.

Routledge, Clay. "Suicides Have Increased. Is This an Existential Crisis?" *New York Times*, 23 June 2018.

Saraswati, Swami Satyananda. *Kundalini Tantra*. Munger, Bihar, India: Yoga Publications Trust, 2003.

Scharmer, Otto, and Katrin Kaufer. *Leading from the Emerging Future: From Ego-System to Eco-System Economies*. San Francisco: Berrett-Koehler, 2013.

Schwartzkopf, Stacey, and Kathryn E. Sampeck, eds. *Substance and Seduction: Ingested Commodities in Early Modern Mesoamerica*. Austin: Univ. of Texas Press, 2017.

Sclove, Richard E. *Democracy and Technology*. New York: Guilford Press, 1995.

Sclove, Richard. "Town Meetings on Technology: Consensus Conferences as Democratic Participation." In *Science, Technology & Democracy*. Edited by Daniel Lee Kleinman. Albany: State Univ. of New York Press, 2000, pp. 33–48. http://richardsclove.com/publications.

Sclove, Richard E. "Cybersobriety: How a Commercially Driven Internet Threatens the Foundations of Democratic Self-Governance and What to Do About It." In *Community Practice in the Network Society: Local Action/Global Interaction*. Edited by Peter Day and Douglas Schuler. London and New York: Routledge, 2004, pp. 36–51. http://richardsclove.com/publications.

Sclove, Richard. *Reinventing Technology Assessment: A 21st Century Model.* Washington, DC: Woodrow Wilson International Center for Scholars, April 2010. http://richardsclove.com/publications.

Shah, Idries. *World Tales.* New York: Harcourt Brace Jovanovich, 1979.

Shahjahan, Riyad A., and Kimberly A. Haverkos. "Revealing the Secular Fence of Knowledge: Towards Reimagining Spiritual Ways of Knowing and Being in the Academy." In *Indigenous Philosophies and Critical Education: A Reader.* Edited by George. J. Sefa Dei. New York: Peter Lang, 2011, pp. 367–85.

Shammas, Carole. "Changes in English and Anglo-American Consumption from 1550 to 1800." In Brewer and Porter, *Consumption and the World of Goods*, pp. 177–205.

Smith, Adam. *The Theory of Moral Sentiments.* 6th ed. 2 vols. London: A. Strahan and T. Cadell, 1790.

Speth, James Gustave. *America the Possible: Manifesto for a New Economy.* New Haven: Yale Univ. Press, 2012.

Sukthankar, V. S. *On the Meaning of the Mahābhārata.* Bombay: Asiatic Society of Bombay, 1957.

Taylor, Charles. *Sources of the Self: The Making of Modern Identity.* Cambridge: Harvard Univ. Press, 1989.

Thompson, E. P. *The Making of the English Working Class.* Middlesex: Penguin, 1980.

Thompson, E. P. *Customs in Common: Studies in Traditional Popular Culture.* New York: The New Press, 1993.

Tigunait, Pandit Rajmani. *Tantra Unveiled: Seducing the Forces of Matter & Spirit.* Honesdale: Himalayan Institute Press, 2007.

Trentmann, Frank. *Empire of Things: How We Became a World of Consumers, from the Fifteenth Century to the Twenty-First.* New York: Harper, 2016.

Tuchman, Barbara. *A Distant Mirror: The Calamitous 14th Century.* New York: Ballantine Books, 1978.

Turkle, Sherry. *Alone Together: Why We Expect More from Technology and Less from Each Other.* New York: Basic Books, 2011.

Twenge, Jean M., Brian H. Spitzberg, and W. Keith Campbell. "Less In-Person Social Interaction with Peers Among U.S. Adolescents in the 21st Century and Links to Loneliness." *Journal of Social and Personal Relationships*, vol. 36, no. 6 (2019), pp. 1892–1913.

Urban, Hugh B. *Tantra: Sex, Secrecy, Politics, and Power in the Study of Religion.* Berkeley: Univ. of California Press, 2003.

van Buitenen, J. A. B., trans. and ed. *The Mahābhārata* Vol. 1, *The Book of the Beginning.* Chicago: Univ. of Chicago Press, 1973.

van Buitenen, J. A. B., trans. and ed. *The Mahābhārata* Vol. 2, *Book 2— The Book of the Assembly Hall, and Book 3—The Book of the Forest.* Chicago: Univ. of Chicago Press, 1975.

van Buitenen, J. A. B., trans. and ed. *The Mahābhārata* Vol. 3. *Book 4—The Book of Virata, and Book 5—The Book of the Effort*. Chicago: Univ. of Chicago Press, 1978.

van Buitenen, J. A. B., trans. and ed. *The Bhagavadgītā in the Mahābhārata*. Chicago: Univ. of Chicago Press, 1981.

Vieten, Cassandra, Helané Wahbeh, B. Rael Cahn, et al. "Future Directions in Meditation Research: Recommendations for Expanding the Field of Contemplative Science." *PLoS ONE*, vol. 13, no. 11 (2018), https://doi.org/10.1371/journal.pone.0205740.

Warner, Jessica, Minghao Her, Gerhard Gmel, and Jürgen Rehm. "Can Legislation Prevent Debauchery?: Mother Gin and Public Health in 18th-Century England." *American Journal of Public Health*, vol. 91, no. 3 (March 2001), pp. 375–84.

Washburn, Michael. *The Ego and the Dynamic Ground: A Transpersonal Theory of Human Development*. 2nd ed. Albany: State Univ. of New York, 1995.

Waters, Tony. *The Persistence of Subsistence Agriculture: Life Beneath the Level of the Marketplace*. Lanham, MD: Lexington Books, 2007.

Weinberger, A. H., M. Gbedemah, A. M. Martinez, et al. "Trends in Depression Prevalence in the USA from 2005 to 2015: Widening Disparities in Vulnerable Groups." *Psychological Medicine*, vol. 48, no. 8 (June 2018), pp. 1308–15.

White, David Gordon. *The Alchemical Body: Siddha Traditions in Medieval India*. Chicago: Univ. of Chicago Press, 1996.

White, David Gordon. *Kiss of the Yoginī: "Tantric Sex" in Its South Asian Contexts*. Chicago: Univ. of Chicago Press, 2003.

White, David Gordon. "Yoga, Brief History of an Idea." In *Yoga in Practice*. Edited by David Gordon White. Princeton: Princeton Univ. Press, 2012.

Wilber, Ken. *Integral Psychology: Consciousness, Spirit, Psychology, Therapy*. Boston and London: Shambhala, 2000.

Woods, Julian F. *Destiny and Human Initiative in the Mahabharata*. Albany: State Univ. of New York Press, 2001.

Wu, Tim. "That Flour You Bought Could Be the Future of the U.S. Economy." *New York Times*, 24 July 2020.

Yaden, David Bryce, Jonathan Haidt, Ralph W. Hood, et al. "The Varieties of Self-Transcendent Experience." *Review of General Psychology*, vol. 21, no. 2 (June 2017), pp. 143–60.

Yaden, David B. and Roland R. Griffiths. "The Subjective Effects of Psychedelics Are Necessary for Their Enduring Therapeutic Effects." *ACS Pharmacology & Translational Science*, vol. 4, no. 2 (9 April 2021), pp. 568-72.

Zuboff, Shoshana. *The Age of Surveillance Capitalism: The Fight for a Human Future at the New Frontier of Power*. New York: Hachette Book Group, 2019.

Index

Author Interview

THE BACKSTORY

Karavelle Press: How did you come to tackle this project? Why don't you start off by describing your process for decoding the *Mahabharata*.

Richard Sclove: My process? The short answer is standard scholarship mixed with a little assist from the gods.

As I say in Chapter 1, the inspiration for the book floated up during a silent meditation retreat. I already knew the *Mahabharata*'s basic plot from having read a couple of children's versions. But I realized that to tease out the authors' allegorical meaning, I needed to read an unabridged translation.[1]

I've heard that it typically takes scholars five years to master the *Mahabharata*'s thousands of pages well enough to begin conducting original research about it. But that wasn't exactly my experience. As I started reading about the Pandavas' early years, right away I noticed that their lives oscillated between adventures out in the wilderness and then conflict with their cousins, the Kauravas.

Meanwhile, over the years I had read many translations of the *Bhagavad Gita.* This led me to assume, quite naturally, that the Pandavas represent the higher self—the soul—and the opposing Kauravas symbolize the ego. From that, it seemed obvious that the *Mahabharata* is portraying a pathway of psychospiritual growth.

But when I started to diagram that path, wham! Suddenly I was staring at a picture of the human subtle body as understood in Hinduism: ascending chakras connected by three intertwined energy channels. Whoa, I thought, does the epic's structure reflect an esoteric understanding of human psychophysiology? Soon I was off and running, working out my decryption of Yudhishthira's dice match.

The oddest thing about this process is that up to that point it involved no great effort. As I followed the Pandavas' journey, I found myself slipping into an altered state of consciousness. Nothing wildly dramatic—no ethereal music or visions of angels. But I had the sense that I wasn't so much interpreting the text as that it was disclosing itself. Somehow, although I was reading the story for the first time, simultaneously I was peeling away the hidden structure. The structure just sort of fell out into my lap. Later I came to think of this process as a kind of "alchemy of interpretation." Reading the text was altering my mental state in a way that allowed the text to reveal itself in new ways.

As I moved on from decoding the *Mahabharata* to decoding modern civilization, this process shifted. I began to feel as though I was engaged in a collaborative process with some type of higher intelligence. Whether this was "the one consciousness that is everything" (that's a Hindu notion), or Jung's collective unconscious, or simply a deep place within my own unconscious mind, I can't say. Although the last strikes me as the least likely.

I was also highly energized—taking lots of catnaps, while sleeping little at night. Creative insights were pouring in from "elsewhere" at a furious pace. This happened especially when I took a long run in the woods with Haley, our mini-goldendoodle, and during my dreams. I'd wake up and it might take forty-five minutes just to write down what I'd worked out in my sleep.

I call this process "collaborative" because it wasn't like I was just sitting back and transcribing dictation. This wasn't channeling. I had a collaborator—or at least there was a collaborating force—but I discovered that I needed to contribute my own creativity, sundry facts about the world, and plenty of sweat effort.

Does the fact that this was a collaboration mean that the other intelligence is "higher" but not omniscient? Did it need me to fill in the holes in what it knows? Or was it withholding certain knowledge, perhaps for my benefit? It didn't say.

As the collaboration stretched out over weeks, it became exhausting. But I also "knew" that my altered state would come to an end as soon as I completed a first draft of the book. That happened after producing a seven-hundred-page manuscript in eleven weeks.

I've been through an experience like this several times in my life. In each case, a first draft pours out as a kind of messy intuitive gush— genuine insights mixed in with many false guesses and digressions. After that initial burst of creativity—in which I'm sure I've solved many mysteries of the universe—reality sets in, and then there's a long slog to transform the initial gush into something that feels ready to share with the world.

It's still a long leap from wondering why Yudhishthira gambles to connecting that with modern psychology, history, and political economy. How do you account for making that jump?

Well, in a way I was working out the solution to a problem that had been gnawing at me for several decades.

Back in 1978, when I was twenty-four, I landed a job as the research assistant to a national energy policy study sponsored by the Ford Foundation. I was qualified for the position because I had just finished up a master's degree in nuclear engineering at MIT. (No, I never planned to be a nuclear engineer. Concerned about the social and environmental effects of nuclear power, I'd pursued a credential so that I could be a critic.)

The twenty senior members of the Ford Foundation study team were a seriously elite, establishment bunch. They included half a dozen Harvard professors (mostly economists, among them Nobel Prize–winner Ken Arrow and future Nobel Prize–winner Tom Schelling), Edward Fried (the US executive director of the World Bank), two former nuclear-weapons designers (*New Yorker*–profiled Ted Taylor—reborn now as a solar-energy enthusiast—and Dick Garwin, a senior scientist at IBM), and John Sawhill (the president of New York University and onetime director of the Federal Energy Administration). McGeorge Bundy ("Mac," I soon learned)—the Ford Foundation's president, who before that was the national security advisor to Presidents John F. Kennedy and Lyndon Johnson and the dean of faculty at Harvard—had initiated the project and participated in all our monthly meetings.

It was a heady experience . . . in all ways but one: it turned out that I was not in close alignment with the group's approach to public-policy analysis. To begin with, I was jarred to discover that the team addressed almost every policy issue by reducing it to economic considerations. From my standpoint, this filtered out all the flesh-and-blood social dimensions of policy decisions—how people's lives would be affected beyond their pocketbooks or economic preferences. Soon I wondered why an elite club of middle-aged white guys was entitled to a vastly bigger voice in policymaking than all the people whose lives would be affected. Shouldn't democracy have a place in this process? Finally, I found the entire exercise soul-crushing.

One year into the project, I wrote to one of my former professors, political theorist Langdon Winner:

> I'm much bothered by what I can see happening to my mind during this project. I find myself—still partly as a game, but also insidiously—beginning to translate an extraordinary range of phenomena into monetary or cost-benefit terms. I find myself thinking, "If I do

this for him or her, what will I get in return, how much does it cost me to do it, and how much will the return be worth to me in, say, monetary terms." I kid not. I realize that such calculus cannot begin to encompass the complexity of reality, and yet at the same time that one begins to assimilate ultra-instrumental modes of thinking about the world, one—me, I—begin to lose the ability to comprehend my life and the world in other terms (more feeling-ful, empathetic, artistic, poetic, real, honest). Somehow when I read speeches by the President, editorials by scientists and economists, and who-knows-what-else, I get this sinking feeling that we've been taken in by economic rationality, so-called systematic analysis, commercial logic. No true feeling, caring, love, or even thought. No true sense of community—whether of immediate family and friends or of the whole of humanity. No remembrance of what it feels like to be skilled in providing for our own needs. No remembrance of what a stream sounds like, the smell of the earth in springtime, the taste of a moist wind—things which are not "valuable" but which to me are memorable, precious, worth fighting to preserve, still alive.

As the project wound down in May 1979, the mainstream professional world was, temporarily, my oyster. The well-connected senior participants all appreciated my efforts. Without applying, I was offered jobs in two different branches of the US Department of Energy. I applied to doctoral programs at the University of California at Berkeley, Princeton, Harvard, and MIT. I was accepted into all of them. NYU president John Sawhill asked me to come there, where I could pursue my PhD studies while sharing a research assistantship between him and Mac Bundy (who was about to retire from the Ford Foundation to become a professor of history). Mac took me aside and said that he hoped I'd join him in moving on to NYU. I understood that I was being groomed to become a junior member of the Old Boy Network.

After some tormented inner struggle, I opted to return to MIT, this time as a graduate student in political science. My reasons were complex, but central was a sense that MIT, despite some drawbacks in basic humaneness, was good about leaving you alone to find your own way. I had a goal in mind, albeit not one that I could articulate with precision. I knew that I wanted to work on alternative approaches to policy analysis, to critique the economic-grounded approaches that I found soul-deadening and the technocratic approaches that were antidemocratic, and to see if I could contribute to coming up with something better.

I was setting out on what has turned out to be a lifelong quest to save the world and, I suppose, my own soul in the process. (Or has it been vice versa?) This is one reason that I was predisposed to leap easily from pondering Yudhishthira's addiction to the madness of modern civilization. In one guise or another that madness had been on my mind for a long time.

Does that mean it took you forty years to begin coming up with an answer to your quest?

No, there have been many steps along the way. I'll tell you about one that has been especially influential in setting me up to write this book.

By 1982 I had finished up the mandatory course work toward my PhD degree, and I was scouting around for a dissertation topic. Thanks to my work on the Ford Foundation study, Professor Dorothy Zinberg, down the road at Harvard's John F. Kennedy School of Government, invited me to contribute a chapter to a book she was editing about the social dimensions of energy policy. Naturally, I chose to work on finding a way to counter the predilection of mainstream economics to reduce all policymaking to economic calculus. But how could I do this convincingly, especially speaking to academic elites who'd established their careers by building up this way of thinking?

Working late one night in my office at MIT's Center for International Studies, I began struggling to see if I could use Immanuel Kant's moral philosophy to counter mainstream economic analysis. I was thinking about Kant really, really hard, including his ideas about reality (which inform his moral theory). Kant says that we can never know reality "as it truly is." Instead, what we know is inevitably shaped by the structure of our minds, which includes hardwired concepts such as three-dimensional space, linear time, and causality. Kant believed that these concepts are innate, universal, and unchanging.

Kant's idea that we have foundational concepts built into our minds sounded right. But I very much doubted that these concepts are the same for all cultures and that they never change. For one thing, I'd read Kant's lectures on anthropology, and I knew that he didn't know much about other cultures. As an example: Contrary to Kant's theory, the Trobrianders of Malinowski's day lived timelessly in the present; what we call past and future they knew only as aspects of "now." As one result, they didn't experience causality. (If there's no past or future, then there are no "past" causes to produce "subsequent" consequences.) And modern physics has decisively overturned Kant's belief—borrowed from Descartes and Newton—in the invariability of linear time (special relativity), space as distinct from time (relativity's "space-time"), and mechanical or determinate causality (quantum mechanics).[2]

But all that's at the level of ideas. If my own mental structures are neither fixed nor universal, then why does reality appear to me specifically as it does? Could it somehow appear otherwise, and, if so, is there any reason to privilege the way that it ordinarily appears?

This wasn't an idle academic exercise. I was chewing on these ideas with ferocious determination and passion, seeking a deep passage beyond the demoralizing soullessness of modern economics. And then, as I was thinking so very hard about Kant's foundational concepts . . . my own foundational mental structures started to   F   L $_\text{E}$ x

During the next six weeks, everything became different. I had slipped into another reality. Immediately, the book-lined walls of my office seemed to freeze into hyperreality, and I had the sense that momentarily they might shatter and dissolve, or that I might even be able to walk through them. Fearing that I might die, I resisted that dissolution.

Notwithstanding that resistance, my altered state of consciousness persisted. In the coming few weeks I didn't need to sleep much. I could absorb books rapidly on many topics and see easily how complex ideas from one domain related to those in another, ostensibly far-removed.

That first night I had a breakthrough in seeing how I could use Kant's philosophy to work out a new approach to policymaking. (This was an earlier instance of the alchemy of interpretation working its magic.) In three weeks, I churned out a primitive 130-page essay—an intuitive gush akin to my first draft of *Escaping Maya's Palace*. I then spent four years unpacking those pages into a doctoral dissertation that later became a book, *Democracy and Technology*, that won an award from the American Political Science Association.

Immediately after finishing that first draft, I participated in a weekend psychological and spiritual retreat at the former Spring Hill community in Ashby, Massachusetts. I'd signed up two months earlier at a girlfriend's urging. At one point on Saturday morning the leaders divided the thirty-odd participants into pairs. You sat on the floor opposite your partner and took turns silently and nonreactively witnessing for one another. When it was your turn to speak, your assignment was to gaze into your partner's eyes and say what you saw.

I was sitting opposite a bearded young man about my own age. It was my turn to talk. One of the retreat leaders, a psychotherapist named Kevin, came over and said, "You seem to be stuck."

Still in my altered state of consciousness, I explained, "I don't believe my own eyes. What I see is bullshit. I don't want to see bullshit and I don't want to say bullshit. I want to see what is *really* there."

"Well," Kevin suggested mildly, "what's stopping you? Why don't you go ahead and see what's really there?"

Apparently, Kevin's words gave me the permission that I'd needed. I stared into my partner's eyes, his face faded from its previous normal coloration to hues of gray, and then his eyes didn't waver or alter as his face was replaced by the face of a kind of monstrous goat with several extra eyes.

"I see a weird-looking goat," I said.

For the next three weeks, whenever I slightly squinted directly into someone's eyes, the same basic phenomenon would happen. The face would fade to gray, the eyes would stay the same, and another face, or else a succession of faces, would appear surrounding those unaltered eyes. Sometimes it helped to gently hold the other person's hands while looking.

When I looked into Kevin's eyes, he was staring patiently back toward me in the form of a large fish, like a grouper, floating placidly where a moment before his normal human head had been. The grouper's mouth pursed open and closed, while its side fins fanned rhythmically. When I told him the kinds of things I was seeing, Kevin's reaction was, "Oh, those are just past lives." Possibly, but I wasn't sure that was entirely right.

As an MIT student, I approached all this partly with a scientist's mind. First, formulate a testable hypothesis: Am I going crazy? Are these conventional hallucinations?

I tested those hypotheses and quickly rejected them as not fitting the facts. The strongest confounding evidence was that when I shared what I was seeing, too often my partner was amazed, reporting that there was some substantial truth being revealed that I couldn't possibly have known beforehand.

For instance, I was living in a group house on Ash Street, near Harvard Square and the Charles River in Cambridge. A few nights after returning from Spring Hill, I squinted into the eyes of a new housemate while sitting on the gray carpet in her room up on the third floor. I had hardly spoken with this woman before, so I basically knew nothing about her. Her face faded out: "I see a Siamese cat," I reported.

"I don't believe it!" she cried. She walked behind me to her bookcase and pulled out a couple of illustrated volumes about cats: "Cats are my thing!"

We tried again and this time I saw the Mona Lisa. "Oh my god," she blurted. "I was an art-history major and that's my painting!"

"Crazy hallucinations" don't usually elicit that kind of reaction, and I was getting lots of such reactions.

And there were other unusual experiences. For instance, a week after returning from Spring Hill, I wanted to talk with Dorothy Zinberg about transforming my 130-page gush into a chapter for her book. For some reason, I didn't try to call her. Instead, even though it was the weekend, I pedaled my twelve-year-old Peugeot ten-speed bike three miles along the Charles River to her office at the Kennedy School. I took the elevator to the fourth floor and—damn!—the magic wasn't working. She wasn't there; her door was locked.

And then I heard her distinctive voice, laughing just around the corner. I called out; she didn't answer. I walked toward her. She seemed to be walking away, always just out of sight. She kept laughing, and I followed her laugh. I walked down five flights of stairs into the Kennedy School's basement-level library, where I'd never been before, always following the laugh, straight to where . . . I ran into Dorothy. "Were you laughing just now?" I asked.

"No," she said, her face scanning mine quizzically. I imagine she was thinking, "Why would I have been laughing in a library, an enforced-silence zone?" We went back to her office and discussed my chapter.

In 1982, when all this was happening, I was twenty-eight years old. I'd been interested in spirituality since I was nineteen, and I had read a certain number of spiritual books, including the Bible, Carlos Castaneda's *The Teachings of Don Juan, Chuang Tzu*, the *Bhagavad Gita*, and Idries Shah's *Tales of the Dervishes*. But at that time, I understood spirituality mostly in intellectual terms. I'd taken a tai chi course in college and occasionally done a guided group meditation. But I had never had a spiritual teacher, taken a meditation course, or adopted a spiritual practice.

The upshot is that I didn't have much guidance for interpreting or integrating what I was experiencing. I was sure that I was having a spiritual experience and I found it exhilarating. I felt blissful, deeply at peace, and that I was navigating the world with a new, finely attuned moral compass. But other than that, I wasn't sure what was happening.

And then after six weeks, I returned to my normal state of consciousness.

Twenty years later I met Sally Kempton, a Hindu spiritual teacher. When I told her my story, she explained that I was describing a spontaneous kundalini awakening. The shifting faces that I had seen? Third-eye activation. It turns out that seeing altered faces during a kundalini awakening is a rare phenomenon but not a unique one. For instance, at about the same time that I was seeing altered faces, so was a midwestern college professor named Dorothy Walters, right down to a weird goat (in her case, a satyr).[3]

Soon I was meditating regularly and reading books about kundalini awakening and Hinduism generally. This later fed into my involvement with the *Mahabharata*, including knowing when I was looking at a tantric map of the human body. My MIT spiritual experience also helped me know how to navigate the altered states I slipped into while writing this book.

Meanwhile, I'd known since I wrote it that there was a gap in *Democracy and Technology*. One thrust of the book is that economic and technological decisions combine to become social structures. This phenomenon stands out among many that economic theory overlooks. I also intuited that among the follow-on consequences, there must be effects on psychological and spiritual development—and I suspected they weren't all good. But I didn't know how to discover what they were.

That hole in *Democracy and Technology* was still nagging at the back of my mind when I began pondering Yudhishthira's anomalous behavior during the dice match and connecting it with modern circumstances.

***Escaping Maya's Palace* spans an unusually wide range of disciplines. How has your scholarship become so broadly interdisciplinary?**

It started with clam chowder. I began my college career as an undergraduate physics major at Middlebury College in Vermont. In September 1973 I transferred to Hampshire College in western Massachusetts, allured by their commitment to encouraging interdisciplinary learning and research.

In my case, this was communicated most directly by my assigned academic adviser—physicist and pioneering electronic-synthesizer musician Everett Hafner. The first time I went to see him, I encountered a friendly, bearded and bespectacled middle-aged man who was busy heating up homemade New England clam chowder over a Bunsen burner in his laboratory. We waited for it to come to a simmer, and then he generously shared his bounty. Everett thanked me for coming and said we should meet again sometime.

Huh? I was confused about what to do with my life and what to start studying at Hampshire. When does the "advice" part of being an advisee happen?

I made another appointment, this time resolved that I wouldn't let Everett pull off any more of that spacey-science-guy routine to divert us from straightening me out. I was hardly into my spiel when Everett gave me an assignment: "Go back to your room, take a blank piece of a paper, and draw a big circle. Then place each academic discipline along the edge of the circle in its proper order in relation to all the other disciplines. Great to see you!"

Cool idea. I worked on it and came back with a circle showing about thirty disciplines arranged logically around the edge. I decided that certain applied-professional fields, such as law and architecture, didn't fit along the circle, so I drew them on a flat plane intersecting the circle at a right angle.

Everett smiled. I smiled and never looked back. Without saying anything more, he'd taught me that all the disciplines are interrelated and not to take the distinctions very seriously.

Over the years, I've come up with a few handy tricks for doing interdisciplinary research. I figured out the first one while I was still at Hampshire. It turns out that if you need to know something about a new discipline, you can learn a surprising amount just by skimming an introductory textbook. (I tried it first for hydrogeophysics, while I was researching the hazards of high-level nuclear waste management.) In many disciplines, even a freshman-level text will convey about 80 percent of what the discipline knows. Of course, learning the remaining 20 percent might take years. But 80 percent is often enough for the purposes of interdisciplinary research.

Another trick: physicist Ted Taylor, from the Ford Foundation project, taught me that when you start tangling with a new research question about which you're clueless, it's a good idea to restrain yourself from reading what other people have already concluded. Otherwise, you'll be indoctrinated into the received wisdom, which inhibits bringing originality to a problem.

Third trick (partly contradicting the second): praise the goddesses for Google Scholar. When I'm venturing into a new topic area, I hunt around for an academic article related to the question I'm planning to investigate. Any academic article. When you find one, Google Scholar magically shows you every published scholarly article or book that cites it. Sifting through those cites, you're moving forward in time, finding your way to the most recent research . . . and to most of what is known so far about the topic you want to understand.

Final trick: when you're trying to learn about a new topic, you also need to know when to stop. My rough rule of thumb is that when three articles in a row don't teach me anything new that I need to know, then I probably know enough to move on to the next question.

Unfortunately, *Escaping Maya's Palace* covers too much terrain for me to have been able to fully comply with that rule of thumb. When I couldn't, I relied as much as possible on the kindness of experts in various fields. But eventually I ran out of people I could pester to review draft chapters, so I'll have to wait for future readers to tell me what I got wrong. I don't like violating my own rule, but I console myself with thinking that the questions I'm addressing matter and I've done the best I could.

One more question: You write about "the Taboo" against integrating a post-egoic perspective into scholarship. Why were you willing to transgress that taboo?

I suppose I have a certain innate readiness, reinforced by my Hampshire education, to challenge received wisdom. It also matters that I'm an independent scholar. If I were in academia, there would be a lot of pressure to stay in line.

My resolve to challenge conventional thinking, when that seems called for, has been put to the test a time or two. For instance, back in 1982 when I met with my PhD committee to discuss expanding my Zinberg chapter into a dissertation, the committee promptly blew apart. Two members said yes, but the two policy analysts resigned. One was Carl Kaysen, the head of MIT's Science, Technology, and Society Program (and previously deputy national security advisor under Mac Bundy and then the director of the Institute for Advanced Studies in Princeton, where he succeeded J. Robert Oppenheimer). A short while later, Carl cornered me in a corridor and threatened that if I pursued this dissertation topic, he'd make sure that I never got a job anywhere.

That made my choice clear: I could have conventional success replete with an infinite supply of comfy ego strokes or I could keep my integrity intact. I decided to prioritize saving my soul. I stuck with my thesis topic.

And that's how I got myself disinvited from the Old Boy Network. Which hasn't worked out badly after all.

About the Author

Richard Sclove has served as the director of strategic development at the Mind and Life Institute, cofounded by the Dalai Lama, and as a project director at the Center for Contemplative Mind in Society. He also founded the Loka Institute, a nonprofit organization dedicated to making science and technology responsive to democratically decided social priorities.

He earned his bachelor's degree from experimental and inter-disciplinary Hampshire College and his PhD in political theory and MS in nuclear engineering from MIT. He was awarded an endowed postdoctoral fellowship in economics at the University of California-Berkeley and is an elected fellow of the American Association for the Advancement of Science.

Dr. Sclove has published in venues ranging from the *Washington Post, Christian Science Monitor, Adbusters, Huffington Post, Yes! Magazine,* and *Utne Reader* to the *Chronicle of Higher Education, Technology Review, Science,* and *Issues in Science & Technology.* His first book, *Democracy and Technology,* won the Don K. Price Award of the American Political Science Association honoring the "year's best book in science, technology and politics," and it continues to be cited as a seminal work in its field.

Richard and his family spent the academic year 2006–07 living in Bal Ashram—an ashram and orphanage beside the Ganges River in the ancient city of Varanasi, India.

Communications with the author—including requests for speaking engagements as well as critiques or suggestions for improving the book—are welcome and may be submitted via the websites www.RichardSclove.com or www.EscapingMayasPalace.com.

CPSIA information can be obtained
at www.ICGtesting.com
Printed in the USA
BVHW010531060622
638965BV00014B/298